THE NORTH PACIFIC TRIANGLE
THE UNITED STATES, JAPAN, A..._
CENTURY'S END

Withdrawn

The emergence of a significant new partnership involving Canada, Japan, and the United States has been largely ignored by students of international relations and Canadian foreign policy. This collection of essays by scholars and policy-makers explores the evolving alliance and illustrates its growing strength in a collective global leadership.

The essays examine the three market-oriented democracies in their changing roles towards each other and show how they have moved beyond their separate, special, bilateral relationships into a dynamic three-way engagement. Their intersections in trade, investment, business negotiations, peacekeeping, and environmental affairs are analysed from a range of perspectives from various disciplines, including political science, management studies, economics, geography, and history. A compelling view unfolds: in the context of a rapidly globalizing economic system, and amid the economic crisis that beset Asia and Japan in 1997, this triumvirate continues to strengthen and flourish, adding its influence to the creation of a new world order.

MICHAEL FRY is Professor and former Director of the School of International Relations, University of Southern California.
JOHN KIRTON is Associate Professor of Political Science and Research Associate at the Centre for International Studies, University of Toronto.
MITSURU KUROSAWA is Professor of International Law and International Relations, Osaka School of International Public Policy, Faculty of Law, Osaka University.

The North Pacific Triangle: The United States, Japan, and Canada at Century's End

Edited by
Michael Fry, John Kirton, and Mitsuru Kurosawa

UNIVERSITY OF TORONTO PRESS
Toronto Buffalo London

© University of Toronto Press Incorporated 1998
Toronto Buffalo London
Printed in Canada

ISBN 0-8020-4212-0 (cloth)
ISBN 0-8020-8065-0 (paper)

∞

Printed on acid-free paper

Canadian Cataloguing in Publication Data

Main entry under title:

The North Pacific triangle : the United States, Japan, and Canada at century's end

Based on a conference held in Tokyo, Japan, Dec. 1993.
Includes bibliographical references and index.
ISBN 0-8020-4212-0 (bound)   ISBN 0-8020-8065-0 (pbk.)

1. Canada – Relations – Japan.   2. Canada – Relations – United States.
3. Japan – Relations – Canada.   4. Japan – Relations – United States.
5. United States – Relations – Canada.   6. United States – Relations – Japan.
I. Fry, Michael G., 1934–   .   II. Kirton, John J.   III. Kurosawa, Mitsuru.

JZ1242.N67 1998   327   C98-930704-2

University of Toronto Press acknowledges the support of the Canada Council and the
Ontario Arts Council to its publishing program.

This book has been published with the financial assistance of the School of International
Relations, University of Southern California, Los Angeles.

Contents

TABLES   viii
FIGURES   x
CONTRIBUTORS   xi
PREFACE   xv

Introduction   1

1 The New North Pacific Triangle   3
MICHAEL FRY, JOHN KIRTON, and MITSURU KUROSAWA

I The Economic and Business Relationship   15

2 The 'Nixon Shokku' Revisited: Japanese and Canadian Foreign Economic
Policies Compared   17
DAIZO SAKURADA

3 Managing Macroeconomic Relations with the United States: Japanese and
Canadian Experiences   36
TSUYOSHI KAWASAKI

4 Japanese–American Trade Negotiations: The Structural Impediments
Initiative   60
MICHAEL W. DONNELLY

5 Japanese Direct Investment in Canada: Patterns and Prospects   85
DAVID W. EDGINGTON

6 Japan's Post-Bubble Economic Changes: Implications for the United States and Canada 106
RICHARD WRIGHT

7 Business Negotiations: Comparing the U.S.–Japan and Canada–Japan Experiences 140
ROSALIE TUNG

II **The Political and Security Relationship** 165

8 Cooperative Security in the North Pacific 167
FRANK LANGDON

9 The Future of the U.S.–Japan Security Relationship: A Canadian Perspective 185
DAVID A. WELCH

10 Japanese and Canadian Peacekeeping Participation: The American Dimension 196
MITSURU KUROSAWA

11 Environmental Issues: A New International Agenda and Related Domestic Experience 209
PAUL PARKER

III **Managing the New Relationship** 235

12 Managing Canada–Japan Relations 237
JAMES H. TAYLOR

13 Canada–Japan Forum 2000: A Novel Exercise in Diplomacy 251
MICHAEL GRAHAM FRY

14 In the Spirit of Nitobe and Norman: Circularity in Japanese and Canadian Approaches to Regional Institution Building 277
LAWRENCE T. WOODS

15 The Emerging Pacific Partnership: Japan, Canada, and the United States at
the G-7 Summit   292
JOHN KIRTON

ABBREVIATIONS   315
BIBLIOGRAPHY   319
INDEX   359

Tables

3.1 Two Factors Shaping the Nature of Macroeconomic Diplomacy in the 1960s and 1980s

3.2 Three Cases of Macroeconomic Diplomacy

3.3 Outcomes of the Cases

4.1 Agenda for Structural Impediments Initiative

4.2 Chronology of SII Negotiations

5.1 Annual Japanese DFI in Canada and the United States, FY 1980–95 (U.S.$millions)

5.2 Cumulative Japanese Direct Investment in Canada, FY 1952–93 by Major Industrial Sector (U.S.$millions)

5.3 Japanese Investments in the British Columbia Forest Products Industry (Date of Establishment)

5.4 Japanese Investments in the Canadian Pulp and Paper Industry, 1985–93

5.5 Japanese-Affiliated Auto Assembly Plants in Southern Ontario and the United States

5.6 Major Hotel/Resort Properties, and Golf Courses Purchased/Developed by Japanese Investors in British Columbia, 1986–93

11.1 Consumption of Chlorofluorocarbons and Halons, 1986–93

11.2 CO_2 Emissions from Fossil Fuel Combustion and Cement Manufacturing, 1960–95

11.3 Concentration of SO_2 at Selected Major Cities, 1980–92

11.4 Total SO_2 Emissions by Source, 1970–92

11.5 Selected Lakes and Rivers Annual Mean Concentration of Phosphorus, 1970–93

11.6 Nationally Designated Protected Areas and National Parks, 1990

11.7 Internationally Designated Heritage and Habitat Areas, 1992

11.8 Official Development Assistance, 1970–95

15.1 Relative Capability of Major Powers in the International System,
1950–95, Ratio of U.S. GNP in Current U.S.$ Exchange Rates
15.2 Seven-Power Summit Success
15.3 Compliance with Summit Macroeconomic/Energy Agreements by Year,
1975–89
15.4 Compliance with Summit Macroeconomic/Energy Agreements by
Country, 1975–89
15.5 Assessment of National Summit Success in Canadian Élite Editorials

Figures

2.1 Canada–U.S. Dyad and Japan–U.S. Dyad during the Nixon Shocks
    Negotiations
6.1 Trend in Stock Prices
6.2 Stock Index Divided by GNP
6.3 Urban Land Price Index Divided by GNP
6.4 Official Discount Rate
6.5 Growth in GNP and Money Supply
6.6 Oil Price Trend
6.7 Return on Capital in the Private Sector
6.8 Nominal GDP Growth Rate by Country
6.9 Trade Account Trends by Country
6.10 Japanese Capital Outflows
6.11 Foreign Assets Held by Selected OECD Countries
6.12 Trends in Household Savings Ratio by Selected Countries
6.13 Elderly Population Ratio by Selected Country
6.14 Government Net Debt as a Proportion of GDP by Selected Country
6.15 Overseas Production Ratios by Selected Country
6.16 Japanese Direct Investment Abroad, by Destination
6.17 GDP Growth Rate Forecasts by Selected Country
7.1 Conceptual Paradigm of International Business Negotiations

Contributors

Michael W. Donnelly is Professor of Political Science and Associate Dean of Arts and Science at the University of Toronto. He has written on contemporary Japan's politics and agriculture, foreign policy, the political economy of nuclear power, American trade relations, conflict management, and Canadian economic relations. In addition to numerous book chapters, his articles have appeared in *Pacific Affairs*, *The Pacific Review*, *International Journal*, *Current History*, and *Shokuryo Seisaku Kenkyu*.

David W. Edgington is Associate Professor of Geography at the University of British Columbia. His research centres on Japanese trade and foreign investment in the Pacific Rim, and Japanese urban and regional restructuring. He is the author of *Japanese Business Down Under: Patterns of Investment in Australia* (London: Routledge 1990), and numerous articles on Japan and Canada.

Michael Graham Fry is Professor at and former Director of the School of International Relations at the University of Southern California. His most recent publications include *Statesmen as Historians* (London & New York: Pinter and Columbia University Press 1991) and *Power, Personalities and Policies: Essays in Honor of Donald Cameron Watt* (London: Frank Cass 1992). He is a historian of the international system and has published widely on North Atlantic, Middle East, and Asia Pacific affairs.

Tsuyoshi Kawasaki is Assistant Professor of Political Science and Interdisciplinary Studies at Simon Fraser University. His research interests include Japanese foreign policy, international relations theory, and the international relations of the Asia-Pacific region. His articles have appeared in *Journal of Public Policy* and *The Pacific Review*.

John Kirton is Associate Professor of Political Science, a Research Associate of the Centre for International Studies, and Director of the G7 Research Group at the University of Toronto. He is the co-editor of *The Triangle of Pacific States* (Tokyo: Sairyusha Press 1995), *Building a New Global Order: Emerging Trends in International Security* (Toronto: Oxford University Press 1993), *Canadian Foreign Policy: Selected Cases* (Toronto: Prentice-Hall 1992), and co-author of *Canada as a Principal Power: A Study in Foreign Policy and International Relations* (Toronto: John Wiley 1983). He is a specialist on Canada–United States relations and Canada-Japan relations.

Mitsuru Kurosawa is Professor of International Law and International Relations at the Osaka School of International Public Policy, Osaka University, and a Professor at the Faculty of Law, Osaka University. He is co-editor of *The Triangle of Pacific States* (Tokyo: Sairyusha Press 1995), editor of *In Search of a New International Order* (Tokyo: Sinzansha Press 1994), and author of *Nuclear Disarmament and International Law* (Tokyo: Yushindo Press 1992), *International Disarmament Law: A New Framework* (Tokyo: Yushindo Press 1986) and *Contemporary International Law on Disarmament* (Niigata: Nishimura Publishing 1986). He is a specialist on international security issues, including nuclear disarmament, non-proliferation, and peacekeeping.

Frank Langdon is Professor Emeritus of Political Science and a Research Associate of the Institute of International Relations at the University of British Columbia. He writes on political, military, and economic relations of the Asia-Pacific region with an emphasis on Japan and its ties to Canada and the United States. Recent publications include 'Canada's Goals in the Asia Pacific,' *The Pacific Review* 8 (1995). He is co-editor of *Japan in the Posthegemonic World* (Boulder: L. Rienner 1993).

Paul Parker is Associate Professor of Geography and Director of the Local Economic Development Program at the University of Waterloo. He is editor of *Pacific Coal Trade: Energy or Environmental Priorities* (Canberra: Australia–Japan Research Centre 1993) and three earlier books. He specializes in environmental policy, Japanese trade, and impact assessment.

Daizo Sakurada is Associate Professor of International Relations at the Faculty of Integrated Arts and Sciences of the University of Tokushima, and Visiting Research Fellow at the Institute of American and Canadian Studies, Sophia University. He is author of *Japan and the Management of the International Political Economy* (Toronto: Centre for International Studies, University of Toronto 1989), has contributed a chapter to Mitsuru Kurosawa and John Kirton, eds., *The Triangle of Pacific States* (Tokyo: Sairyusha Press 1995), and written articles in journals such as *Gaiko Jiho (Revue Diplomatique), Kokusai Seiji (International Relations)*, and *Asia-Pacific Review*. His interests are in comparative foreign policy among Canada, the United States, and Japan, and in international relations theory.

James H. Taylor is the former Canadian Ambassador to Japan (1989–93) and NATO (1983–85), a former Undersecretary of State for External Affairs (1985–89), the Prime Minister's Personal Representative for the 1989 Economic Summit, and currently the Chancellor of McMaster University. He is the author of *The New World of International Institutions* (Toronto: CIIA 1993).

Rosalie Tung is a Fellow of the Royal Society of Canada and the Ming and Stella Wong Professor of International Business, Faculty of Business Administration, Simon Fraser University. She has authored eight books and has published widely on the subjects of international management and organizational theory in many leading journals.

David A. Welch is Associate Professor of Political Science at the University of Toronto. During the preparation of his chapter he was Visiting Associate Professor of International Relations (Research), Thomas J. Watson Jr. Institute for International Studies, Brown University (1996–97) and Visiting Scholar, Center for International Affairs, Harvard University (1996–97). He is the author of *Justice and the Genesis of War* (New York: Cambridge University Press 1993) and co-author of *Cuba on the Brink: Castro, the Missile Crisis and the Soviet Collapse* (New York: Pantheon Books 1993). His articles have appeared in *Ethics and International Affairs, Foreign Affairs, International Journal, International Security, Security Studies*, and *The Journal of Conflict Resolution*.

Lawrence T. Woods is Associate Professor of International Studies at the University of Northern British Columbia. His articles have appeared in *Asian Survey, Pacific Affairs, Pacific Review, Australian Journal of International Affairs, Études Internationales, International Studies Notes, Current Politics and Economics of Japan*, and *Journal of Developing Societies*. His book, *Asia-Pacific Diplomacy: Nongovernmental Organizations and International Relations*, was published by UBC Press in 1993.

Richard Wright is Professor of International Business and Finance in the Faculty of Management, McGill University. He is the author of *Japanese Business* *in Canada: The Elusive Alliance* (Montreal: Institute for Research on Public Policy 1984) and *Japanese Finance in Transformation: Implications for Canada* (Ottawa: Canada–Japan Trade Council 1994), and co-author of *The Second Wave: Japan's Global Assault on Financial Services* (London: Waterlow 1987), and *Accessing Japanese Debt Markets* (Ottawa: Canada–Japan Trade Council 1990).

Preface

This book is the result of a mutually reinforcing and rewarding collaboration between two networks of scholars exploring the relationship between and among the United States, Japan, and Canada. The first network, led by Mitsuru Kurosawa of Osaka University and John Kirton of the University of Toronto, sought to expand its ongoing work on 'Comparing Japanese and Canadian Approaches to Dealing with the United States' to take fuller account of recent developments in the post–Cold War, globalizing international system, and to place the United States more fully as a dynamic and central actor at the forefront of the emerging North Pacific Triangle. The second network, led by Michael Fry of the University of Southern California, aimed at enriching its initial concern with Japanese–Canadian relations by more fully taking into account the impact of American actions and perspectives on that bilateral relationship. This resulting work is thus one that treats in a balanced fashion the three bilateral relationships that constitute the North Pacific Triangle, and does so in a way that highlights the intense and interdependent dynamics of their emerging triangular community.

This work is the result of thorough research, review, and revision over several years. It originated in a conference in Tokyo in December 1993 (funded in the form of The Canada–Japan Research Award) and the subsequent publication of the revised papers in Japanese as *Taiheiyo Kokka no Toraianguru* (*The Triangle of Pacific States*) (Tokyo: Sairyusha Press 1995). We are grateful to Atsuo Takeuchi of Sairyusha Press for his permission to publish in the current volume revised and extended versions of five of the chapters first published in the 1995 book, which was awarded the Canadian Prime Minister's Award for Publishing in Japan. A large number of additional chapters were commissioned in 1995 for the current volume, and prepared, reviewed, and revised during the subsequent three years.

Of the many scholars who made a major contribution to this book we would like to highlight in particular Michael Donnelly, who first suggested and subsequently arranged the merger of the two research networks for this project, and Daizo Sakurada, for his outstanding initiative and dedication in driving forward the ongoing research enterprise of which this project is a part. Both are exemplars of our underlying commitment to collaborative research among American, Japanese, and Canadian scholars as a means of improving understanding of the complex dynamics of the Pacific region as the next century dawns.

We are also grateful for the support provided by the staff of our respective institutions: the University of Southern California's School of International Relations; the University of Toronto's Centre for International Studies, and Osaka University's School of International Public Policy. We are particularly appreciative of the exceptional assistance rendered during the research stage by Marc Sharrett and during the final editorial stages by Cecilia Brain, Mary Lynne Bratti, Joan Golding, and Rashida Chee-A-Kwai at the Centre for International Studies. We owe much to our editors at the University of Toronto Press, Virgil Duff and Robert Ferguson, for their support, advice, and patience. We acknowledge with gratitude the financial support of the Government of Canada through Brian Long of the Academic Relations Division of the Department of Foreign Affairs and International Trade, of the Research Fund of the School of International Relations at the University of Southern California, of those organizations assisting the research of the individual chapters, and of our colleagues serving as anonymous reviewers of our grant applications and the resulting manuscript. Above all we thank our families for their understanding during the long periods of time in which we were absorbed in the research, writing, and final editing of this book.

We dedicate this work, with great pleasure, to the Right Honourable Joe Clark, who during his time as Canada's Prime Minister and Secretary of State for External Affairs did so much to wisely manage and presciently develop the relationship between and among the three major powers of the North Pacific Triangle.

MICHAEL FRY, LOS ANGELES
JOHN KIRTON, TORONTO
MITSURU KUROSAWA, OSAKA

JULY 1997

INTRODUCTION

1

The New North Pacific Triangle

MICHAEL FRY, JOHN KIRTON, AND MITSURU KUROSAWA

For the past half-century, the management of relations with the United States has been the primary challenge for both Japan and Canada in their foreign, and at times even domestic, affairs. But during the past decade, America's relationship with its two major Pacific partners has become a central question for the United States, and the entire international community as well. The end of the Soviet Union and the Cold War, the consequent shift of attention to economic and social issues in an age of intense globalization, and the rise of Japan and Canada alongside the United States as major powers in these realms has increasingly put United States–Japanese–Canadian relations, in their bilateral, regional, and multilateral dimensions, at centre stage in all three countries and in other consequential capitals. The emergence of regionalism in the international system, led by an ever deeper, broader, and more self-absorbed European Union, has given the three major market-oriented democracies in the Pacific a heightened appreciation of their common interests and led them into closer contact, coalition creation, and community building. At the same time, the demise of Cold War–bred alliance solidarity and structures has called into question the premises and processes that have long guided the three countries in their security relations with one another, and forced them to search for new ways to manage and shape the post–Cold War order.

To many observers, this transition has been a conflict-ridden process centred on growing economic tensions between the United States and Japan. American demands for Japanese financial assistance during the 1990–91 Gulf War and to finance Russian reforms, a steady succession of acrimonious U.S.-initiated trade negotiations with Japan, and the recurrent American push for a higher Japanese yen have indeed been a preoccupation of American foreign policy in the 1990s. Such crusades, reinforced by disputes over the American military presence in Japan and Japan's reluctant support for America's global security endeavours, have often captured the attention and aroused the emotion of publics in both countries. But beneath the drama, there are three broader, more basic, and potentially much more significant processes at work.

The first is a broadening web of interaction as America's once separate, special bilateral relationships with Japan and Canada individually are giving way to a more interactive, triangular configuration. As long ago as 15 August 1971, America's unilateral suspension of gold convertibility for the U.S. dollar, its demand for foreign currencies to float upward, and its imposition of a 10 per cent surcharge on dutiable imports into the United States forced Canada and Japan, as the major exporters to the U.S. market, to come together. They did so at first, reluctantly and hesitantly, to cope with this shock to their economic health, and subsequently, with some enthusiasm, to diversify their relations with and thus reduce their dependence on the United States. During subsequent decades, in leading sectors such as investment, these ties of Japanese–Canadian diversification, and thus the traditionally fragile, third leg of the trans-Pacific triangle, have flourished. Now America's conduct of its bilateral relationship with either Japan or Canada often involves consideration of, or dealings with, the other. Longstanding Canadian concerns that the United States would 'sideswipe' Canadian interests in negotiating bilateral arrangements with Japan have been joined in the 1980s by American worries that Japan's new direct investments in North America might disproportionately flow north rather than south of the United States–Canada border, and in the 1990s by Japanese fears that American–Canadian arrangements under first the Canada–United States Free Trade Agreement (FTA) and then the North American Free Trade Agreement (NAFTA) might exclude Japan in a harmful way.

A second transformation has been the movement of the trilateral relationship from its economic foundations into a much broader sphere of endeavour, including the major issues of regional and global peace, security, arms control, and war. Throughout the long decades of the Cold War, Japanese and Canadian diplomats had dealt with each other and with their American counterparts in multilateral forums on a host of global political issues, such as relations with and diplomatic recognition of the People's Republic of China, and security issues such as United Nations disarmament and arms control efforts. The new Cold War of the 1980s brought a deeper concern and dialogue about the management of East–West relations. However, the post–Cold War world of the 1990s, inaugurated by the 1990–91 Gulf War, has seen a veritable explosion of the agenda and intensification of contact and cooperation. Japan has joined Canada in peacekeeping in proximate Cambodia and distant Mozambique; confronted issues of Pacific security, new nuclear challenges, and a perceived threat from North Korea; defined a new relationship with Russia; and undertaken more ambitious global arms control initiatives, notably an effort to inhibit military spending among recipients of assistance from multilateral development banks and to curb the use of antipersonnel landmines. At the same time, both of the historic bilateral pillars of Pacific security – the U.S.–Japan security treaty, and the Canada–U.S. defence relationship, centred in the North American Aerospace Defence Command (NORAD) – have been questioned by policy élites and publics in all three countries.

Third, the three North Pacific powers have moved from earlier diplomatic conflicts and efforts at cooperation into ambitious quests in community building as they have pioneered the creation and development of the international institutions of the post–Cold War era. Their initial activities from 1976 onward in the Group of Seven (G7) major industrial democracies have been joined by their leadership in the Asia Pacific Economic Cooperation Forum (APEC) from 1989 (at the ministerial level) and 1993 (at the leaders level), and most recently in a host of political and security forums: the North Pacific Co-operative Security Dialogue (NPCSD), the Council for Security Co-operation in Asia Pacific (CSCAP), the Association of Southeast Asian Nations Post Ministerial Conference (ASEAN-PMC), and the ASEAN Regional Forum (ARF). Here the United States, Japan, and Canada have variously sought, as major powers and global players of increasing international importance, to manage their bilateral and regional differences and to protect and promote their distinctive values, but above all to forward their common interests in shaping the institutions and order of the global community of the twenty-first century.

With these transformations have come important changes in the way the three North Pacific powers have related to one another. Historically, both Canada and Japan dealt with a vastly more powerful United States as important and independent, but often supportive and deferential, supplicants. They received in return the exemptions and rewards that their respective special relationships brought. The 1971 surcharge crisis and accompanying decline of America's global pre-eminence enhanced the Canadian and Japanese need to constrain a unilateralist America, but also to strengthen ties between themselves for improved self-protection. Only in the 1990s has a more complete array of roles emerged. Japan and Canada are now variously competitors for American attention, resources, and designation as its most important partner, common crusaders in the perennial struggle to keep America open and outward-looking, associates that can share techniques on the successful management of relations with an always-challenging America, allies who can forge their own bonds with or without the United States, and colleagues and competitors in shaping the new Asia-Pacific and global order.

In turn, America's relationship with both Canada and Japan has changed in consequential ways. Largely gone is America's responsibility and role as protector from a potentially predatory Soviet Union or remnant Russia. Gone with this role is the resulting position of Canada and Japan as loyal allies on the outer perimeter of the American security sphere, respectively defending the U.S. homeland and Western nuclear deterrent from an over-the-pole attack and maintaining the Pacific Ocean as an American lake. In its place has emerged a recognition of the need for Japanese, and the value of Canadian, cooperation in the construction of the new, still undefined and amorphous Asia-Pacific security order, especially as a new Asian arms race and tensions created by a still politically unreformed China and isolated North Korea mount. At the same time, America has heightened its appreciation of the value of Japanese and Canadian investment, markets, and products for its own prosperity, even as it adjusts uneasily to its fading global pre-eminence with harsh demands that particular economic imbalances be redressed.

These challenges of trilateral, comprehensive community building in the post–Cold War, globalizing world are compounded by profound changes in the domestic coherence and self-confidence of the three countries. In the United States, the 1994 advent and 1996 confirmation of an inward-looking Republican Congressional majority committed to deficit reduction has constrained America's capacity for enlightened international leadership and institution building. In Japan, the 1990s end of the post–World War II economic miracle – reflected in prolonged economic stagnation, rising unemployment, collapsing financial institutions, natural and human shocks, and major political realignment – has produced a new defensiveness or paralysis, even as more assertive leaders have come to the fore. And in Canada, fundamental questions about the country's prospects of continuing as a cohesive federal state have arisen, just as Canada has begun to restore its international competitiveness and moved to place relations with the Asia-Pacific region at the forefront of its new foreign policy vision.

This book explores this new relationship among the United States, Japan, and Canada in the post–Cold War world of the 1990s and the changing roles of each country towards the others as the twenty-first century approaches. It has three central purposes.

Firstly and most broadly, it seeks to chart the changing patterns of interaction between and among the United States, Japan, and Canada over recent decades in order to highlight the trends and transformations taking place in the post–Cold War, globalizing international system at the end of the twentieth century.

Secondly, it seeks to compare the changing approaches of Japan and Canada to managing their relationship with the United States, to assess the effectiveness of the strategies and techniques employed by each, and to suggest how the most successful can be adapted for use by the other. As part of this exercise in policy analysis, prescription, and learning, it also points to ways in which an ever-central United States will and can conduct its relationship with its two leading Pacific partners for mutual and general benefit.

Thirdly, it explores how the growing United States–Japan–Canada transpacific community is serving and can serve as the foundation for larger efforts at regional and global order building to meet the needs of the twenty-first-century world. It examines the trade, investment, and other economic implications for the United States and Canada of a domestically transforming and demographically aging Japan, and how their shifting transpacific economic ties alter the basis for regional community building. It also analyses the common political, security, and ecological challenges the three countries confront in the new era, and the new institutions they are constructing to cope with them.

Understanding this new triangular dynamic requires moving beyond a reliance on the many existing studies of the individual bilateral relationships between the United States and Japan, the United States and Canada, and Japan and Canada.[1] This book thus offers analyses in which the intersections and interdependencies among these bilateral relationships, the new trilateral processes, and the regional community building based on these, occupy centre stage. Understanding these new triangular relationships builds on earlier studies of the three countries' new foreign policy approaches, concerns that are of central interest to scholars of international relations and related domestic politics.[2] However, securing a more complete understanding of their current complexities and evolving character, particularly in the post–Cold War system, requires a multidimensional and multidisciplinary enterprise. Thus, this book assembles the insights of scholarly specialists in Canada, Japan, and the United States across the disciplinary expanses of economics, business, law, diplomacy, political science, and geography.[3] Their contributions are united not by any a priori commitment to a single theoretical model or methodological approach but by a common conviction that Japan in particular and the United States and Canada more generally are currently experiencing a profound transformation based on connections between their domestic and foreign policies, and their economic and political–security concerns. To identify the depth, direction, and durability of these transformations amidst the fluctuations of current moods, policy debates, and government posturing, this book grounds its contemporary analysis in new interpretations of earlier turning points and periods and looks ahead to the prospects and possibilities that await.

This book begins, in its first section, by exploring the economic foundations of the triangular relationship, with a focus on trade, investment, the macroeconomic pillars of exchange rate, monetary and fiscal policy, and business negotiations.

In Chapter 2, Daizo Sakurada examines the immediate response to, and subsequent policy redirection of Japan and Canada arising from, one of the decisive events in the post–World War II international system and U.S.–Canada–Japan relationship: America's August 1971 imposition of an import surcharge and suspension of the convertibility of the U.S. dollar into gold. Sakurada notes the particular shock these moves produced for America's two largest trading partners, Canada and Japan, the divergent response of the two countries, and the greater success that Canada enjoyed as it succeeded in lifting the surcharge, preserving the vital Autopact, and maintaining its existing exchange rate regime, while Japan acquiesced in its textile dispute and accepted a large upward revaluation of the yen.

In Chapter 3, Tsuyoshi Kawasaki moves from the immediate turning point to the longer trend, comparing the experience of Japan and Canada in influencing United States macroeconomic policy during the 1960s, 1970s, and 1980s. Recognizing that overwhelming American preponderance in relevant capabilities left the smaller Pacific partners little room for policy freedom and diplomatic manoeuvre, Kawasaki argues that financial market forces occasionally produced economic conditions or 'windows of opportunity' that Japan and Canada could and did use to their advantage.

In Chapter 4, Michael Donnelly focuses on how opportunities were converted into outcomes as the post–Cold War period dawned. He probes in detail the bargaining between the United States and Japan in the Structural Impediments Initiative of 1989–90. Focusing on the bilateral strategic interaction and process of joint decision making, Donnelly argues that the general conditions of asymmetric competitive interdependence led to a bargaining approach of 'authoritative prescription' by a United States on the offensive and 'minimal deferential adjustment' by a Japan on the defensive. A bilateral summit, an election victory by Japan's ruling Liberal Democratic Party, and the use of interest bargaining, integrative compromise, attitudinal change, and intra-state accommodation finally produced an agreement that reflected the essential interests of and benefited both sides.

In Chapter 5, David Edgington explores the recent pattern and current prospects of Japanese direct investment in Canada. Concluding that Canada's traditional 2 per cent share of Japanese FDI could fall to only .2 per cent over the next decade, he points to the opportunities provided by NAFTA's provisions and the explosion of Japanese tourism, with Canada as a favoured destination, as forces that could offset this trend.

In Chapter 6, Richard Wright looks more deeply within Japan to assess the implications of its 'post-bubble' economic changes and rapidly aging society for both the United States and Canada. He predicts a short-term continuation or widening of Japan's external trade surplus, a sharp decline in Japanese domestic and overseas investment, a shift from portfolio towards direct foreign investments, a move from North America and Europe towards Asia as a preferred destination, and a sharper focus on maximizing return on equity. Despite these trends, however, the United States will benefit from Japan's greater preference for locating its 'transplants' south of the Canada–United States border, while Canada can seize new export opportunities in building products; processed foods; and financial, engineering, and construction services; and can more easily afford a business or investment presence in Japan.

In Chapter 7, Rosalie Tung looks beyond government policy to explore how the business communities in all three countries are negotiating to form joint ventures and other partnerships. After outlining a conceptual paradigm of cross-national business negotiations, she examines survey research results on U.S.–Japan and Canada–Japan negotiations to identify the factors that lead to success and failure. She concludes that the prospects of success can be enhanced if North American businesspeople negotiating with the Japanese show patience, trust, and respect for cross-cultural differences; study the market, industry, and particular needs of prospective Japanese partners; and maintain dialogue at all levels. While changes in the Japan of the 1990s may suggest to some that these cultural factors will be of diminishing force, they are in many respects similar to those highlighted by Donnelly in U.S.–Japan negotiations at the intergovernmental level.

The second section of this book deals with security and political issues. It focuses on Japan's increasing involvement in areas and roles in which the United States and Canada have long specialized, and the new relationships with its transpacific partners that Japan's growing global involvement has created.

In Chapter 8, Frank Langdon outlines the still dangerous post–Cold War security challenge facing the United States, Japan, and Canada in the Asia-Pacific region and their respective responses to managing the many conflicts within it. Comparing the United States' continuing preference for bilateral military alliances with Canada's thrust for a regional and multilateral cooperative security dialogue, and with Japan's new acceptance of a global, if still non-belligerent, security role, Langdon reviews the new defence policies unveiled in all three countries in 1995. He identifies a movement in all three countries towards greater involvement and de facto cooperation. He concludes that the United States, Japan, and Canada are all essentially status quo powers that have come to welcome the multilateral approach through confidence and security-building mechanisms pioneered by Canada. Langdon suggests, however, that the region still requires a subregional North Pacific security forum to supplement the recently created broader dialogues.

In Chapter 9, David Welch deals with the future of the critical U.S.–Japan security relationship, and Canada's perspective on how it will and should evolve. He argues that despite the Canadian government's official silence on the subject, it views the U.S.–Japan Security Treaty as an effective, indeed vital, vehicle for fostering Japanese security, U.S.–Japanese cooperation, and stability in northern Asia-Pacific, and prefers the new multilateral mechanisms it is fostering to reinforce rather than replace this historic bilateral pillar. Looking ahead, as long as the treaty continues to provide the substance and symbol of American commitment, Ottawa is open to any adjustments that meet U.S. and Japanese current needs.

In Chapter 10, Mitsuru Kurosawa reviews Canadian, Japanese, and American involvement in, and approaches to, United Nations peacekeeping from its start at Suez in 1956 to the present proliferation of such activity in the post–Cold War period. Contrasting Canada's seminal role in pioneering such activity with Japan's late and still somewhat hesitant involvement in the 1990s, he finds that the causes of these differences lie in Canada's foreign policy tradition of multilateralism and Japan's preference for U.S.-focused bilateralism. Kurosawa concludes that Japan has much to learn from Canada in this new era.

In Chapter 11, Paul Parker takes up the 'new' security issue, and common public preoccupation, of protecting the global environment. He argues that differing geophysical characteristics, domestic politics, industrial structures, and environmental group strength have given the United States, Japan, and Canada different positions and relationships on major international and domestic environmental issues, and propelled each country into the lead in particular areas. Thus the United States was in the vanguard in stratospheric ozone, natural protected areas, world heritage and biosphere reserves, and environmental impact assessment; Canada in greenhouse gas emissions, acid rain, water quality, and wetlands protection; and Japan in sulphur dioxide and nitrogen oxide and official development assistance for environmental purposes. Parker points to the recent dialogues between Japan and Canada on strengthened environmental cooperation and the potential for partnership in such critical areas as the North Pacific fisheries.

The third and final section deals with the ways the three Pacific powers have moved to manage their deeper and broader relationships, both through innovative bilateral political mechanisms and the shaping and creation of international institutions.

In Chapter 12, James Taylor focuses on the overall Japan–Canada relationship and the way in which the two governments have managed the intensifying, broadening, and deepening interconnections between the two countries. Noting that the large array of complex and harmonious relations between the two societies often unfold beyond government management, Taylor emphasizes three recent initiatives by the Canadian government: to engage Japan in a multilateral, academically delivered North Pacific Cooperative Security Dialogue at the end of the Cold War; to enhance Canada's value-added exports through an expanded diplomatic presence; and to reassure major Japanese investors in Canada of the latter's stability. The success achieved by some of these initiatives has been reinforced by a host of new programs introduced by Japan.

In Chapter 13, Michael Fry addresses one innovative management technique, the Canada–Japan Forum 2000 joint eminent persons' group created by the two governments in May 1991. Noting Canada's enthusiasm and Japan's initial reluctance for the venture, he describes the work and recommendations of the Forum in its four component areas of political, economic, international, and cultural affairs. Fry concludes that, despite changes of government in both countries, the exercise had results in the fields of Canada's exports to Japan, Japanese investment in Canada, environmental stewardship in the North Pacific, and cooperation in the Uruguay Round and G-7. Such accomplishments are all the more valuable, he argues, in light of the Chrétien government's enthusiasm for China, Japan's growing concentration on the Asian rather than the North American region, and the enhanced need for democratic polities to legitimate their foreign policies in the post–Cold War era.

In Chapter 14, Lawrence Woods examines current Japanese and Canadian approaches to institution building in the Asia-Pacific region. Drawing upon the earlier experience of Inazo Nitobe and Herbert Norman in the Institute of Pacific Relations from 1925 to 1960, he traces the evolution of regional nongovernmental diplomacy through the Pacific Trade and Development Conference (PAFTAD) and the Pacific Basin Economic Council (PBEC) in the mid-1960s, and the tripartite Pacific Economic Cooperation Council (PECC) in 1980. In the 1990s, the American attempt to dominate the agenda of the APEC, established in 1989, led Japan to pioneer the ASEAN-centred, intergovernmental ARF, which began operating in July 1994, and inspired Canada to develop the nongovernmental CSCAP. Despite these differences in emphasis, Woods concludes, the compatibility between Japan's concept of comprehensive security and Canada's concept of cooperative security is leading to a mutually reinforcing, two-track dialogue and partnership.

In Chapter 15, John Kirton examines American, Japanese, and Canadian cooperation within the global forum of the G-7 summit, and the way a trilateral Pacific partnership has strengthened since the 1975 inception of the forum. He argues that over the Summit's first twenty-one years, Japan and Canada have slowly moved towards more equal involvement, initiative, and cooperation, at times without, or over the initial opposition of, the United States. However, such cooperation, evident in the shaping of the Summit as an institution and in multilateral trade liberalization, remains less than the profound changes in global and G-7 relative capability would predict or permit. This unfulfilled potential for partnership is largely due to the differing political philosophies of leaders in the two countries, and the Eurocentric focus of the Canadian prime ministers from Quebec.

Taken together, these chapters present a portrait of a rich and rapidly changing trans-Pacific triangle in which longstanding domestic assumptions and foreign policy approaches are being rethought and substantially revised. As this process is still in its early stages, it is premature to declare with confidence the direction these changes will cumulatively take or the new order they will produce. But from the analyses in these chapters, several trends are clear.

The first is the effective end of America's separate if special bilateral relationships with Japan and Canada respectively in both the security and economic realms. With them have gone the pattern of economic 'exceptionalism' for global security support that the combination of American ascendency and the Cold War bred. Although the rising security threats across the Pacific mean America will remain aware of the need for its most reliable allies, the probable threats are less to the United States itself than to its Pacific allies. This fact will reduce the willingness of a less economically ascendant America to bear a disproportionate share of the security burden.

The second trend is the emergence of Japan as a global player and global power – in short, an international actor increasingly resembling its two transpacific partners who have long been in this position. Japan's rapidly rising wealth and intensifying globalization have given it system-leading responsibilities for international development assistance, and for the stable functioning of the international financial and multilateral trade system. Moreover, its modern military capabilities combined with the new security challenges of the post–Cold War period have propelled it into a global security role, as its peacekeeping deployments demonstrate. Not surprisingly, these major changes in Japanese foreign policy, taking place despite the country's economic stagnation in the first half of the 1990s, have given rise to agonizing domestic debates over foreign policy of the sort long familiar to Americans and Canadians.

The third trend is the resulting advent of a more equal, globally relevant partnership among the three leading market-oriented Pacific democracies. Japan and Canada have become more assertive and more successful in their relationship with the United States. Yet only rarely have they combined to mount initiatives that do not include, or that actively oppose, the United States. In particular there are few signs that Japan or Canada would welcome the emergence of Japan as the core of a Pacific system or global order that would rival those being pioneered by or involving the United States. Here the post–Cold War international system has generated less a sense of freedom and opportunity on the part of Japan and Canada than a cautious emphasis on stability in the face of a still dangerous Asia-Pacific region.

A fourth trend has thus been the intensification of American, Japanese, and Canadian diplomacy to shape a new regional order for the Asia-Pacific region, to strengthen collective management of the global order, and to manage bilateral differences within these broader, rapidly developing regimes. Although each of the three Pacific partners has convergent rather than common or competitive interests in these ventures, their combination has led to a hitherto successful leadership coalition in promoting new regional and plurilateral institutions. As powers of global relevance, the three have thus far avoided the development of a post–Cold War institutional order, based on narrowly conceived geographic regionalism, in favour of transregional institutions that embrace countries of enormously diverse character. As the twenty-first century approaches, the demands of a rapidly globalizing international economic system and an increasingly dangerous security challenge in Asia suggest that this emerging partnership in collective global leadership will only strengthen.

NOTES

1 On the U.S.–Japan bilateral relationship see Destler and Sato, eds., *Coping with U.S.–Japanese Economic Conflicts*; Encarnation, *Rivals Beyond Trade*; Buckley, *U.S.–Japan Alliance Diplomacy, 1945–1990*; Bergsten and Noland, *Reconcilable Differences*; and Saxonhouse, *The Economics of the U.S.–Japan Framework Talks*. On the U.S.–Canada bilateral relationship see Doran, *Forgotten Partnership*; and Leyton-Brown and Jockel, eds., 'Weathering the Calm.' On the Japan–Canada bilateral relationship see Hay, ed., *Canadian Perspectives*; Langdon, *The Politics of Canadian–Japanese*; Pringsheim, *Neighbours across the Pacific*; Schultz and Miwa, *Canada and Japan*; Japan–Canada Forum 2000, *Partnership across the Pacific*; and Holroyd and Coates, *Pacific Partners*.

2 The major previous works on the triangular U.S.–Japan–Canada relationship are Dobson, ed., *Canadian–Japanese Economic Relations*; Stern, ed., *Trade and Investment Relations*; Matthew and Boownsey, eds. *Japan's Relations with North America*; Doran et al., *Pacific Partners*; Kurosawa and Kirton, eds., *Taiheiyo Kokkano Toraianguru*; and Hawes, *Atlantic Past, Pacific Future*.

3 This group of scholars includes two colleagues and collaborators who have published their important work as Terry Ursacki and Ilan Vertinsky, 'Canada–Japan Trade.'

I. THE ECONOMIC AND BUSINESS RELATIONSHIP

2

The 'Nixon Shokku' Revisited: Japanese and Canadian Foreign Economic Policies Compared

DAIZO SAKURADA

Introduction

No unilateral U.S. policy has caused as fundamental a shift in the international political economy as the so-called Nixon Shokku (Shocks) of 15 August 1971.[1] By forcibly suspending the U.S. dollar's convertibility to gold and imposing a 10 per cent surcharge on all dutiable goods coming into the United States, the Nixon regime precipitated conflict with its close allies. It also destroyed the Bretton Woods international monetary system. Canada and Japan, the United States' largest and second-largest trading partners, were particularly damaged. Both took steps to counteract the Shocks. The outcomes of Ottawa's and Tokyo's policies, however, were divergent: in the end, Canada achieved more than Japan without making any apparent concessions. Specifically, Japan acquiesced in its 'textile wrangle' with the United States and accepted an unexpectedly large upward revaluation of the yen vis-à-vis the dollar. The Canadians, on the other hand, succeeded in lifting the surcharge with the lucrative Canada–U.S. Autopact intact.

This case is of special scholarly interest for two reasons. First, the importance of the event means it should attract more attention from political scientists and international relations (IR) scholars. There has been an accumulation of analyses of the event by economists, but not much interpretation of the bargaining outcomes between the Canada–U.S. and the Japan–U.S. dyads. Also, a more theoretically rigorous comparative study of the American allies' response to unilateral U.S. foreign economic pressure is possible because this enforcement was multilateral in the sense that all of the U.S. trading partners were affected evenly at the same time. For these reasons, this topic should be taken up as a crucial case study for universally applicable theory building in the field of IR as well as for studying comparative foreign policy in Canada–U.S.–Japan triangular relations.

There exists, in the works of Joanne Gowa and John Odell, some scholarly literature about Washington's decision-making process leading to the August announcement. Tokyo's decision-making process during the crisis has also been described in detail by Ushio Shiota, Kunio Yanagida, Robert Angel, and Tsuyoshi Kawasaki. Such Canadianists as Osvald Croci, Peter Dobell, John Kirton, and Robert Bothwell, and J.L. Granatstein and Robert Bothwell, also delineate Ottawa's diplomatic relations with its giant neighbour during this period.[2] But, in the English-language literature, no attempt has been made so far to compare and analyse the two most important countries' policy responses to this case of 'multilaterally enforced U.S. unilateralism.' The purpose of this chapter is to fill this vacuum both empirically and theoretically. Based on primary and secondary materials concerning the incident and interviews with former policy-makers, this chapter will describe and compare the policy responses of these two 'friends' of Washington.

The Canadian and Japanese negotiations with America over this issue supports Stephen Krasner's concept of the 'national interest.' Krasner, in *Defending the National Interest*, presumes the existence of a national interest in each state.[3] National interest is the 'preferences' of a state's central decision-makers related to general societal goals. National interest, Krasner argues, persists over time and has a consistent ranking of component values. States, according to this view, are autonomous actors seeking their own interests. Krasner's identification of the 'national interest' is valid in the treatment of Canadian and Japanese responses to the Shocks because there were no significantly conflicting views in either society about the aims of their diplomatic negotiations with the United States.

Still, the 'national interest' is an ambiguous term considering that the preferences of central decision-makers may change both over time and as a result of external influences during the course of diplomatic interactions. For clarity, this chapter deliberately sets a limit on the period of this case. August 1971, when President Richard Nixon delivered his historic speech, is considered the beginning of the crisis. By December 1971, when the import surcharge was lifted, the Shocks were virtually over.

This chapter first describes the stages leading to the solution of the Nixon crisis. Then, the important question of why Canada and Japan responded to the American economic measures as they did will be theoretically addressed. Here, the dependent variable is the difference between the policy outcome of the Canada–U.S. dyad versus the Japan–U.S. dyad: Canada did achieve its 'national interest,' while Japan failed to do so.

Further, in explaining the foreign economic policy responses to the August crisis, this chapter will use four frameworks or models as independent variables and examine their explanatory powers.[4] The first two models employed in this chapter are a simplified version of Allison's Model II ('organizational process' model), and a simplified Model III (the 'governmental politics' model). Constructed as antitheses of the 'unitary-rational assumption' of a state's external behaviour, these models fundamentally emphasize the deficiencies emanating from the domestic policy-making process of each government. Thus, the more the policy-making process of either Tokyo or Ottawa showed reactions reflecting Allison's Model II and/or III to Nixon's enforcement of his measures, the worse its bargaining outcomes against Washington would likely be.

Another model was created by Charles Doran in his book *Forgotten Partnership*. Going beyond the interdependence debate of the 1970s, he proposed the concept of 'intervulnerability' as a proper conceptual framework to explain Canada's better-than-expected performance in its handling of U.S. relations.

The last model examined is the 'complex interdependence' model of Robert Keohane and Joseph Nye. This model is composed of three main characteristics: the minor role of military force in the resolution of disputes, an absence of hierarchy among issues, and multiple channels of contact between societies. As demonstrated below, this chapter revives the complex interdependence model as the most relevant independent variable to explain the divergent bargaining outcomes between the two dyads.

Background to the Shocks

Until the late 1960s, Washington had regarded both its political and economic interests as being served by a prompt recovery of the European and Japanese economies.[5] Consequently, the United States had shouldered the burden to help stabilize the international trade and monetary system. This meant its trade system had basically been directed at encouraging free trade all over the world through the General Agreement on Tariffs and Trade (GATT), and its monetary policy had been largely based on a 'benign neglect' of the Bretton Woods monetary system of fixed exchange rates. This attitude began to change with the escalation of the Vietnam War and the budget deficits caused by President Lyndon Johnson's expansionary 'Great Society' program. The result was a huge capital outflow from the United States. American dollars flooded world financial markets and U.S. inflation was transmitted to the West European countries, Japan, and Canada through the monetary system. These nations were compelled to accept inflated dollars at face value under the fixed exchange rate system. As a reserve currency economy, the United States was free to generate more international money (dollars) as long as dollar-holders retained the view that the value of the dollar would be 'as good as gold.'

By the summer of 1971, however, it was clear that confidence in the dollar had been greatly shaken. The U.S. economy had gone through a recession in 1970. The Nixon regime's stimulus to the domestic economy unleashed renewed inflationary forces, resulting in the further undermining of confidence in the dollar, which, in turn, caused chaos in foreign exchange markets. The Nixon administration was under pressure to convert a gigantic volume of inflated dollars into gold. Since the U.S. gold reserve was not sufficient, the international monetary system of fixed exchange rates with the dollar as the key currency was threatened with collapse.

Increasing speculative attacks on the dollar in mid-August, coupled with the first American trade deficit in 1970 since 1893 and a disappointing report on American economic recovery, convinced Washington of the need to resort to drastic unilateral measures to prevent the outflow of gold and to shift to other economic partners the burdens of leadership in the international political economy. This was even more significant as the Nixon regime was increasingly being accused of mismanaging the domestic economy. Preservation of American autonomy in foreign economic policy became high on the agenda of the Nixon Cabinet, which was intent on winning re-election the following year.

Against this backdrop, President Richard Nixon delivered his 'New Economic Policy' on the night of 15 August 1971.[6] It was a bombshell: no American allies had been informed, let alone consulted, prior to the announcement. Perceived to be the greatest threats to the Canadian and Japanese economies were the imposition of the 10 per cent import surcharge and an unpegging of the U.S. dollar from gold. The latter measure was interpreted to undervalue the U.S. dollar vis-à-vis the currencies of its trade surplus nations so as to reduce the U.S. trade deficit. This meant major economic costs to the export-oriented Canadian and Japanese economies.

One caveat, however, must be noted in the comparison of Canada–U.S. negotiations and Japan–U.S. negotiations towards a diplomatic settlement. Both Canada and Japan considered the measures very harmful to their economic expansion and protested accordingly. However, the main focus of Canadian–American negotiations was trade-oriented, whereas that of Japanese–American negotiations was over the extent to which the undervalued Japanese yen should or should not be revalued vis-à-vis the U.S. dollar. The fact that the Canadian dollar had been floating against the U.S. dollar since June 1970, with a resulting appreciation of the Canadian currency, strengthened the Canadian negotiators' bargaining position against their American counterparts.

The different nature of the 'issue' as perceived in Ottawa and Tokyo cautions against disregarding the two dyads' differences. Nevertheless, as revealed in interviews with Simon Reisman, chief negotiator on the Canadian side, America did exert pressure to appreciate and peg the Canadian dollar against the U.S. dollar.[7] Therefore, both American allies were in a similar and comparable position of being urged to appreciate their currencies against the U.S. dollar, as well as to grant trade concessions to the United States.

The Canadian Response

The Trudeau government had launched some independent Canadian foreign policy initiatives before the Shocks. Ottawa's recognition of Beijing in October 1970 spared Trudeau the first Nixon Shock dropped on the regime of Japan's Eisaku Sato in July 1971. Trudeau's visit to the Soviet Union produced a Soviet–Canada détente in the form of a protocol of consultation. These and other actions, like the halving of Canadian North American Treaty Organization (NATO) forces in Europe, and the introduction of the Arctic Waters Pollution Prevention Act to establish Canadian sovereignty over the North, were not welcomed in Washington: some American officials feared the precedent-setting effects of Canada's independent moves. Still, the Canadian actions were nothing more than mere irritants, not resulting in outright diplomatic confrontations across the 49th Parallel or becoming a reason not to exempt Canada from the Nixon measures.[8]

The fact that Canada–U.S. relations suffered no major territorial or commercial disputes meant that the Nixon measures were shocks, in the genuine meaning of the word, for Ottawa's decision-makers at the time of his speech.[9] Canada depended on American markets for some 70 per cent of its exports, so it seemed that Canada could be the largest victim of American unilateralism. The federal government estimated that at least a quarter of Canada's exports to the United States would be subject to the 10 per cent import surcharge, that is, between $2.5 billion and $3 billion out of the 1970 total of $10.5 billion in exports to the United States. At the beginning, 40,000 to 100,000 Canadians were predicted to lose their jobs due to the damage caused by the surcharge.

The first governmental response began with the policy prescription drafted by Deputy Minister of Finance Simon Reisman and other officials. At a meeting to consider countermoves, the point was made that the United States had inadvertently taken economic measures without giving due consideration to Canada's situation. Canada should make a proper representation in Washington and put its own case forward: Canada deserved an exemption from the surcharge. This prescription reflected the 'special relationship' between Canada and the United States in the past: in 1963, 1965, and 1968, when the United States imposed such unilateral macroeconomic measures as the Interest Equalization Tax and other regulatory policies, Canada had been able to obtain de facto exemptions by emphasizing the 'intervulnerable' economic structure it shared with its southern neigbour. Canadian policy-makers thought that the intervulnerable economic conditions could at least offer a compelling argument to use against American decision-makers in the 1960s.[10] Asking for an exemption was almost semi-automatically decided at the meeting.[11] The policy recommendations were accepted by the Cabinet and became Canada's official position.

External Affairs Minister Mitchell Sharp stated at the first press conference that the Nixon measures were taken to alleviate unfair exchange rates and discriminatory restrictions against American export products. He added that Canada fulfilled neither condition, and should not, therefore, be subject to the surtax: Canada was, indeed, innocent. This perspective was reiterated by Finance Minister Edgar Benson and Trade Minister Jean-Luc Pepin later in Washington when they met Secretary of the Treasury John Connolly, the main culprit of the American action. From then on, the main Canadian arguments for an exemption, including Prime Minister Trudeau's, can be summarized as follows:

1/ The Canadian dollar had been floating freely since June 1970 and had appreciated against the U.S. dollar by 6 to 7 per cent.
2/ Canada had no noticeable trade barriers preventing the sale of American products; in fact, Canada had decided to speed up the import liberalization plans agreed to in the GATT Kennedy Round.
3/ It may have been true that Canada had a trade surplus of $1.12 billion in 1970, but it had actually run a current account deficit of $165 million with the United States.
4/ The intervulnerable nature of both economies meant that the deterioration of the Canadian economy as a result of the surtax would lead to a decrease in imports from the United States, and this would badly affect, rather than rebuild, the American economy.

The Canadian government threatened neither retaliations nor countermeasures like a depreciation of the Canadian dollar or the imposition of a countervailing import surtax. Rather, just like Japan, Canada would domestically take some economic measures in the form of tax cuts and the Employment Support Act.

The Canadian position was slightly different from that of Japan, which tried to avoid a large appreciation of the yen, and that of Europe, which pushed for a devaluation of the U.S. dollar through an increase in the price of gold. Canada agreed with the United States on the need for a better realignment of currencies and the elimination of trade barriers, but did hope that the United States would abolish the import surcharge without appreciating the Canadian dollar. This stance was based on the conviction that Canada was 'caught between' the international commercial and monetary disputes between the United States, on the one hand, and Japan and Europe, on the other, even though Canada itself had already undertaken currency realignment and trade liberalization.

This did not mean, however, that Canada would serve as a mere 'spokesperson' for America in the international arena. Ottawa was under enormous pressure from various domestic groups like the business community, the opposition parties, and labour to soften the impending damage caused by the American economic measures. Washington was also not so soft on Ottawa, strongly pushing Ottawa to acquiesce in granting trade concessions like changing the safeguard clause in the Autopact and repegging the Canadian dollar at a higher level against the U.S. dollar. Canada, of course, did not budge.

The circumstances that promoted Ottawa's diplomatic breakthrough were set before the December Smithsonian meeting.[12] Canada was able to act as if it were a unitary-rational actor with no serious dissenting voices emerging domestically. This was crucially important for Canada, the lesser power, to make up for its inferior overall capabilities vis-à-vis the United States, the larger one. Lobbying activities by Trudeau's Cabinet ministers took the form of speeches emphasizing Canada's innocence. These steadily penetrated American society.

By the start of the December meeting, the transnational or transgovernmental actors' moves were in full swing: the Canadian–American Committee issued a statement calling for the exemption of Canada from the surtax with the proviso that the trade balance with the United States was improved and that Canada reconsider the Autopact. Senator Gratton O'Leary paid a private visit to Washington in October to explain Canada's reasons for concern to his friends on Capitol Hill. The Canada–United States Interparliamentary Group heard about Canada's difficulties as well. As a result of this lobbying by Canadians, a resolution was forwarded advocating the exemption of Canada and Mexico from the surcharge. Although it fell short of passage in Congress, it signified that the U.S. domestic process was not monolithically supportive of the Nixon–Connolly method of dealing with Canada. Besides, some members of the media sympathized with the Canadian arguments for a floating dollar and nondiscriminatory trade policy. For example, a *New York Times* editorial on 7 November insisted, 'It would be well for Americans to understand why Canada believes it merited exemption from the Nixon economic actions and the threat they pose to Canadian political and economic stability.'

Compared with the Japan–U.S. dyad, largely unaffected by transnational/transgovernmental activities, the split in the American decision-making process created by these 'multiple channels of contact' helped Canada upstage the

United States. Indeed, the Nixon regime included Ottawa's transgovernmental allies like Arthur Burns, chairman of the Federal Reserve Board (FRB), and Henry Kissinger, national security adviser. They were both worried about Connolly's 'coming-on-strong' approach towards the allies. The hardliners' actions were backfiring, they thought. The U.S. economic and/or strategic relationship might be damaged by the Treasury Department's intransigence towards American allies. Denmark had already started to impose its own 10 per cent import surcharge; more retaliatory measures might be in the offing. Some Wall Street friends of Nixon's were also warning him of the dangers of his 'New Economic Policy.' In consequence, by mid-November, Nixon decided to listen to the dovish opinions advocated by Kissinger and Burns. How to exit from the policy was now a valid question.

Ivan Head, Kissinger's Canadian counterpart, set the final stage for the removal of the measures. Two meetings were planned for 6 December at the White House.[13] The lower-level meeting between Canadian and American officials headed by the Canadian Finance Minister and the American Treasury Secretary was disastrous. But the one in the Oval Office between the Trudeau–Head and Nixon–Kissinger pairs produced just what Canada wanted from the United States. Trudeau asked if the U.S. government had decided that Canada must never be in surplus with the United States. That would mean that Canada had no choice but to sell more of itself (e.g., stocks and natural resources) to the Americans in order to finance its debts to them. If so, then Ottawa would be forced to draw its own conclusions and might formulate policies unfavourable to America. With the help of Kissinger, according to Head, Nixon agreed not to prevent Canada from acquiring a trade surplus with the United States, and assured Canada of its identity. In practice, this meant that the Americans would lift the surtax against Canada down the road. This top-level tacit understanding made Canada's bargaining position very strong at the Smithsonian.

The Japanese Response

Japanese–American relations had not been in good condition when the second Nixon Shocks assaulted the Sato regime. Nixon's abrupt announcement on 15 July that he would visit Red China had been the first Nixon Shock for the pro-Taipei Sato, eroding his political position and strength within the ruling Liberal Democratic Party (LDP). The Japan–U.S. textile wrangle had also received criticism from inside as well as outside Japan. Certainly, the Japanese desire to see the Okinawa reversion treaty ratified by the U.S. Senate constrained Sato's independent moves against Washington. Against this backdrop, there did exist within the Japanese Ministry of Finance (MOF) and the Bank of Japan (BOJ) a desire to voluntarily appreciate the now undervalued Japanese yen. The government stuck to avoiding appreciating the yen at any cost. In order to deflate foreign disapproval of Japan's closed markets and to resist external pressure to change the parity of the yen, Japan had already issued on 4 June an 'eight-point program to avoid yen revaluation.' In the midst of grudgingly implementing this market liberalization plan, Tokyo heard Nixon's historic speech.[14]

The 'New Economic Policy' catalysed an MOF-led policy-making process in Japan.[15] In particular, the highly technical nature of the yen–dollar exchange rate prevented public opinion from compelling politicians to forcefully intervene in the policy-making process. As a result, the Prime Minister and other related ministers could not wield effective leadership on the issue. In sum, the Shocks were not treated as a golden opportunity to alter the fundamental economic strategies of Japan, but to passively push for the status quo as much as possible.

Japan was the only major country to keep its foreign exchange market open despite strong dissenting voices within the MOF. The money market was inundated with dollar-selling. Consequently, the BOJ bought about $42.8 billion to maintain parity of $1 to ¥360 before it decided to close the market. The eight-point program was kept intact, but Tokyo also determined to request that Washington drop the surcharge as soon as possible. In addition, to feel out the reactions of European countries and the possibility of aligning with Europe against the United States, a special envoy was dispatched to France and the United States. The envoy himself, however, soon realized the impossibility of maintaining yen–dollar parity. Meanwhile, pro-adjustment forces within the MOF gained strength. On the envoy's return to Japan, the government proclaimed a floating exchange system after the temporary closure.

The United States and other countries mainly welcomed this move, but soon began rebuking Japan's managed floating system as a dirty float. Actually, Tokyo saw to it that the yen would rise as gradually as possible to cushion against the impact of revaluation. The prospective damage caused by American unilateralism was not small. The Japanese Ministry of International Trade and Industry (MITI) predicted an annual loss of $4.5 billion in exports and a 2.2 per cent reduction in gross national product (GNP). The government tried to compensate for this economic stagnation by giving favours to small and medium-sized companies and adopting various fiscal stimuli to inflate the economy.[16]

The national interest of Japan as perceived by the Sato government was to minimize the change of parity as much as possible and secure a lifting of the surtax as soon as possible. Instead of launching an initiative to stabilize the international economic system, Tokyo responded to the shifting international environment passively. Sato's pro-U.S. stance on other issues like the representation of Taiwan instead of Red China in the United Nations General Assembly did not change. Furthermore, Japan backed down on the textile export regulation issue on 15 October. The United States, on the other hand, also made its conciliatory moves: in Anchorage, Nixon himself welcomed Emperor Hirohito on his way to Europe, and the Okinawa revision treaty was ratified in the Senate.[17]

The initial American negotiating stance was to turn around a $13 billion balance of payments deficit by such measures as the realignment of key currencies, reduction of trade barries, and defence burden-sharing. Japan was forced to edge towards accepting foreign demands as it went through various international conferences. A 15 November meeting held inside the MOF suggested a 12 per cent appreciation of the yen to the dollar: the figure would supposedly translate into about a $6.5 billion improvement in the trade surplus for the United States.

As noted in the case of Canada's response, resistance within the Nixon regime to Connolly's hardline stance was mounting by the end of November. The Rome G-10 meeting and the Nixon-Pompidou summit paved the way for a settlement of the issue.[18] The former saw Connolly agreeing to drop the surtax when a proper realignment of currencies would be made. He also accepted the idea of a contraction of the U.S. trade deficit from $13 billion to $9 billion. In this context, Burns suggested a 20 per cent revaluation of the yen to the dollar to BOJ Governor Tadashi Sasaki. Since 13 per cent was the highest that the Japanese could go, an agreement was not reached between the two. Still, 15 per cent was now recognized as a realistic rate for adjustment after the Rome conference. Besides, the defence burden-sharing issue was solved with the major European NATO members' agreeing to a $1 billion annual increase in defence budgets. The American–French confrontation aired for the first time the American pledge to devalue the price of the dollar against gold. In return, the French promised to cooperate with the Americans in realigning the major currencies.

The Smithsonian Settlement[19]

What was good for the Nixon team before the Smithsonian was the reassurance from the main leaders of the U.S. Congress that the United States could speak with one voice on this issue. On the other hand, Japan was in an inferior bargaining position, its weakness underlined by the failure of the last-minute Honolulu Japan–U.S. commercial talks. Commercial concessions to avoid a large revaluation of the yen as hoped for by the MOF were not given by MITI and the Ministry of Agriculture, which had vested domestic interests. Canada, as seen, was in a better position to deal with the Americans.

To avoid the large appreciation of the Japanese yen, the Honolulu trade talks continued while the G-10 ministers met at the Smithsonian. Japan's interests and stance at the meetings can be summed up as follows. The revaluation of the yen was the last thing the government wanted, and 15 per cent was the largest acceptable adjustment target. The parallel trade talks had to be used as a bargaining chip to cushion against the pressure for a larger revaluation. Finance Minister Mikio Mizuta had the authority to negotiate with his counterpart, and no other ministers were to intervene.

The Americans first proposed a 19 per cent revaluation of the Japanese yen against the dollar. The Japanese logic against this was defensive: this figure would worsen the Japanese recession, and a weak Japanese economy could not tolerate such a monetary burden. This logic, however, did not appeal to foreign minds. In addition, the lack of consensus among the participating European states destroyed the possibility of a Euro-Japanese alliance against the United States as well. Mizuta, in the bargaining process, recognized that the 17 per cent line was necessary for a settlement. In the final negotiation, 16.88 per cent appreciation of the yen to the dollar or parity changed to $1= ¥308 was the answer. It was evaluated as a larger-than-expected figure by the Japanese at the time. One official recalled ordering his lieutenant to interrupt the bargaining and come back home when he knew the figure (though this did not actually occur). Nevertheless, the Japanese economy absorbed the shock effects of this parity change and grew in the long run.

Canada's interest at the Smithsonian was to have the participants approve of the floating Canadian dollar with the surtax lifted. Reisman, the chief negotiator representing Canada, remembered Connally being tough on Canada with a request to peg the Canadian dollar at $1.06 to $1.07 to the U.S. dollar. The Canadian team responded that the special economic interactions between Canada and the United States would require the maintenance of free float for Canada. It also assured that the Bank of Canada would intervene in the money markets only when there emerged large rate fluctuations. Ultimately, Canada was alone in being exempted from repegging its currency – certainly good news for Canada. Ottawa confidently anticipated that, in lieu of the currency realignment and lifting of the surcharge, the Canadian dollar would follow the U.S. dollar downward, thereby strengthening Canada's competitive position in the American market; this would enhance its capacity to export to Europe and Japan. In retrospect, the trade irritants between Canada and its neighbour did not dissipate with the fading of the Shocks, but the Autopact, one of the greatest focal points for negotiations at that time, was not abandoned and is still alive today.

Conclusion: Theoretical Explanation

Four possible conceptual frameworks can be utilized to explain the dependent variable: the divergence in bargaining outcomes between the Canada–U.S. and the Japan–U.S. dyads. Japan's response to the Nixon Shocks turned out to be trade concessions in the form of voluntary textile export restraints and a very large revaluation of the yen. Yet, Canada very skilfully avoided granting any apparent concessions and achieved its national objective of lifting the surtax. What accounts for these results?

Model III ('governmental politics') as envisaged by Allison suggests that policy outcomes reflect the conclusion of 'pulling and hauling' between major players in the game.[20] As a result, no strong and effective leadership can be wielded in the case of a governmental-politics-driven decision-making process. Accordingly, the state cannot act as if it were a unitary-rational actor, and the bargaining outcome is thus not necessarily optimal. Allison's Model II ('organizational process') also points out the existence and importance of 'standard operating procedures' (SOPs) in making and implementing a decision. Decision-making based on SOPs tends to be incremental, and may even constrain an indispensable brave shift of decisions.

The initial Japanese and Canadian responses to the Shocks can be explained by these models to some extent. Both models defined above are a negative factor for any policy innovation. The more similar the decision-making process of a responding nation to the ideal type of Model II and/or III, the less effectively the nation could deal with the United States, ultimately resulting in policy inertia or even a disastrous failure.

The Japanese MOF's decision to maintain the status quo by keeping the money market open (and, therefore, to buy rapidly depreciating U.S. dollars in large amounts) reflected 'pulling and hauling' between domestic bureaucrats with no SOPs. Prime Minister Sato and other Cabinet members' involvement in the decision-making process seems to have been almost nil.[21] This post-Shock adhesion to the status quo policy, however, was replaced by the purely reactive response of grudgingly accepting the revaluation of the yen. Soon after the yen began floating, division of opinions within the government about how to handle the crisis faded out. The settlement of the issue was provided not by Sato's active involvement and leadership but by a semi-consensus in the MOF that the realignment of currencies was necessary even if Japan had to accept a larger-than-expected revaluation. The role of the powerful BOJ in this crisis was to 'implement' the decisions made largely by the MOF, as was the case with all foreign exchange dealings.[22] There is no evidence that the rupture between the MOF and the BOJ on the issue brought about the inertia in the decision-making process. In sum, the governmental politics model cannot fully explain Japan's failure when the pulling and hauling did not seriously affect the decision-making process. Particularly, the crucially important Smithsonian meeting did not see Japan's bureaucratic infighting over jurisdiction: the bargaining power was concentrated in the negotiating team.

A similar observation can be made about Canada's response. Betraying the prediction of Model III, 'pulling and hauling' did not seriously influence the process in Ottawa. But the primary decision to send an envoy to Washington made at the initial meeting organized by Reisman was a 'conditioned reflex' based on past SOPs of the Canada–U.S. 'special relationship.' In this sense, the importance of SOP-based decision making as conceived by Model II is relevant. But like Japan, the passage of time saw Canada acting as if it were a unitary-rational actor. When the requests for an exemption based on the SOP failed, Ottawa soon organized a special task force to coordinate Canada's response and investigated every possible means to defend its national interest.[23]

How relevant is the concept of intervulnerability? If Canada–U.S. economic relations, as the official Canadian line repeatedly asserted, were 'intervulnerable,' meaning the surcharge and other unilateral economic pressure were self-defeating for the United States, Washington could give Canada the benefit of the doubt while not giving it to Japan. Besides, the Nixon regime could justify to the general American public an exemption for Canada on the basis of the intervulnerable nature of the two economies. Indeed, Canada's logic in appealing to the Americans was a warning that the new economic policy as applied to Canada was damaging to the U.S. economy as well as to the Canadian one. But it is unclear to what extent this logic was accepted by the Americans. Rather, what persuaded Nixon was Trudeau's emphasis on the structural importance of a 'trade surplus' for Canada, not intervulnerability. In contrast, the case of the 1963 Interest Equalization Tax may be more convincingly explained by the intervulnerable economic structure.[24]

The complex interdependence model is thus the most suitable framework for explaining the dependent variable in the surcharge case.[25] The minor role of the military, one of the conditions of this model, applied evenly to Canada and Japan: the United States did not use or threaten to use military forces in resolving this issue, nor did it attempt to pull out its forces from Japan or to abolish the North American Air Defence Command (NORAD) due to the stubbornness of its allies.

But, the absence of a hierarchy among issues or the blurring of high politics and low politics is an important element in explaining the different results of negotiations. For both Canada and Japan, any hierarchy among issues towards the United States dissipated before the Smithsonian: resolution of the Nixon Shocks was as important as any other major issues.

Figure 2.1: Canada–U.S. Dyad and Japan–U.S. Dyad during the Nixon Shocks
Negotiations

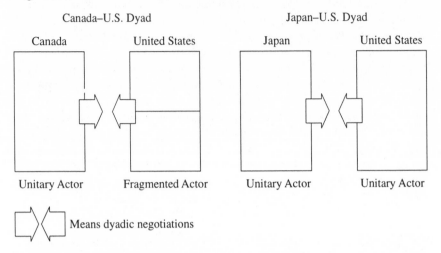

Within the Nixon Cabinet, however, high politics represented by Kissinger
(and, in a sense, Burns) finally dominated low politics represented by Connolly
and his associates. In retrospect, this happened just before the American diplomatic breakthrough towards China and the Soviet Union, when a revision of the
new economic policy was being considered. Kissinger, for one, confided in his
memoirs that he was no expert on economic matters (low politics) and
expressed his fear of economic concerns prevailing over the high politics of
security.[26] Naturally, his interests and actions agreed with those of Trudeau
rather than Connolly. In other words, Canada, with an absence of a hierarchy of
issues among high politics and low politics, discovered room for manoeuvre in
a U.S. Cabinet constrained by the primacy of high politics over low politics.
This condition alone, however, does not explain the dependent variable completely. If, as suggested, the primacy of cohesion of the political alliance was
more crucial than economic conflicts with allies, Japan could have been more
successful in handling its international monetary diplomacy, probably with the
assistance of Kissinger's intervention.

Here the concept of multiple channels of contact among societies becomes
vital. The speeches and interviews conducted by Canadian ministers and officials, the statement of the Canadian–American Committee, and lobbying activities by Canadian Members of Parliament with their American counterparts and
others all contributed to a more accommodating attitude in America towards
Canada than towards Japan on this issue.[27] The existence of de facto 'transgov-

ernmental allies' like Kissinger and Burns played a decisive role in defending the Canadian national interest.[28] The result was the Canada–U.S. dyad, closer to the ideal type of complex interdependence, producing a bargaining outcome closer to the interests of the lesser partner than the Japan–U.S. dyad, remote from the ideal of complex interdependence. In short, as shown in Figure 2.1, multiple channels of contact between Canada and the United States disaggregated the U.S. decision-making process in Canada's case, whereas the fewer channels of contact between the allies across the Pacific did not do so. The United States acted as a fragmented actor vis-à-vis Canada; towards Japan, it was more unitary.[29] That is why the American preponderance of capabilities vis-à-vis Japan was more impressive, and resulted in better bargaining outcomes for the larger power, than in the case of the Canada–U.S. dyad during the Nixon Shocks.

NOTES

1 This chapter draws on material first published in Japanese in *Kokusai Seiji (International Relations)* 107 (September 1994), 114–80. The author would like to thank Professors Kenichiro Hirano, Akihiko Tanaka, Hiroaki Kato, Tamiko Kurihara, and Tsuyoshi Kawasaki for their valuable comments on the earlier draft.

2 For the description of this incident from the U.S. side, see Gowa, *Closing the Gold Window*, and Odell, *U.S. International Monetary Policy*. Tokyo's accounts are represented by Shiota, *Kasumigaseki ga Furueta Hi*; Yanagida, *Nippon wa Moeteiruka*; Angel, *Explaining Economic Policy Failure*, and Kawasaki, 'Policy Ideas and Change.' For Ottawa's response, see Croci, 'The American Friend'; Dobell, *Canada in World Affairs*; Kirton and Bothwell, 'A Proud and Powerful Country,' and Granatstein and Bothwell, *Pirouette*, esp. 61–70.

3 See Krasner, *Defending the National Interest*, esp. 35.

4 See respectively Allison, *Essence of Decision*; Doran, *Forgotten Partnership*; and Keohane and Nye, *Power and Interdependence*, for the basic conceptual frameworks used here. Allison and Morton Halperin later combined Allison's Models II and III into an overarching model called the 'Bureaucratic Politics' model, but this chapter separately deals with the models because each is based on distinct 'defining properties' and 'internal logic.' For this point, see Allison and Halperin, 'Bureaucratic Politics'; Bendor and Hammond, 'Rethinking Allison's Models,' esp. 304. Contrary to Bendor and Hammond's assertion (313) that Model II should not necessarily focus on 'the negative, constraining effects of organizational routine,' this chapter basically regards Model II–like behaviour as damaging to a rational policy-making process.

5 For the following account on the background leading up to the Nixon Shocks, see

Cohen, *Uneasy Partnership*, 87; Gilpin, *The Political Economy*, 138–41; Illgen, *Autonomy and Interdependence*, 79–82; Keohane, 'The Theory of Hegemonic Stability,' esp. 150; Gowa; and Shiota, 31.

6 For the actual text of Nixon's speech, see Nixon, *Public Papers of the President*, 886–91.

7 Interview between Simon Reisman and John Kirton, 27 August 1979, and interview between Simon Reisman and Daizo Sakurada, 8 September 1993.

8 See especially Thordarson, *Trudeau and Foreign Policy*; Kirton and Bothwell, 116–17; and Granatstein and Bothwell, 183–86, 194–95 for the Canada–U.S. diplomatic background before the shocks.

9 The Canadian responses to the Shocks before the December Smithsonian meeting are based on the *New York Times,* 15 September 1971; Stewart, 'The Week of the Great Ultimatum'; Canadian Institute of International Affairs (CIIA), *International Canada*, July & August, September, October, November 1971, 157–64, 173–81, 201–3 214–18; Canada, Department of External Affairs, *External Affairs,* September, October 1971, 326–35, 382–88; Canada, Department of External Affairs, *Statements and Speeches,* 71/23; Senate, *Proceedings of the Standing Committee on Foreign Affairs*, 25 March 1975, 17–18; Croci, 13–24; Granatstein and Bothwell, 61–68; interview between Simon Reisman and John Kirton, and interview between Simon Reisman and Daizo Sakurada.

10 Based on interview between Mitchell Sharp and Daizo Sakurada, 7 September 1993; interview between Simon Reisman and John Kirton; and interview between Simon Reisman and Daizo Sakurada. See also Sharp's account during this period in Sharp, *Which Reminds Me*, esp. 179–80.

11 A journalist who investigated this matter used the term 'a conditioned reflex' to delineate this decision-making. See Stewart.

12 For the situation leading to the Smithsonian meeting, see esp. Brandon, *The Retreat of American Power*, esp. 230–36; Solomon, *The International Monetary System*, 198–204; The Canadian–American Committee, *The U.S. Import Surcharge and Canada,* 4–7; *New York Times*, 17 November 1971; Odell, 280–83; Kirton and Bothwell, 118–19; interview between John Kirton and Philip Trezise, 15 April 1981; interview between Simon Reisman and John Kirton; interview between Simon Reisman and Daizo Sakurada.

13 For Nixon–Trudeau and Kissinger–Head meetings, see Martin, *The Presidents and Prime Ministers*, 237–38; interview between Rufus Smith and John Kirton, 8 April 1981; interview between Ivan Head and Daizo Sakurada, 8 March 1993; Kirton and Bothwell, 116–17; Granatstein and Bothwell, 68–70; Dobell, 24–29; and CIIA, 231–32.

14 For the background to the Shocks and the situations of both the MOF and BOJ, see

Taizo Hayashi, 'Arufa (Enkiriage) Sagyo Shimatsuki'; idem, 'Enkiriage Sagyo no Zasetsu Kara Furoto made'; Yoshino, *En to Doru: Endaka eno Kiseki to Haikei*, 168–70; Yamamoto, *Sengo Nihon Gaikoshi 5*, 136–37; Ushiba, *Gaiko no Shunkan*, 140–41, and Shiota, esp. 113–14.

15 For the initial Japanese response to the Shocks prior to the closing of the yen–dollar markets, see Kashiwagi, *Gekidoki no Tsuuka Gaiko*, esp. 4; Sagami, 'Tenno Heika to En no Kiriage,' esp. 54–65; *Asahi Shimbun*, 17 August 1971; Shiota, 17, 65, 102–9, 219–21; and Angel, 124–41.

16 See Kase, *Kokusai Tsuuku Kiki*, 49; Hayami, *Hendo Sobasei 10 Nen*, 35–42; *Asahi Shimbun*, 28 August 1971; Yamamoto, 154; and Angel, *Economic Policy Failure*, 156–58.

17 For the Japan–U.S. diplomatic relationship, see Hirano, *Gaiko Kisha Nikki: Fukuda Gaiko no Ichi Nen*, 33–90, and Meyer, *Assignment: Tokyo*, 156–57. For the Japanese stance on the economic issue, see Ekonomisuto, ed., *Sengo Sangyoshi eno Shogen 4*, 210; Volcker and Gyohten, *Changing Fortunes*, 91–95. See also Yoshino, 214–32.

18 For the Rome G-10 meeting and Nixon–Pompidou summit, see Reston, *The Lone Star*, 425–29; Angel, 236–42; Kashiwagi, 143–45; Yamamoto, 166–70; Ekonomisuto, 210–11; Kase, 63–65; and Volcker and Gyohten, 84–88.

19 The account of the Smithsonian settlement is based on NHK Shuzaihan, *Nippon no Jyoken Mane 1*, 208–17; Ando, *Sekinin to Genkai Jou*, 82–86, 99–114, 122–24, 135–42, 204–5; *Asahi Shimbun*, 20 and 21 December 1970 (morning and evening editions); Kashiwagi, 16, 22, 149–52, 164–65; Ekonomisuto, ed., 211–14; Yamamoto, 171–78; Volcker and Gyohten, 88–90, 96–100; Saywell, ed., *Canadian Annual Review of Politics and Public Affairs 1972*, 259–63; ibid., 1973, 221–24, 232–36; Summary of the Address and Answers by Mitchell Sharp to the Canada–U.S. Relations Colloquium at the University of Toronto, 23 November 1979; Dobell, 28–29; Granatstein and Bothwell, 70; CIIA, 242–43; interview between Reisman and Kirton, and interview between Reisman and Sakurada.

20 For the recent criticisms of Allison's Models, see Welch, 'The Organizational Process,' 112–46; and Bendor and Hammond. To be exact, this chapter utilizes simplified versions of Models II and III. In addition to Allison's *Essence of Decision*, Rosati, 'Developing a Systematic Decision-Making Framework,' 234–52, and Sato, *Taigai Seisaku*, 35–54, are used for the theoretical simplification of the amended Allison's models.

21 No effective Japanese political leadership on this issue can be found during this time. See Angel, Conclusion, for the assessment of political leadership.

22 See BOJ Governor Sasaki's account on the issue, as cited in Angel, 275.

23 Under its Informal Access Program, the author consulted the files of the Canadian Department of External Affairs and International Trade in September 1993. No sub-

stantial evidence of a serious division of opinion about the ways to cushion against the adverse effects of the import surcharge could be found. The Canadian government during the crisis was also shown to be very adept at synchronizing lobbying activities in favour of dropping the surtax. See esp. Canada, Department of External Affairs and International Trade, Historical Section, File No. 35–1–USA-1971–SITREP, Vols. 1–11.

24 At least, this was the interpretation by the Canadian side for its reactions to the 1960s unilateral measures by the United States. For a different interpretation, see Chapter 3 in this volume.

25 For the detailed examination of the 'complex interdependence' model, see Keohane and Nye, esp. Chap. 2, and 104–5, 217; Yamamoto, *Kokusaiteki Sogoizon*, 22–23; Yamakage, 'Sogoizonron,' esp. 120–2; Daizo Sakurada, 'Sengo Kanada Gaiko Seisaku no Rironteki Tenkai'; and Sato, *Taigai Seisaku*, 120–22. As Keohane and Nye suggested in their *Power and Interdependence*, one can utilize four models in Chap. 3 (economic process, overall power structure, issues structure, and international organization) as independent variables for explaining international regime change. An empirical case study using the above four models can be found in John Volger, 'Interdependence, Power, and the World,' 200–25. This chapter, however, approached this issue differently by employing complex interdependence as an explanatory conceptual framework.

26 See Kissinger, *White House Years*, 950, 956–97. See also Kirton and Bothwell, 119, for a more neutral account of the inside story in the Nixon administration.

27 John Petty, Connolly's right-hand man in the Treasury during the crisis, was very negative about Canada's transnational/transgovernmental interference in the U.S. domestic process. Interview between John Petty and Daizo Sakurada, 17 September 1993. But Canada's activities in American society made de facto ratification of Canada's privileges after the Smithsonian bargaining (floating of the Canadian dollar and withdrawal of surtax) easier. In other words, Canadian penetration contributed better to American acceptance of Canadian gains at the Level II (domestic) negotiation. For the concept of Level I and II interactions, see Putnam, '*Diplomacy and Domestic Politics*,' 427–60, and Evans, Jacobson, and Putnam, eds., *Double-Edged Diplomacy*.

28 For the concept of transgovernmental/transnational relations, see Keohane and Nye, 'Transgovernmental Relations and International Organizations,' esp. 49; and Fox, Hero, and Nye, eds., *Canada and the United States*.

29 Canada's unitary behaviour on this issue is also proven by Quebec's perception: Quebec regarded the crisis as a rallying point for federal–provincial collaboration under the leadership of Ottawa rather than a nationalistic chance to voice its own views. This conclusion was obtained by analysing Quebec's attitudes during the

crisis. See Sakurada and Elmhirst, 'The Myth of Constraints.' A similar observation about Canada's coherence against the United States was made by Dickerman in his 'Transgovernment Challenge and Response.' The parallel empirical example of negotiations between a 'united Canada versus fragmented United States' can be found in Wagner and O'Neil, 'Canadian Penetration of the American Political Process.'

3

Managing Macroeconomic Relations with the United States: Japanese and Canadian Experiences

TSUYOSHI KAWASAKI

This chapter compares Japanese and Canadian experiences in coping with, and influencing, U.S. macroeconomic diplomacy. U.S.–Japan relations underwent intensive negotiations on macroeconomic issues particularly, if not exclusively, during the decade of 1977–87 (hereafter referred to as the 1980s). Although Washington and Ottawa were occupied with the Free Trade Agreement during the 1980s, they had to settle their disagreements on U.S. balance of payments measures during the 1960s. In the past, each dyad has been studied separately. By analysing this set of dyads together, this chapter attempts to deepen understanding of the complex political economy of macroeconomic relations in the two dyads and among nations more generally.

Comparing the two dyads in the context of macroeconomic diplomacy reveals that they have more common features than is often implicitly assumed. A conventional view, held particularly among the Japanese, is that U.S.–Canada relations enjoy the status of a 'special relationship' based on close cultural and historical conditions. In sharp contrast, U.S.–Japan relations have more fragile foundations because of cultural and racial differences. This chapter's analysis shows that the 'specialness' of U.S.–Canada relations, even during its highest point in the 1960s, was less than is usually assumed. Somewhat surprisingly, the macroeconomic policy problems that Ottawa faced in dealing with Washington during the 1960s have many more common dimensions than often assumed with the problems that confronted Japanese macroeconomic policymakers negotiating with Americans in the 1980s.

The central empirical puzzle that this chapter attempts to solve is this question: Why is it that despite the international power superiority of the United States, Washington's macroeconomic policy changed in the direction of accommodating Tokyo's and/or Ottawa's requests on some occasions? A conventional, mainstream approach focusing on national power – the realist approach to international relations – would predict that Washington should have maintained its policy intact all along vis-à-vis Tokyo and Ottawa. But in both U.S.–Canada relations in the 1960s and U.S.–Japan relations in the 1980s, such an expectation is not supported by the evidence. How is this anomaly explained?

This chapter argues that Ottawa and Tokyo had windows of opportunities to circumvent what would have otherwise been the overwhelming effect of U.S. international power, and that these windows were generated by economic conditions in financial markets. Only when such economic conditions threatened the perceived interest of Washington did the probability increase for Ottawa and Tokyo to persuade Washington to change its original policy and to accommodate their demands. Verbal persuasions – such as appealing to the 'special relationship' or common interests – alone were not strong enough to change the original U.S. position. Canada and Japan's credibility had to be backed by 'hard' economic realities. In the broader literature of international political economy, these findings support the thesis that global financial forces are an independent and powerful structural factor shaping the policy outcomes of national governments in the contemporary world political economy.[1] This paper advances this thesis by presenting new empirical evidence in the area of macroeconomic diplomacy and negotiations.

This chapter is organized as follows. It first provides an overview of macroeconomic relations in the two dyads since the 1960s. This background analysis explains why intensive macroeconomic negotiations clustered in the 1960s for the U.S.–Canada relationship and in the 1978–88 period for the U.S.–Japan relationship. The chapter then comparatively analyses the U.S.–Canada and the U.S.–Japan cases. It concludes by considering the theoretical and policy implications of its findings.

Throughout this chapter, the term 'macroeconomic policy' is used rather broadly to refer to the particular set of measures used to correct the balance of payments imbalances among nations. These include fiscal, monetary (i.e., interest rate), exchange rate, and capital control measures. This definition does not include trade measures and sector-specific structural measures. Capital control measures here primarily mean those concerned with portfolio investment, but when relevant, the term includes direct investment as well. In short, macroeconomic policy as defined in this chapter concerns the set of non-trade, short-term measures that are aimed at rectifying balance of payments imbalances. In this context, the term is used interchangeably with 'balance of payments policy.'

Changes in the International Economic System and Their Consequences for Macroeconomic Diplomacy

One salient feature of the contemporary U.S.–Canada economic relationship (that is, since the early 1980s) is that macroeconomic policy rarely becomes an issue for negotiation. This is in sharp contrast to the contemporary U.S.–Japan economic relationship. Examinations of public records and policy surveys, as well as personal interviews with a then top Canadian Ministry of Finance official, support this conclusion.[2]

At first glance, the absence of U.S.–Canada macroeconomic diplomacy in the 1980s is not difficult to explain. The key causes are the minor importance of Canada (due to its small economic size) in Group of Seven (G-7) summit meetings on the issue of macroeconomic coordination; and Canada's geographical proximity to the United States coupled with the virtual integration of the Canadian economy into the U.S. economy. In short, as the question of macroeconomic coordination emerged as a global issue since the mid-1970s, the Canadian economy was neither large enough nor independent enough to be counted as a global economic power. Only Japan, the United States, and Germany belonged to the 'major league' responsible for managing global capitalism.

It is not that disagreements were quietly solved between Ottawa and Washington on macroeconomic issues; rather, major disagreements as such did not exist in the first place. As far as the issue of macroeconomic coordination was concerned, Washington's attention was directed at the two other 'global partners' that tended to accumulate huge trade surpluses. In this picture, Canada was Washington's backyard. Instead, the U.S.-Canada economic agenda in the 1980s was occupied by trade-investment issues, that is, issues regarding access to trade and investment markets, which culminated in the conclusion of the Free Trade Agreement. Accordingly, it is not surprising that there are few recent writings on U.S.–Canada macroeconomic diplomacy.[3] Broader political studies on macroeconomic coordination, furthermore, rarely analyse Canada's situation in an in-depth manner.[4]

The above analysis concerning the absence of U.S.–Canada macroeconomic diplomacy in the 1980s is plausible but remains incomplete. Looking back on post–World War II history, Washington and Ottawa did have negotiations in the 1960s over the unilateral U.S. capital control initiatives that were aimed at correcting U.S. balance of payments deficits. These negotiations were concerned with the 1963 Interest Equalization Tax, the 1965 Voluntary Capital Control, and the 1968 Mandatory Capital Control of the United States. Tokyo also had to cope with the same U.S. initiatives during the 1960s. Thus, a critical, and interesting, question is: Why did macroeconomic negotiations disappear from the U.S.–Canada negotiation agenda, but remain in the U.S.–Japanese negotiation agenda?

Canada was 'small and insignificant' in the global economic scene both in the 1960s and in the 1980s. This fact would lead one to expect that in neither decade would macroeconomic issues appear on the U.S.–Canada negotiation agenda. Yet such an expectation is not supported by the evidence. Why, then, did macroeconomic negotiation occur between Washington and Ottawa in the 1960s but not in the 1980s? At the same time, why did macroeconomic issues remain in U.S.–Japan negotiations since the 1960s? To answer these questions, we must carefully compare conditions surrounding U.S. macroeconomic diplomacy between the 1960s and the 1980s.

There are two key factors that shaped the nature of macroeconomic diplomacy between the United States and its trade partners: the international distribution of economic power and the level of economic interdependence, particularly interdependence through capital flow. We can hypothesize two propositions. First, the hegemonic distribution of economic power (i.e., one giant nation among numerous weak nations) tends to induce the hegemonic nation to take unilateral actions to unspecified nations when that nation wants to correct its balance of payments problems. As the distribution of economic power shifts in the direction of more equal distribution, the former hegemonic power is more likely to take consultative actions towards specific partners, particularly rising powers that accumulate trade surpluses with it. Thus, macroeconomic diplomacy under the hegemonic distribution of economic power tends to be characterized by small powers 'swarming' around the hegemonic power competing for winning exemptions after the latter nation has taken some unilateral action. In sharp contrast, under a more egalitarian distribution of economic power, the action of the hegemonic power is more constrained and characterized by continual negotiations with its few partners, leaving out smaller nations from this negotiation circle.

While the distribution of economic power shapes the manner in which macroeconomic diplomacy is conducted, the level of economic interdependence influences the content of macroeconomic diplomacy. Thus, the second hypothesis is this: the higher level of economic interdependence that exists among nations, the more likely it is that domestic policy (such as fiscal and monetary policy) become negotiation issues among them. In other words, when the level of economic interdependence is low, macroeconomic negotiations among nations are characterized by more external policies, such as exchange rate policy and capital control policy, on their agenda.[5]

When a balance of payments imbalance emerges between nations, they will take measures, unilaterally or through negotiations, to rectify it. In doing so, these nations tend to attempt, as much as possible, to manipulate those measures that do not directly affect domestic economic management. Put another way, the nations tend to maintain domestic autonomy or independence intact in dealing with external imbalances, preferring exchange rate policy and capital control policy to fiscal policy and monetary policy.

TABLE 3.1
Two factors shaping the nature of macroeconomic diplomacy in the 1960s and 1980s

	Power distribution	Economic interdependence
1960s	Hegemonic	Low
1980s	Oligopolistic	High

When the level of economic interdependence between nations is low, their domestic economies are less exposed to the world economy, and the magnitude of their balance of payments imbalances remains modest in relation to the overall size of their economies. These external imbalances can be coped with by using exchange rate policy and capital control policy, without sacrificing domestic autonomy. The domestic costs of rectifying external imbalances are low in this situation. But as the level of economic interdependence increases, these costs grow. In such a situation, the domestic economies are more exposed to external influences and the size of balance of payments imbalances tends to be larger. The manipulation of exchange rate and capital control policy alone will not be sufficient in reducing the external imbalances; more domestic measures such as fiscal and monetary policy must be used to tackle the problem. In addition, if there is an enormous flow of short-term capital circulating around the globe, it may make governments' capital control measures less effective in changing their external imbalances.

Thus, we have two hypotheses about the manner and content of macroeconomic diplomacy, hypotheses based on the distribution of economic power and the level of economic interdependence, respectively. I argue that macroeconomic diplomacy in the 1960s was influenced by the hegemonic distribution of economic power and the relatively low level of economic interdependence. In sharp contrast, macroeconomic diplomacy in the 1980s was conditioned by a more equal or oligopolistic power distribution and a higher level of economic interdependence (see Table 3.1).

According to these two hypotheses, we can interpret the nature of macroeconomic diplomacy in the 1960s and 1980s as follows. In the 1960s, the United States was the preponderant world economic power, standing tall among small powers including Canada and Japan. At the same time, the level of economic interdependence (i.e., both trade and capital flow linkage among nations) was relatively low. Under these two conditions, the policy initiatives of the Kennedy and the Johnson administrations to correct U.S. balance of payments problems were characterized (1) by their unilateral and globalist approach, that is, by unilateral actions aimed at unspecified nations, and (2) by their focus on capital control as coping measures (U.S. exchange rate policy was constrained by the Bretton Woods rule of fixed exchange rates). In the 1980s, on the other hand, the United States was one of three oligopolistic powers — the others being Japan and Germany – and was more exposed to international economic transactions than in the previous decades. Under these conditions, the macroeconomic diplomacy of the Reagan administration in the face of huge U.S. balance of payments deficits was featured (1) by negotiations with Japan and Germany, two other economic giants, and (2) by its scope to include fiscal and monetary policy.

In this explanatory framework, it is not surprising that U.S.–Canadian macroeconomic diplomacy occurred in the 1960s but not in the 1980s. In the 1960s, Ottawa, as did other governments of small powers including Tokyo, requested of Washington that Canada be exempted from unilateral U.S. capital control measures. In the 1980s, the focus of Washington's macroeconomic diplomacy shifted to negotiation with Japan and Germany on fiscal and monetary policy, leaving out Canada, and other smaller nations, from the tripartite negotiation. As for Japan, the nature of its macroeconomic diplomacy with the United States changed as its power position rose in the world economy and as the level of U.S. exposure to Japanese economic influences (trade and capital flow) increased. In the 1960s, Japan was one of those small nations requesting exemptions from U.S. capital control measures. In the 1980s, it had changed into one of the key negotiators of the United States on the issue of fiscal and monetary adjustments. Japan had macroeconomic diplomacy in both decades; but the character of that diplomacy is sharply different between them.

Identifying the Cases

The previous section has identified three cases:

1/ U.S.–Canada macroeconomic diplomacy in the 1960s,
2/ U.S.–Japan macroeconomic diplomacy in the 1960s, and
3/ U.S.–Japan macroeconomic diplomacy in the 1980s.

It has also specified the differences in the context of macroeconomic diplomacy between the 1960s and the 1980s (see Table 3.2).

At this point, each of these three cases should be outlined briefly.

Case 1: U.S.–Canada Macroeconomic Diplomacy in the 1960s

In the 1960s, the administration of John F. Kennedy, and later that of Lyndon B.

TABLE 3.2
Three cases of macroeconomic diplomacy

Q: Did macroeconomic policy become a diplomatic issue?

	In the 1960s	In the 1980s
U.S.–Canada relations	Yes*	No
U.S.–Japan relations	Yes*	Yes**

*Ottawa and Tokyo responded to U.S. unilateral and
globalistic capital control policy.
**Tokyo negotiated with Washington on fiscal and
monetary policy.

Johnson, became quite concerned with capital outflow from the United States. Although the United States enjoyed trade surpluses, its excessive capital outflow was a potential threat to the international currency status of the U.S. dollar. Under the Bretton Woods monetary system, which was a fixed exchange rate system, the U.S. dollar was linked with gold at a fixed conversion rate, and Washington was obliged to exchange the U.S. dollar for gold upon receiving requests to do so from foreigners. As the amount of U.S. capital outflow increased, Washington became more concerned about the possibility that its gold reserve would become dangerously low, jeopardizing the foundation of the Bretton Woods monetary system.

Addressing this problem, the Kennedy administration resorted to limiting the outflow of U.S. private investment. It first introduced, with its balance of payments report of 18 July 1963, taxes on U.S. private portfolio investment going abroad. This Interest Equalization Tax, however, was not effective enough. Accordingly, President Johnson, who came into power after Kennedy's assassination in 1963, introduced the Voluntary Capital Control measures in his 10 February 1965 balance of payments report, in addition to extending the Interest Equalization Tax for two more years. He then had to resort to the Mandatory Capital Control measures on 1 January 1968. These three sets of measures caused deep concern in the nations that relied on raising capital in the New York capital market, because the measures seriously limited the access to the world's best market for borrowing money. Furthermore, the 1965 and 1968 capital control measures covered U.S. direct foreign investment, constraining the overseas activities of U.S. multinational corporations. Canada needed U.S. capital not only for stimulating its economic growth (in the form of inviting and maintaining U.S.-owned manufacturing plants on its soil), but also for sustaining its provincial governments' projects on social and economic infrastructure. Thus in terms of both portfolio and direct investment, the three sets of U.S. measures generated strong concerns in Canada about the health of a Canadian economy that was dependent on U.S. capital.

On all occasions in 1963, 1965, and 1968, Ottawa sent a delegation to Washington in an attempt to gain an exemption from the U.S. capital control measures. Its primary goal was to keep its access to U.S. capital, whether in the rich New York capital market or in U.S. multinational corporations. After relatively short negotiations, and with certain costs, Ottawa won at least partial exemptions in all of the three occasions.[6]

Case 2: U.S.–Japan Macroeconomic Diplomacy in the 1960s

Japan was also dependent on the New York capital market for its post–World War II economic reconstruction and expansion. For example, it had borrowed approximately $176 million (U.S.) in the period 1959–63.[7] In the wake of the 1963 Interest Equalization Tax, Tokyo sent, as did Ottawa, a delegation to Washington to win an exemption. But in sharp contrast to the Canadian success, the Japanese plea was firmly rejected by the U.S. Treasury Department. Toyoo Gyohten, a former top official at the Japanese Ministry of Finance (MOF), characterizes the U.S. reaction as follows: 'The United States Treasury was very tough, very uncompromising. It failed to show any sign of sympathy. So we had to come back empty-handed.'[8] When President Johnson extended the Interest Equalization Tax in February 1965, Japan was finally granted an exemption of $100 million per annum in raising capital in the United States.[9]

In comparison with Canada, Japan was much less dependent on U.S. foreign direct investment, so that the Voluntary and Mandatory Capital Control measures were not a major concern for Japan. But when the Johnson administration introduced the Mandatory Capital Control measures in 1968, it requested the government of Eisaku Sato to cooperate with its efforts to reduce capital outflow. After a month-long negotiation, the Japanese government agreed to strengthen its effort to raise capital in European capital markets, which would help to reduce capital outflow from the New York capital market.[10]

Case 3: U.S.–Japan Macroeconomic Diplomacy in the 1980s

Macroeconomic diplomacy after 1977 had very different characteristics from that of the 1960s. First, the Bretton Woods monetary system of fixed exchange rates had disappeared by the mid-1970s, replaced with a floating exchange rate system.[11] This fact made exchange rate policy a critical component of macroeconomic policy and negotiations. Second, G-7 summit meetings started in 1975 and became institutionalized since then.[12] This forum, coupled with more ad hoc gatherings of finance ministers of the G-7 nations, became the focal point of macroeconomic diplomacy among advanced capitalist nations in general, and among the United States, Japan, and Germany in particular.

More important, as was pointed out earlier in this chapter, were the following two underlying characteristics of macroeconomic diplomacy in the 1980s: the relative decline of U.S. economic power vis-à-vis Japan and Germany, and the high level of economic interdependence. The first factor, which was obviously helped by the aforementioned G-7 mechanism, led the United States to employ a more focused negotiation approach with specific nations (especially Japan and Germany), rather than the previous unilateral and globalistic approach, in its macroeconomic diplomacy. The second factor, the rise of economic interdependence, led to the emergence of fiscal and monetary policy (replacing capital control policy) as the central item in the macroeconomic negotiation agenda among advanced capitalist nations. At the same time, it resulted in huge U.S. trade deficits with Japan. These structural changes culminated in the recurrence of macroeconomic negotiations between the United States and Japan (and to a lesser extent between the United States and Germany) on the question of how to rectify U.S. trade deficits with Japan. Canada, meanwhile, receded into the background in this new global picture.

Washington and Tokyo had two rounds of macroeconomic negotiations during the period under consideration: between the administration of Jimmy Carter and the governments of Takeo Fukuda and Masayoshi Ohira in 1977–79; and between the administration of Ronald Reagan and the government of Yasuhiro Nakasone in 1985–87. In both periods, the bilateral negotiations centred around whether Japan was ready to take expansionary fiscal and monetary measures in exchange for a U.S. commitment to stabilize the dollar–yen exchange rate. The United States encouraged the foreign exchange market to drive the yen higher, generating a massive deflationary economic pressure on Japan's export-oriented manufacturing sector. The overall deterioration of the Japanese economy, in turn, pressed the Japanese government to introduce expansionary fiscal and monetary measures, as requested by Washington.

Theoretically, U.S. trade deficits with Japan could be reduced either by Washington's deflationary fiscal and monetary measures, or by Tokyo's expansionary fiscal and monetary measures, or by both. The first option was costly for the United States because it would increase the unemployment rate in the U.S. economy. In Japan, the powerful MOF, concerned with budget deficits, was opposed to the second option. Thus, the final outcome of the U.S.–Japan negotiations depended on the power relationship between the two nations. And

TABLE 3.3
Outcomes of the cases

Q: Did the United States significantly shift its original policy
in the direction of Ottawa's/Tokyo's interest?

	In the 1960s	In the 1980s
With Canada	Yes	N/A
With Japan	No*	No and yes**

*Japan could not immediately win an exemption from the
Interest Equalization Tax. U.S. foreign direct investment
measures were irrelevant to Japan.
**In both 1977–79 and 1985–87, the United States did not
change its original policy at first, but later did.

as was described above, the United States had the upper hand over Japan, successfully manipulating the foreign exchange market.

But a careful analysis shows that the United States did not always prevail despite its advantage. There were occasions when the United States had to take the first option. Sometimes Japan conceded, and at other times the United States changed its original anti-deflationary position. Whereas the Fukuda government faced rapid yen appreciation and introduced a large-scale fiscal expansion package in late 1977, the Ohira government, which came to power in December 1978, could successfully circumvent the U.S. pressure to follow Fukuda's path. Meanwhile, in November 1978, the Carter administration clearly reversed its previous policy: it stopped encouraging the yen's appreciation and restrained its own fiscal and monetary measures.[13]

In 1985–87, a similar pattern took place. In the face of the yen's rapid appreciation, the Nakasone government finally lifted its previous commitment to an austere fiscal policy and introduced a large-scale fiscal expansion package in the spring of 1987. Meanwhile, the Reagan administration had begun to refrain from encouraging the yen's appreciation since late 1986. And in October 1987, the Reagan administration clearly restrained its fiscal and monetary policy.[14]

With this outline of the empirical cases, it is possible to summarize their outcomes in Table 3.3. Here, our interest is in whether the United States shifted its original policy in the direction of Ottawa's or Tokyo's interest. Given the power superiority of the United States vis-à-vis Canada and Japan, it would not be surprising to find Washington doing what it wanted despite the negative effects that such an action would have on Canada and Japan. But if Washington changed its original policy to accommodate the interest of Canada and/or Japan, that fact requires explanation.

Such an unexpected change of U.S. policy could be called 'success' for Canada or for Japan; if it did not occur, then the case in question is 'failure.' In other words, it can be concluded (1) that in the 1960s, Canada succeeded and Japan failed; and (2) that Japan's record in the 1980s is a mixture of success and failure. In inferring causes of success and failure, it is useful to employ what Alexander George called 'structured, focused comparison.' Here one carefully compares a set of cases under similar circumstances, controls as many potential causal variables as possible in this process, and attempts to isolate a group of causal variables that determines policy success or failure.[15] According to this guideline, it is prudent to examine the 1960s and the 1980s separately. Thus one compares, first, the case of Canadian success (Case 1 above) and the case of Japanese failure (Case 2 above) in the 1960s. Second, the hypothesis drawn from this first comparison of the 1960s should be tested in explaining Japan's success and failure in macroeconomic diplomacy towards the United States in the 1980s (Case 3 above).[16]

Explaining and Comparing Outcomes

The 1960s

The best case to use to compare Canadian and Japanese experiences vis-à-vis U.S. unilateralism in the 1960s is the case of the 1963 Income Equalization Tax. The cases of 1965 and 1968 on U.S. foreign direct investment policy are less relevant because Tokyo, unlike Ottawa, was not seriously concerned with the U.S. policy. In response to the 1963 U.S. portfolio investment control initiative, both Ottawa and Tokyo sent their delegations to Washington for exemptions. Shortly after its request, Ottawa more or less won an exemption, but it was not until February 1965 that Tokyo won an exemption. This contrast between Canadian success and Japanese failure is striking. What explains the difference?

One could argue that Ottawa enjoyed a 'special relationship' with Washington, whereas Tokyo did not, and that this difference was crucial for Ottawa's success in winning an exemption. The U.S.–Canada economic relationships in the 1960s was 'easy, informal, extensive, responsive and, in short, friendly.'[17] Kal Holsti wrote in 1971 that U.S.–Canadian diplomatic culture produced 'a sense of mutual empathy and responsiveness between the two governments, and a propensity to limit conflict behavior to very low levels of intensity – occasional threats and official protests, but not violence.'[18] Indeed, quiet negotiations through close personal contacts were the dominant practice between

Washington and Ottawa. Furthermore, there were norms – although they were not perfectly complied with – of exceptionally easy mutual communication; advance consultation; a technical, problem-solving approach to diplomatic issues; and no explicit threats and issue linkage. The logic of the U.S.–Canada 'special relationship' assumed that, unlike usual international relations, there was a long-term, if not short-term, harmony of interest between the United States and Canada because of their unusually close economic and cultural ties.[19]

The Canadian delegation led by Louis Rasminsky, the Bank of Canada Governor, did emphasize that the United States shared the same economic destiny with Canada when he requested an exemption from the Interest Equalization Tax in Washington. He argued that the U.S. measure was self-defeating and short-sighted because it hurt the Canadian economy, which would in turn damage the U.S. economy immediately. In addition, the Canadian delegation avoided any retaliation in requesting an exemption.[20] This strategy seemed to work perfectly; Washington did grant an exemption to Ottawa. On the other hand, the absence of a 'special relationship' between the United States and Japan can explain why Washington rejected Tokyo's similar request in a quite cold manner, as was noted earlier.

A close analysis of Washington's action, however, strongly suggests that such an analysis focusing on the 'special relationship' may be misleading. From Washington's perspective, the exemption was granted not as a symbolic gesture of international friendship, but as a result of bargaining. Indeed Ottawa did pay a price: setting a ceiling on its foreign exchange reserves. From the U.S. perspective, the goal of the Interest Equalization Tax was to reduce capital flow out of the United States. The Tax was designed to increase the costs of foreign sales of bonds and equities in the New York capital market. After negotiations with Ottawa, Washington lifted the restrictions against Canadian bonds and equities sold in the United States (i.e., an exemption). In return, Ottawa was asked to make contributions to Washington's endeavour. Washington wanted a concrete assurance from Ottawa that the latter would make tangible contributions towards the solution of the former's capital outflow problem.

One potential cooperative measure was for Ottawa to impose limits on the capital-raising activities of Canadian provincial governments in the United States, so that capital flow from the United States to Canada could be restricted. When Washington suggested this measure, Ottawa refused, saying that such a direct intervention by Ottawa in provincial affairs would be highly problematic in terms of Canadian domestic politics. So a compromise was reached: Washington would monitor the foreign exchange reserve (i.e., U.S. dollar reserves) of Ottawa, which indirectly indicated the level of capital flow from the United States to Canada.[21] To the Canadian delegation, this condition was 'minimal, hardly a significant impingement on the future freedom of action of Canadian governments.'[22] As it turned out, 'the eventual granting of an exemption left a residue of resentment among [U.S.] Treasury officials that Canada had been the undeserving recipient of an untoward act of generosity.'[23]

According to this bargaining-focused interpretation, therefore, Ottawa 'won' an exemption through bargaining with Washington, rather than through persuading Washington. U.S. officials never fully understood the logic presented by Rasminsky.[24] It is thus not surprising that they continued to take unilateral capital control measures in 1965 and 1968, neither of which exempted Canada initially. According to Gerald Wright, the Canadian officials involved were fully aware of the unsympathetic attitude of the U.S. side.

It was the conviction of most of the Canadian officials who participated in the bilateral negotiations in the 1960s that their American counterparts never understood the operation of the linkages binding the two economic systems, never grasped the degree of interdependence that the two countries had come to share, and never drew the appropriate implications for United States policy.[25]

What then led U.S. officials to grant an exemption to Canada? It was partly Ottawa's promise to make contributions to the U.S. goal of slowing capital outflow from the United States. The price of having continuous access to the U.S. capital market was the erosion of Canadian economic independence. That is to say, Ottawa accepted the U.S. request that Canadian capital control policy would be subjected to Washington's direction.[26] But there was another, perhaps more important, factor that triggered the U.S. decision to grant an exemption: a financial crisis in Canada.

Financial turmoil in Canada, which was caused by the U.S. announcement of the Interest Equalization Tax, 'had already convinced the authors of the tax to exempt new Canadian issues [of bonds in the New York market].'[27] A similar event took place in the case of the 1968 Mandatory Capital Control measures: 'Again, as in 1963, it was the disarray of the Canadian financial community that swayed the American authorities.'[28] In both cases, 'The actual, and anticipated, reactions of financial markets to the successive American programs decisively influenced the way the two governments dealt with each other ...'[29]

At the negotiation table, U.S. officials may not have understood the Canadian arguments that the two North American nations were closely linked by massive economic forces, and that the smooth flow of these economic forces was vital to the interests of both the United States and Canada.[30] The U.S. officials thought such arguments were Ottawa's ploy to gain favourable treatment. They understood the arguments quite well, however, when their own policy actually backfired and began to hurt their national interest. In the face of the financial turmoil and the offer of cooperation from Ottawa, Washington decided to grant an exemption to Canada.

The Canadian rhetoric about the harmony of interest between the two nations was not, by itself, powerful enough for the U.S. officials to grant this exemption. Nor did Ottawa's offer to help Washington solve the U.S. problem induce Washington to change its original policy. The serious financial turmoil provided Ottawa with a window of opportunity to push Washington for policy change. The close linkage between the Canadian and the U.S. economies mattered only because it made the financial turmoil more serious a threat to Washington than it would have been otherwise.

Comparing the Canadian case with the Japanese case is instructive here. Japan also offered cooperative measures and experienced financial turmoils, but it was granted no immediate exemption by Washington. Japan failed to win an immediate exemption because the financial turmoil in Tokyo did not significantly threaten the health of the U.S. economy. This in turn was a function of the insignificant position of the Japanese economy in U.S. foreign economic policy. Thus, the proposition that Japan had no special relationship with the United States is not significant in explaining the Japanese case. Rather, the Japanese failure was due to the weak link between the U.S. and the Japanese economies.

This conclusion leads to the following hypothesis: A nation negotiating with the United States has the highest possibility to induce Washington to change the original U.S. macroeconomic policy when economic conditions become seriously harmful to Washington's original policy goal. Neither preaching to U.S. officials about how self-defeating their measures are, nor promising cooperation to solve their problems, can induce them to change their original policy. But economic pain can. Lesser nations are unlikely to be able to change U.S. macroeconomic policy by their national power alone. Whether they are fortunate to have the help of economic forces is a crucial factor in determining whether their macroeconomic diplomacy towards the United States will be successful.

The 1980s

The hypothesis developed in the previous section can be confirmed by the Japanese experiences of the 1980s in coping with U.S. macroeconomic diplomacy. The Fukuda government failed to maintain its original austerity-oriented fiscal policy change. In sharp contrast, the Ohira government succeeded in pursuing a similar policy. Both faced U.S. diplomatic pressure for policy change. A major factor, if not the only factor, explaining the difference between the two Japanese governments is the role of economic forces in the foreign exchange market.[31] That is, the Ohira government did not face rapid yen appreciations, which the Carter administration had encouraged throughout Fukuda's tenure as prime minister. In contrast, in the face of waves of yen appreciation, the Fukuda government changed its original austerity-oriented fiscal policy and introduced a large-scale fiscal expansion package in late 1977.

Since the summer of 1977, private investors had been buying yen and selling dollars in the foreign exchange market in light of large Japanese trade surpluses and huge U.S. trade deficits. The Carter administration welcomed this market direction because it wanted to reduce huge U.S. trade deficits with Japan by discouraging Japanese exports to the United States. The administration even encouraged this trend by publicly announcing its willingness to see the dollar fall further. This was called 'talking down the dollar' tactics or 'the dollar weapon.'[32] The Japanese government faced this frontal assault, and Prime Minister Fukuda eventually made a concession by changing its original fiscal policy in late 1977.

By October 1978, however, the U.S. administration was increasingly suffering from the negative results of its 'talking down the dollar' tactics: its inflation problem was aggravated and its exchange rate policy was backfiring. On 1 November 1978, the Carter Administration dramatically changed its policy stance by intervening in the foreign exchange market to prop up the dollar and by significantly constraining its original expansionary macroeconomic measures. It no longer could allow the dollar to drop against the yen in the foreign exchange market. After this incident, Ohira came into power (in December 1978). Under the circumstances, the Ohira government had a 'breathing space' and successfully defended its anti-reflationary policy.[33]

Thus, a change in U.S. macroeconomic policy, which had been frequently requested by Tokyo but consistently rejected by Washington, took place, but not because Japan had the power to impose its will on the United States. Rather, it was because of a 'change of tide,' so to speak, in the foreign exchange market. In fact, the Fukuda government had a great opportunity to push the Carter Administration for policy change in the fall of 1978. In the face of the inflation problem caused by the previous U.S. exchange rate policy, the Carter Administration was sharply divided between two groups, the proponents and the opponents of macroeconomic policy change. But the internal division apparently was not clear from the outside. Thus the Fukuda government failed to push the Carter Administration forcefully for policy change at that time.[34] The Fukuda government did not exploit a window of opportunity that was provided by economic forces in the foreign exchange market. Later these forces themselves finally induced the Carter Administration to change its macroeconomic policy.

A similar pattern was repeated in 1985–87.[35] The Reagan Administration drove the dollar down against the yen in the foreign exchange market after the Plaza Accord of September 1985. In the face of rapid yen appreciation, the Nakasone government finally changed its original macroeconomic policy, in a quite dramatic manner, in the spring of 1987.[36] After this 'victory,' however, the Reagan Administration faced the same problem the Carter Administration had a decade earlier; this time, financial market forces were much more powerful.

Private investors had become increasingly frustrated about the unwillingness of the Reagan administration to reduce the so-called 'twin deficits' (i.e., huge U.S. trade and budget deficits). On 19 October 1987, they began to sell massive amounts of their stocks on the New York Stock Exchange after learning of a policy disagreement between Washington and Bonn. This Black Monday financial panic shook the foundation of financial markets in the United States. The Reagan administration was immediately forced to regain private investors' confidence in U.S. macroeconomic policy by announcing its more serious commitment to deficit reduction.[37]

Until then, President Reagan had had only a half-hearted commitment to deficit reduction. Although the U.S. Congress had introduced the Gramm-Rudman-Hollings law, which was aimed at cutting the huge budget deficits, the president's reaction to it was far from enthusiastic. But the financial crash forced the president to cooperate more seriously with Congress on this policy problem. Immediately after Black Monday, Reagan made the following announcement: 'Today, I signed the preliminary sequester order under the Gramm-Rudman-Hollings law. However, I think it is preferable, if possible, that the executive and legislative branches reach agreement on a budget deficit reduction package.'[38]

As was true for the Carter Administration, the Reagan Administration successfully shifted the burden of adjustment in correcting the U.S.–Japan trade imbalances to Tokyo. The key policy tool of the two administrations was exchange rate policy. By encouraging private investors to drive the dollar down and the yen up, both administrations could generate powerful deflationary pressure in the Japanese economy, which in turn induced the Japanese government to introduce expansionary macroeconomic measures. While avoiding painful domestic deflation, the Carter and Reagan administrations could reduce U.S. trade deficits with Japan as the Japanese economy grew faster and Japanese exports to the United States slowed down. But as in the case of the Carter Administration, the Reagan Administration's exchange rate policy eventually backfired. Private investors in the financial markets turned around and forced the Carter and the Reagan administrations to adjust their macroeconomic policies in order to correct U.S. trade (and budget) deficits.

Furthermore, even before the financial backfire, one can detect the important power of economic forces in the U.S.–Japan macroeconomic diplomacy of 1985–87. In the case of U.S.–Canada negotiations in 1963–68, economic forces were crucial for the weaker side, that is, Ottawa, to win some concessions from Washington. In the U.S.–Japan case of 1985–87 as well, economic forces significantly helped Tokyo to change Washington's policy in its desired direction.

After the Group of Five Finance Ministers (including the Japanese finance minister and the U.S. treasury secretary) agreed to encourage dollar devaluation in the Plaza Accord, the dollar began to fall in the foreign exchange market.[39] As it kept falling, however, the interests of Washington and Tokyo began to diverge. Tokyo wanted less dollar devaluation; Washington wanted more. Washington began its commitment to stop the dollar devaluation as a bargaining chip against Tokyo. It wanted Tokyo to change its austerity-oriented fiscal policy. Tokyo, however, was not willing to make any commitment concerning its fiscal policy. Instead, it attempted to use its promise to implement expansionary monetary policy as a bargaining chip in getting a U.S. commitment to exchange rate stabilization. In the face of Washington's 'talk down the dollar' tactics, however, Tokyo was forced to stand in a defensive position. This bargaining process took place throughout 1986.[40]

Tokyo eventually accepted the U.S. terms and agreed to make a commitment to change its macroeconomic policy in exchange for a U.S. commitment to stop the dollar's fall. These official commitments were formalized at the Louvre Accord of February 1987. A deal was struck that was based on the Japanese concession on macroeconomic policy and the U.S. concession on exchange rate policy. U.S. macroeconomic policy was not on the negotiating table; the Reagan administration successfully avoided making any commitment to change its macroeconomic policy.[41]

Despite the fundamental asymmetry in its content, the Louvre Agreement was still a minor success for the Nakasone government in that the Reagan administration finally made a commitment to stop dollar devaluation. This was made possible largely due to the change of conditions in the foreign exchange market. That is to say, Tokyo alone did not have enough bargaining power to force Washington to make an exchange rate policy commitment. Theoretically, Washington could have forced Tokyo to change Japanese macroeconomic policy without giving up the U.S. exchange rate policy stance that could be used to gain further concessions from Tokyo.

But Washington had to abandon the 'whip' because its exchange rate policy was increasingly becoming less viable. As the dollar kept dropping, the danger of a bottomless fall became more realistic. This would have precipitated the U.S. economy into a serious recession. Given this power of economic forces in the foreign exchange market, Washington had no alternative but to sit down with Tokyo to make a commitment to stop the dollar's fall.

As was pointed out in the previous section, Ottawa was greatly assisted by financial panics in winning concessions from Washington in the 1960s. Similarly, Tokyo modestly benefited from financial market forces in negotiating with Washington in early 1987, although it was also suffering from the deflationary pressure generated by the same forces. Financial market forces provided Ottawa and Tokyo with rare opportunities to gain some concessions from Washington. These would have been much more difficult to obtain given the U.S. power superiority vis-à-vis Canada and Japan.

Conclusions

Financial market forces played a critical role in U.S.–Canada and U.S.–Japan macroeconomic diplomacy. First, along with the relative decline of U.S. economic power, the rise of financial market forces as a key agent of economic interdependence fundamentally changed the nature of macroeconomic diplomacy between the 1960s and the 1980s. This structural change in the international economic system is the key to understanding why Canada disappeared from the global picture of macroeconomic diplomacy in the 1980s.

Second, the role of financial market forces is the key to isolating the specific conditions under which weaker nations like Canada and Japan could still win some concessions from the United States in their macroeconomic diplomacy. Despite significant differences in historical and geographical conditions between U.S.–Canada and U.S.–Japan macroeconomic diplomacy, in both cases financial market forces provided the weaker nation with a window of opportunity to change the macroeconomic policy of the stronger nation.

The argument focusing on the role of economic forces as a cause of Washington's policy change can be contrasted with two other arguments: (1) the argument emphasizing the role of diplomatic culture, and (2) the one stressing the role of international institutions. First, this discussion of U.S.–Canada macroeconomic diplomacy in the 1960s has carefully concluded that the so-called U.S.–Canada special relationship was not a decisive factor for Washington to exempt Ottawa from its capital control measures. Power and interest, rather than culture and norms, were the language that U.S. officials understood.

Second, although this chapter did not fully deal with the role of international institutions in the cases, their impact on policy making also was not significant. For the case of U.S.–Canada macroeconomic diplomacy in the 1960s, Maureen Appel Molot's thorough study concludes that bilateral institutions, such as the Joint Canada-United States Committee on Trade and Economic Affairs and the

Canada–United States Balance of Payments Committee, played quite limited roles.[42] In the case of U.S.–Japan macroeconomic diplomacy as well, little evidence is available to show that Washington's calculation of its core interest vis-à-vis Tokyo was fundamentally influenced by such institutions as Group of Seven summit meetings. To use the language of international relations theory, Realist analysis (which emphasizes power and interest as causal factors), rather than Neoliberal Institutionalist analysis (which emphasizes the role of norms and institutions in international politics), has more explanatory power in our cases.[43]

In general, these findings support what David Andrews calls the 'capital mobility hypothesis,' that is, the hypothesis that 'when capital is highly mobile across international borders, the sustainable macroeconomic policy options available to states are systematically circumscribed.'[44] At the same time, however, our analysis offers at least two caveats in advancing this hypothesis.

First, at the level of the international system, the rise of mobile capital has changed the content of the macroeconomic negotiation agenda; meanwhile, the relative decline of U.S. hegemony has altered the manner in which the United States has conducted its macroeconomic diplomacy. Thus, to fully understand the changed nature of macroeconomic diplomacy of, and towards, the United States since the 1960s, one must take into account both the rise of financial market forces and the relative decline of U.S. economic power. Contrary to this conclusion, the capital mobility hypothesis, prima facie, focuses mostly on the former change, leaving the impression that a key change in the structure of the postwar international monetary system has occurred only in terms of capital mobility. The current findings confirm that analysts should more explicitly address the impact of the international distribution of economic power in analysing macroeconomic diplomacy.

Second, at the level of bilateral relations, this analysis suggests that the significance of financial market forces in macroeconomic diplomacy may vary across bilateral relations even in the same time period, and even in the same international exchange rate regime. (Recall the analysis of the 1960s.) This point is not fully appreciated in the current literature of the capital mobility hypothesis that tends to focus on the international level. Comparative studies of bilateral relations may be a new research frontier. In future research, in particular, more careful comparative analysis of domestic politics in macroeconomic diplomacy should be conducted.[45] This study has found that financial market forces opened up windows of opportunity for Canada and Japan against the United States. Yet, having this opportunity did not guarantee a favourable U.S. policy change. (Recall, for example, the Fukuda government's 'failure' to exploit the division in the Carter Administration in late 1978.) Under what conditions can a lesser state successfully exploit the window of opportunity generated by financial market forces? This is one of the questions that should be addressed in the future.

Finally, some policy implications should be noted. The analysis suggests that financial market forces are elusive double-edged swords to governments engaged in macroeconomic diplomacy.[46] As Tokyo found in the 1980s, market forces are like waves – depending on market conditions, they may hurt you or benefit you. Washington learned a similar lesson; its attempt to manipulate these forces was ultimately self-defeating. Currently, an enormous amount of capital circulates around the globe, and no one government can fully control this flow. A particular government may be lucky to have a window of opportunity provided by financial market forces to press another government for a change in macroeconomic policy. But the former government may soon experience the economic tide reversing in favour of the latter government.

Furthermore, financial market forces may generate long-term economic problems initially unexpected by governments engaged in macroeconomic diplomacy. Japan's so-called 'bubble economy' is a case in point. In the course of macroeconomic diplomacy vis-à-vis the United States after the Plaza Accord, Tokyo cut its discount rate to extremely low levels, which stimulated speculative investments in the real estate and stock markets of Japan – hence the 'bubble economy' of the late 1980s. This 'bubble' burst in the early 1990s, and since then, Japan has been experiencing serious economic problems, including the highest unemployment rate in its postwar history.

Financial market forces are a formidable force for governments in contemporary macroeconomic diplomacy, whether in terms of their short-term elusiveness or in terms of their ability to cause unexpected economic problems. The policy lesson that can be drawn from the case studies must be a modest one: it is not about how to control and use powerful market forces, but how to live with them in an economically interdependent world.

NOTES

1 An earlier version of this chapter was read at the Canada–Japan Research Award Workshop, 'Comparing Japanese and Canadian Approaches to the United States,' Tokyo, 17 December 1993. I thank the conference participants, especially Daizo Sakurada. I am also grateful for financial support given by the Canada–Japan Research Award. The views expressed in this chapter are solely mine. The most recent analysis of the autonomous finance thesis can be found in Andrews, 'Capital Mobility and State Autonomy,' 193–218.

2 The literature examined include *Canadian Annual Review of Politics and Public Affairs*, various years; *Public Papers of the Presidents*, since the Carter years;

Canada among Nations, edited by scholars at Carleton University; as well as comprehensive newspaper clippings in the John Holmes Library at the Canadian Institute of International Affairs in Toronto.

3 Instead, the literature on Canadian macroeconomic policy usually focuses (1) on the relationship between electoral and business cycles and (2) on the political accountability of macroeconomic policy making.

4 See, for example, Destler and Henning, *Dollar Politics*; Funabashi, *Managing the Dollar*, 2nd ed.; Funabashi, *Tsuka Retsu Retsu*; and Putnam and Bayne, *Hanging Together*. An important exception is Dobson, *Economic Policy Coordination*.

5 See Webb, 'International Economic Structures,' 309–42.

6 Molot, 'The Role of Institutions,' 164–93; Wright, 'Persuasive Influence,' 137–63; Wright, 'Cooperation and Independence'; Wright, 'Capital Movements and Government Control,' 671–88.

7 Volcker and Gyohten, *Changing Fortunes*, 52.

8 Volcker and Gyohten, *Changing Fortunes*, 53.

9 Ibid., *Nihon Keizai Shimbun*, 11 February 1965, 1.

10 *Nihon Keizai Shimbun*, 27 January 1968, 1.

11 For the demise of the Bretton Woods monetary system, see Gowa, *Closing the Gold Window*; Odell, *U.S. International Monetary Policy*, Chaps. 4 and 5. Also see Chapter 2 in this volume.

12 See Putnam and Bayne, *Hanging Together*.

13 For the 1977–79 episode, see Destler and Mitsuyu, 'Locomotives on Different Tracks'; Kawasaki, 'Pressing Japan for Fiscal Expansion'; Putnam and Bayne, *Hanging Together*, Chaps. 4 and 5; Putnam and Henning, 'The Bonn Summit of 1978'; Volcker and Gyohten, *Changing Fortunes*, Chap. 5.

14 For the 1985–87 episode, see Destler and Henning, *Dollar Politics*; Funabashi, *Managing the Dollar* and *Tsuka Retsu Retsu*; Kawasaki, 'In Defence of Economic Sovereignty'; Kawasaki, 'Managing Macroeconomic Adjustments'; Shiota, *1,000 Nichi no Joho*; Yuasa, *En to Doru no Kobo*; Volcker and Gyothen, *Changing Fortunes*, Chaps. 8 and 9. In the summer of 1993, the author conducted personal interviews with a small number of persons who were close to Japanese policy making in the 1977–79 and 1985–87 periods; results are included in this chapter.

15 George, 'Case Studies.' The following three general conditions of 'success' were also taken into account: (1) It took a reasonably short time for a U.S. policy to change in the face of a foreign request to do so. (2) The degree of the U.S. policy change is significant in light of the original foreign request. (3) The costs that Ottawa or Tokyo paid for the U.S. policy change were reasonable to these lesser powers. For a different set of standards for determining policy success in U.S.–Canada relations, see Nye, 'Transnational Relations and Interstate Conflicts,' 961–96.

16 Both in 1977–79 and 1985–87, Japan experienced one success and one failure. Thus, in the 1977–87 period as a whole, it had two successes and two failures.

17 Peyton Lyon's words in Canada, Senate, 6.

18 Holsti, 'Canada and the United States,' 390.

19 For the U.S.–Canada 'special relationship,' see also Barry, 'The Politics of "Exceptionalism"'; Canada, *Canada–United States Relations*; Cuff and Granatstein, 'Canada and the Perils of "Exemptionalism"'; Dickey, 'The Relationship in Rhetoric'; Doran, *Forgotten Partnership*; and Merchant and Heeney, *Principles for Partnership*.

20 For the details of the Canadian strategy, see Wright, 'Persuasive Influence,' 144–45, 150–53.

21 For this dimension of the U.S.–Canadian negotiation, see Wright, 'Persuasive Influence,' 145–47. On the background analysis of Canadian dependence on the U.S. capital market, see Wright and Molot, 'Capital Movements and Government Control,' 671–75.

22 Wright, 'Persuasive Influence,' 146.

23 Ibid.

24 Ibid., 153–55, 158.

25 Ibid., 154. Based on extensive interviews with U.S. and Canadian officials, Wright's 'Cooperation and Independence' analyses all the 1963, 1965, and 1968 capital control negotiations.

26 At first, as was pointed out earlier, this cost seemed to be minimal to Ottawa. Yet, it turned out that it became an increasingly heavy burden on the Canadian economy. In 1965, for example, Ottawa began to discourage the foreign borrowing activities of Canadian banks. This was done in exchange for another exemption from U.S. capital control measures (the 1965 Voluntary Capital Control measures). In 1968, Washington granted yet another exemption to Canada from its Mandatory Capital Control measures on the condition that Ottawa strengthen its control over foreign borrowing activities in Canada. These processes eroded Canadian freedom of action in capital markets and deepened the integration of the Canadian economy into the U.S. economy as a subordinate actor. On the costs of winning exemptions, see Molot, 'The Role of Institutions,' 167–69; Wright, 'Persuasive Influence,' 149–50; Wright and Molot, 'Capital Movements and Government Control,' 680–82.

27 Wright and Molot, 'Capital Movements and Government Control,' 676.

28 Ibid., 679.

29 Ibid., 685.

30 For a different interpretation, see Plumptre, *Three Decades of Decision*, esp. 204–19.

31 Another major factor is the changing position of the prime minister in Japanese fiscal policy making. For a further analysis on this point, see Kawasaki, 'Managing Macroeconomic Adjustments,' Chaps. 3 and 4.

32 Parboni, 'The Dollar Weapon.'
33 For this episode, see Kawasaki, 'Pressing Japan for Fiscal Expansion.' Interviews with people who worked closely with Ohira indicate that Prime Minister Ohira was committed to austerity-oriented fiscal policy. The absence of rapid yen appreciations worked favourably for him in pursuing his fiscal policy.
34 For this episode, see Putnam and Henning, 'The Bonn Summit of 1978,' 79–80.
35 See Kawasaki, 'In Defence of Economic Sovereignty.'
36 As was true for the Fukuda government a decade earlier, the timing of this policy change was greatly influenced by the changing position of the prime minister in Japanese fiscal policy making. According to my interviews with former Japanese officials, the shift of prime ministerial support from the austerity-oriented Ministry of Finance to the expenditure-oriented Liberal Democratic Party was a decisive factor in causing the Japanese fiscal policy change.
37 For this episode see Destler and Henning, *Dollar Politics,* 63.
38 Quoted in Destler and Henning, *Dollar Politics*, 78, note 65, originally appearing in *New York Times*, 21 October 1987.
39 On the Plaza Accord, see Funabashi, *Managing the Dollar*, Chap. 1, and *Tsuka Retsu Retsu*, Chap. 1. Throughout the 1985–87 period, the Bank of Japan was a junior partner of the MOF, and the latter essentially guided Japanese monetary policy. See Ota's memoir in Ota, *Kokusai Kinyu Genba Kara no Shogen*. Ota was a Bank of Japan official who was heavily involved in Japanese monetary policy making during the period concerned.
40 For a detailed analysis, see Kawasaki, 'In Defence of Sovereignty.'
41 Kawasaki, 'In Defence of Sovereignty.'
42 See Molot, 'The Role of Institutions.'
43 On the other debate between the Realist and Neoliberal Institutionalist positions, see Baldwin, *Neorealism and Neoliberalism*; Keohane, *International Institutions and State Power*; Powell, 'Anarchy in International Relations Theory.'
44 Andrews, 'Capital Mobility and State Autonomy,' 193.
45 One potential model to be employed is Robert Putnam's 'two-level games.' See Putnam, 'Diplomacy and Domestic Politics'; and Evans, Jacobson, and Putnam, eds., *Double-Edged Diplomacy*.
46 While this paper has focused on government-to-government negotiations, there has been another kind of macroeconomic diplomacy in recent years: the one between governments and financial markets (i.e., a massive number of private investors). As many governments have accumulated huge budget deficits, they have become more reliant on bond markets and have become more vulnerable to financial market forces. This is more difficult than the old government-to-government diplomacy, because the ultimate victory in the new macroeconomic diplomacy can be achieved only by self-discipline: to reduce budget deficits by cutting government expenditure

and/or raising taxes. Canada in the 1980s was not involved in macroeconomic diplomacy with the United States, as was pointed out, but it started this new type of macroeconomic diplomacy. It remains to be seen whether Canada will ultimately win in this diplomatic game.

4

Japanese–American Trade Negotiations: The Structural Impediments Initiative

MICHAEL W. DONNELLY

Bilateral political bargaining is deeply embedded in the everyday fabric of Japanese–American economic relations. As transnational relations have proliferated and mutual economic dependence has deepened, and as the manifold benefits of commercial ties across the Pacific have spread across both national economies, the political forays by politicians and bureaucratic officials into the heartland of economic activity have also expanded dramatically. At times it seems that almost any aspect of domestic and cross-border commercial life can become the object of petty haggling. While considered to be a mode of joint deliberation and decision making of last resort, the least efficient and potentially most destructive way for nations to deal with economic controversies, Japan and America have nonetheless been engaging in ad hoc, bilateral bargaining for over two decades.[1]

In recent years the most important negotiations have focused on trade and especially on the character of the Japanese marketplace. Approximately forty-five major trade agreements were reached through bargaining from 1980 to 1996.[2] Many more formal and informal 'commitments' and 'understandings' have also been made. The objects of dispute have ranged from rice, cellular phones, and medical technology to apples, semiconductors, public works, and flat glass. Intertwined in the politics of all these settlements are larger questions concerning the evolving character of international economic management at the end of the twentieth century. In a period of rapid increases in international economic exchanges, as globalization requires more ambitious multilateral cooperation, why have these two governments persisted in pursuing aggressive bilateralism? What mechanisms of dispute resolution have been tried as these two countries cope with economic frictions associated with structural adjustment and growing economic interdependence?

Political Bargaining and Structural Impediments

The central assumption of this chapter is that one cannot understand present-day international economic adjustments without comprehending how political bargaining between national governments takes place. No firmly established theory of international bargaining awaits the analyst of bargaining-based economic negotiations. Instead of scholarly consensus, an untidy array of research programs crowd the intellectual landscape, ranging from descriptive accounts of how governments advance their diplomatic strategies to mathematized paradigms formulated by political scientists who aspire to neatly package the regularities of human behaviour into a handful of game-theoretic variables.[3]

The secondary literature on Japanese–American negotiations is for the most part qualitatively analytical or only modestly theoretical.[4] The most widely accepted view is that Japanese foreign policy is reactive to external forces, thereby tempting the American government in response to private-sector complaints to launch aggressive campaigns of foreign pressure (*gaiatsu*) in order to persuade and even compel Japan to change. Since political pressure does not always work, a growing empirical literature seeks to explain the variation in outcomes.[5]

Rather than adopt a single, preconstructed framework or take up the issue of why *gaiatsu* does or does not work, this analysis maps how the American and Japanese governments attempt to cope with economic interdependence. This chapter's concern is not to explain in a definitive way the specific substantive results of bargaining, nor to suggest when and how *gaiatsu* will improve the likelihood of America achieving its ends. It simply offers a pre-theoretical understanding of the complex admixture of conflict and cooperation that marks the bilateral bargaining process. In doing so the analysis sheds light on the bargaining strategies of the Japanese government in a way that is not usually the case in most of the secondary literature.[6]

The chapter deals with the Structural Impediment Initiative (hereafter, SII) embarked on by the two governments in July 1989 and formally completed in June 1990. The settlement included a follow-up mechanism that required that the two governments review regularly progress in the areas in which agreement was reached, permit additional discussion of 'problem' areas, and allow consideration of further actions. Two additional annual reports were subsequently issued.[7] Under President Clinton the American government subsequently adopted a revised and much more aggressive strategic approach to Japan.

The SII was the centrepiece of the Bush administration's effort to deal with America's 'Japan problem' at a time when tensions were close to an all-time high. The most important innovation in U.S.-Japan trade negotiations hitherto attempted, the negotiations were designed to designate actions for dealing with structural economic problems, in both countries, considered as impediments to trade and balance of payments adjustments. SII has been the most explicit attempt by the two governments to address in political negotiations underlying structural differences in the two economies. Interactions were difficult and, at times, rancorous, as they were not simply discussing questions regarding trade imbalances but, most fundamentally, an American attempt to make the Japanese economy more 'open, transparent, and fair.' The talks produced widely varying results.

The essence of a bargaining situation is that the ability of any participant to gain an end is dependent to an important degree on the choices and decisions of others. Bilateral political bargaining is thus a means (though not the only one and not intrinsically positive in results) by which economically and politically interdependent governments search for advantages while coming to mutually acceptable agreements. Bargaining takes place in a situation of 'reciprocally contingent choice.'[8] Both governments were divided internally by 'turf' battles among subunits and by policy coalitions rooted in conflicting ideologies, organizational goals, and personal ambitions. At key moments decisions were made by top-level policy-makers, including subcabinet government officials and political leaders. A great deal of preparatory work and policy debate, however, involved working-level officials, including, in some cases, transgovernmental coalitions and the quiet manoeuvrings of influential politicians.

What were the major political circumstances that conditioned how the two governments sought mutually acceptable agreements? In outline, they include: (1) governmental subunits, on both sides, with conflicting ideas and preferences regarding how best to understand and deal with the 'dispute' that sometimes formed transgovernmental alliances; (2) parties to the conflict that attempted to influence how others estimated their own preferences by using power, information, and face-to-face persuasion; (3) agreement achieved partially as a function of bargaining tactics both at the bargaining table and beyond; (4) a process of bilateral interaction that was a multilevel game of horizontal (cross-border) and vertical bargaining (intragovernmental); a large number of participants not formally seated at the table; (5) for both governments, strong pressure to establish 'common zones' of potential agreement since policy élites came to believe that their interests in the end would be served by appearing to do something positive; and (6) final decisions designed to ensure that bilateral relations did not degenerate into uncontrollable political conflict, even as the outcomes were not designed to embody 'efficient' solutions to objective economic problems.

Bargaining and negotiations of this sort are best understood as rooted in a broad political and social context; involving a good deal of ritual, empty words and veiled threats; and moving by a piecemeal process of trial and error rather than according to the rational convergence of positions held by unified parties. To be effective, the strategies adopted by all parties have to fit in a productive way with the domestic politics of the other parties involved in the negotiations.[9] In the case of the United States, for example, this meant a need for energetic sponsors in Tokyo and broad support within the bureaucracy, the business community, the Liberal Democratic Party (LDP), the Office of Prime Minister, and the press. Japan also needed support from the White House, Cabinet members, government departments, Congress, and the national and local media. What is conceded or gained at the table will also depend on what is acceptable among political, economic, and bureaucratic constituents at home. Sometimes, too, strategies of negotiation will be shaped as a way to retain power and influence in domestic politics as much as they are adopted to persuade the other side to concede.

This analysis is not a detailed description of what occurred at each formal negotiation or in the various public and private discussions, of which there were many. A good deal of extremely detailed and reliable scholarship has told the story well.[10] The principle effort here is more analytical than descriptive, reflecting an attempt to understand in a specific empirical context what Susan Strange declares to be at the heart of the study of political economy: 'The way things are managed, how they got to be managed in that particular way, and what choices this leaves realistically open for the future.'[11] The following questions are addressed:

1/ What is the larger political and economic context of Japanese–American economic interdependence?
2/ What prompted Japan and the United States to enter into SII?
3/ How did the two sides define and frame their interests and objectives with respect to the negotiations?
4/ How best can one characterize the bargaining process? How was the deal done?
5/ What was the nature of the agreement? What larger lessons can be drawn regarding SII?

The Political Uncertainties of Asymmetrical Competitive Interdependence

Japan began to emerge as a truly global economic power in the early 1970s. America's irreversible decline as a hegemonic power became progressively obvious as well. Not politically, economically, or even psychologically were policy élites, in either country, fully prepared to cope with the unrelenting pressures for economic adjustment which followed. In a milieu of growing Japanese economic strength and frustrating economic difficulties for the United States, bilateral friction and the need for new forms of accommodation were inevitable.

In many ways Japanese–American relations were transformed into a form of competitive and extremely complex interdependence.[12] By any standard of measurement the two nations are economically interconnected, their well-being reciprocally intertwined through trade, direct and indirect investment, joint ventures, and a host of other commercial, technological, military, educational, cultural, and intellectual links. Multiple channels of human contact and a growing number of cross-national political alliances often blur clear lines of 'national,' 'bilateral,' and even 'international.' In many respects, mutual dependence was based on the respective national strengths of the two nations. Nonetheless, policy adjustment to structural changes and deepening interdependence had been anything but smooth. Judging by the political rhetoric in the late 1980s the relationship was approaching a state of stress and crisis.[13]

American frustrations were partially rooted in some serious economic asymmetries in the ties of interdependence. Politically the two nations were only emerging from a dominant–subordinate political framework established over forty years earlier by the San Francisco system. An American security presence in Asia in the late 1990s is still the major premise of Japan's defence and economic policies, and a major reason why the American side can take the offensive on many bilateral disputes even if Japan received very little in return at the negotiating table. By the late 1980s bilateral imbalances in the relationship were growing, especially in areas of trade. During most of the decade Japan's annual bilateral trade surplus with the United States averaged about U.S.$50 billion a year. Most economists agreed that the causes of American deficits and Japanese surpluses were largely rooted in macroeconomic factors: exchange rates, interest rates, savings and investment levels, and differences in business cycles. But despite adjustments in macroeconomic policies, the American deficit remained stubbornly high. Japan was running an overall trade balance at a time when the United States was recording record deficits.

While Japanese overseas investment had surged during the decade, especially in the United States, foreign investment in Japan remained extremely modest. Asymmetrical interdependence was also keenly competitive, as reflected in the commercial success of Japanese firms in the United States. As Japanese imports surged, a large number of U.S. firms, industry associations, labour organizations, and Congressional politicians were calling for protection and more aggressive trade negotiations.

What gave the bilateral relationship a ferocious character at times was the scope and speed of the economic transformation. Moreover, new forms of competitive asymmetrical interdependence in the 1980s developed within the context of an odd complementarity between the two national economies. The United States was marked throughout the decade by low savings and investment rates, severe budgetary deficits, high capital costs, an overvalued currency, very short corporate time horizons, low levels of expenditure on research and development, and severe doubt about the country's educational standards. Japan boasted extraordinarily high levels of savings and investment, a healthier budgetary balance, low capital costs, an undervalued yen, high levels of non-military research and development expenditures, stable workplace relations, high levels of educational achievement, and a private sector performing very well. In many ways, Japan's strengths meshed with America's weaknesses.

Moreover, interdependence brought with it increased visibility of national differences. A widely held belief among American officials, academics, politicians, and intellectuals to this day holds that the American and Japanese markets are in many respects quite different in relation to national values, economic ideology, the nature of business firms, financial markets, interactions between governments and the private sector, vertical and horizontal linkages among companies, and in everyday business practices.[14] As American–Japanese ties expanded, the two societies became more aware of the institutional differences that separated them.

As Schoppa and Naka have demonstrated so well, there was no consensus in the United States on how best to understand America's 'Japan problem,' even as most could agree that mutual dependence was shifting in Japan's favour. Nor was there a consensus in Washington on what measures might be undertaken to deal with the unavoidable economic challenge. The range of potential political options to use in actively seeking to reduce trade deficits and open up Japanese markets was thus broad: U.S. trade law remedies, including the so-called Super 301 provisions of the 1988 Trade Act; voluntary import and export agreements; extraterritorial application of U.S. law; threats of protectionist legislation, countervailing duty and antidumping investigations; direct bilateral pressure to eliminate sector-specific barriers; multilateral talks within the General Agreements on Tariffs and Trade (GATT) and other international forums; an emphasis on 'deadlines' and 'results' in new bilateral trade agreements; further attention on the macroeconomic causes of trade imbalances; and direct discussions on the structural causes of persistent imbalances.[15] There was even some talk about a free trade agreement between the two countries.

The trade conflict was thus connected to a larger political and ideological debate regarding the nature of the international trading system and the conditions of economic competition as they evolved in the two countries. An abundant secondary literature suggests that fundamental differences in domestic structures and national ideological beliefs separate Japan and the United States. Diplomacy can also be shaped in unpredictable ways by conditions of 'parallel politics': pluralistic, segmented, and relatively competitive policy 'subgovernments'; internally divided and decentralized political parties; strong and well-entrenched interest groups; locally oriented office-holders; and political arrangements that help to keep policy responsive to the grievances of constituents harmed by the workings of the marketplace or threatened by new forms of economic competition.[16]

Getting to the Talks

It is common practice that the United States will take the offensive in negotiations by announcing that some aspect of the Japanese market or government policy requires adjustment, reform, or abolition. On the other hand, a reluctant response of some kind to trade-related and other American-initiated talks is widely considered by Tokyo to be the political cost of maintaining a friendly relationship given the country's political and security dependence on the United States and the overall economic importance of the American market. Many critics have argued that the American government is often the real 'political opposition' in Japanese politics, and that pressure from Washington provides an excuse for leaders of the LDP under the strong leadership of the prime minister to intervene in policy making by narrow subgovernments in a way that counteracts the entrenched power of privileged but narrow economic interests.

The Bush Administration's negotiating strategy regarding SII was based on the assumption that traditional adjustment mechanisms would not produce significant changes in Japan's external surplus. It was decided by the new administration that a new approach to Japan was necessary, one that would help lower the overall trade imbalance and also reduce structural barriers blocking potential American exports.[17]

Bilateral tensions over trade and investment were severe. The widespread view in Washington was that structural barriers existed across many sectors in the Japanese economy that obstructed imports and distorted the 'efficient' functioning of the economy. These structural impediments closed out foreign competition, prevented the transmission of normal market signals, robbed consumers of the benefits of free-market economic competition, and inhibited normal market corrections in trade imbalances. As a consequence, more open markets were essential in Japan, even if they would not solve America's bilateral current account and trade deficits, which, for the most part, were macroeconomic in nature and essentially produced at home.

The political assumption was that the Japanese government bore a good deal of the responsibility for opening its nation's markets to the world but that officials were conservative by nature, excessively protective of vested interests, and unwilling to embark on domestic policy change. As always, strong and consistent pressure on Japan would be necessary to force policy changes. In moments of candour, American negotiators sometimes suggested that if the spirit of free trade was to survive in the United States then success in Japan was crucial. Throughout the negotiation, SII negotiations were used by the Bush Administration to counter protectionist demands in Congress. But to be convincing, very specific results were necessary.

The idea for the talks apparently originated in the Department of Treasury, although the need for worldwide 'structural reform' of trade regimes had been a topic of academic and government talks for years at economic summits, GATT hearings, sessions of the G7 finance ministers, and discussions of the International Monetary Fund and the Organization of Economic Cooperation and Development. Japanese officials had also been seriously considering 'structural' talks of some kind. Indeed, a number of subcabinet-level 'structural-adjustment' discussions had already been conducted between Japan and the United States in previous years.

There continued to be considerable disagreement both within the Bush Administration and also in Congress on what should be done about Japan. The President's Advisory Committee on Trade Policy and Negotiations in 1989 urged that the administration undertake a 'results-oriented' approach, including threats of retaliation if necessary.[18] Some officials in agencies like the Department of Commerce and the United States Trade Representative (USTR) preferred a results-oriented approach. On the other hand, Carla Hills, head of USTR, and Linn Williams, her deputy in charge of trade talks, were opponents of 'managed trade.'[19] The Departments of State and Defence tended to see the relationship with Japan within a larger geo-strategic setting, thus downplaying economic tensions. The position of the Department of Treasury reflected special concern about structural barriers to macroeconomic adjustments. Behind the new initiative was considerable Congressional pressure on the administration to get a lot 'tougher' with Japan, even if it meant drawing away from the principles of free trade.[20]

The final American decision to embark on the talks was preceded by off-the-record talks with Japan, beginning with the Ministry of Finance. SII was directly connected to the application of Section 301 of the Trade and Tariff Act of 1974 as amended by the Omnibus Trade and Competitiveness Act of 1988. The Bush Administration had little choice but to name Japan a priority country under provisions of the new act. However, despite widespread sentiment favouring strong measures towards Japan, only three products and two trade practices were targeted for investigation. What made this cautious outcome more acceptable to critics in Washington, including some members of the administration, was the president's endorsement of SII. It was widely accepted that the new talks would be dealt with in tandem with Super 301 discussions. Indeed, it was a way for the United States to carry out Super 301–type investigations without the heavy threat of immediate retaliation. By staking out a position between relative 'free trade' and numerically targeted 'managed trade,' the White House aimed at showing Congress that it could take decisive action, enhance its ability to press Japan, yet all the while retain its own political prerogatives in Washington to determine U.S. government policies towards Japan.[21]

Prime Minister Sosuke Uno and President George Bush agreed to the talks during a brief June meeting in Paris during the annual Economic Summit. Why did Japan go along with an idea that was in many bureaucratic quarters strongly disliked? Officials in Tokyo recognized that both governments had to address Japan's trade surplus in some sort of policy forum. But they opposed any notion of 'results-oriented' discussions and rejected the idea that 'structural impediments' could be modified in a short period of time. They also did not like Super 301, calling it a unilateral policy undermining the very basis of the international trading system. In talks at the subcabinet level Japanese participants told their American counterparts to take their Super 301 complaints to GATT. While declaring that it would not talk within the threatening legal framework of 301, the Japanese government finally indicated a willingness to discuss the three products, but not under 'any kind of threat.'

Part of the Japanese game plan may also have been to concede enough to the Bush Administration in the SII so that the White House could withstand Congressional pressure to place Japan on the Super 301 list once again in 1990. In any case, Japanese leaders were grievously weakened at home by the Recruit Cosmos Scandal and hardly in a political position to act tough with their most important political, economic, and military ally. They understood that there were important voices of moderation within the Bush Administration that warned against weakening the larger political and military alliance with Japan in the name of 'fair trade.' Moreover, Japan was divided too, with some government officials and business organizations in favour of more liberalization of the marketplace. While not at all certain on where the 'initiative' would lead, the LDP government had little choice but to go along with the American proposal, which was reported in the mass media as nothing less than an attempt to 'remake' Japan. In fact, many Japanese officials believed that they had 'dodged the first bullet' when the United States decided to limit the application of Super

301, welcomed the opportunity to discuss American structural impediments, and were prepared to show some 'blood-stained efforts' to reduce the trade surplus.

Forming a Comprehensive Bilateral Agenda

No precedents or standard benchmarks existed to mark how to proceed. By agreement the talks would be comprehensive, move along in a variety of sectoral areas, and examine structural problems in the economies of both countries. The Japanese side initially rejected the nomenclature of Structural Impediment Initiative because it implied that structural impediments actually existed. In the end they relented, especially when the American side pressed to have the discussion be called 'negotiations.' But throughout the bargaining SII was translated into the Japanese language by the press and government officials as *Nichi-Bei Kozo Mondai Kyogi* (Japanese–American Discussions of Structural Problems), eliminating the harsh idea of impediments and suggesting instead that the two sides would simply discuss their differences. The Japanese also warned that they were not engaged in any sort of 'results-oriented' discussions or that subjects under discussion should be treated as actionable under U.S. trade law. The Americans replied that another round of fruitless talks was not acceptable and that the talks should move along with tight deadlines, including a midterm report on the discussions by April 1990 or just before Washington would again make a decision about whether or not to list Japan under the provisions of Super 301.

The situation was complicated in late July when the LDP lost its majority in elections for the House of Councillors. Prime Minister Uno resigned following the loss and in light of personal scandals. He was replaced by Toshiki Kaifu, who had a weak power base in the LDP. A major factor was the unhappiness of many consumers and taxpayers with the country's ruling political party. Until elections were held for the House of Representatives in February 1990, when the LDP won a resounding victory, it was extremely difficult for the government to undertake any new policy departures. In fact, no substantive progress was made in the bilateral meetings until then. At least at the bargaining table, discussions did not become negotiations until after the elections.

In any case, after a certain amount of semantic quibbling and procedural wrangling the two sides finally met formally for the first time in Tokyo in September. The American side of the SII working group was co-chaired by subcabinet officials from State, Treasury and USTR. Officials from the Departments of Justice and Commerce and the President's Council of Economic Advisers were also in regular attendance. The Japanese side was headed by vice-ministerial officials from Foreign Affairs, Finance, and International Trade and Industry.

TABLE 4.1
Agenda for structural impediments initiative

American concerns	Japanese concerns
Savings and investment patterns	Investment–savings balance
Land policies	Corporate investment and productivity
Distribution system	Government regulations
Price mechanism	Research and development
Exclusionary business practices	Export and promotion
Keiretsu relationships	Education and workforce education

Officials from the Economic Planning Agency and the Fair Trade Commission also were present. Altogether, ten agencies of the American government and close to twenty from the Japanese participated, depending on policy jurisdictions and issues raised for discussion. The formal meetings often had 100 or more people in the room, moving in and out. In the end, of course, this meant that at times restricted meetings among the principals took place under considerable secrecy, including small meetings in Bern, Hawaii, and a suburb of Washington, DC. Throughout the SII process subunits of both governments were in contact with their counterparts across the Pacific.

Table 4.1 outlines the agenda brought to the table by the two sides.[22]

In a word, the American side focused on a set of 'structural impediments' believed to keep foreign firms out of Japan. In rhetorical terms, the U.S. approach reflected assumptions of how Japan might change to more closely approximate the workings of an open, free, and accessible market economy. The content of the American agenda was not unexpected, reflecting as it did a deliberate attempt to base proposals on ideas already widely discussed in Japan by industrial federations and the popular press or already recommended by various government commissions. Japanese criticism of American business, on the other hand, was mostly a repetition of the list of defects found in any standard critique of the American economy. Indeed, in discussions the American side found a good deal with which to agree. What made the negotiations rather unique is that the two sides put into the official record views about business and economic arrangements normally considered inappropriate for discussion in intergovernmental negotiations.

The policy agenda was thus a full one. American officials recognized that the issues they brought to the table were complex, touching on practices deeply embedded in the Japanese economy. The talks were not without substantial irony. Even among supporters of SII few believed that implementation of the American agenda would lead to a quick reduction of the nation's trade deficit with Japan, since it reflected predominantly a macroeconomic misalignment and not foreign restrictions. On the other hand, reforms suggested by the Japanese would probably help eliminate substantially the U.S. deficit.

Influential members of Congress wanted 'results-oriented' negotiations: measurable goals, timetables for action, and fairly definitive results. Ambassador Carla Hills was more compromising, declaring on many occasions that what could be best hoped for from Japan was 'an initial down payment, with a blueprint of additional steps.' In Congressional testimony and in various public utterances members of the Administration admitted that changes in Japan would take time, time to build a consensus, time to pass new laws, time to phase in reforms.[23]

Strategic and Tactical Interaction

Robert Putnam has shown how negotiations between governments are often simultaneous two-level games. As he and his collaborators have noted, positions at the 'table' – the strategies of negotiators – usually emerge from within the bureaucratic politics of each government, which is sometimes divided internally even as the team of negotiators is dealing with the other side.[24] The chief negotiators may have 'silent' opponents as well as supporters, on both sides of the table. It is important to emphasize that international agreements require acceptance both by domestic constituents at home and by the constituents of the players directly across the table. In this case, SII prompted a complicated set of vertical and horizontal interactions conducted simultaneously among governmental units and élite politicians. Often these interactions amounted to transgovernmental coalitions among subunits of different governments, demonstrating that for all participants successful bargaining strategies will be those that work well within the domestic politics of the other side. Building on the insights of Putnam's two-level game approach, Schoppa suggests how intergovernmental bargaining is 'nested' within an even broader constellation of political forces reflective of the mixed nature of the international economic context as well as the complex uncertainties of domestic politics.[25]

In the case of SII, then, neither 'state' was exclusively the sole agent involved in bargaining – a lot of activity to influence and persuade was happening away from the bargaining table – nor were single government units in a position to impose their will inside and outside of government before and even after a decision was reached. Conditions of interdependence and the formation of transnational coalitions blurred even further any simple notion of two 'sides' engaging in goal-seeking behaviour or the idea of two-level games exclusively played in one country. In some ways, it was not certain on either side of the Pacific who was on which side.

Table 4.2 outlines the chronology of SII negotiations.

TABLE 4.2
Chronology of SII negotiations

29 May 1989	United States names Japan as 'priority country' under Omnibus Trade and Competitive Act (Super 301).
14 June 1989	President Bush and Prime Minister Uno agree on SII talks at Economic Summit held in Paris.
23 July 1989	Liberal Democratic Party loses majority in Upper House.
4–5 September 1989	First SII meetings held in Tokyo.
23 October 1989	Liberal Democratic Party establishes special economic research committee on structural adjustment.
6–7 November 1989	Second SII meeting in Washington.
18 February 1990	LDP retains majority in Lower House.
22–23 February 1990	Third SII meeting in Tokyo.
3 March 1990	Prime Minister Kaifu meets with President Bush in Palm Springs, California, to discuss progress in SII talks.
12 March 1990	Former Prime Minister Takeshita visits Washington, meets with President Bush, and discusses SII talks.
21 March 1990	Informal SII talks in suburbs of Washington, DC.
2–5 April 1990	Fourth SII meeting in Washington; midterm report issued.
24–25 May 1990	Informal SII meeting in Hawaii.
25–28 June 1990	Fifth and final SII meeting in Tokyo; final report issued.

The chronology implies that events unfolded in an automatic way. In fact, bilateral negotiations of this sort are highly fluid and often unstructured even during much of the process of discussion, involving as they often do many groups with different 'utilities' and capacities to influence what happens before some sort of formal 'agreement' is finally reached. Since no consistent set of enforceable rules exists, and neither side can unilaterally impose its will, the Japanese and American governments most often have no choice but to continually talk. Most negotiated agreements between the two governments have not been subject to formal ratification at home. An apparent 'solution' can be illusory or short-term because business ties linking the two countries are not unchanging, agreements are often extremely abstract, and the ongoing political struggle at home continues over an appropriate 'Japan strategy' or 'cope with America' strategy.

As the 'offensive' side the Americans had a number of presumed advantages over the 'defensive' side. These included the ability to seize the initiative and set the overall agenda, including the selection of products, commercial practices, or government policies in Japan to be discussed; present inflated if not phoney demands; establish deadlines; escalate demands; create outside pressures on the Japanese government by mobilizing consumers and other interests behind American demands; and dominate the way in which issues would be discussed and linked together. The offence should also have more manoeuvrability during the discussions, be able to better adjust to the dynamics of the bargaining, be better placed to make the first concessions, be able to concentrate more effectively on its bargaining resources, and, when finally forced to concede something, to 'receive less' rather than 'give up a lot.'[26]

Very often American demands and pressures for change are accepted with a certain degree of 'legitimacy' in Japan, especially if there is already a sizeable coalition of influential domestic economic and political forces in favour of Washington's position.[27] The reverse is rarely, if ever, so. Overt Japanese pressure is not expected or accorded any 'legitimacy' in the United States even if there is important support for Tokyo's stance. So in the beginning Japan is on the defence. As the 'defensive' side, the Japanese consider prenegotiations especially important, if for no other reason than to lock the United States into early agreements, if not to reduce the feasible zone of ultimate compromise. For the defence information is crucial, meticulous planning is an absolute requisite, delays are probably useful, and behind-the-scenes negotiations are preferable given the defensive struggle. All the bargainer's cherished values of unity, commitment and resolve are also important, especially if the offensive side reveals itself to be uncertain, divided, and impatient. Often in a Japanese style of defensive action, intermediaries are important, great efforts are made to reduce the big issues to manageable units, watchful waiting is a habit, early commitments in the actual discussions are avoided, and agreements are kept as vague and general as possible.

The secondary literature is almost unanimous in judging that the American side has special advantages by being the more 'powerful' of the two nations and so able to take the offensive. Michael H. Armacost, who was the American ambassador in Tokyo, has written that American pressure was 'palpable, overt, and apparently one-sided.'[28] He also writes that 'the Japanese capacity to resist pressure or to absorb it without yielding was about as skilful as I have ever seen.'[29] He writes further,

In undertaking lobbying – that is, in applying pressure – the Japanese enjoyed a distinct advantage: Given the disparity in market access, they were normally seeking to prevent new trade restrictions in the United States, while we were seeking to remove old ones in their country. In the U.S. political system, veto points are legion, hence Japanese representatives could quietly shop around for an amendment here, a procedural delay there, a veto elsewhere, in order to block new trade restrictions. And they encountered little difficulty in recruiting capable help, since many former U.S. trade officials were readily available for an appropriate retainer.[30]

In the case of both sides, tacit rules of accommodation have been established as a result of many decades of routine consultation, cooperation, and negotiations. Lies are avoided, information is exchanged, and discussions proceed in a reasonable manner with considerable effort made first to uncover the 'facts' by forming collaborative, issue-oriented teams of working-level officials. In recent times, the opponent's political difficulties are not obviously exploited, even as attempts are made to influence domestic interests in favour of the foreign demand. In some ways, the two negotiating teams formed a tacit alliance against protectionist forces in the American Congress. Motives of the other side are not impugned, and both sides negotiate with sufficient 'good faith' that some kind of agreement will have to be reached that is consistent with wider multilateral rules and the need to sustain the American–Japanese global partnership. Reviewing Japan's record of response to U.S. pressure, George has written that Japan 'has been quite successful in developing a set of responses that modify these pressures for its own purposes, molding them in a more acceptable direction in light of domestic obstacles and its own national interest and offering a blend of concession and noncompliance.'[31]

The operational principle in Japan is thus to grant authority to the United States to generally prescribe, while retaining the political and economic flexibility suited to what is considered to be a reasonable concession. This is especially so on market-access questions. Of course, it is impossible to encapsulate the complete range of strategic and tactical behaviour of various participants and place them into a neat set of mutually exclusive generalizations. What follows are what seem to have been the main assumptions of the American strategic approach in SII once formal talks began in September 1989 and continued to June 1990:[32]

- By presenting a comprehensive agenda, break down the deep-rooted sectionalism that fragments the Japanese bureaucracy and bring domestic agencies to the international bargaining table to discuss their areas of jurisdiction. The Economic Planning Agency and the Fair Trade Commission would probably support some of the American agenda.
- It is easier for both the Japanese and the American side to make trade-offs if policy areas are broad and many parts of both governments are involved.
- Build a constituency in Japan beyond the walls of government that will support market-opening measures; a supportive media is important and consumers will be sympathetic if the merits of the American proposals are explained. For example, the issues of high prices in Japan and the need for new infrastructure were emphasized.
- Press for more transparency and accountability in Japanese government policies and regulatory practices to help build a favourable public constituency.

- While manoeuvring beyond the bureaucracy, do not undermine officials; recognize that the Japanese government is not unified and that leadership is not always strong, but also realize that officialdom's cooperation is a fundamental requisite for reform.
- Use data, reports, and reforms previously proposed by the Japanese government, business organizations, and academics as the basis of the American-proposed agenda. In that way you build on an existing domestic constituency.[33]
- Avoid giving away your bottom line too early, and certainly don't set specific targets or numbers as these figures can be politically exploited by the other side. Besides, a 'rush to decision' might create controversy among the American negotiators over how to rank priorities.
- Keep Congress on board during the negotiations, since the administration was under immediate pressure to produce specific results, but not in a way that individual lawmakers or committees could influence specific negotiation decisions and choices.
- Refer to the Big Threats: Super 301, the Congress, the forces in favour of 'managed trade' in the United States.
- Sound reasonable to soften *gaiatsu*; emphasize that the talks should be a two-way street and that the United States must address its own structural problems.
- Cooperate with Japanese officials in gathering and analysing data regarding the Japanese economy, including comparative price surveys.
- Don't undermine the LDP, especially in light of general elections for the Lower House scheduled for 18 February 1990. In the end, support of the LDP and prime minister Kaifu will be crucial. Moreover, the Prime Minister is sympathetic to many of the items on the American agenda. A socialist government would be a disaster for the United States.
- Use well-established channels of communication and old friendships to help bridge differences; secret talks are especially necessary since formal hearings are open.
- Remind Tokyo that the fault will be Japan's if SII fails.
- Keep up the direct pressure and the campaign of public education in order to meet the February deadline for an interim report.
- Remain unified in the face of potential Japanese unity; it is much easier to deal with Japan if a broad consensus within the executive branch is set early and maintained throughout the discussions.
- Have President Bush communicate directly with Prime Minister Kaifu so that the Japanese ministries will see the necessity for compromise.

How far the American side believed that Japan could be moved towards the

United States' various positions on the issues is somewhat obscure since intended negotiated outcomes were uncertain, perhaps even for those who were directly making the 'demands.' The public record gives ample evidence that it was generally assumed by the Americans that 'structural impediments' were only one cause of trade deficits, that the Japanese government's position to undertake change was somewhat limited, that many of the concrete proposals for change were extremely difficult for some of the nation's politicians and bureaucrats, and that it would take years before the final results of any structural adjustments would be clear.

The Japanese had little choice but to be defensive. What tactical assumptions did they use during the six months of bargaining?

- Do not give in to American 'pressure'; staunchly defend constituency interests and above all remain unified.
- Remind the Administration that the two sides must think big, putting the bilateral relationship into a 'global' perspective that links the two sides to common political, security, economic, and policy aspirations. Many officials in Washington will agree.
- Point out that the American agenda is based on misunderstandings, are too abstract, are matters of domestic policy, and are beyond the reach of government policy, which in any case is consistent with international practices.
- Warn that the idea of reciprocity in trade will take the world back to the practices of the 1930s.
- Quietly mobilize the support of American business and members of the informed élite, including policy communities and politicians who recognize the dangers in political demands that violate the ideals of free trade.
- Avoid displaying of an obvious bargaining strategy; what the other side does not notice gives you more flexibility. Continue also to say 'no' in an indirect fashion.
- Remind the Americans that their trade deficit is best explained by their own domestic deficiencies: 'It's your fault, not ours!'
- Emphasize that reform and change are already taking place; such an approach shows that Japan is acting in good faith, while also narrowing the 'range' for further accommodation.
- Probe the other side in discussions and in Washington to set obtainable goals; most important is to discover Washington's bottom line and then to work out a position below these expectations.
- Stall based on the assumption that the United States has no trade policy, administrations change, America's agenda is constantly in flux, the government has a short attention span, no real interests in follow-up, and no single approach to Japan.

- Redefine the agenda whenever possible to make adjusting and compromise easier for the American side. (Of course, the American side was using the same ploy.)
- Use American pressure as a way to engineer whatever compromises are necessary at home.
- Do not let agreements undermine the authority of bureaucracy or the electoral appeal of LDP politicians.
- Stay unified and on the defensive to outlast the other side even if it means a game of 'chicken.' If you let concessions dribble out you draw attention to your freedom of action.
- Limit the damage, exploit all loopholes, and make sure that change is in the form of 'positive adjustment.'
- Let a minor crisis develop both to draw the Americans out and also to help build a consensus at home that something will have to be done.
- Let the politicians decide after public support has been stabilized. In doing this, some blame for concessions can be transferred to the United States.

For months there was little but stalemate. The third round of discussions held in February 1990 were reported as a failure in the press. The American side agreed. For the most part SII was more 'talk' than 'negotiation,' even as Washington had narrowed down an initial 240-item list of demands to three major areas. There was no formal movement on the Japanese side. To increase the pressure on Japan, President Bush invited Prime Minister Kaifu, on very short notice, for a personal two-day visit on March 2–3 in Palm Springs, California. Apparently the invitation was arranged outside official Japanese channels. The meeting was probably crucial as it helped to break what had become a bilateral deadlock. According to various press reports, the president pressed the prime minister to recognize how important the trade issues were, not only to the entire U.S.–Japan relationship but to global trade more generally. He clearly sought to energize Japanese efforts both on SII and the sectoral issues being discussed under Super 301.

When the worried prime minister returned home he quickly set up a Cabinet-level task force. Within a week a bureaucratically drafted package was ready for the leaders of the LDP. Summit diplomacy in California and the practical politics of the LDP following its electoral victory moved the officials towards finalizing an interim report, which was presented at the fourth meeting held in early April.

The Japanese effort was generally satisfactory to the United States. U.S. Trade Representative Carla Hills called it a 'good blueprint, sufficient to call a down payment.' Later in the month Ambassador Hills announced that Japan would not be targeted a second time for market-access negotiations under Super

301. Successful negotiations held in parallel with SII permitted agreement on the outstanding issues related to supercomputers, satellites, and wood product.

While Tokyo had responded to the United States in fair detail, difficult issues remained regarding investment in public works, the distribution system, and what Americans are fond of calling 'exclusive business practices.' Formal and informal discussions continued for weeks. In late May the American side once again complained about lack of progress, even after informal talks had been held in Hawaii. Six members of Bush's Cabinet sent letters to their Japanese counterparts outlining why Tokyo's plans fell short. A major demand was that Japan spend 10 per cent of its GNP on public works over the ensuing ten years.

The fifth and final meetings opened in Tokyo on 25 June 1990. Marathon discussions lasted four days. The major disagreement revolved around levels of Japanese public investment. In a last-minute compromise, the Bush Administration dropped its campaign to have Japan boost its investment by 10 per cent. The deadlock was broken following discussions involving the president and the prime minister and the intervention of Kanemaru Shin, widely regarded at the time as boss of a group of LDP politicians with close ties to the construction industry. He was also the single most important supporter of Kaifu among LDP leaders. The LDP saw merit in an American demand that would require the Japanese government to significantly increase its public infrastructure budget. Against the strong preference of the Ministry of Finance, Kanemaru backed an expenditure level of ¥430 trillion in public investment over a ten-year period. The press suggested that side-deals were also promised by Japan in the areas of defence policies, overseas investment, and foreign business activities.

When the final joint report was issued in June, to bring to a close the formal bargaining on SII, the U.S.–Japan Working Group stated that the Agreement

contains significant, extensive efforts and actions by both governments that should contribute to further reductions in external payments imbalances. These actions should also lead to more efficient, competitive, and open markets, promote sustained economic growth and enhance the quality of life in both Japan and the United States.[34]

In the end, powerful politicians in Japan helped the two governments reach a final agreement after pressing and prodding each other with allies in the their own government and in Washington.

Conclusion

Unlike the case of Canada and the United States, no legally defined free trade agreement links Japan with the United States. Multilateral ways of dealing directly with bilateral trade disputes – such as through GATT, the World Trade Organization, or G7 coordination – for the most part have not been seen as satisfactory by either government. Both sides long ago rejected relegating bilateral economic ties to the fate of unregulated markets. A tempting option is direct, face-to-face, political bargaining.

By structuring the analysis in terms of the strategic interaction of two interdependent but divided governments a more complex portrait emerges than is usually provided of Japan's responses to American initiatives. SII demonstrates that the Japanese can and do devise their own bargaining strategies and that their tactics cannot be reduced simply to the question of how they resist or deflect foreign pressure. What gives the negotiation process its complex, sometimes even bizarre, quality in the multilevel games is that four dimensions of activities are commingled in most Japanese–American bargaining situations.[35]

Interest bargaining is intended as a way to influence a policy or commercial practice that brings bilateral interests into direct conflict. While not necessarily fixed-sum clashes in the sense that gains of one firm or sector become losses for another, nonetheless the rules of the marketplace will probably change, creating new competitive conditions. Many of the American demands in SII would have a direct impact on the Japanese economy, whether on savings and investment, the cost of market entry for foreign firms, the way in which private business is conducted (*keiretsu*), or the price of imported products. Schoppa writes with some exaggeration that the 'list of interests adversely affected by U.S. proposals looked like a 'who's who' of the rich and powerful in Japanese politics.'[36] It was also an attack on some vulnerable, uncompetitive, small and medium-sized industries in Japan. The joint decision process for resolving conflicts is interest bargaining in the sense that the two sides must confront the possibilities of clear winners and losers. This is the most widely studied aspect of bilateral negotiations, epitomized by a great deal of the rational-choice literature in political science.

Not all behaviour in negotiations can be interpreted as a fundamental clash of interest. *Integrative bargaining* refers to attempts to bring about agreements that suit the purposes of at least some of the major participants. Tactics aimed at pursuing the instrumental goals in interest bargaining are modified as parties to the dispute recognize that they are locked into a long-term political and economic alliance of complex interdependence in which neither country is united and potential coalitions can be put together from both sides. For example, Naka suggests that SII can be seen as an 'imperfect three-actor game' in which the common goal of both governments was to prevent the American Congress from enacting protectionist measures including various forms of managed trade.[37] Again, the Bush Administration identified a successful GATT round as a high priority, and this required support from the Japanese side. On the other hand, the Ministry of Foreign Affairs, the Economic Planning Agency, and even the Ministry of International Trade and Industry all supported some aspects of deregulation, liberalization, and structural adjustment in the Japanese economy regardless of the American position. As Naka has shown in persuasive detail, talking and negotiating during SII resulted in complex forms of transgovernmental alliances linking working-level officials across national boundaries.

Bargaining also involves attempts to influence the beliefs, ideologies, attitudes, and fundamental practices of the other side. Both sides also used negotiations as a way to produce *attitudinal and perceptual changes*, either to reduce hostility, increase friendly feelings, nurture a more favourable media, de-emphasize differences, or simply build up a political atmosphere permissive to compromise and concessions. Political debate was rich in ideas related to a consumer-oriented economy, deregulation, enforcement of antimonopoly laws, and domestic demand-led growth, or why a nation's quality of life could be enhanced through a more open, transparent, and fair economy. The American ambassador reported that 'I made our case in scores of public speeches, briefings for editorial writers, lunches for businesspeople and academics, and one-on-one meetings with people influential in politics and the bureaucracy.'[38] Japanese diplomats were also active. Extensive consultations took place horizontally on each side and within transgovernmental and transnational networks linking the two countries. Working-level officials shared information and knowledge, exchanged ideas, and worked together in developing specific details and alternatives for potential agreement.

Finally, as suggested by Putnam, bilateral negotiation also involve *intra-state accommodation* as teams of negotiators deal with the problems of reaching an internal consensus regarding what is happening at the bargaining table. Taking his inspiration from Graham Allison, Naka has demonstrated how inadequate it can be to assume in SII the existence of unitary national governments in international negotiations. Japanese agencies were not always on the same side regarding major issues discussed in SII.[39] Nor were American agencies. Government on both sides appeared as a 'constellation' of loosely allied units, each with its own organizational goals, standard operating procedures, programs, and political repertoires. They fought quietly among themselves and sometimes formed 'alliances' with governmental agencies on the other side.

Each element of a negotiation of this sort has its own logic, implies particular tactics and strategies, and does not always fit with the other dimensions. A tactical move to achieve a particular goal may be detrimental to the same side in other aspects of the negotiating situation. Nor is there any guarantee that both sides will arrive at the tactical and strategic balance among these values in matching ways. The observer seeking a comprehensive explanation of all the results requires the combined wisdom provided by realism, with its preference for power and rational-choice analysis; the framework of transgovernmental and transnationalism, with an emphasis on how world politics in almost every issue area is permeated by cross-border networks; theories of domestic and especially bureaucratic politics; and the ideas of epistemic communities that underscore the importance of joint learning across borders and the formation of new 'regimes.'

Reviews of SII regarding the concrete results remained mixed.[40] Each side pledged to take far-reaching measures in the areas under discussion. The Japanese side promised increases in infrastructure spending, land reform measures, liberalization of the Large-Retail Store Law, more rigorous enforcement of the Anti-Monopoly Law, and efforts to make *keiretsu* groups more transparent. The United States promised measures to raise the level of domestic savings, reduction of the federal government's fiscal deficit, encouragement of higher levels of civilian research and development, more export promotion efforts, and improvement of job-training programs.

Very few observers expected short-term gains in exports from the United States to Japan. Never during the negotiations did either side really believe that the 'trade imbalance' could be immediately resolved through discussion and agreement. At the same time a great deal of scepticism existed about the implementation of the SII agreement by either side. In immediate political terms what mattered most was that the Bush Administration had to show Congress and sections of the nation's business community that some kind of blueprint for action – a commitment from Tokyo for reform in six targeted areas and some first step towards change – had been delivered. While going along with this, the Japanese government helped shape an agreement for reform in Japan that received considerable domestic support, did not include any major compromises to American views regarding the structural features of an ideal 'capitalist economy,' and left a good deal of room for future manoeuvre. In the months that followed, it was extremely difficult to decide beyond doubt which individuals, groups, firms, industries, or even government had 'won' or 'lost.' There is little evidence that the Japanese side sought to placate the United States by endangering the fundamental strengths of its economy.[41]

The agendas discussed at the table and more widely in the media reflect deep-rooted differences that, because of politics as much as comparative economic success, have become more salient even as the two economies have become more interdependent than ever. In formally addressing these differences, under the rubric of 'structural impediments,' the boundaries of the political have been significantly expanded. Is this a good way for the two countries to deal with problems of structural adjustment? The evidence is certainly mixed. Picking out the faults and failings of another nation and making them the basis of bilateral discussions and possible negotiated change is surely risky. A number of larger changes in the world have subsequently created some broader options to move beyond narrow bilateralism: the end of the Cold War; the creation of strengthened multilateral solutions to economic disputes, including especially the World Trade Organization (WTO); and the growing regionalization of the Asia-Pacific economy. The Japanese side has always had the capacity to say 'no' directly as subsequently shown in negotiations with the Clinton Administration during the Economic Framework talks when Washington attempted to move from a rule-based approach to one that emphasized results. The American government was forced to compromise, and the MITI officials started to declare that the 'era of bilateralism' is over. It is too early to confirm their prediction.

NOTES

1   Oye, *Economic Discrimination and Political Exchange*. Both governments have made a point of emphasizing that politically negotiated agreements were settled on a most favoured nation basis so that they would potentially benefit all countries. On the other hand, many of the agreements have gone well beyond subject areas covered by multilateral rules.
2   The American Chamber of Commerce, *Making Trade Talks Work*.
3   Competing schools of researchers have been building a view that negotiations among nations can best be viewed as art; a mode of conflict management; a reflection of the balance of power among nations, including ideas of hegemonic stability and 'cooperation under anarchy'; a rational game of calculated gains and losses; how political leaders frame decisions especially in light of laboratory experiments in cognitive psychology regarding loss-avoidance; a process of decision-making; a challenge of diplomatic management or economic statecraft; an institutionally or legally bound set of dispute-resolution mechanisms; coordination through 'epistemic communities'; a challenge of interdependence in world politics; or simply a matter of two-level political games. A useful collection of essays is Young, *Negotiation Analysis*. Also useful is Walton and McKersie, *A Behavioral Theory of Labor Negotiations*.
4   The literature is vast. Among the most suggestive are Campbell, 'Japan and the United States,' and George, 'Japan's America Problem.'
5   The following studies deal with the question in considerable detail and are notable exceptions to the generally non-theoretical character of much research on Japanese–American relations: Schoppa, *Bargaining with Japan*; Naka, *Predicting Outcomes*; and Mikanagi, *Japan's Trade Policy*. Of course, for decades scholars have argued that the growth of economic interdependence has made the exercise of political power in interstate negotiations extremely subtle. The classic statement is Keohane and Nye, *Power and Interdependence*.

6 The most convincing comparison of how Japanese and American firms employ different political strategies in shaping bilateral economic ties is Katzenstein and Tsujinaka, '"Bullying," "Buying," and "Binding."' In brief, they argue that American firms complain and Washington bullies, while Japanese firms adapt to the American market and their government compromises.

7 U.S. Government, *Joint Report of the U.S.–Japan Working Group*; U.S. Government, *First Annual Report of the U.S.–Japan Working Group*; U.S. Government, *Second Annual Report of the U.S.–Japan Working Group*.

8 Ned Lebow, *The Art of Bargaining*, 11.

9 A substantial theoretical literature focuses on domestic politics, economic interdependence, and bargaining. For a recent discussion see Keohane and Milner, eds., *Internationalization and Domestic Politics*.

10 The most complete studies are Schoppa, *Bargaining with Japan*, and Naka, *Predicting Outcomes*. The author has also done considerable field research on SII.

11 Strange, *States and Markets*, 18.

12 There is a substantial literature on this topic. See especially Keohane and Nye, *Power and Interdependence*; and Brown, *Globalization and Interdependence*.

13 Armacost, *Friends or Rivals?*

14 Lincoln, *Japan's Unequal Trade*; Tyson, *Who's Bashing Whom?*; Prestowitz, *Trading Places*; Bergsten and Noland, *Reconcilable Differences*.

15 Schoppa, *Bargaining with Japan*, 49–85.

16 Kernell, ed., *Parallel Politics*.

17 For a detailed analysis of the state of American politics at the time of the birth of SII see Schoppa, *Bargaining with Japan*, especially Chap. 3; Naka, *Predicting Outcomes*; Armacost, *Friends or Rivals?*; and Janow, 'Trading with an Ally.' The best economic studies are Yamamura, ed., *Policy and Trade Issues* and his second edited collection *Japan's Economic Structure*. See also a special edition on the trade crisis in *The Journal of Japanese Studies*, 13 (Summer 1987). Studies by Mikanagi, Destler, and Cohen show that many of the ideas associated with the American agenda for SII were hardly new. See Mikanagi, *Japan's Trade Policy*; Destler, *American Trade Politics*; and Cohen, *The Making of United States International Economic Policy*.

18 Advisory Committee on Trade Policy and Negotiations, *Analysis of the U.S.–Japan Trade Problem*.

19 Interview with Linn Williams, 1991.

20 Naka has analysed the viewpoints of governmental subunits in great detail. His judgements parallel my own somewhat less complete reading of publicly available information.

21 Schoppa writes that the American strategy was dictated by three major considerations: 'Bush's desire to use the SII talks to mend his fraying Republican free trade coalition; his negotiating team's desire to minimize conflict among themselves while

taking advantage of conflict among actors on the Japanese side; and the efforts of Japanese actors to use *gaiatsu* to secure their sectional policy objectives.' Schoppa, *Bargaining with Japan*, 51.

22 For a detailed discussion see Naka, *Predicting Outcomes*, Chap. 2, and Schoppa, *Bargaining with Japan*, Chap. 4.
23 United States Government, *United States–Japan Structural*.
24 Evans, Jacobson, and Putnam, eds., *Double-Edged Diplomacy*. The idea that a chief negotiator is the recipient of two sets of demands has been widely recognized for many decades in the literature on labour negotiations. See Walton and McKersie, *A Behavioral Theory of Labor Negotiations*.
25 Schoppa, *Bargaining with Japan*.
26 Any study of Japanese negotiating practices must acknowledge the eloquent and brilliant work of Michael Blaker. See Blaker, *Japanese International Negotiating Style*.
27 This is a point heavily emphasized in Schoppa, *Bargaining with Japan*.
28 Armacost, *Friends or Rivals?* 68.
29 Ibid., 69.
30 Ibid., 71.
31 George, 'Japan's America Problem,' 16.
32 The author was in Tokyo during the SII. In addition to the U.S. government documents and secondary resources cited above, the most valuable sources of information included Japan Economic Institute, *JEI Reports*, various issues; Japan, Tsusho Sangyo Chosa Kai, ed., *Nichibei Kozo Mondai Kyogi Saishu Hokoku*; Japanese newspapers, including *Asahi Shimbun*, *Nihon Keizai Shimbun*, and *Japan Times*; and the *New York Times*. A number of interviews with journalists were also conducted.
33 The central importance of linking strategies and tactics to the right domestic constituents is a point never forgotten in the analysis by Schoppa, *Bargaining with Japan*.
34 U.S. Government, *Joint Report of the U.S.–Japan Working Group*, 1.
35 See Walton and McKersie, *A Behavioral Theory of Labor Negotiations*.
36 Schoppa, *Bargaining with Japan*, 12.
37 Naka, *Predicting Outcomes*, Chap. 4.
38 Armacost, *Friends or Rivals*, 51.
39 Naka, *Predicting Outcomes*, Chap. 6. See Allison's views in Allison, *Essence of Decision*.
40 A reading of the two annual reports of the U.S.–Japan Working Group referred to in note 7 is a useful place to start. Schoppa and Naka have also attempted to measure the 'results.' My bottom line judgement is that SII as process and its results directly and indirectly deeply shaped the reform process in Japan in the way that no previous or subsequent bilateral negotiation has.
41 No commentator has suggested that SII brought an historic breakthrough in bilateral relations.

5

Japanese Direct Investment in Canada: Patterns and Prospects

DAVID W. EDGINGTON

Introduction

A significant characteristic of Japanese–Canadian relations over the last fifteen years or so has been the steady rise of a Japanese business presence in Canada. As Japanese firms began to invest overseas in earnest following the yen revaluation (*endaka*) in 1985–86, the number of Japanese companies operating in Canada grew rapidly. This growth in direct foreign investment (DFI) and corporate start-ups represented a 'new wave' of Japanese business activity.[1] It involved not only higher amounts of investments by value, but also increasingly sophisticated forms of Japanese involvement.[2] The recent wave of DFI ended dramatically with the bursting of the Japanese 'bubble economy' and the severe recession in Japan that commenced in 1991. Nonetheless, it represented a clear break from previous Japan–Canada investment relations based mainly on minority holdings in primary resources, such as coal, copper, and timber, as well as the local sales and distribution companies of major Japanese producers.[3]

The ten years up to the mid-1990s saw Japan expand its share of total foreign-controlled assets in Canada, edging into third position behind the United States and Britain and accounting for some 4 per cent of Canada's total foreign investment.[4] Overall, recent Japanese direct investment flows to Canada have followed global trends of Japanese DFI, peaking in fiscal year (FY) 1989 at U.S.$1.36 billion and falling thereafter to just U.S.$562 million in fiscal 1993, U.S.$492 million in fiscal 1994, and U.S.$568 million in fiscal 1995 (see Table 5.1). In total, the cumulative sum of U.S.$8.82 billion invested in Canada represents approximately 2 per cent of worldwide Japanese DFI.[5] During this recent period of expansion Japanese companies began operating fully owned subsidiaries in a much wider range of production and service areas than previously. Compared with traditional concentrations in the resource sectors, from

TABLE 5.1
Annual Japanese DFI in Canada and the United States,
FY 1980–95 (U.S.$ millions)

Fiscal year	Canada (A)	United States (B)	(A)/(B)
1980	112	1,484	7.5 %
1981	167	2,354	7.1 %
1982	167	2,736	6.1 %
1983	136	2,565	5.3 %
1984	184	3,359	5.5 %
1985	100	5,395	1.9 %
1986	276	10,165	2.7 %
1987	653	14,704	4.4 %
1988	626	21,704	2.9 %
1989	1,362	32,540	4.2 %
1990	1,064	26,128	4.1 %
1991	797	18,026	4.4 %
1992	753	13,819	5.4 %
1993	562	14,725	3.8 %
1994	492	17,331	2.8 %
1995	568	22,193	2.6 %

Source: Bank of Japan, unpublished data.

1985 onward there was a much broader spectrum of Japanese investment, such as car assembly and auto parts in Ontario, processing of wood fibre into pulp and newsprint in British Columbia and Alberta, technology-intensive manufacturing close to Ottawa, and management of hotels in resort regions such as Whistler and Banff.[6] In the 1990s this *tsunami* of investment slowed to a trickle, yet further investments were announced in auto plants. There is also the possibility that new fields such as prefabricated housing-related investment might increase in the future.[7] The Japan External Trade Organization (JETRO) reported that over 38,000 people were employed by about 400 Japanese-affiliated companies operating in Canada in 1996. Most of these, 85.1 per cent, were located in Ontario, British Columbia, or Quebec.[8]

The broader context for this new Japan–Canada relationship lies, of course, in the globalization of Japanese manufacturing and commercial enterprises brought on by *endaka* and overseas restrictions on exports.[9] Moreover, the rise of trade groupings and formalized trade blocks has been a significant influence.[10] As will be shown, Japanese DFI in Canada cannot now be treated without reference to the recently concluded North American Free Trade Agreement

(NAFTA) and its predecessor the Canada–U.S. Free Trade Agreement (FTA). One must examine Japanese investment in Canada within these contextual settings to reveal the particular sectors that Japan has been interested in, and to identify the various factors that are likely to shape further rounds of investment up to the end of the century.[11]

The discussion that follows assumes that Japanese DFI constitutes, on balance, a positive element in Canada's development due to the additional jobs and economic stimulus it provides. Concerns have been raised from time to time over the adverse affects of Japanese multinational behaviour; examples include restrictions imposed by parent companies on their subsidiaries over the sourcing of inputs and destination of exports, the transfer of inappropriate technology, transfer pricing abuses, and so on.[12] Yet, in the main, Japanese companies have been welcome and eagerly sought by Canadian federal and provincial governments.[13] In fact, Canadian authorities have been increasingly worried about maintaining Canada's so-called traditional '10 per cent share' of cumulative Japanese DFI in North America, based on Canada's perceived share of the combined North American market.[14] During the 1970s, when Japan's resource-oriented overseas investments were at their height, Canada did indeed achieve something approaching 10 per cent of Japanese investment in North America. But as indicated in Table 5.1, from the early 1980s Canada secured substantially smaller annual shares and only 2.6 per cent of Japanese DFI in the United States during fiscal 1995. This was due primarily to changing Japanese domestic priorities – away from energy- and resource-consuming 'smokestack' industries towards a technology-intensive economic structure, one that Canada has been less able to supply.[15]

Japan, Canada, and NAFTA

There has long been a high level of interdependence between the Canadian and Japanese economies and that of the United States. The notion that Japan–Canada relations must be seen within a 'triangular perspective' is also not new, and in the previous decade the Canada–U.S. Free Trade Agreement dominated the debate over Japanese investment flows into Canada.[16] Currently, it is important that Japanese investment interest in Canada be assessed within the context of the North American Free Trade Agreement, enacted in 1993. North America as a whole has continued to lead the dollar value of Japanese overseas business expansion, and at the end of fiscal year 1993 the three NAFTA countries (Canada, the United States, and Mexico) together accounted for nearly 45 per cent of all Japanese direct foreign investment. However, within the NAFTA region the distribution of Japanese interest has been far from even. The United States, with around 70 per cent of this region's population and 88 per cent of its combined gross domestic product (GDP), has continued to capture over 90 per cent of Japan's total investment in NAFTA.[17]

An analysis of cumulative Japanese DFI by different sectors among the three NAFTA countries is revealing.[18] Mexico received over 85 per cent of its Japanese DFI in resources (mainly mining and oil) and manufacturing (mainly auto assembly). The United States, by comparison, received over 70 per cent of its cumulative investment from Japan in services (e.g., commerce, finance, and real estate). Canada, on the other hand, recorded a more even distribution among the three sectors. The cumulative distribution in Canada for fiscal year 1993 is shown in Table 5.2, which indicates 11.1 per cent in resources, 43.6 per cent in manufacturing, and 45.3 per cent in services. By and large, these patterns reflect different investment motivations by Japanese firms, and also different perceptions of the role played by each country within NAFTA. Thus, at a broad level Japanese companies have used Canada more heavily as a source of natural resources for their own domestic economy than either the United States or Mexico. By comparison, virtually all investment in the United States was oriented to final sales in the local market, either in the form of import-substituting manufacturing or in the form of financial services and real estate. In Mexico, transport equipment (auto assembly) was the dominant sector, aimed at the local market as well as the United States. During the 1980s, the United States replaced Mexico as the chief target market for Japanese producers expanding their operations in Mexico, either from border town *maquiladoras* or from other locations.[19]

For Japan, the huge NAFTA market will continue to be important even though recent investment trends favour cheap wage locations in nearby Asian countries. Moreover, JETRO has predicted that, with the higher yen in the mid-1990s diminishing export profits, there will be a continued need for Japanese overseas production.[20] However, compared with the rush into foreign investment following the Plaza Accord of 1985 (which caused the yen to begin its steep ascent against foreign currencies), Japanese business has now adopted a more cautious approach to DFI in North America. This is due to the recession in Japan and the sharp deterioration of corporate profits. Thus, rather than setting up new factories in North America, companies are now more likely to increase production incrementally at existing bases, improve local sourcing of parts and raw materials, and consign even research and design activities to NAFTA to improve their overall global competitiveness.[21] With this new strategy, an important factor from a Canadian, Mexican, or U.S. perspective is which part of the NAFTA 'factory' they might obtain when it comes time for Japanese firms to expand. Accordingly, in order to forecast Canada's chances of attracting future investment the chapter now examines recent trends in Japanese DFI by

TABLE 5.2
Cumulative Japanese direct investment in Canada,
FY 1952–93 by major industrial sector (U.S.$ millions)

	Value	Per cent
Resources		
Agriculture/Forestry	72.2	0.9
Fisheries	4.4	0.0
Mining	786.8	10.1
Subtotal	(863.4)	(11.1)
Manufacturing		
Food processing	66.8	0.1
Textiles	216.3	2.8
Pulp and paper	1,700.2	21.9
Chemicals	81.6	1.1
Steel and other metals	235.8	3.0
Machinery	185.5	2.4
Electrical machinery	234.2	3.0
Transport equipment	538.1	6.9
Other	129.3	1.7
Subtotal	(3,386.7)	(43.6)
Services		
Construction	41.0	0.1
Commerce	706.6	9.1
Finance/Insurance	771.1	9.9
Services	913.1	11.8
Transport	30.1	0.4
Real estate	954.3	12.2
Others	102.0	1.3
Subtotal	(3,434.6)	(45.3)
Total	7,769.5	100.0

Note: Numbers may not add to 100 per cent because
of rounding.
Source: Bank of Japan, unpublished data.

individual industries. Three representative investment areas have been chosen
from the resources, manufacturing, and service sectors.

Lumber and Pulp Mill Investments

Beyond the influence of continental relations, Japan's trade links with Canada
in part continue to drive its investments in this country. Since the mid-1980s,

exports of forest products to Japan grew dramatically overall. Demand in this sector was especially strong from the late 1980s because of the rapid expansion in Japanese industrial and consumer markets. For example, the national level of housing starts in Japan surpassed that of the United States in the early 1990s. Throughout this period Canada continued to be the most important source for Japan's lumber requirements, and, conversely, Japan remained Canada's largest offshore market for softwood lumber.[22] Between 1991 and 1993 exports of lumber almost doubled in value (mainly West Coast softwood cut to Japanese housing dimensions), replacing coal as the top valued Canadian export, and accounting for roughly 25 per cent of all Canadian sales to Japan. Wood pulp remained the number three exported commodity by dollar value.[23] The forest products sector as a whole made up 42 per cent of Canadian exports to Japan in 1995.[24]

In response to this dramatic increase in trade, Japanese timber product companies expanded their operations in Canada (see Table 5.3). For instance, from the mid-1980s there were many examples of Japanese timber companies establishing small-to-medium specialty product sawmills in British Columbia. By way of illustration, Elk Wood Specialties Ltd., a Japanese company, set up a custom sawmill in 1988 at Maple Ridge, BC, at an estimated cost of about $2 million, with all output destined for Japan. This project allowed Elk Wood's Japanese customers to buy special Japanese metric dimension lumber for traditional Japanese house construction (rather than conventional North American $2' \times 4'$ lumber), and so saved handling and land storage costs in Japan. This move was also necessary due to the critical shortage of timber mill labour in Japan, which led to significantly higher production costs for sawn timber.[25] Other developments included the opening of representative offices by companies dealing in prefabricated timber homes (such as Sanwa House and Daiwa House) and specialist timber merchants such as Yamane Lumber.[26]

While these new investments in Canadian lumber facilities are significant, they have been overshadowed by over $2 billion invested since the mid-1980s in major BC and Alberta pulp and newsprint projects (see Table 5.4). Increased costs in Japan led to pulp and paper firms deciding to upgrade their domestic plants for the production of more value-added paper while shifting their pulp-making capacity overseas. Due to the greater availability of commercial timber Canada was considered the most favoured location for new pulp mills within North America. In particular, the promotion of northern Alberta's forest resources by the provincial government led to two massive mill investments by Japanese corporations, targeting stands of aspen, a fast growing pulp-specific timber species.[27]

One of these was the Daishowa Corporation, which constructed an enormous hardwood kraft pulp mill near Peace River at an estimated cost of around

TABLE 5.3
Japanese investments in the British Columbia forest products industry
(date of establishment)

Trading Companies (Sōgō Shōsha) with lumber divisions

Vancouver office of Canadian subsidiary

Mitsui	1956
Okura	1957
Nissho Iwai	1959
Marubeni	1960
Mitsubishi	1960
Sumitomo	1961
Itochu	1969
Kanematsu	1972
Nichimen Canada	1974
Tomen	1974

Other investments

Itochu	1968	CIPA Lumber Co., Japanese dimension sawmill, Nanaimo, BC
	1993	Delta Plywood, plywood veneer producer, Delta, BC
Mitsubishi	1968	Crestbrook Forest Industries Ltd., an integrated timber and pulp producer, Cranbrooke, BC (33% equity)
	1980	Mayo Forest Products Ltd., Japanese dimension sawmill, Nanaimo, BC (40% equity)
Marubeni	1972	Daishowa-Marubeni Pty. Ltd. sawmilling operation in Quesnel, BC (25% equity)
	1992	High Level Forest Products Pty. Ltd. 2 × 4 sawmilling operation in northern Alberta (50% equity)
Mitsui	1994	Anderson Forest Mill Pty. Ltd. custom cut sawmill

Timber wholesalers

Emachu	1975	Elk Trading Company, Vancouver
	1988	Elk Wood Co., Custom Cutting Saw Mill, Maple Ridge, BC
Nichiei	1987	Vancouver representative office
Yamane Lumber	1987	Vancouver representative office
Haseman	1993	Vancouver representative office
Tenryu	1993	Vancouver representative office
Toyoshima Trading	1993	Vancouver representative office

Large-scale building companies

Sankyo-Kokusaku	1976	Vancouver representative office
Misawa Home	1979	Vancouver representative office
Mitsui Home	1980	Vancouver representative office
	1993	Lumber sorting and pre-cut plant, Langley, BC
Sumitomo Forestry	1985	Vancouver representative office
Sanwa Home	1986	Vancouver representative office
Daiwa House	1989	Vancouver representative office

Source: Edgington and Hayter, 'International Trade, Production Chains and Corporate Strategies.'

TABLE 5.4
Japanese investments in the Canadian pulp and paper industry, 1985–93

British Columbia		
Oji Paper		
(joint venture with Canfor)	$1,300m (upgrading)	Howe Sound, BC
Cariboo Pulp and Paper Co.		
(50–50 joint venture between		
Daishowa-Marubeni and Weldwood)	$60m (expansion)	Quesnel, BC
Quesnel River Pulp Co.		
(50–50 joint venture between		
Daishowa Canada and West Fraser		
Timber Co.)	$80m (expansion)	Quesnel, BC
Alberta		
Daishowa Canada	$500m (new pulp mill)	Peace River, Northern Alberta
Alberta-Pacific Forest Industries		
(Crestbrook: Mitsubishi/		Athabasca,
Honshu Paper Co.)	$1,300m (new pulp mill)	Northern Alberta
Quebec		
Daishowa International		
(existing timber/paper mill)	$215m (upgrading)	Quebec City

Source: Edgington, 'Japanese Direct Investment in Canada.'

$500 million, and having an annual capacity of 340,000 tons. Daishowa's pulp mill began operations in 1991, but has been plagued by low pulp prices, financial problems in Japan, pressure from environmentalists, as well as land claims from the local Lubicon Indian band.[28] The second gigantic pulp mill was built for the Japanese-run Alberta-Pacific (Alpac) consortium on the Athabasca River after substantial modifications to reduce contaminants from the pulp bleaching process. This plant, which cost roughly $1.3 billion, commenced operations in 1993 with an annual production capacity of 500,000 tons per annum, making it the largest of its kind.[29] A third mill was upgraded for Oji Paper Company at Howe Sound in British Columbia at a cost of about $500 million. This facility is a joint venture with Canfor Corporation, and is operated as Oji's major North American newsprint factory. It is expected that all of the newsprint produced will replace similar capacity driven out of Japan due to the higher costs of production.[30]

Further rounds of Western Canadian forest industry megaprojects are extremely unlikely. Indeed, the large Alpac project is probably the last of its size in the world, due to increasing operating costs, tougher environmental standards, and growing environmental awareness.[31] Moreover, pulp prices have plummeted since this new production capacity has been in place. Better prospects lie in the area of lumber and plywood investments. The increased use of North American pre-cut softwood timber has led Japanese timber industry firms, as well as prefabricated housing manufacturers, to secure more long-term resources from Canada. These groups may consider further selective purchases of timber mill operations in British Columbia and Alberta that can cut lumber to Japanese sizes and quality standards, or other investments into value-added wood products and prefabricated housing systems.[32] This is particularly the case as the trade in logs from Oregon and Washington, a more traditional supply base, becomes more problematic due to increased environmental constraints. In 1993, such an investment was made by CIPA Lumber Co. (owned by Japan's Itochu Corporation), into a veneer processing plant in Vancouver. The mill produces veneer primarily for export markets in Japan and the United States, and CIPA established plans to add a plywood and engineered wood plant to take advantage of higher demand and prices. In the same year Mitsui Home, which has a twenty-year history of importing 2 × 4 North American timber into Japan for its prefabricated housing operations, invested in a BC sorting and pre-cut factory, and Mitsui trading corporation invested in its own custom cut mill (see Table 5.3).

The Automobile Industry

For Canada, Japanese investment in automobiles has been the second most significant sector in manufacturing behind that of timber products and pulp. There are now three Japanese auto plants operating in Canada. A Honda plant in Alliston, Ontario, opened in November 1986, and that produces both coupe and three-door models of the Honda Civic. A Toyota facility in Cambridge, Ontario, began production in November 1988, and manufactures four-door Corollas. CAMI Automotive, a joint venture between Suzuki and General Motors Canada, opened at Ingersoll, Ontario, in April 1989, concentrating on small cars and four-wheel-drive utility vehicles. Over the last decade, these three ventures have invested around $1.5 billion in Canadian production facilities. At the time of their inauguration they were seen as a sign of renewed interest by Japanese investors in Canada; they accounted for about 25 per cent of Japanese total auto assembly investment in North America, and constituted about 20 per cent of production in the so-called 'transplant' Japanese auto production factories. This despite the fact that Canada constituted only 10 per cent of the joint U.S.–Canada market.[33] By 1992 these plants produced an estimated 319,000 units per year and exported around 78 per cent of their output to the United States.[34] Many other smaller industrial companies have been set up by Japanese firms in southern Ontario, some resulting from the Japanese take-over of U.S. subsidiaries in Canada. But these are dwarfed in size by the three Japanese car assembly transplants.[35]

It should be noted that the triangular relationship among Japan, the United States, and Canada has nowhere been more problematic than in the auto production sector. To begin with, in order to attract Japanese investment to Canada rather than the United States, the Canadian government negotiated special import duty reductions for imported auto parts and components in return for guaranteed levels of output and exports. The Canada–U.S. Free Trade Agreement (which commenced operation in 1989) disrupted this arrangement, however, as it aimed to phase out the duty reductions by the middle of the 1990s.[36] Toyota and Honda especially felt discriminated against by this action, as they entered Canada as assemblers with the initial knowledge and expectation that they could bring in parts from Japan duty free. Due to U.S. coercion this privilege was taken away unilaterally by the FTA through a 50 per cent local content rule, which was subsequently raised to 62.5 per cent by NAFTA.

Further problems arose for the transplants in 1991–92, when the U.S. Customs Service retroactively ruled that 90,000 two-door Honda Civic squarebacks assembled in Ontario were not eligible for duty-free entry into the United States. It ruled that Hondas shipped south from the Ontario plant at Alliston in the first fifteen months after the FTA took effect failed to meet the 50 per cent North American content requirement, which meant that Honda owed duties amounting to 2.5 per cent of the value of the cars (about U.S.$17 million).[37] In response, Honda, together with the Canadian government, argued that the U.S. Customs Service chose not to look at the local content of Honda's cars as a whole, and in particular incorrectly rejected Honda's engines as not being made in North America. The engines used for assembly in Canada were in fact made of aluminium ingots fabricated at Honda's plant in Ohio, yet the Customs Service did not count the processing cost of these major components when calculating Honda's local-content ratio. If full engine processing costs were included, Honda officials estimated that the total local content was really 69 per cent as opposed to the Customs service claim of only 46 per cent. All told, the actions against the Honda Civics exported from Canada were widely seen as an effort to force Japanese automakers in the United States to buy American-made parts; this case study illustrates how bilateral disputes directly involving only Japan and the United States often catch Canadian operations in a crossfire.[38]

The ambiguities surrounding local content regulations were solved by NAFTA to Honda's favour, and the valuable duty exemption for imported parts to the Japanese transplants in Canada was extended to 1996. Nevertheless, at the time of NAFTA's introduction many Japanese commentators argued that the rather arbitrary 25 per cent increase in North American content requirement to

62.5 per cent would slow down Japanese investment in Canada. Given the higher external tariff on auto parts in Canada (reduced in 1995) and the eventual loss of duty remission, the feeling was that Canada would be hardest hit by the changes because Japanese production was geared primarily towards the U.S. market.[39] By comparison, Mexico was not expected to be affected as seriously, as Japanese producers in that market (currently Nissan and Honda) publicly stated that their factory output would not be directed towards sales in the United States or Canada, and so would not be affected by the domestic content provisions of NAFTA.[40]

Nonetheless, events since 1993, especially the increased yen-based costs in Japan caused by an appreciating currency and ballooning unit labour costs, have impelled Japanese auto companies to seek even higher levels of production within NAFTA markets.[41] Honda released plans in 1994 to increase total Canadian assembly output by about 20 per cent to 120,000 units annually by 1997. A new model at the Ontario plant was planned for release in 1996 (a Canadian version of the Acura), which comprised the first vehicle designed exclusively for the Canadian market from a Japanese manufacturer. An additional capacity investment of $20 million was expected to bring the total investment in the Ontario facility to around $490 million, involving an additional eighty new jobs, and plans were made to export Canadian-made Civics to Taiwan and Brazil.[42] Company executives reported that the low-valued Canadian dollar, ample land, and the elimination of tariffs on parts imported to build vehicles (which had been 9.2 per cent prior to 1995) were responsible for the decision to expand production in Canada.[43]

At the same time, however, Honda announced a much larger U.S.$245 million expansion to its Ohio operations in the United States, involving 600 new jobs; mainly to develop a 50 per cent increase in engine manufacturing capacity and to set up a new production line to raise output by 18 per cent to around 720,000 vehicles. In addition, a further 250 workers were to be hired at Honda's U.S. research and development facilities in Ohio and California, and U.S.$50 million was to be invested in a new Mexican assembly plant that was expected to create 250 jobs and start making cars in November 1995. The heavy U.S. slant in this new round of investment, compared with Honda's obvious bias towards Canadian production in the mid-1980s, was seen as an attempt to appease U.S. irritation over Japan's huge trade imbalance in auto vehicles and parts.[44]

Still, production at Japanese plants in Canada reached over 390,000 units in 1995, of which about 83 per cent were exported mostly to the United States.[45] There are now more motor vehicles exported from Japanese-affiliated plants in Canada than are imported into Canada by Japanese automakers from Japan, the United States, and Mexico. This adds significantly to Canada's automobile trade surplus. Honda Canada announced in 1995 an investment of $300 million to build

TABLE 5.5
Japanese-affiliated auto assembly plants in Southern Ontario and the U.S.

Honda
Location: Alliston, 95 km northwest of Toronto
Beginning of manufacturing activity: November 1986
Production capacity: 120,000 cars per year
Employment: 1,750
Products: Civic, Acura 1.6EL, (New) Minivan

Honda in the United States

Marysville, Ohio	Anna, Ohio	East Liberty, Ohio
November 1982	July 1985	December 1989
380,000 cars	575,000 engines	220,000 cars
5,200 persons	2,100 persons	1,900 persons
Accord		Civic

Toyota
Location: Cambridge, 95 km southwest of Toronto
Beginning of manufacturing activity: November 1988
Production capacity: 85,000 cars per year
Employment: 1,000
Products: Corolla, (New) Sporty Coupe

Toyota in the United States

Fremont, CA (NUMMI)	Georgetown, KY	
December 1982	May 1985	September 1988
300,000 cars	240,000 cars	300,000 engines
4,200 persons	4,300 persons	500 persons
Corolla (Prizm)	Camry	

CAMI: Suzuki and General Motors
Location: Ingersoll, 95 km southwest of Toronto
Beginning of manufacturing activity: April 1989
Production capacity: 200,000 cars per year
Employment: 2,400
Products: (Geo) Metro, Tracker, (Suzuki) Swift, Sidekick

Source: K. Nagao, 'Globalization Processes of Japanese Automobile Production.'

a new minivan plant in Alliston, Ontario, beginning in 1998 with a capacity of 120,000 units and a workforce of 1,200.[46] Toyota Motor Manufacturing Canada Inc. commenced its own $600 million expansion plans in 1994 to add a second plant in Cambridge, Ontario, that will expand its workforce by 1,100 and double its capacity to 200,000 units a year when in operation. A Toyota engine plant began production at Cambridge in 1995, and a further $400 million investment was announced in 1997. Toyota Canada will make a new generation of the Corolla sedan and a new coupe model designed in North America, the Toyota Solara. The existing Toyota plant was rated by J.D. Power as the first plant for quality in North America in 1995, and the Canadian Honda plant was rated fourth.[47]

Despite these recent investments tension over the provisions of NAFTA still exists. Between them the two Japanese companies will have spent close to $1 billion on the recent expansions, and they are demanding tariff concessions from the Canadian government on vehicles they import in return for their investments. Japanese automakers in Canada have continued to press the federal government to reduce the 7.3 per cent tariff on fully imported vehicles imported from outside North America, arguing that the investments they have made here entitle them to the same treatment as the U.S. Big Three, which can import vehicles duty-free from anywhere in the world because of commitments made under the 1965 Auto Pact. Both Toyota and Honda will meet all Auto Pact requirements to quality as domestic manufacturing by the time their expanded plants are running in the fall of 1998. By contrast, the leaders of the 'Big Three' have strongly opposed the federal government for considering an elimination of the tariff.[48]

Tourism and Real Estate Investments

During the 1980s, the Japanese government encouraged its citizens to travel overseas in an effort to reduce the country's burgeoning trade surpluses. A 'Ten Million Program,' initiated in 1987, aimed at encouraging ten million Japanese consumers to spend more time and money on travel by 1992. Over and above this planned increase, the number of Japanese outbound travellers – including tourists and business travellers – exceeded the goal of ten million two years ahead of schedule in 1990.[49] Apart from the period of the Gulf War, Japanese overseas travel has continued to grow. In the first half of 1995, a record 6,821,000 Japanese travelled overseas, up 8.2 per cent from the same period in 1994, according to the Japan National Tourist Organization (JNTO). An estimated fifteen million Japanese went abroad in 1995.[50]

Canadian sites such as Banff and Niagara Falls have been favoured tourist destinations for the Japanese since the early 1970s. From the late 1980s the new wave of international tourism, together with the high-valued yen against the Canadian currency, caused total Japanese visitors to this country to jump from just 139,000 in 1985 to 474,000 in 1990 and 668,000 in 1996, overtaking visitor numbers from more traditional sources such as the United Kingdom.[51] In fact, Canada's share of the Japanese tourism market has grown faster over this period than overall market growth. While Japanese tourists are now visiting all parts of Canada, BC and Alberta have benefited most. In particular, the sharp increase in Japanese visitors to British Columbia enabled tourism to overtake mining as the second-largest sector of BC's economy behind forestry. Since 1988, the greatest increase in Japanese visitors to Canada has taken place in the winter months (November–February) due to the greater number of skiing packages available to Japanese tourists at Whistler and Banff.[52]

Japanese property investors soon followed the boom in Japanese tourism worldwide. In British Columbia they were active during the boom years of Japan's 'economic bubble' (1986–90) in selectively buying hotels in Vancouver and properties such as golf courses at tourist resorts close by (see Table 5.6). Hotel acquisitions in Banff also took place beginning in 1988.[53]

A prime example of Japanese interest in BC recreational areas is the international-class Whistler ski resort, just 80 km north of Vancouver, which Japanese skiers have chosen as their favorite international destination over Vail and Aspen in the United States.[54] Japan, which reportedly has twelve million skiers – more than in the whole of North America – has provided a large market for Whistler. By 1990 it was estimated that Canada had attracted 70 per cent of Japan's overseas ski market, and that more than one-third of Whistler hotel bookings were made to Japanese tour wholesalers. In the winter of 1993–94, some 69,700 room nights were generated by Japanese skiers in Whistler. This represents a 174 per cent increase since 1988–89, a period in which five of the twenty-six hotels at this resort were bought by Japanese firms.[55] In 1992, as Whistler moved ahead of Vail as the top ski destination in North America, Nippon Cable, reputedly the largest manufacturer of Doppelmayr lift systems in the world, acquired 23 per cent of Blackcombe Skiing Enterprises, providing sufficient capital for a five-year $25 million resort expansion plan at Whistler to go ahead.[56] The continued increase in Japanese tourism in British Columbia has so far drawn Japanese investment primarily to the Vancouver-Whistler-Victoria 'Golden Triangle' region. Thus a report by Colliers International revealed that of well-known 'brand name' hotels (i.e., three stars and above), Japanese owners controlled 29 per cent of hotels in Vancouver, 40 per cent in Whistler, and 30 per cent in Victoria.[57]

Apart from hotels and resorts, and a small amount of condominiums, Japanese property investment in Canada in the late 1980s and early 1990s was surprisingly restrained. For example, Canadian cities did not experience any of the aggressive large-scale 'trophy' office purchases such as occurred in New York or Los Angeles over the 1980s. Probably the only example is Nippon Life Insurance Co., which opened a special subsidiary company in Toronto, NLI Properties Canada Inc., in 1985 to search for possible real estate investments. Toronto at that time was undoubtedly one of the best office property markets in North America. Yet in the period up to 1991 NLI participated in just one syndi-

TABLE 5.6

Major hotel/resort properties and golf courses purchased/developed by Japanese investors in British Columbia, 1986–93

Japanese investor	Name	Location	Year
Hotels/Resorts			
Toky	Pan Pacific	Vancouver	1986
Itoman	Harrison Hot Springs	Harrison Hot Springs	1987*
Listel	International Lodge	Whistler	1987
Aoki	Westin Hotel	Vancouver	1988
IPEC/ICEC	Nancy Greene Olympic Lodge (incl. Crystal Lodge)	Whistler	1988*
IPEC	Harbour Towers Hotel	Victoria	1988
Mutsumi	Whistler Fairways Hotel and Resort	Whistler	1988*
Okabe	Coast Hotel/Motel Chain	Vancouver, 12 other BC locations	1988
Okabe	Ramada Renaissance Hotel	Vancouver	1988
Palios	O'Doul's Hotel	Vancouver	1989*
Chotokan	Radium Hot-Springs Resort	Radium Hot Springs	1989
Yamanouchi Pharmaceutical	Chateau Whistler (80% share)	Whistler	1989
Libest	Westbrook Whistler	Whistler	1990
Maiami Canada	Ming Court Hotel	Vancouver	1990
Crossroads Enterprise	Royal Oak Inn	Victoria	1991
Golf Courses			
Sail View	Carnoustie Golf Course	Vancouver	1990
Meadow Gardens	The Fort Golf and Country Club	Fort Langley	1991
Green Life	Meadow Gardens Golf Course	Pitt Meadows	1991
Skylark	Swaneset Bay Resort	Pitt Meadows	1992
Tanabe Beach	Furry Creek	Britannia	1993

*Sold to another Japanese investor in 1992–93.
Source: Edgington, 'Japanese Real Estate Investment,' 292–305.

cated real estate deal involving Toronto's Richmond Adelaide Centre commercial complex.[58] Besides the relative conservatism of Japanese real estate investors towards Canada, another major constraint on Japanese acquisitions of office buildings in both Toronto and Vancouver was the scarcity of suitable 'A' grade downtown property for sale. In the downtown areas of cities such as Toronto and Vancouver, the traditional Canadian pension fund companies that own most office buildings were reluctant to sell during the prosperous 1980s. Consequently, it was hard for Japanese investors to find appropriate property on the market. The largest single Japanese investment deal in Canadian real estate in the boom period comprised the Hong Kong Bank of Canada Building in Vancouver, which was sold in 1989 to Sun Enterprises of Tokyo for $130 million.[59]

Nearly all Japanese real estate investment in Canada ended rather suddenly at the end of 1990 due to the drying up of easy bank finance in Japan. The cheap money that spawned the hotel megadeals in Vancouver, Banff, and Whistler disappeared along with the fall in the value of stock and land assets in Japan. Some properties were in fact placed quietly on the market in 1992–93 and sold privately to other Japanese investors to avoid 'losing face.'[60]

Conclusion

During the last ten years or so, Japanese investors sent huge volumes of capital overseas in search of investment opportunities, especially during the second half of the 1980s, but cut back after the spectacular bursting of the 'bubble economy' in 1991.[61] When assessing future patterns of Japanese investment, regard must be given to likely prospective demand for Canadian resources, the unfolding of NAFTA, the locational preferences of Japanese manufacturers, and whether Canada can maintain its share of Japanese overseas tourism. Another consideration is how long the 'post-bubble' recession will last in Japan. A squeeze on finances in the home market and declining revenues and profits mean that the investment capacity of Japanese firms will continue to be greatly diminished. Furthermore, the geographic destination of Japanese overseas investment flows are set to change dramatically in the years ahead: much less is likely to flow to North America and Europe, and much more to other Asian countries. Apart from the need for Japanese firms to lower production costs and remain competitive, this shifting emphasis is also a function of the enormously greater growth potential seen in Asia and the relatively poor performance of recent Japanese investments elsewhere.[62] Yet the fixation of the Japanese with the United States makes it difficult for Canada to gain much additional investment attention. Nor do this country's constitutional agonies commend it to the Japanese. If separation of Quebec occurs, the Japanese will worry, as they always do, about political instability and changing rules.

The combination of these tendencies could be disastrous for Canada. As Canada struggles to stay connected with a more technologically focused and affluent Japan, indications are that Canada is becoming more peripheral. Japanese direct investment worldwide declined during FY 1989–92, yet recovered over the next three years (up 48.5 per cent) to FY 1995 in dollar terms, mainly due to the yen's rapid appreciation. But while Japanese investment in the United States followed the global trend and increased by 60.6 per cent, it fell in Canada by 25.9 per cent over the same period, down to pre-1987 levels in nominal dollar terms (see Table 5.1).[63] Recent JETRO surveys confirm these aggregate figures: only nine new Japanese firms were established in Canada during 1993, six during 1994, and six during 1995, indicating that investment interest in this country has been marking time.[64] Unless special measures are taken these trends suggest that Canada's traditional 2 per cent share of total Japanese DFI might well fall to 0.2 per cent over the coming ten years.

As the Canadian economy emerges from the early 1990s recession, it must find ways of avoiding further economic difficulties by quickly taking up new technological innovations and gaining access to high-growth Asia-Pacific markets.[65] Strengthening ties with Japan will be one component of securing a more prosperous future. For manufacturing regions in Central Canada, government policy should give special attention to attracting joint ventures and technological cooperation between Japanese and Canadian companies. In order to build up the technological base of Canadian manufacturing the objective must be not simply to force Japanese firms to produce more goods in NAFTA, but to secure for Canada its more sophisticated technological operations, including research and development, with Canadian workers. A particularly pressing issue is that, at present, too few Japanese companies in Canada appear to be able to take advantage of NAFTA. Thus in 1995 Japanese electronics firms Hitachi and Sanyo moved their television assembly operations out of Quebec and Ontario, switching production to either Mexico or the southern United States. In 1996, Mitsubishi Electronics closed its small-scale television tube plant in Ontario, citing severe competition with lower-cost Korean producers based in the United States.[66]

Still, according to the JETRO survey cited earlier, close to 90 per cent of the Japanese affiliates engaged in manufacturing in Canada reported they were exporting to the United States, and half of these sent 50 per cent of their production south of the border. Firms in the bearings, electrical and electronic equipment, and machinery sectors recorded increased exports to the United States and Mexico because of the elimination or reduction of tariffs.[67] These survey results suggest that under the right conditions NAFTA can work for Canada and raise the level of exports from Japanese-controlled plants in this country.

For British Columbia and Alberta, attracting future growth in tourism investment and associated service sectors appears more promising, especially as it is forecast that by the year 2000 over twenty million Japanese will travel overseas annually. Recent reports have estimated that for Canada this could mean tripling Japanese arrivals from around 500,000 in the early 1990s to 1.5 million each year.[68] While there are several questions as to how such a dramatic expansion could be arranged, increased numbers of Japanese visitors may well lead to the rise of Japanese investments in services such as retailing, language education, health centres for Japanese seniors (the so-called 'silver' market), and so on, later in the decade. British Columbia in particular should experience higher levels of Japanese investment interest as North America's Pacific Northwest is deemed generally to provide an attractive business environment and high quality of life resulting in a steady in-migration of new residents.[69]

NOTES

1 Edgington, '"The New Wave."'
2 See Rugman, *Japanese Direct Investment*; Morris, 'Japanese Manufacturing Investment'; Edgington, 'Japanese Direct Investment.'
3 See Langdon, *The Politics of Canadian–Japanese*; Wright, *Japanese Business in Canada*; Blain and Norcliffe, 'Japanese Investment.'
4 Statistics Canada, Cat. 67-202.
5 Japanese Foreign Press Center, *Direct Overseas Investment*.
6 Mark, 'Japanese Direct Investment in Canada'; Brazeau, *The Directory of Canadian Business*; Richardson, 'Reaping the Yen'; Government of Ontario, *Japanese Investment Profile*; JETRO, *Directory of Japanese-Affiliated Companies*; Holroyd and Coates, *Pacific Partners*.
7 Keenan, Jang, and Freeman, 'Canada Still Luring Investment.'
8 JETRO, 'Eighth Annual JETRO Survey.'
9 Morris, 'Globalisation and Global Localisation'; Emmot, *Japan's Global Reach*; Edgington, 'The Globalisation of Japanese Manufacturing,' 87–106.
10 McMillan, *Building Blocks or Trade Blocks*.
11 See Craib, 'NAFTA's Implications'; Edgington and Fruin, 'NAFTA and Japanese Investment'; Edgington, 'Japanese Manufacturing Companies.'
12 Edgington, 'Japanese Manufacturing in Australia.'
13 This relatively relaxed attitude towards Japanese investment can be contrasted with the mistrust of United States multinational corporations in Canada that occurred during the 1960s and 1970s, and mistrust of Japanese DFI in the United States during the 1980s. The difference reflects, of course, recent shifts in perceptions and actions of most governments in Canada towards multinationals, due mainly to their links with the global economy and the demand for new sources of technology; see Investment Canada, 'Foreign Multinationals and Canada's International Competitiveness.' Interestingly, throughout the period under review Canada has offered, arguably, a warmer climate for Japanese investment than the United States through avoiding the 'Japan-bashing' sentiments associated with the States' fear of increased inward investment; see Franz and Collins, *Selling Out*.

14 Rugman, *Japanese Direct Investment*; Edgington, 'Japanese Direct Investment.'

15 Hay, *Manufactures*.

16 See Dobson, 'A Canadian Perspective'; Sato, 'A Japanese Perspective'; Stern, ed., *Trade and Investment Relations*; Edgington, 'Japanese Perceptions.' The likely impact of U.S.–Japan trade conflict on Canada's trading relations with Japan is considered by Ursacki and Vertinsky, 'Canada–Japan Trade.'

17 See Edgington and Fruin, 'NAFTA and Japanese Investment.'

18 Ibid.

19 Ibid.

20 JETRO, *JETRO White Paper on Foreign Direct Investment 1994*; JETRO, *JETRO White Paper on Foreign Direct Investment 1997*.

21 Florida and Kenney, 'The Globalization of Japanese R and D.'

22 Robertson and Waggener, 'The Japanese Market for Softwood.'

23 *Canada–Japan Trade Council Newsletter*, January–December 1993, and March–April 1994.

24 Tiessen, *Canada–Japan Trade Perspectives*.

25 Interview with K. Kanno, Executive Vice-President, Elk Trading Co. Ltd., Vancouver, January 1994.

26 Edgington and Hayter, 'International Trade.'

27 Nikiforuk and Struzik, 'The Great Forest Sell-Off'; Pratt and Urquart, *The Last Great Forest*.

28 Nikiforuk and Struzik, 'The Great Forest Sell-Off'; Pratt and Urquart, *The Last Great Forest*. In 1992 Daishowa Paper entered a joint venture with Marubeni Corporation, its major trading company, to operate its Western Canadian holdings under the auspices of Daishowa Marubeni International Ltd. (DMI). DMI has recently reported it will proceed with plans to build a $900 million lightweight coated paper mill in Peace River, Alberta; see 'Daishowa Marubeni to Invest $900 Million in Canada,' 6.

29 Interview with Kiyoshi Fujieda, President, MC Forest Investment Inc, Vancouver, 21 January 1994.

30 Interview with G.C. Thomson, Controller, Howe Sound Pulp and Paper Ltd., Vancouver, March 1996.

31 Pratt and Urquart, *The Last Great Forest*.

32 Cartwright, *Canadian Wood and Building Product*; Canada–Japan Trade Council, ed., *Japan's Changing Needs*.

33 Edgington, *Japanese Direct Investment in Canada*.

34 JAMA, *JAMA Canada Annual Report 1993*.

35 See Edgington, 'Japanese Manufacturing.'

36 Edgington, *Japanese Direct Investment in Canada*.

37 'Honda: Is It an American Car?'

38 'Local Content Should Not Be Used.'

39 See JAMA, *JAMA Canada Annual Report 1993*; Edgington and Fruin, *NAFTA and Japanese Investment*.

40 Matsumoto, 'Politically Wary Honda.'

41 Sumiya, 'Toyota to Hike North American Output.'

42 Honda Announcement, 19 July 1994.

43 Keenan, 'Ottawa Dropping Tariff for Honda,' A1 and A21.

44 *Financial Post*, 20 July 1994.

45 JAMA, *JAMA Canada Annual Report 1996*.

46 'Honda Expands Canadian Operations,' 5.

47 See Ennis, 'Canada Set for a Bigger Share'; Keenan, 'Ontario Toyota Plant'; Keenan, 'Toyota Plans $400 Million Retooling.' Cami Automotive Inc., the joint venture of General Motors of Canada Ltd. and Suzuki Motor Corporation, has not expanded its operations as sales of its small cars – including the Geo Metro and Suzuki Sidekick – have slumped. However, in its favour the Ingersoll, Ontario, plant helps GM meet U.S. regulations for CAFE – corporate average fuel economy. See Jack, 'Sales Surge Forecast.'

48 Jack, 'Toyota Chief: We're Canadian.'

49 Japan, Ministry of Transport, *Annual Report on the Transport Economy*.

50 Umeda, 'Strong Yen Boosts,' 138–39.

51 Statistics Canada, Cat. 66-001.

52 See Edgington, 'The Economic Impact of Tourism,' 7–14; *Canada–Japan Trade Council Newsletter*, March–April 1996.

53 Edgington, 'Japanese Real Estate Investment.'

54 Interview with P. Clark, Manager, Market Research, Whistler Resort Association, June 1993.

55 Edgington, 'Japanese Real Estate Investment.'

56 *Vancouver Courier*, 18 October 1992.

57 Colliers International Hotel Realty, *The West Coast Hotel Investment Report*.

58 Interview with Y. Susaki, President, NLI International Canada, Toronto, December 1991.

59 Edgington, *Japanese Property Investors*.

60 Ibid.

61 See Wood, *The Bubble Economy*; Wright, *Japanese Finance in Transformation*.

62 Courtis, 'Japan's Tilt to Asia,' 4. Within NAFTA, Japanese investors up until 1994 had not shown much interest in Mexico as a low-cost production location, but DFI in fiscal 1994 suddenly jumped more than tenfold and overtook DFI in Canada, while dropping again in fiscal 1995; see 'The Japanese Have a Yen,' 71; Orme, *Understanding NAFTA*; Japanese Foreign Press Center, *Direct Overseas Investment*.

63 See also JETRO, *JETRO White Paper on Foreign Direct Investment 1997*.

64 JETRO, *Eighth Annual JETRO Survey*.

65 See for example Crane, *The Next Canadian Century.*
66 'Two Japanese Firms Moving,' 10; Waldie, 'Canada Losing Sole TV.'
67 JETRO, *Eighth Annual JETRO Survey.*
68 Thornell and Pringsheim, *Japanese Travel to Canada*; Tourism Canada, *Meeting Highlights*; Tourism Canada, *Proceedings, Canada–Japan Tourism Conference.*
69 Edgington, 'Trade, Investment and the New Regionalism.'

6

Japan's Post-Bubble Economic Changes: Implications for the United States and Canada[1]

RICHARD WRIGHT

Introduction

In the late 1980s, Japan's economy soared to unprecedented heights in terms of Gross National Product (GNP), market share, and asset prices. During this period, Japan became rightly viewed as the world's money machine, exporting on average more than $100 billion of long-term capital per year from 1985 to 1989. Both the United States and Canada became increasingly reliant on inflows of Japanese capital. For Canadians, the flow was especially critical: by 1991 Japanese investors held 25 per cent of all foreign-held Canadian bonds, up from less than 2 per cent a decade earlier, and Japan ranked third, after the United States and Britain, as a source of foreign direct investment in Canada.[2]

The subsequent Japanese economic downturn and the collapse in asset values since 1990 has resulted in a reassessment of Japan's position as a global economic power and has raised serious questions about Japan's ability to sustain its position as the world's largest foreign investor. The implications are profound both for Japan and for countries such as the United States and Canada that had come to rely on sustained inflows of Japanese capital.

The Ride Up

Between 1986 and 1991, Japan demonstrated an astonishing surge of economic vitality. In the longest and most robust growth period Japan has seen in the post-war era, the Japanese economy grew the equivalent of France's GNP each year.

Even before the economic take-off of the mid-1980s, Japan's financial assets had been growing more rapidly than the economy in general. From 1985 to 1990, however, the gap between the financial and the real economies widened dramatically. By the time the Nikkei stock index reached its peak of 38,915 on

Figure 6.1: Trend in Stock Prices

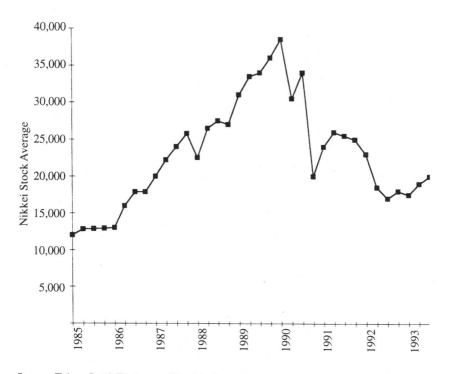

Source: Tokyo Stock Exchange, *Monthly Statistics Report.*

31 December 1989, it had multiplied 5.5 times since the beginning of the decade (Figure 6.1). The Tokyo stock market represented an astonishing 42 per cent of global stock market capitalization, compared with only 15 per cent in 1980. Of the 1,136 companies listed on the first section of the Tokyo Stock Exchange (TSE), 716 had price/earnings multiples greater than 50.[3] As a proportion of GNP, stock prices tripled during the decade (Figure 6.2). If one accepts the premise that stock market appreciation should be related to growth in the real economy, Japan's equity markets had become grossly overvalued.

Similarly, land prices soared at a pace much faster than GNP in the late 1980s (Figure 6.3). In the United States, the ratio of land prices to GNP has fluctuated between .56 and .86 since 1970.[4] In Japan, it stayed between 2.2 and 3.2 in 1970–75 before surging to 5.7 by the end of 1989.[5] Land prices in the Tokyo metropolitan area skyrocketed 45 per cent in 1986, followed by a 61 per cent

Figure 6.2: Stock Index Divided by GNP

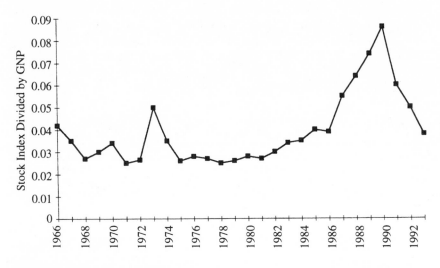

Source: Japanese Ministry of Finance.

jump in 1987. The property market boom spread quickly to other major Japanese cities such as Osaka, where prices rose 50 per cent in 1989. By the time property values peaked in 1990, they had reached 2.7 times their 1985 level. Just the increase alone in national property values between 1985 and 1990 (estimated at ¥1,385 trillion) amounted to practically three times the size of Japan's nominal GNP.[6]

At the height of the bubble, Japan's Management and Coordination Agency estimated Japan's total supply of land to be worth some ¥2,400 trillion, or nearly five times the estimated ¥500 trillion value of land in the United States.[7] Based on these appraisals, the value of metropolitan Tokyo was equivalent to that of the entire United States, and the grounds of the Imperial Palace alone were worth more than all of Canada!

What caused this phenomenal surge in Japanese asset values? The initial impetus behind the asset price inflation was a combination of several conditions prevailing in both the Japanese financial environment and other financial markets at the time, among them low interest rates, financial deregulation, and oil price changes. But this potent mixture exploded in Japan as a consequence of two characteristics that distinguish the Japanese financial system in particular: lending decisions based on collateral values rather than cash flow, and exten-

Figure 6.3: Urban Land Price Index Divided by GNP

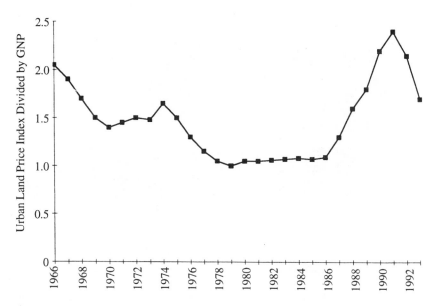

sive cross-shareholdings. The influence of each of these conditions is considered in the following sections.

Low Interest Rates

The bubble economy had its roots in the September 1985 Plaza Accord, in which central bankers agreed to raise the value of the yen to reduce Japan's trade surplus. As a result, Japanese firms that were competing in 1985 at an average exchange rate of 239 yen per dollar had to be competitive in 1986 with an average exchange rate of 169 yen to the dollar. Fearing a detrimental impact of the high yen on the domestic economy, the Bank of Japan adopted a policy of low interest rates and expanding money supply. In the thirteen-month span from January 1986 to February 1987, the official discount rate was pared from 5 per cent to 2.5 per cent, the lowest rate ever to that time. It remained there for twenty-seven months, until May 1989, when the rate was raised to 3.25 per cent (Figure 6.4). The money supply expanded at a double-digit pace for four years running, from 1987 through 1990 (Figure 6.5). As a consequence, Japanese companies accelerated their investments in plant and equipment. Between 1986 and 1991, they invested approximately U.S.$3 trillion in plant and capital

Figure 6.4: Official Discount Rate

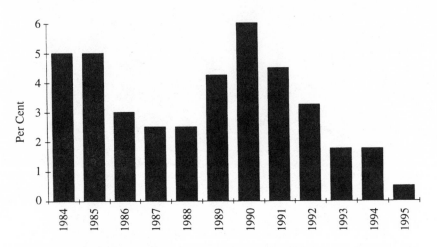

Source: The Economist Intelligence Unit, *Japan Profile*, 1995 and 1991; JETRO, *Business Facts and Figures 1996*.

equipment, and committed another U.S.$600 billion to research and development.[8] Vast amounts of cash also flowed into the stock and real estate markets.

Deregulation and Financial Engineering

The rise in stock and property values stimulated by low interest rates was powerfully reinforced by innovative financing practices that grew out of the financial market deregulation that occurred in Japan during the late 1980s. Deregulation helped to create an environment conducive to the active corporate pursuit of so-called *zaitech* or 'fund engineering,' particularly experimentation with new, low-cost ways of raising capital through the issue of equity-linked debt. Between 1981 and 1985 issues of equities and equity-related instruments, such as convertible and warrant bonds, accounted for only a quarter of Japanese companies' source of funds; by 1989 they accounted for more than 70 per cent.[9] With a continuously rising stock market, investors would inevitably convert these equity-linked bonds to stock, receiving their returns in the form of capital gains rather than coupon interest. Companies could issue convertible bonds with confidence that they would never have to refinance them, nor, given the sustained rise in share prices, were they unduly concerned with the dilution of their shares.

Figure 6.5: Growth in GNP and Money Supply

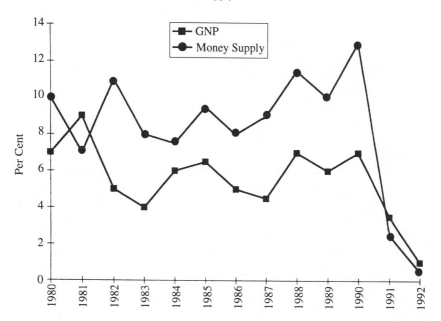

Corporate financial managers took advantage of these fund-raising and investment conditions in various ways. First, companies capitalized on the then-high price of their stock to raise funds at extremely low cost through equity financing; then they reinvested the funds in stocks, mutual funds, or large time deposits. Larger firms, with a more diversified range of fund-raising methods at their disposal, would have financial institutions such as banks underwrite their commercial paper issues, then reinvest the funds procured that way in large-denomination time deposits paying higher interest than the commercial paper.[10]

As a consequence of all of this, listed companies in Japan had access to extraordinarily cheap capital. In 1989, it cost listed Japanese companies a nominal average of only 0.4 per cent a year to raise money domestically through warrant bonds or convertible bonds, and even less if they sold them overseas and swapped the proceeds for yen.[11] Listed companies raised ¥25 trillion through such issues in 1989, more than twice their total net profits. In fact, the net interest expense paid by listed manufacturers in the six months leading up to September 1989 was −.09%; that is, they received more from interest-bearing instruments than they paid out on borrowings.

A number of circumstances particular to the Japanese business environment supported this widespread corporate shift to financial engineering. First, compared with their North American counterparts, Japanese firms in the manufacturing sector have been characterized by relatively high ratios of liquidity to total assets, ranging around 15 per cent on average. In the second half of the 1980s, however, that figure surged to more than 20 per cent. By contrast, in the United States, where efforts in financial deregulation got off to a much earlier start, the comparable liquidity ratio has held steady at around 6 per cent, with little or no significant deviation since the mid-1960s.[12] This fact suggests, by and large, that the speculative financial management strategies embraced by many Japanese firms have not been pursued in the United States.

Second, shareholders have little influence or control over a company's management in Japan. They are not always able to stop a firm from retaining capital surpluses or engaging in investment-oriented financial engineering practices that have nothing to do with its main line of business. In North America, by contrast, shareholders have a greater degree of control over company management, and, barring exceptional circumstances, they generally view company retention of surplus capital as counter to the objective of maximizing shareholder benefits.

A third factor contributing to the large-scale financial engineering is the relative ease with which cash could be raised by equity financing in Japan. Dividend yields in Japan have traditionally been extremely low (the average pre-tax return on equity earned by Japanese firms between 1970 and 1991 was 18.2 per cent), and cross-shareholding arrangements with other firms help to minimize the risk of being bought out. Again, this is in contrast to North America, where dividend yields are higher (averaging 24.5 per cent for the comparable period), and where equity financing typically heightens the buy-out risk faced by the owners of a business.[13]

In summary, equity financing was a low-cost means of raising funds essentially because expectations that stocks were headed up had the effect of lifting the expected rate of return on investments in stock. This in turn kept interest rates low, at least for a while. This was facilitated by severe competition in the deposit market, with rival banks bidding against each other to attract corporate depositors. With this extremely low cost of funds, business firms raised much more capital than was necessary for investment in productive assets, ploughing the excess into increasingly speculative real estate investments and stock funds. By 1990, these funds totalled more than $300 billion and were a significant factor supporting high stock valuations.[14] The rising stock market assured a continuous supply of inexpensive investment capital, thus reinforcing even further the upward trend in stock and real estate prices.

Figure 6.6: Oil Price Trend

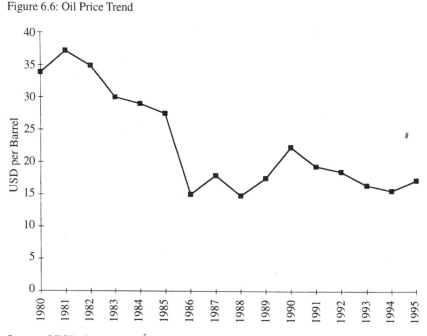

Source: OECD, *Perspective Économique de l'OECD.*

Oil Price Decreases

Conditions external to Japan, particularly changes in world oil prices, also contributed significantly to the surge of liquidity and asset values in Japan during the late 1980s. World oil prices crashed in 1986 (Figure 6.6). As a consequence, Japan's bill for imported oil fell 44 per cent, from U.S.$34.6 billion in 1985 to U.S.$19.5 billion in 1986. This U.S.$15 billion windfall represented 17.7 per cent of Japan's 1986 current account surplus. Clearly, Japan was materially more wealthy as a result. This newfound wealth was a further stimulus to increased domestic and foreign investment.

The influence of external forces such as oil price changes, over which Japan had little or no control, should temper somewhat the type of fawning view expressed by *The Economist*: 'Since Japan combined this asset price inflation with stable goods prices and appreciating currencies, it achieved a possibly unprecedented feat: through reckless creation of financial credit, it printed the means to buy real assets from foreigners.'[15]

Collateral-Based Lending Practices

With attractive new financing options available as a result of financial deregulation, large Japanese companies became increasingly reluctant in the 1980s to borrow from banks for their funding needs. The dependence of manufacturing firms on bank loans fell from 38.4 per cent in 1975 to 25.2 per cent by 1989.[16] Banks and other financial institutions consequently became much more aggressive in their lending practices as they fought to retain their market shares. At the same time, however, liberalization of large deposit rates, begun in 1985, increased the banks' financing costs, leading to a much greater managerial emphasis on profitability than before. In consequence, the composition of bank loan portfolios began to shift. Loans to small businesses and individuals (so-called 'consumer lending') increased, as did long-term loans, all of which offered higher profit margins but also greater risk. Even more significantly, real estate–related loans, including those to nonbanks, increased from 17.8 per cent of total bank assets in 1984 to 28.8 per cent in 1989.[17]

In contrast to Western countries, where banks usually base their lending decisions on the borrower's ability to generate cash flow, Japanese banks base their property lending decisions primarily on the market value of the borrower's collateral. Accurate market values are difficult to determine in the illiquid Japanese property market. The transactions that took place in the bubble era were of an increasingly speculative nature, and thus a poor guide to the intrinsic value of the property. Nevertheless, even with these uncertain values, Japanese banks were so eager to swell their balance sheets in the late 1980s that they occasionally advanced up to 100 per cent or more of the collateral's assessed value, in contrast to a historical rate of 70 to 80 per cent.[18] Furthermore, a single property could sometimes be used to obtain loans from several institutions totalling far more than the value of the property. The bottom line is that these aggressive bank lending practices put ever more yen into the hands of speculators who used it to ramp up real estate and stock market prices even higher.

Cross-Shareholdings

A well-documented feature of the Japanese financial system is its extensive cross-shareholdings.[19] In contrast to the norms of many other financial systems, Japanese banks are entitled to hold shares of their customers and related *keiretsu* members. In fact, Japanese banks hold 18 per cent of all equity securities in Japan. This characteristic of the Japanese financial system has a significant impact on share price behaviour since, under rules of the Bank for

International Settlements (BIS), a bank is allowed to allocate to its capital base 45 per cent of unrealized capital gains on its portfolio of negotiable securities. The rising Japanese stock markets of the late 1980s increased the capital base of banks and hence their supply of loanable funds. Similarly, higher stock valuations increased the collateral base of borrowers and thus their ability to borrow even more to invest in the inflated real estate and stock markets.

Cross-shareholdings also make the Japanese stock market more volatile. As 70 per cent of all equity is held by long-term institutional shareholders, the actual market float is closer to 30 per cent of total stock holdings.[20] Relatively little buying or selling pressure is needed to register significant gains or losses in market values. Through their impact on bank lending and stock price volatility, *keiretsu* cross-shareholdings played a key, although seldom noted, role in the growth of asset values.

Link between Stock Prices and Land Prices

Another often-cited justification for stratospheric Japanese stock valuations was the unrealized capital gains on land held by corporations. When buying a share, investors bought not only a stake in the firm's business, but also a share of the increasingly valuable land on which the company was based. In this way, higher land prices resulted in higher stock prices. Similarly, higher stock prices fed back into the property market, as stock portfolios could be used as collateral for more property speculation. The banks not only had ready loan demand from well-capitalized clients, but the banks' own expanding asset bases increased their supply of loanable funds.

A study by Japan's Economic Planning Agency applied a multivariable, auto-regressive econometric model to explore the relationship between real estate prices, long-term interest rates, and share price levels.[21] For the overall period 1970–90, real estate prices accounted for less than 1 per cent of share price movements; for 1982–88, however, property prices were found to explain over 60 per cent of share price movements, dramatically illustrating the strong interrelationships between these markets in Japan.

Summary

Most discussions about the reasons behind the Japanese asset bubble focus primarily on low interest rates and the growth in money supply. The bubble is viewed simply as 'too much money chasing too few assets.' This section has elaborated further upon the source of the increased wealth, both *perceived* (e.g., increases in stock and land values resulting from financial liberalization and financial engineering) and *real* (e.g., oil price decreases); and also on those elements of Japan's industrial structure and financial system, such as extensive cross-shareholdings and collateral-based lending practices, that made the bubble a reality. Land and stock values are inextricably linked in Japan, each feeding into and reinforcing the other. The apparently separate nature of these markets helped to conceal the weak justification for asset values as long as everything kept going up.

The Ride Down

At first, overall inflation was not a major issue since the revaluation of the yen and the drop in oil prices reduced the price of imports. In 1989, however, industrial production in Japan increased 9 per cent and job offers exceeded the number of job seekers by 48 per cent. The labour shortage placed upward pressure on wage rates, and inflation rose towards 4 per cent.[22] Furthermore, Japanese were becoming increasingly resentful at being priced out of the housing market. In Tokyo and other major metropolitan districts, the cost of a new home rose to more than ten times the annual income of the average salaried worker, making it all but impossible for many to buy a home during their lifetimes.[23] Irrational investments were clearly being made by Japanese companies, both in excess capacity at home and in unwise acquisitions and projects abroad. (As an example, one Japanese resort development in Hawaii reportedly would have needed at least 80 per cent capacity utilization at $700 a night to break even.) In short, the economy was dangerously overheating.

Consequently, the first major act of Yasushi Mieno, the new governor of the Bank of Japan, was to raise the overnight discount rate from 3.75 per cent to 4.25 per cent on Christmas Day, 1989, eight days after he was appointed, and again to 5.25 per cent in March 1990 (see Figure 6.4). The Ministry of Finance joined the central bank in clamping down on speculative excesses by imposing a tax on idle land in an effort to cool down the property market. Further restrictions were made on the growth of bank lending to the real estate sector.

The impact was sure and quick, as the same reinforcing spirals that drove property and stock values ever higher in the late 1980s went into reverse. The stock market peaked on 31 December 1989 at 38,915 within four days of Mieno's first interest rate increase. Before bottoming out at 14,309 in September 1992, 63 per cent of the market's value had been wiped out, the largest margin of decline on record (see Figure 6.1). Stock prices crashed quickly to near pre-bubble levels. Although some of the lost ground has subsequently been recaptured, the Tokyo Stock Index remains at little more than half of its value at the peak of the bubble.

Excesses in the real estate market are not being worked out as quickly. According to Japan's National Land Agency, Tokyo real estate prices have dropped only 12 per cent from their late 1989 high, although most independent analysts estimate the average fall in national land values so far at 25 to 30 per cent. Analysts suggest that property prices in Tokyo and Osaka will have to fall by as much as 60 per cent from their 1990 peak before attaining a level that could be sustained by the growth in national income. The Research Institute of Construction and Economy forecasts that it will take twenty years of 4 to 6 per cent economic growth before national income and property prices fall once again into line.[24]

Ironically, the Achilles heel of the Japanese financial system has been the extensive cross-shareholding so often held up as a foundation of Japan's competitive edge. As discussed above, the capital base of Japanese banks, and hence their lending capacity, is tied closely to the level of the stock market. With the tumbling market, banks were no longer able to supply the funds for real estate speculators and their upward-spiralling speculative schemes. A wall of debt came crashing down on even legitimate borrowers who could no longer make their loan payments or find buyers for their overpriced properties. Asset markets entered a deflationary spiral that has only partially run its course. Because of these interdependencies, a significant drop in property prices has the potential to drag the stock market down even further along with it. However, the probability of this occurring seems quite low. The government has at its disposal many levers capable of artificially maintaining property values. Given the fragility of the current Japanese economy (as well as the importance of Japanese inheritance taxes, which are based on asset values), the government is likely to continue exercising such options as needed to moderate any precipitous decline in property values.

Domestic Consequences of the Downturn

The Japanese economy is undergoing two profound adjustments as a consequence of the bubble and its subsequent collapse. The first is the natural reaction to the excesses of the credit boom of the late 1980s. It takes the form of asset price deflation, lower credit growth, and a gradual restructuring of the financial services industry. The second adjustment is less recognized but ultimately much more important: Japanese businesses are coming to accept that the country's long-term rate of economic growth will be much slower than before.[25] This belief will call for significant changes in employment, management, and corporate strategy. But most of all, it implies a sharp decline in both domestic and overseas investment.

Financial Effects

Deteriorating Position of Banks
The cure for the financial excesses of the late 1980s will be a bitter pill for Japan's financial services industry to swallow. The tremendous volume of real estate–related loans extended by banks and nonbanks during the bubble period accounted for a sharply increased share of total loans outstanding. As a result, when land prices suddenly plunged, the banking sector was left with an enormously enlarged burden of non-performing assets. By the end of 1992, the nation's city, long-term credit, and trust banks together held ¥396 trillion in outstanding loans, of which at least ¥12 trillion were estimated to be non-performing.[26] In addition, the collapse in stock prices effectively generated devaluation losses or unrealized losses on equity holdings and other assets, hurting bank earnings in the process. By the end of the bubble period in late 1989, banking institutions in the above three categories had run up a combined total of ¥55.4 trillion in unrealized gains on their holdings in equity; by September 1992 that total had declined to only ¥14.6 trillion.[27] This margin of loss is widely seen as severely undermining the financial health of Japan's banking sector, all the more so because the industry has long counted on unrealized gains from equity holdings to buttress its earnings picture.

Financial Industry Rationalization
With the value of their asset bases and share portfolios now decimated, banks are being forced to rationalize, both by increasing their asset base and by cutting costs. The creation of Sakura Bank through the merger of Taiyo Kobe Bank and Mitsui Bank in 1990, of Asahi Bank through the merger of Kyowa and Saitama Banks in 1991, and the recent merger of Mitsubishi Bank and Bank of Tokyo to form Tokyo Mitsubishi Bank are examples of a trend that is sure to be replayed over the next few years. One senior Japanese banker estimates that the eleven existing city banks will eventually be reduced in number to only six; the seven trust banks will be cut to three; the three long-term credit banks will have to reorient themselves completely into providers of specialist financial technology along the lines of some American investment banks; and the number of regional banks will be cut in half.[28]

The banks are lobbying the Ministry of Finance (MOF) to further deregulate financial markets to allow them to enter new business areas. New deregulation plans announced by the Japanese government in November 1996 call for more open financial markets to make Tokyo 'an international market comparable to the New York and London markets by the year 2001' by changing the laws covering banking, insurance, foreign exchange, and related areas. A major consequence of the proposed changes would be the elimination of the barriers that have long segmented commercial and investment banking in Japan.[29] Should the banks gain greater entry into corporate underwriting, they would stand a good chance of recapturing some of their better corporate customers who left them to raise funds in the Euromarkets in the heady 1980s.

Macroeconomic Impact

Of greater concern than the health of the financial institutions themselves may be the macroeconomic effects of their reduced lending. Bank lending in Japan grew at an average annual rate of 9.2 per cent between fiscal years 1985 and 1989. The pace has, however, slackened dramatically with the current economic downswing: in January 1993, lending grew only 2.2 per cent over the same month of the year before.[30] What is more, in reaction to the stall in lending, money supply growth since the end of the second half of 1990 has headed sharply lower (see Figure 6.5). It has been suggested that banks could end up taking an overly cautious attitude on lending, ultimately creating a credit environment that stifles business activity in the real economy, forestalling recovery in the process.

Interestingly, the decline in the importance of banking relationships that typified the free-wheeling bubble era may in fact be reversing with the recession. As long as access to equity-linked debt remains restricted, firms will again become more reliant on their main banks. Depending on how long investors' memories are, the poor returns and questionable selling practices associated with the bubble days will impede the redevelopment of the equity-linked market. Moreover, it is unlikely that companies will unload bank shares, no matter how low the yield, for fear of cutting themselves off from credit in an uncertain environment.

Although Japanese financial institutions are in a precarious position, their current problems will almost certainly work themselves out, albeit quite painfully for some. Stronger, more powerful financial institutions with a broader line of permissible activities will continue as strong partners of Japanese industrial borrowers and as formidable competitors abroad. The system is becoming more manageable once again, enabling the MOF to regain control of economic levers that they lost when so many firms were raising funds directly from investors and replacing the services of banks.

Economic and Managerial Effects

Although the pain of post-bubble adjustments has so far fallen mainly on the capital-strapped banks and other financial institutions, fundamental changes are occurring throughout the entire Japanese industrial system. What was originally seen as a financial adjustment designed to curb the dizzying spiral of land and stock prices has triggered a substantial reduction of the economy's paper wealth, profoundly affecting consumer confidence, business investment, and the general economic outlook.

Consumer spending and capital investment were the two factors most influencing the direction of the business cycle during the bubble period. Annual GNP growth averaged 5.1 per cent between 1986 and 1989; of that, consumer spending accounted for an estimated 2.5 points and capital spending for 2.3 points.[31] Both of these influences are undergoing significant transformations in the post-bubble era, as explained below.

Consumer Spending

The rise in net financial assets, mainly in stock prices, during the bubble period of the late 1980s is estimated by the Bank of Japan to have added one percentage point on average to growth in consumer spending each year from 1987 to 1990.[32] The comparable margin of growth attributable to this wealth effect over the period from 1980 to 1986 averaged only 0.6 per cent, thus highlighting the sharply strengthened effect of soaring stock prices on consumer spending in the second half of the 1980s.

Consumer confidence has been deeply shaken by the sudden decrease of Japan's financial wealth and the prospect of a long-term economic slowdown. Consumers have cut back on spending, especially on durable goods, and have become much more conscientious in their spending habits. Department store sales have dropped drastically as consumers switch to discount chain stores, where sales growth has accelerated since 1991.[33] Domestic vehicle sales fell each year from 1990 to 1994, and still remain well below pre-bubble levels.[34] Even without massive lay-offs, there will be a further decline in take-home pay for employees as Japanese companies continue to slash costs as overtime accounts for about 10 per cent of the average pay packet and bonuses for up to 30 per cent.

Paradoxically, the shift in consumption patterns and the demand for greater value added may actually enhance the ability of some foreign firms to sell in Japan as Japanese consumers begin to shop more carefully and to compare the relative costs of imported and domestically produced products. A number of foreign imports have already benefited from this trend.

Capital Investment

The most far-reaching transformation resulting from the post-bubble recession in Japan is the decline in Japanese business investment. This is a natural consequence not of the speculative boom in the markets for equity and property

Figure 6.7: Return on Capital in the Private Sector

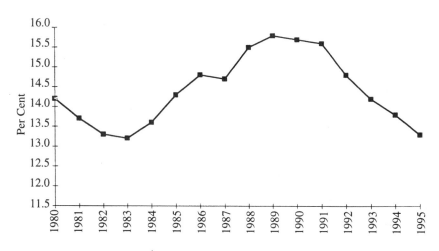

Source: OECD, *Perspective Économique de l'OECD.*

per se, but of the massive binge of capital spending driven by the availability of cheap finance.

It is estimated that capital investment accounted for over two-thirds of Japan's GNP growth between late 1986 and early 1991.[35] The difficulty in maintaining such a high level of domestic investment is clear from Japan's deteriorating ratio of capital to output (Figure 6.7): it takes more and more investment to deliver a given increase in output.

This fact has its counterpart in Japan's declining long-term growth rate (Figure 6.8). The growth trend of real GDP in the decade before the 1973–74 oil shock was nearly 9 per cent a year; since 1993 the rate has been less than 1 per cent, and it is likely to remain under 2 per cent for the foreseeable future.

Experience in Europe and America suggests that a ratio of capital spending to GNP of about 12 to 15 per cent is typical for a mature economy.[36] Japan's ratio peaked at 22 per cent in 1991. Since then major companies such as Toyota and Nissan have announced steep reductions in investment, and further severe cuts seem inevitable, with consequences for both employment and consumer confidence. Toshiba, for example, has ranked more than 100 of its business units by profitability and targeted the bottom one-third for contraction or closure.[37] Similarly, mammoth Nippon Telegraph & Telephone Company, Japan's largest company, has announced plans to shrink its payroll by more than 10 per cent – possibly 30,000 people – over three years. Gone too will be many of the com-

Figure 6.8: Nominal GDP Growth Rate by Country

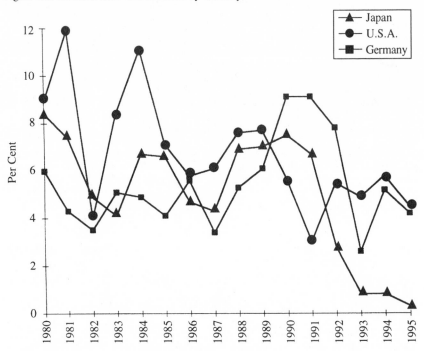

Source: OECD, *Perspective Économique de l'OECD*.

pany's 1,300 sales outlets.[38] Some forecasters expect capital spending to fall by almost half before this adjustment is complete, particularly as cuts spread into the service sectors.

Restructure and Renewal

So far the pain of Japan's recession has been taken mostly in reduced overtime and bonus payments for workers rather than in outright firings. Unemployment, only 2 per cent at the height of the bubble, remains officially under 3.5 per cent, even after six years of recession.[39] But after several consecutive years of declining profits, many Japanese companies now realize that they went too far in their excesses of the late 1980s. Many will have to restructure, jettisoning some of the luxuries of the past several years and cutting costs to the bone, transforming their businesses to put profits ahead of market share.

    The actions of Japan's financial authorities in bursting the bubble clearly had

Figure 6.9: Trade Account Trends by Country

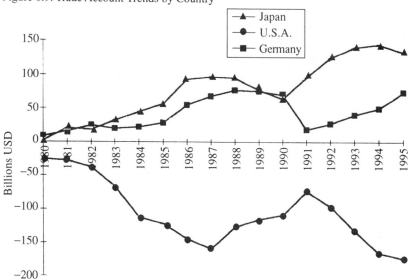

Source: OECD, *Perspective Économique de l'OECD*.

sociopolitical as well as purely economic aims. To many, it had been clear for some time that the bubble breached the social contract of Japanese society, threatened bureaucratic legitimacy, and tore at the heart of the Japanese ethos of frugality, perseverance, and eventual reward. The post-bubble adjustments will, essentially, mark a return to these time-honoured virtues – ultimately making Japanese firms leaner and meaner competitors than ever before.

External Consequences of the Recession

Impact on Trade Flows

One likely effect of the post-bubble recession is a continuation or even widening of Japan's external trade surplus, at least in the short term (Figure 6.9). Pressures for growing surpluses exist on both sides of the trade equation. With consumer spending down in Japan (see above), domestic demand for imports will remain depressed until economic prosperity returns.

This sharply lower domestic demand comes at a time of growing excess capacity in Japanese industry. It is estimated that only 65 per cent of Japan's manufacturing capacity is currently being utilized.[40] Even more significantly, many Japanese manufacturing firms now have much higher break-even points than before as a consequence of the spate of investments in robotics and other automated production processes during the bubble period. This combination of low domestic demand, growing excess capacity, and high break-even points is forcing Japanese companies to push ever harder for exports, seeking bigger market shares in those countries experiencing more prosperous economic conditions. Neighbouring Asian countries are growing at a tremendous rate and are hungry for Japanese goods and technology. North America also offers new opportunities as it continues its sustained economic growth. As in the past, Japan is attempting to export its way out of its current economic slump, forcing its current account surpluses ever wider.

Upward movements in the value of the yen will likely do little to reverse the widening trade imbalance. Japanese trade patterns have never been very responsive to changes in exchange rates. Despite textbook theory, relative prices in Japan have tended to move towards actual exchange rates rather than vice versa. After the yen soared in the 1980s, for example, Japanese companies were quick to cut costs and to invest in productivity-enhancing machinery, maintaining their competitiveness. One implication of this is that exchange rate changes alone will do relatively little to prune Japan's trade surplus. History suggests that changes in relative domestic demand have a bigger influence on trade balances than do currency movements.[41] So unless Japan's domestic demand grows faster than that of its trading partners – unlikely in the short run, given the severity of the current economic slowdown – Japan's current account surplus is not likely to shrink significantly in the foreseeable future.

Impact on Capital Flows

The post-bubble adjustments in Japan are likely to have a more immediate impact on Japan's long-term capital movements than on its trade flows. Figure 6.10 illustrates both the stimulating effect of Japan's financial bubble on Japanese foreign investment flows, and also the equally dramatic constraining effect of the post-bubble transformations. During the late 1980s, Japan was by far the world's largest foreign investor, exporting on average more than $100 billion a year, to become the world's largest holder of foreign assets (Figure 6.11). Since land and stock prices began to crash in 1991, however, the rate of new investments abroad has slowed, although there is recent evidence of a pick-up. Some Japanese firms have even liquidated investments made abroad (especially in the United States and Europe) during the bubble, both because their returns were low and because funds were critically needed at home and in other Asian markets.

Figure 6.10: Japanese Capital Outflows

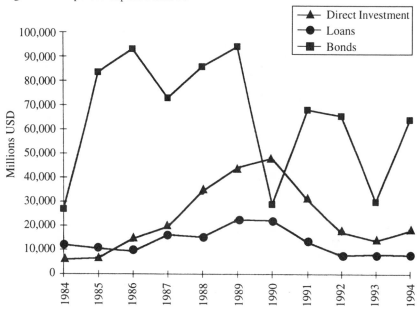

Source: OECD, *Perspective Économique de l'OECD.*

Does the end of the bubble mark the end of Japan's days as a major supplier of capital to the world, or will Japan revert back to its earlier role as a sustained capital exporter once the post-bubble adjustments have worked themselves out? The answer depends partly on the time frame involved.

In the short term, Japan's sustained trade surpluses (discussed above) will continue to generate additional liquidity for Japan, and will therefore contribute to continued capital overabundance there. This ongoing liquidity generation, combined with the low return on domestic investment capital in Japan (see above), suggests that Japan will continue at least for the next few years to be a net exporter of long-term capital, although certainly at a lower overall magnitude than in the bubble era.

Understanding and forecasting Japan's external capital flow position beyond the immediate post-bubble recessionary adjustment period requires consideration of more fundamental underlying economic and demographic conditions shaping the longer term. The following discussion considers both the domestic *supply* of funds and the domestic *demand* for funds in Japan, which together will shape Japan's external capital flows over the longer term.

Figure 6.11: Foreign Assets Held by Selected OECD Countries

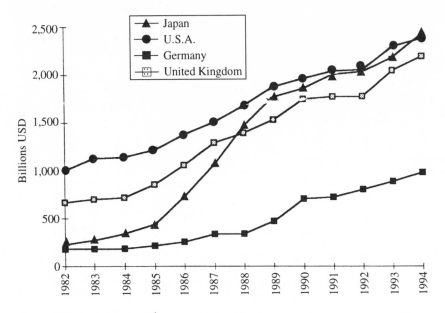

Source: OECD, *Perspective Économique de l'OECD.*

The Domestic Supply of Funds

In Japan, as elsewhere, the domestic supply of capital (i.e., the aggregate domestic demand for investment assets) is essentially a function of household savings. Although household savings rates have been declining in Japan for some time, the Japanese continue to save a higher proportion of their incomes than people of any other industrialized country (Figure 6.12). This high savings rate has been a significant factor in enabling Japanese companies to invest heavily in their manufacturing capabilities by tapping a large pool of cheap capital.

Japan's high savings rate is explained at least in part by demographic factors unique to Japan. Japan currently has the highest percentage of its population (approximately 65 per cent) in the workforce of any major country.[42] Facing the prospect of retirement in a country notorious for low pensions, older Japanese consume a relatively small portion of their disposable income, choosing instead to put away savings towards their retirement.

This savings pattern will change dramatically, however, due to the rapid aging of Japan's population. According to demographic forecasts, by the year

Figure 6.12: Trends in Household Savings Ratio by Selected Country

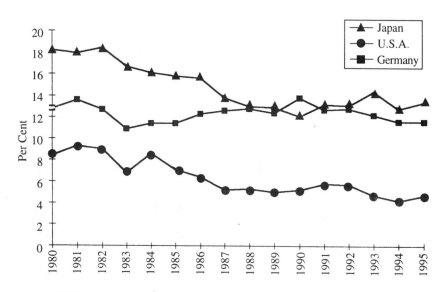

Source: OECD, *Perspective Économique de l'OECD.*

2020 Japan will have reversed its position, having the highest proportion of elderly people in its population (approximately 25 per cent) of any Organization for Economic Cooperation and Development (OECD) country (Figure 6.13). Japanese will then become aggregate *dissavers* as they draw upon their savings to support their retirement. At some point, forecast around the year 2010, Japan will likely become a net *importer* of capital as retirees begin liquidating investment assets to fund their current consumption. Until such time, however, savings levels in Japan, albeit drifting downward, will remain among the world's highest.

The Domestic Demand for Funds

This sustained *supply* of domestic funds generated by household savings through the medium term must be compared with the likely *demand* for investment funds – which is, in turn, a combined function of the need for investment funds by the private business sector, and of the borrowing needs of governments.

As discussed earlier, productivity gains in Japan's business sector have

Figure 6.13: Elderly Population Ratio by Selected Country

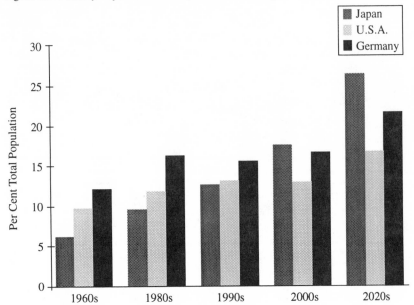

Source: *Japan Economic Almanac, The Nikkei Weekly.*

become much more difficult to maintain through new investments. As a consequence, the domestic capital investment needs of Japanese companies have
dropped dramatically and will likely remain low well beyond the current recessionary period. Thus, the aggregate domestic demand for investment capital by
Japan's private sector will probably remain well below recent levels for many
years into the future.

Trends in the borrowing needs of Japan's public sector in the decades ahead
are more difficult to predict. The Japanese government has been spending mas-
sively in an attempt to jump-start the economy out of its current recession.[43]
The cumulative effect of the various government stimulus packages has caused
Japan's budget deficits to rise steadily since 1992.[44]

On the other hand, the Japanese have traditionally held public indebtedness
to the lowest levels of any industrialized country (Figure 6.14). Even the widely
proclaimed $140 billion package of tax cuts and other stimulative measures
announced in early 1994 are limited to one year and will eventually be offset by
increases in other forms of taxation.[45] While the demands of an aging popula-

Figure 6.14: Government Net Debt as a Proportion of GDP by Selected Country

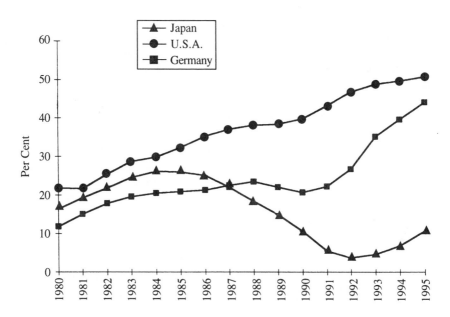

Source: OECD, *Perspective Économique de l'OECD.*

tion will unquestionably place a growing financial burden on government, the tradition of governmental frugality seems deep-seated in Japan, and there is little reason to doubt that once the Japanese economy has pulled out of its current recession governmental spending and indebtedness will drop back towards their traditionally low levels. Thus, the aggregate demand for funds by the public sector in Japan is also likely to remain moderate in the future.

Conclusion

For the medium term, at least, the declining investment needs of both business and government in Japan will reduce the aggregate domestic demand for investable funds. This anticipated decline in the domestic demand for funds should roughly offset the gradual drop in personal savings caused by the aging of the Japanese population. Consequently, new domestic savings in Japan and new domestic investment in Japan are likely to diminish roughly in proportion through the next decade.[46] After that, however, the supply of funds from domestic savings will begin to decline much more rapidly due to the net dissaving of elderly Japanese. Thus at some point, probably soon after the turn of the century, Japan is likely to reverse its present position, becoming a net capital *importer.* This new surplus (or net import) position on Japan's capital account must, of course, be offset by a corresponding but opposite net *deficit* position on the *current* account, meaning that Japan will of necessity become a net importer of goods and services at some point in the not too distant future.

The Changing Character of External Investment Flows

Although Japan should remain a net overseas investor for at least another decade, significant changes are likely to occur in the nature, the destination, and the strategic motives of those external investment flows. These changes have significant implications for the United States, Canada, and other traditional recipients of Japanese investments.

Form of Investments

The nature of Japanese overseas investment activity will be altered significantly by the collapse of the bubble. First, there will likely be a shift away from *portfolio* investment towards proportionately more *direct* overseas investment, for several reasons. A great deal of the portfolio investment of the bubble era was made for essentially passive motives: to park the excess cash that so many Japanese companies had at that time in real estate or securities. Portfolio investments will continue to be made for real business purposes, but the 'excess-liquidity' motivation will diminish. Moreover, the continuing trend towards global convergence of interest rates will further reduce the incentive to invest abroad to take advantage of interest rate differentials.

On the other hand, the imperatives for still more *direct* investments abroad by Japanese companies will remain strong. Unless Japan makes major changes in its immigration laws, which seems unlikely, the cost of labour in Japan will grow even more acute, increasing pressure on Japanese firms to shift even more production offshore. The growing threat of trade restrictions against Japanese imports in foreign countries will also keep pressure on Japanese firms to replace exports with direct investments abroad, as will any future appreciation in the value of the yen.

It is significant that despite all of their recent overseas direct investments, Japanese companies presently produce and sell abroad an amount approximately equivalent to less than 8 per cent of Japanese GNP.[47] In contrast, German and American companies produce and sell abroad the equivalent of about

Figure 6.15: Overseas Production Ratios by Selected Country

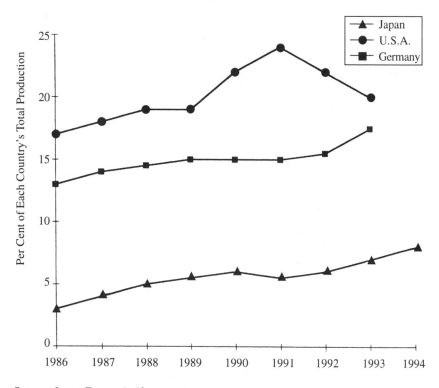

Source: *Japan Economic Almanac.*

17.5 per cent and 20 per cent, respectively, of their home country GNPs (Figure 6.15). There is every reason to expect that Japan's investment profile will continue to move towards closer convergence with those of other industrialized countries, with significant further expansion of overseas production via direct investments abroad.

Recent announcements by several of Japan's largest firms confirm this trend towards greater offshore production. Japan's car makers, for example, are stepping up production abroad. The number of cars made abroad by Toyota rose 17 per cent in 1993 from the year before, while its production in Japan fell by 9 per cent.[48] Each month the company aims to sell in Japan 1,800 cars made at its plant in Kentucky. All in all, Japan's car exports fell by 15.9 per cent in dollar terms in the year to November 1993, while car imports from America shot

Figure 6.16: Japanese Direct Investment Abroad, by Destination

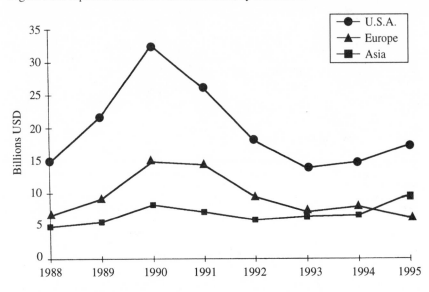

Source: The Economist Intelligence Unit, *Japan Profile*, 1995 and 1997.

up by 70.8 per cent. The situation is similar in electronics. Pioneer, part of the Matsushita group, plans to increase its overseas output from the current 30 per cent of the total to 50 per cent in 1996; while Kenwood, a rival, aims for a boost from 40 per cent to 60 per cent.[49]

Destination of Investments

The *geographic destination* of Japanese overseas investment flows will also shift markedly in the years ahead: much less will flow to North America and Europe, and much more to other Asian countries. This shifting emphasis is a function both of the relatively poor performance of recent Japanese investments elsewhere, and of the enormously greater market growth potential seen in Asia.

Japanese investment in Asia has until recently been motivated mainly by the search for lower labour costs. But now Japanese are eyeing other Asian countries as the world's most dynamic growth markets. While the bulk of Japanese investments in recent years has flowed to the United States and Europe (Figure 6.16), returns on those investments have generally been low. Average pre-tax profits of Japanese manufacturing investments in North America were actually

Figure 6.17: GDP Growth Rate Forecasts by Selected Country

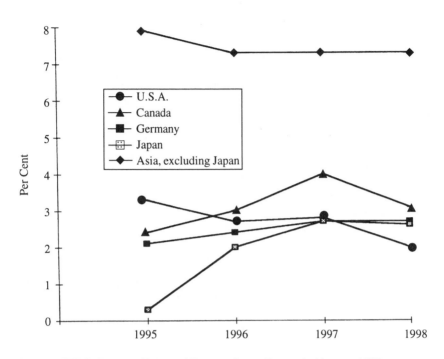

Source: JETRO, *Business Facts and Figures*; *Japan Economic Almanac 1997*;
The Nikkei Weekly; *The Economist*, 31 May.

negative in the early 1990s and only moderately profitable in Europe, while
investments in Asia yielded significantly higher returns.

These differences may well be magnified in the years ahead. While GNP
growth forecasts for North America and Europe range from 2 to 4 per cent,
many Asian countries are experiencing sustained growth rates of 7 per cent or
more (Figure 6.17). Combined with Asia's massive population of over three billion, it is not surprising that both Japanese trade and Japanese investment will
be increasingly drawn towards that region.

Strategic Focus of Investment Decisions

Significant changes are occurring also in the *strategic motives* of Japanese
direct investments as a consequence of the post-bubble adjustments. In the

richer bubble years, Japanese firms could afford the luxury of diversifying their overseas investments partially in response to political and public-opinion considerations (for example, diversifying their North American investments between the United States and Canada). In the leaner, tighter years of the post-bubble era, they will be forced to be much more selective in their investment decisions both at home and abroad, putting greater emphasis than before on *maximizing return on equity* rather than on expanding market share or satisfying political demands. Cost reduction and effective market penetration will become the paramount considerations in future investment location decisions.

Implications for the United States and Canada

The transformations sweeping Japanese finance in the wake of the bubble's collapse have significant consequences for the United States and Canada, both directly as major recipients of Japanese investment flows, and more broadly in their business and economic relations with Japan.

Adverse Consequences

Some of the broad trends in the magnitude and nature of Japanese long-term capital flows outlined above are likely to affect the United States and Canada adversely. While Japan will continue to be a net exporter of long-term capital for another decade or two, the overall magnitude of those capital exports will almost certainly be smaller than in the heady days of the bubble. And even within that reduced global aggregate, a smaller portion than in the past is likely to flow to North America as Japanese firms continue redirecting their priorities towards Asia. In a global context, then, the prospects for increasing or even sustaining the levels of Japanese capital flows to the United States and Canada seem remote – perhaps even more so with Mexico now competing intensely as a destination for Japanese investment in the North American Free Trade area.

The United States and Canada may also be influenced negatively by the changing *nature* of Japan's overseas investment flows. The bulk of Japan's investment flows to the United States, and particularly to Canada, has taken the form of *portfolio* investment rather than direct investment. The discussion above suggests that Japanese capital outflows in the post-bubble era will likely shift away from portfolio investment towards proportionately more *direct* investment. The vast amounts of liquidity that typified the bubble era – much of which was parked abroad in real estate and portfolio investments in the United States and Canada – are unlikely to recur. At the same time, converging interest rates among the world's major financial markets are further reducing the incentive for international portfolio investment for other than portfolio diversification objectives.

The decline of Japanese portfolio investment will be felt most severely in Canada, which once saw 25 per cent of its government bonds in the hands of Japanese investors. The largest institutional investors in Canada have traditionally been Japanese life insurance companies, which are attracted to Canadian bonds in part because they are unlisted and therefore need not be 'marked to market' periodically to reflect changes in their current market values. As Japanese life insurers were precluded until recently from paying dividends from capital gains earnings, they focused mainly on current yields, which tend to be high in Canada, in their investment decisions. A recent rule change permits them for the first time to pay dividends from capital gains as well as from current earnings.[50] It may be more difficult than before for Canada to sustain high levels of portfolio investment from Japanese institutions as their objectives broaden to include capital gains.

The aggregate outlook for Japanese *direct* investments in the United States and Canada is also clouded by the post-bubble transformations in Japanese finance. While the imperative for more direct investment abroad by Japanese firms will continue to grow as costs increase in Japan, those new investments that are made will be targeted much more carefully than before, with significantly greater emphasis placed on bottom-line profit. It has been the hope of many Canadians that the Canada–U.S. Free Trade Agreement and, even more so, the North American Free Trade Agreement, would provide a climate in which Japanese firms choose to invest in Canada as a production site for servicing the entire North American market.[51] In fact, however, the opposite seems to be occurring: increasingly selective in their plant location decisions, Japanese firms looking at possible investment sites in North America will seek increasingly to place their plants either where the factor costs are lowest (most likely Mexico), or where the market is largest (most likely the United States). In most cases, Canada does not qualify on either dimension.[52]

The tendency of Japanese firms to shy away from Canada as a production base for North America will remain strong as long as they continue to perceive the possibility of Japanese subsidiaries in Canada being denied access to the U.S. market, whether because of American protectionism (as in the Honda Canada controversy) or because of other cross-border trade impediments (such as Canadian port strikes). As long as doubt remains about whether Japanese subsidiaries in Canada will in fact have unimpeded access to the United States, many Japanese firms will hedge their bets by investing on the American side of the fence. As perhaps a significant indicator of this trend, Honda Motor Co. has announced plans to increase North American production by 18.4 per cent in 1994, but its Canadian plant will increase output by only 2.4 per cent. A Honda spokesperson said, 'We will produce cars at places where we can sell.'[53]

New Opportunities and New Challenges

At the same time, the post-bubble transformations in Japan may offer new opportunities to alert North American business leaders. One of the broadest consequences of the bubble's collapse and the resulting pressures for more deregulation will be a gradual transfer of power from the hands of entrenched bureaucrats to those of elected politicians and to market forces, a trend already under way.[54] Ultimately, this will lead to further easing of barriers to the import of foreign goods and services in response to consumer demands. This opening will offer new export opportunities in the Japanese market for a variety of North American firms, particularly in areas such as building products, leisure and recreational products, and processed foods.[55]

New opportunities may open in Japan also for North American firms in service industries. The post-bubble pressures to accelerate the pace of financial deregulation in Japan (see above) mean that foreign-based banks and securities companies will be able to offer a broader range of financial products and services in Japan, and to operate in a much less collusive competitive arena than in the past.[56] New market opportunities may open also for North American engineering and construction firms, which will be able in the future to bid more easily on major construction projects in Japan.[57]

The financial collapse and economic belt-tightening in Japan is also causing major shifts in consumer purchasing habits of potential significance to North American businesses. In the wake of the post-bubble decline in real wages and lower job security, Japanese consumers are developing much more value-added consciousness in their purchases. They are increasingly balking at paying inflated prices to buy from high-cost domestic Japanese producers.[58] This can mean all sorts of new opportunities for exports to Japan for alert American and Canadian consumer products producers able to offer good value in their products. Another significant post-bubble trend is the weakening of traditional *keiretsu* ties among Japanese companies. Japanese companies that felt obligated in the past to purchase inputs from related companies, even at higher cost, are increasingly seeking the best deals as cost considerations loom larger in their purchasing decisions. North American capital goods manufacturers offering quality goods at competitive prices may discover new market opportunities that were previously precluded by the tight *keiretsu* ties.

The post-bubble crash in the price of financial assets in Japan offers a unique window of opportunity for American and Canadian firms seeking to establish a greater direct presence in Japan. North American companies seeking to build or expand plants in Japan or to enter into partnerships with Japanese firms can now acquire shares of Japanese firms at a fraction of their former cost.[59] Moreover, property values, traditionally among the most formidable obstacles to foreign firms seeking a direct presence in Japan, have sunk to their lowest levels in years. Even the ability of non-Japanese firms to hire competent Japanese personnel in Japan may be facilitated by the growing abundance of Japanese managers laid off or given early retirement by Japanese companies.

Although the overall magnitude of Japanese investments in the United States, and even more so in Canada, is likely to diminish as a consequence of the post-bubble financial adjustments in Japan, the *quality* of those investments that do flow there may actually be enhanced. Japanese firms face intense pressure to improve their profit performance in the post-bubble era, leading many of them to shift production offshore in search of lower production costs. In areas where Americans or Canadians have inherent cost advantages, Japanese firms may seek to lower costs by upgrading their local processing. A prime example is in Canada's resource-related sectors, where Japanese firms seem likely to increase domestic value added, mainly through joint ventures or other collaborative arrangements with Canadian firms. This may lead not only to new inflows of Japanese capital, but also to a significantly greater transfer of valuable technology and management skills.[60]

Conclusions

It is not within the scope of this analysis to recommend how the United States and Canada should seek to attract additional Japanese investment. This has been done extensively elsewhere.[61] This analysis has, however, pointed to major transformations taking place in Japan's financial and business systems that may significantly affect the nature and patterns of Japanese business activity in North America.

On the one hand, Americans and Canadians face the prospect of a significant decline in the overall magnitude of Japanese investment flows, to which they must adjust. On the other hand, the changes occurring in Japan offer a host of potential new business opportunities for North American firms: new possibilities for exports of American and Canadian goods and services to the Japanese market; easier entry for American and Canadian companies seeking more direct involvement in Japan; and possibly stronger and deeper involvement of Japanese firms in certain sectors of the U.S. and Canadian economies.

One thing is certain: Japan will never be the same again. Nor will its relationships with the United States and Canada. The nature of Japan's financial involvement with North America is changing inexorably. Americans and Canadians can no longer rely, as they have before, on Japan as a bottomless money machine. For alert American and Canadian companies whose international horizons extend beyond North America, however, the post-bubble transformations sweeping Japan offer both new challenges and significant new potential opportunities.

NOTES

1 The author acknowledges with gratitude the financial support of Pacific 2000 and of the Canada–Japan Trade Council, as well as the generous cooperation of many business executives, governmental officials, and others on both sides of the Pacific. Special thanks are due to Mr Pascal Beaudoin for his outstanding research assistance.
2 Laliberté, 'Foreign Investment in the Canadian,' 3.
3 Wood, *The Bubble Economy*, 8.
4 Ibid., 68.
5 Zielinski and Holloway, *Unequal Equities*, 145.
6 Japan, Ministry of Finance, *The Mechanism and Economic Effects*, 21.
7 Wood, *The Bubble Economy*, 68.
8 World Link, 50; Japan, Ministry of Finance, *The Mechanism and Economic Effects*, 86.
9 *The Economist*, 6 March 1993.
10 Japan, Ministry of Finance, *The Mechanism and Economic Effects*, 21.
11 Zielinski and Holloway, *Unequal Equities*, 150.
12 Japan, Ministry of Finance, *The Mechanism and Economic Effects*, 22.
13 'A Wobbly Time for Japan's Workers,' 31; Japan, Ministry of Finance, *The Mechanism and Economic Effects*, 22.
14 *Fortune*, 18 May 1992.
15 'A Japanese Puzzle,' 74.
16 Japan, Ministry of Finance, *The Mechanism and Economic Effects*, 15.
17 Ibid., 17.
18 Shale, 'The MOF's Get-Fit Class,' 32–36.
19 Wright, 'Hidden Linkages.'
20 Constand, Freitas, and Sullivan, 'Factors Affecting Price-Earnings,' 68–79.
21 Japan, *EPA White Paper, 1989*.
22 Shale, 'The MOF's Get-Fit Class,' 32.
23 Based on information provided by the Bank of Japan.
24 Jonathan Friedland, 'Bust Bankers,' 57–58.
25 *The Economist*, 29 May 1993, 73.

26 Japan, Ministry of Finance, *The Mechanism and Economic Effects*, 57.
27 Ibid., 57.
28 Shale, 'The MOF's Get-Fit Class,' 36.
29 Wright, 'A Big Bang for Japan?' 1–3.
30 Japan, Ministry of Finance, *The Mechanism and Economic Effects*, 6.
31 Ibid., 32.
32 Ibid., 35.
33 *Japan Economic Almanac: 1997*, 128.
34 Ibid., 91.
35 *The Economist*, 29 May 1993, 74.
36 Ibid., 74.
37 *Nikkei Weekly*, 14 June 1993, 8.
38 Bussey, Chandler, and Williams, 'Japanese Recession Prompts Corporations,' 1f.
39 *Japan Economic Almanac: 1997*, 39.
40 'Why America's Levers Will Not Shift Leveraged Japan,' 73.
41 Sanwa Bank, 'The Effects of Increased Domestic Demand,' 3.
42 Sanwa Bank, 'Responding to Risk,' 3.
43 Canada–Japan Trade Council, 'Economic Stimulus,' 5.
44 *The Economist*, 5 February 1994, 74.
45 Blustein, 'Japan Approves Tax-Cut Package,' A11.
46 Horioka, 'Future Trends in Japan's Saving Rate,' 307–30.
47 World Link, May–June 1992.
48 *The Economist*, 18 December 1993, 31.
49 Ibid.
50 *Financial Times*, 26 March 1990.
51 Blank and Fry, 'The Impact of NAFTA on Japan'; Mathieson, 'Pan Pacific Regionalism'; Niosi, 'The Place of Canada'; Westney, 'Japanese Investments.'
52 Wright, 'The Unrealistic Hopes.'
53 *The Globe and Mail*, 19 January 1994.
54 'Is Japan Unreformable?' 18.
55 Canada, Department of Foreign Affairs and International Trade, *Canada's Action Plan*.
56 Wright, 'A Big Bang for Japan?'; Wright, 'Head for the Rising Sun'; Japan Economic Institute, *Japanese Financial Market Reform*.
57 *The Globe and Mail*, 19 January 1994, B2.
58 'The Good News from Japan,' 35.
59 'A Crack in the Wall,' 88; Bussey, Chandler, and Williams, 'Japanese Recession Prompts Corporations,' A8.
60 *Japan Times*, 1 July 1993.
61 Wright, *Japanese Business in Canada*.

7

Business Negotiations: Comparing the U.S.–Japan and Canada–Japan Experiences

ROSALIE TUNG

The growing interdependence of the economies of the North Pacific Triangle has contributed to the surge in collaborative agreements between economic entities from the United States, Japan, and Canada. Collaborative agreements have been made, for example, in licensing, joint ventures, co-production, joint research and development, and co-marketing. The successful negotiation of the terms and conditions for their establishment is a necessary requisite to the formation of such agreements. Even after the successful formation of such collaborative agreements, there is a continuing need for the partners to negotiate on issues and conflicts that may arise over the life of the cooperative effort. Moreover, in the event of the dissolution of the arrangement, the parties have to negotiate the terms of dissolution, including how and what assets and properties will be distributed among the partners. In short, negotiations are pivotal to the formation, continuation, and/or dissolution of a cooperative agreement. One must, therefore, examine the dynamics and processes associated with business negotiations between entities from these three countries.

A Conceptual Paradigm of Cross-National Business Negotiations

In 1988 I presented a conceptual paradigm of international business negotiations that incorporates five dimensions: contextual environment, negotiation context, negotiator characteristics, strategy selection and process/progress, and negotiation outcomes.[1] (See Figure 7.1.)

Contextual Environment

Following Fayerweather and Kapoor, the contextual environment can be viewed under four general categories: political, economic, institutional–legal, and cultural.[2]

Figure 7.1: Conceptual Paradigm of International Business Negotiations

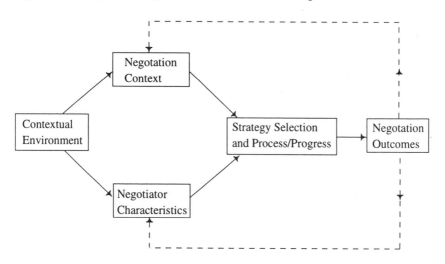

Political Environment
Any cooperative agreement between economic entities from two nations must be examined within the context of the political relations that prevail between the countries. Since the early 1950s, the United States, Japan, and Canada have been political allies in security.

Economic Environment
Political and economic considerations are often inextricably intertwined; hence, the distinctions between the political and economic environments may often be fuzzy. Several observations with regard to U.S.–Canada–Japan economic relationships merit attention.

Between 1989 and 1993, almost 44 per cent of Japan's cumulative outward foreign direct investment (FDI) was destined for North America (41.9 per cent to the United States and 1.85 per cent to Canada). Japanese FDI in Canada is primarily concentrated in natural resources and automotive production, while Japanese FDI in the United States is more diversified. For the same five-year period, slightly over 45 per cent of cumulative FDI in Japan originated from North America (40.67 per cent from the United States and 4.4 per cent from Canada).[3]

Comparatively speaking, while Canada's share of outward and inward FDI to and from Japan is small, Canada does view Japan as an important trading partner. By the end of 1991, almost 28 per cent of Canada's outward FDI in the Asia-Pacific region was located in Japan. Unlike the United States, which is very concerned about Japanese FDI, and hence ownership in 'strategic' industries, Canada is more receptive in most sectors.[4] Despite the fact that Canada's population and economy are roughly one-tenth the size of the United States, at present Canada receives only 4 per cent of Japanese FDI destined for North America. There appears to be plenty of room for improvement. In fact, the Canadian government has stated that it values the economic contribution of foreign-owned companies and will not subject them to the 'political scrutiny focused on some Japanese affiliates in the United States.'[5]

The United States and Canada are each other's largest trading partner. The enactment of the Canada–U.S. Free Trade Agreement (FTA), and then the North American Free Trade Agreement (NAFTA), translates into even closer economic linkages between the two countries.

Among the G-7 countries, the economic characteristics of Canada and Japan are perhaps the most different. Canada maintains the largest export balance in foodstuffs and raw materials, while Japan is largely dependent on imports in these categories.[6] This diametrically opposite economic profile is reflected in the bilateral trade composition between the two countries. The bulk of Canadian exports to Japan are in foodstuffs, natural resources; and raw materials, while Canada imports primarily manufactured products from Japan. The Canadian government recognizes the problems associated with relying too much on exports of raw materials to Japan. In 1991, for example, due in large part to slumping prices of lumber and other building materials, Canadian exports to Japan fell by 11.5 per cent. In May 1993, the Department of Foreign Affairs and International Trade launched an 'Action Plan for Japan' to serve as a blueprint for directing future bilateral trade between the two countries. This plan, updated in January 1994, identified seven sectors in which Canada seeks to increase sales to Japan: building products, fish products, processed food products, auto parts, aerospace industries, tourism, and information technologies.[7] The latter three are new areas targeted for export growth to Japan.

Beginning in the early 1980s, trade tensions between the United States and Japan have taken on political overtones. For example, during the debate in the U.S. Congress over the passage of NAFTA, President Clinton warned that defeat of the measure would result in the Japanese taking advantage of the situation by moving quickly to set up operations in Mexico, thus gaining an edge over U.S. companies. In Canada, in contrast, the debate over NAFTA focused primarily on competition from the United States.

Canada usually plays the role of junior partner in trilateral relationships, and thus its interests may be shortchanged. While Canada has extended 'national treatment' to foreign investors in most sectors, Japanese subsidiaries in Canada fear that they may be singled out as 'Japanese,' not 'Canadian,' in U.S.–Japan trade disputes. This fear was fuelled by the March 1992 U.S. Customs ruling that Honda Civic hatchbacks, produced in Honda's Ontario plant and exported to the United States between January 1989 and March 1990, did not meet the domestic content requirements to qualify for duty-free cross-border trade under the terms of the FTA and, therefore, faced potential fines of $16.5 million. While that dispute was ultimately resolved, Japanese companies have become more convinced that in order to meet U.S. domestic content requirements they must produce in the United States. Another development that has exacerbated this situation is the priority market access negotiations between the United States and Japan, in which the Clinton Administration has called for qualitative and quantitative indicators to assess the inroads made by foreign firms in the Japanese market. Many Canadians believe that 'foreign' means 'United States.' Hence the Canadian government is afraid that new U.S. inroads into the Japanese market will come at the expense of Canadian exports, since the latter has less bargaining clout than the United States.[8]

Institutional–Legal Environment

The institutional–legal environment influences the progress and outcome of business negotiations in three primary ways.

It provides legislation (such as investment, labour–management and tax laws) that affects the nature and form of collaborative agreements. In principle, except for 'strategic' industries, the three countries are relatively open to one another as far as trade and investment are concerned. As noted above, however, there is continuing friction about accessibility to the Japanese market.

The institutional–legal environment influences the partner's attitude towards law and litigation. In the United States and Canada, for instance, contracts are viewed in legalistic terms whereas in Japan, contracts are viewed more in the context of the social relationship that exists between the parties. Similarly, from the Japanese perspective, control (which is of paramount concern to most U.S. enterprises) is viewed in the context of cooperation.[9] These differences in attitude towards law imply that a foreign firm may have to rely upon alternative methods of conflict resolution with Japanese partners.

The institutional–legal environment captures the diversity of institutional settings across countries. In Japan, for example, the relationship between business and government is an intimate one. According to Ballon, 'Japanese social dynamics operate on the basis of interdependence. Whereas Western interaction tends to be of the type, $1 + 1 = 2$, in Japan the formula would be $1 \times 1 = 1$. Thus, in Japan the reality of government and business is not that of two entities to be somehow added up but rather the reality of one coin with two faces. In other words, two distinct but interdependent institutions, namely the government and business, form one reality: Japan.'[10] Foreign firms that seek to negotiate with Japanese entities have to understand this peculiar aspect of the institutional environment in Japan and its implications in terms of whom to include in the negotiation team, what is possible and probable, and what strategies to pursue in the course of the negotiations.

Cultural Environment

Culture can affect negotiations in three ways.

It affects how people process and interpret information. In Japan, for example, there are two types of logic: linear (akin to Aristotelian logic) and indirection. Indirection can be illustrated by the Japanese saying 'When the wind blows, it is good for the makers of wooden tubs.' The logic runs something like this: When it is windy, people become sad. To overcome their melancholy, they play a stringed instrument (shamisen), made of catgut. To make the shamisen, people kill cats, which results in a depletion of the feline population, thus leading to a proliferation in mice. The mice gnaw at the wooden tubs that store grain, damaging them and ultimately resulting in an increased demand for wooden tubs. While the logic may seem convoluted and incomprehensible from the Western perspective, it highlights two significant points: first, the Japanese preoccupation with long-term implications of actions; and second, their ability to perceive relationships between apparently unrelated systems, the wind blowing and the demand for wooden tubs.[11] Differences in logical systems explain how two people from different cultures can view the same situation, an objective reality, and come up with completely different interpretations of what has occurred.

Culture influences people's perception of what is reasonable, right, and acceptable, thus affecting the choice of strategies to be pursued in the negotiation process and the resolution of conflicts. In North America, for example, the concept of 'right' is fundamental and paramount to most types of relationships. Each party insists upon its rights – the right to fire, the right to strike, and the right to higher wages, for example. In Japan, in contrast, the notion of 'right' is a foreign one. When Japan tried to adopt a modern constitution after 1868, it had a difficult time incorporating the term 'right' into the text. Until then, all relationships had been defined in terms of duties and responsibilities. Consequently, despite the incorporation of the term 'right' into the constitution, relationships between two or more entities in the country continued to operate on the traditional basis of mutual obligations. Thus, management has the obligation to take care of labour, while labour has the duty to work hard to fulfil organizational goals.[12]

Culture results in dissimilarities in decision-making and negotiation styles and the choice of methods of conflict resolution.

An assumption is often made that Americans and Canadians are culturally similar.[13] Several studies have challenged this assumption, however, by demonstrating that there can be differences.[14] Despite these findings, it is nonetheless true that Americans and Canadians share more commonalities than differences in terms of how they process and interpret information; in their perception of what is reasonable, right and acceptable; and in their decision-making and negotiating styles and choice of methods of conflict resolution.

Negotiation Context

Negotiation context refers to the structural properties specific to a given negotiation situation, such as motives and criteria, common interests, conflicting interests, nature and complexity of issues to be negotiated, relative balance of power of the partners, clarity of legitimacy boundaries of the issues under negotiation, options to discontinuing negotiation, and the nature of the industry or product.[15]

Motives and Criteria

Accurately gauging motives assists in projecting how accommodating or non-accommodating a particular party to the negotiation will be. If one partner needs the agreement badly enough, it will bend over backwards to meet the terms and demands of the other party. For example, in the negotiations between Boeing Commercial Airplane Company and the Japanese Civil Transport Development Corporation (CTDC, an entity created under the sponsorship of the Japanese government with three working entities: Mitsubishi Heavy Industries, Kawasaki Heavy Industries, and Fuji Heavy Industries) for a joint program for manufacturing Boeing's 767s, the Japanese were very accommodating and acquiesced to most of Boeing's terms, including accepting the U.S. style of confrontation in the negotiating process. In general, the Japanese prefer indirectness so as to avoid possible loss of face on either side.[16] The reason why the Japanese were so accommodating in this case lies in an analysis of CTDC's motives. In the early 1980s, the Japanese government identified aircraft, both military and commercial, as a potential growth industry. Furthermore, the U.S. government had pressured Japan to assume greater responsibility for its own defence. Since there is much complementarity between the production of military aircraft and the production of civilian aircraft in terms of technological know-how and equipment, producing commercial aircraft represents a viable route for recovering the costs of research and development on military defence.

Besides analysing the motives, the criteria used by the parties to assess the feasibility of a project should also be examined. For example, American and

Canadian partners are generally more concerned about short-term profitability. Consequently, the return on investment (ROI) and payback period constitute important criteria. Japanese partners, on the other hand, focus more on the criteria of market share and growth. Other criteria often used to assess the feasibility of a project include the percentage of equity ownership and the ability to exercise management control.

Common Interests

The two parties to a negotiation must have something in common, such as a common desire to develop a new product or to increase production and sales in a given market. In other words, the two parties must have 'something to negotiate for.'[17] During the course of negotiations, however, the two parties may become so engrossed with their differences and conflicts that they tend to lose sight of their commonalities and mutual interests. If and when this occurs, the negotiations often break down because both sides see little incentive to continue the negotiations. Consequently, while attempting to resolve the conflicts between the parties, the partners should always attempt to emphasize the commonalities that exist between them to spur both parties to an amicable resolution of the differences.

Conflicting Interests

These refer to the differences between the parties over issues such as equity share, management control, evaluation of each partner's contribution, and level of technology to be transferred to the venture.

In studies of business negotiations between Americans on the one hand, and Japanese, equity share emerged as one of the most sensitive issues.[18] For the purpose of consolidating their worldwide profit-and-loss statements, U.S. and Canadian firms generally insist on a minimum equity ownership of 51 per cent. In Japan, while there is virtually no legal restriction on the percentage of foreign equity ownership, the issue of equity is still very sensitive. To quote an American executive, the Japanese are very subtle in their objections to any request for a majority equity position by the foreign partner: 'The U.S. firm would say, "We want control." The Japanese would *not* say "No," but the negotiations drag on. All kinds of problems develop. But as soon as you agree to equal or minority partnership, all of a sudden the problems disappear. This is quite common in negotiations in Japan.'[19]

In general, management control is reflected in two areas: representation on the board, and staffing of senior management positions. Representation on the board is generally commensurate with the percentage of equity ownership, though in ventures with a 51/49 split, there is usually an equal number of directors from each side. In such cases, most decisions are made through mutual discussion rather than by vote. This is why building and nurturing good relationships with the Japanese partner is so important to the success of a venture.

The more contentious issue is the staffing of senior management positions. In many ventures between North Americans and Japanese, the former feels that it is imperative to use expatriates to staff certain key positions to maintain adequate control over the technology being transferred and to prevent the Japanese partner from coordinating its joint venture activities, particularly in the areas of finance and personnel, with the rest of the industrial group to which it belongs. In terms of financing, this coordination can be in the form of intra-company loans and borrowing. In the area of personnel, the joint venture company can become a dumping ground for excess personnel from the Japanese partner.

A primary motive for entering into a cooperative agreement with a foreign entity is to complement one's own resources, such as capital, technology, know-how, and market access. In the 50/50 joint venture formed between General Motors and Toyota in the early 1980s to manufacture small cars in Fremont, California, Toyota's contribution was $100 million cash. General Motors' contributions were $11 million cash and the Fremont manufacturing plant. A dollar value has to be assigned to non-cash contributions such as fixed assets. The cash value of such properties is, of course, subject to negotiation.

In many cases, a major motive for entering into a cooperative agreement is to acquire advanced or complementary technology. In the General Motors–Toyota joint venture, a primary motive for GM was to acquire Japanese expertise in small car manufacturing. GM, however, has alleged that Toyota has tried to shield such technology from the venture.

Nature and Complexity of Issues to Be Negotiated

Where the issues under negotiation are numerous and complex, each party has to make constant trade-offs by assessing its priorities and the utility functions of each trade-off. Where the negotiation is serially linked with other problems, one party may make more concessions in a given negotiation so as to maximize outcomes in other related situations.

In general, negotiators tend to be more accommodating, cooperative, and honest in repetitive bargaining situations, as compared to one-shot transactions, because of the prospects of future interactions. In other words, there is a need to maintain a smooth and ongoing relationship between the parties. Consequently, where the negotiations are serially linked or repetitive, the issue of reciprocity or repercussion becomes a major consideration. Furthermore, where the negotiation is serially linked, negotiators tend to tread more cautiously because of the implications that a particular decision may have on subsequent and related occurrences.[20] These linkages may extend to companies that are not presently a party to the negotiation. A partner to a negotiation may be concerned about establishing a precedent to which it could be bound later. For example, prior to Boeing's joint program with CTDC, it had worked only with other manufacturers on a contracting or subcontracting basis. Consequently, Boeing was concerned about the precedent the joint program might set for its future dealings with other domestic or foreign entities. This was the reason for the detailed and long-drawn-out negotiations about the nature and form of the working arrangement between the parties.

Relative Balance of Power

The balance of power determines the extent to which each partner will accommodate or concede to the demands of the other. In the case of the joint production program between Boeing and CTDC, since Boeing possessed the technological know-how it was able to bargain from a position of strength. Consequently, the Japanese partner had to make many concessions, including adapting to the American style of negotiation.

Clarity of Legitimacy Boundaries

The clarity of legitimacy boundaries of the issues under negotiation is determined, to a large extent, by the contextual environment. What may be perceived as legitimate in one country may not be considered so in another. According to a commission that examined corruption for the International Chamber of Commerce in Paris, there are only twelve 'clean' countries in the world, meaning societies where questionable payments (bribery, graft, etc.) are not considered a regular cost of conducting business. The 'clean' countries include the United States, Canada, and the Scandinavian and North European countries.[21] Elsewhere in the world, including in Japan, the use of bribes is considered a normal part of business transactions.

Options to Discontinuing Negotiations

Where there are available options to discontinuing negotiations, either party may be less motivated to work towards an agreement, thus affecting the selection of strategies and hence the progress and outcome of the negotiation. Toyota, for example, initially negotiated with Ford for the possible formation of a joint venture before it turned to General Motors. Where one or both parties perceive the cessation of negotiations as detrimental to their interests, then either or both parties would become more compromising and hence more willing to explore alternative modes of conflict resolution.

Nature of Industry or Product

Given the policy of industrial targeting in Japan, trade and investment in priority industries tend to meet with a more favourable reception. In Canada's 'Action Plan for Japan,' the aerospace industry has been designated one of the growth opportunities for Canadian businesses in Japan.[22] This fits in with Japan's national priorities, since aircraft manufacturing has been targeted as a key industry since the early 1980s.

Negotiator Characteristics

Negotiator characteristics have a direct bearing on the progress and outcome of negotiations because negotiations are, after all, conducted by and between people. Negotiator characteristics fall into five general categories: number of negotiators, whom they represent (whether private, public, or quasi-public), epistemological types, interpersonal relationships, and bilingual team members.

Where there are several negotiators on a team, differences in values and hence opinions may exist within the group. To resolve such intra-group differences, trade-offs and compromises have to be made, thus affecting the selection of strategies to be pursued and hence the progress and outcome of the negotiation. A Japanese negotiation team typically has more members than its American or Canadian counterpart. However, in a Japanese negotiation team, virtually all the talking is done by the chief negotiator. Thus, intra-group differences may be shielded from the opposing team. In American and Canadian negotiation teams, on the other hand, the member who has the expertise on the particular subject under discussion usually takes the lead. Thus differences of opinion may become apparent to the opposing team.

The issue of whom the negotiators represent can influence the selection of strategy, and hence the progress and outcome of negotiations in at least two major ways. First, a negotiator who represents the public or quasi-public sector has a very different set of concerns as compared with a representative from private industry. A negotiator for the public or quasi-public sector, in general, has to consider the implications that his or her decision has on society at large, and how he or she can represent effectively the interests of the public, or at least impart such an impression. A representative of the private sector, on the other hand, is responsible to a narrower constituency, and hence can pursue strategies that maximize organizational rather than societal outcomes.

A second way in which the issue of whom the negotiator represents can influence the progress and outcome of the negotiations pertains to the options available to discontinuing negotiations. In negotiations with the private sector, in case of disagreement, there are more options to discontinuing negotiations. A party can simply cease negotiations and seek another more compatible partner, as Toyota did by turning from Ford to General Motors. This alternative is generally not available in the case of negotiations with the public sector.

Maruyama has classified people into four epistemological types based on how they think and behave: H, I, S, and G.[23] He noted that these types, and mixtures thereof, account for approximately two-thirds of the world's population. While the four types can be found in all countries, one mode tends to dominate in a given society. The H-type ('competitive, classifying, sequential, one-truth, zero-sum'), for example, is more prevalent in the United States and Canada, while the S-type ('cooperative, contextual, many truths, positive-sum') is more dominant in Japan. These epistemological types, of course, influence the way in which people process information and select negotiation strategies.

Besides personality attributes of the negotiators, the choice of strategies is also influenced by the interpersonal relationships that exist between members of the negotiating teams. Where the negotiators trust and respect their counterparts on the opposing team, the issues under negotiation can be more easily defined and narrowed, thus facilitating a meeting of the minds at the negotiating table. Trust, for example, is essential to the successful operation of joint ventures formed between American and Japanese entities.[24]

Where the parties to a negotiation do not speak a common language, the services of an interpreter are generally required, but negotiator characteristics can be confounded by the use of interpreters. Interpreters have been described as 'gatekeepers' because they filter the information that is received by the target audience and can affect that audience's perception of the situation. It is advisable, therefore, to include a bilingual member on one's negotiating team. Such a member can correct mistakes as they occur. Misunderstandings due to inadequate interpretation services impede the progress of negotiations and may completely disrupt them because the perspectives of both sides cannot be presented accurately. Besides interpreting language, a person who is familiar with the other party's culture can also interpret the non-verbal messages for the rest of the team. Moreover, this member may be able to make suggestions about the best way to present certain issues where there are cultural differences.

Strategy Selection and Process/Progress

The negotiation context and negotiator characteristics jointly influence the strategies that are selected by both parties in, first, approaching the negotiation situation, and second, resolving conflicts or differences.

Based on an analysis of East Asian classics, both literary and military, I have identified twelve common themes or principles that guide the Japanese (and other East Asian countries, such as China and Korea) approach to business, including the conduct of business negotiations.[25] They include the following seven, which are relevant to this discussion.

The Importance of Strategies
From the East Asian perspective, there are preferred methods for managing any type of confrontation, business or otherwise. These methods can be arranged in descending order, from most to least desired:

1/ Develop a brilliant strategy to deal a swift and fatal blow to one's adversary/ competitor.
2/ Engage in diplomacy to resolve a confrontation. This includes negotiation, mutual discussion, and the use of intermediaries.
3/ Deploy non-diplomatic means to resolve a confrontation (open warfare). In the business context, this would be expensive and protracted litigation.
4/ Attack a fortified city (waging warfare against a well-established opponent). This is the most risky and costly method.

Mediation, conciliation, and arbitration are preferred, therefore, over litigation. Furthermore, because of the emphasis on strategy, the Japanese tend to play mind games – they ferret out the hidden message in any type of communication (written, verbal, or silent) and develop a strategy to counteract the perceived message. In the West, 'game playing' usually has a negative connotation; in Japan and much of East Asia, however, it is considered an asset.

Transforming an Adversary's Strength into Weakness, and Vice-Versa
This principle is clearly illustrated in Japan's industrial development following World War II. Devastated by the war, Japan rebuilt its economy by purchasing Western technology, thus leap-frogging technological development. The disadvantage of 'starting with virtually nothing' enabled Japan to establish a modern industrial base from which it could compete with the United States and the rest of the West.[26]

Deception as a Means to a Strategic Advantage
While 'strategic misrepresentation' – a form of deception where one side deliberately magnifies the significance of the issue(s) already conceded in order to bargain for better terms in other areas – is also practised in the West, it is more highly regarded in Japan.[27] Because of the Judaeo-Christian influence, Westerners consider deception immoral. In Japan, where there is no indigenous religion akin to Judaism and Christianity, deception has a neutral connotation, that is, it

is amoral and acceptable if it results in a greater good. From the Japanese perspective, the 'greater good' embraces the well-being of the nation-state, the clan (the geographic region from which a person's ancestors came), the extended family, the nuclear family, the corporation (employer), and oneself.

Compromise

According to East Asian philosophy, compromise is often necessary to achieve a goal. Compromise requires an ongoing relationship (whether cooperative or competitive); otherwise, the parties have nothing to trade off. This accounts, at least in part, for the Japanese emphasis on developing ongoing relationships.

Grasping the Interdependent Relationship of Situations

This principle was illustrated in the Japanese saying 'When the wind blows, it is good for the makers of wooden tubs,' discussed earlier.

Patience

Patience was stressed in *Bushido* (the way of military men), which cautions against launching a first strike. Consider the way the sumo wrestlers sit on their haunches to wear down their opponents. Unlike a boxing match, which is filled with action (punches and counterpunches), inaction is a significant part of a sumo wrestling match. This emphasis on patience has accounted, in part, for the often long and drawn-out negotiations with the Japanese.

Flexibility

The emphasis on flexibility accounts, in part, for the Japanese view of written legal contracts as organic documents that can be altered as circumstances change. In the West, a signed contract is considered sacrosanct, with inviolate terms.

Negotiation Outcomes

The outcomes of a given negotiation situation can be assessed along several dimensions. In the event of agreement, the outcome can be measured in terms of negotiator satisfaction and payoffs in the form of joint or individual profits. In the event of a stalemate or deadlock, one has to examine whether alternative strategies can be devised to help break the stalemate. In the event of a complete breakdown between the parties, both partners can withdraw and dissolve the negotiations.

In Figure 7.1, there is a feedback loop from 'negotiation outcomes' to 'negotiation context' and 'negotiator characteristics' because the outcomes of a particular negotiation may be combined with other negotiation situations, and thus may have a cumulative impact on the context in which a future negotiation is conducted and/or the way in which the negotiator perceives and behaves in similar or related negotiations.

U.S.–Japan and Canada–Japan Business Negotiations

Differences in Decision-Making and Negotiating Styles

Most Americans perceive significant differences in decision-making and negotiating styles between themselves and their Japanese partners.[28] The most salient differences are delays in decision-making on the part of the Japanese; personal considerations versus Western logic; lack of decision-making authority among Japanese negotiation team members; avoidance of direct confrontation by the Japanese; and the use of silence.

Canadian companies tend to characterize their own negotiation style as follows: a propensity towards individualism; informal and equality-seeking relationships; directness; expectations of honesty and reciprocity; a marked dislike of silence; a competitive, adversarial, 'persistence pays' view of negotiating; a sequential approach to the handling of various tasks; a legalistic bent; a short, informal approach; and a pride in determination.[29] These ten Canadian characteristics can be analysed in conjunction with the five salient differences identified by the Americans.

Delays in Decision-Making
In Japan, matters do not progress as rapidly as they typically do in the West. Protracted negotiations that extend over several years are fairly common in Japan. Most North Americans who have negotiated with the Japanese will readily acknowledge that patience is a paramount virtue in doing business there. Five factors have contributed to the general slowness in the progress of negotiations:

1/ The Japanese emphasize relationships that are pivotal to all aspects of societal functioning. Relationships are usually developed over years of personal association. The Japanese partner needs time to observe a prospective partner because a business agreement, like a marriage, once entered into is generally viewed as inviolate, and not to be easily discontinued according to the whims of the partners. In American and Canadian companies, there is a tendency to rotate personnel on a more frequent basis. Hence, in the course of protracted negotiations with a Japanese partner for the formation of a cooperative agreement, which may extend for several years, the members of the American and Canadian negotiation teams may change. This fairly frequent rotation of personnel is not conducive to developing relationships, much less trust. Many Japanese have complained that it is difficult to befriend an American or Canadian negotiation team member because by the time they begin to know that person, he or she is transferred elsewhere.

2/ Ninety per cent of the decisions made in Japan are arrived at through consensus. It takes time to reach a consensus.[30]

3/ The Japanese have a longer-term orientation in planning. Japanese tend to look at what will happen ten or twenty years in the future. Hence delays of a few months, or sometimes even years, may appear inconsequential from their perspective.

4/ Language barriers usually result in the use of interpreters. This means that the negotiations may take twice as long with all the interpreting to and from a given language.

5/ Following the principle of inaction identified earlier, the Japanese may often use a delaying strategy in an attempt to arrive at a desired outcome. The use of this stalling technique may stem from a perception that North Americans are generally more eager to reach closure within a relatively short period of time. By stalling, the Japanese hope to wear down their Western counterparts and thereby gain more and better concessions.

Personal Considerations versus Western Logic
Since relationships are pivotal to success in business transactions in Japan, they may not make decisions on the basis of linear logic alone. Their decisions may often be influenced by personal considerations. Indirection also comes into play.

Lack of Decision-Making Authority
Many Japanese negotiating teams do not appear to be vested with decision-making authority and have to consult with higher authority in their respective organizational hierarchies. While this is usually true, sometimes it may be an excuse to buy more time. This apparent lack of decision-making authority has two major implications: first, it results in delays in decision-making; and second, it creates a need to socialize with decision-makers to facilitate the process.

Avoidance of Direct Confrontation
Given the emphasis on face saving in Japan, direct confrontation on issues is generally avoided. While face saving is important in any culture, in Japan it takes on heightened sensitivity. Confrontational techniques that back an oppo-

nent into a corner, thus allowing little room for manoeuvring, should be avoided. The Japanese are generally very polite and do not openly voice or show their displeasure with the manner in which certain things are said or handled. They prefer to hint at issues or be vague in their responses so that if things do not work out, no one will be particularly embarrassed. The Japanese are indirect even in their compliments.

Because of their overriding concern with maintaining harmony, the Japanese tend to avoid extremes and prefer to adopt a middle-of-the-road attitude. Avoiding extremes, combined with the desire to save face, often translates into an aversion to using the word 'no' in conversations. This trait has led some prominent Japanese business leaders, such as Sony Corporation's Akio Morita, to argue that in light of Japan's ascendancy in the global economic arena and heightened 'Japanese bashing' in other industrialized nations, this tradition is outdated.

This avoidance of direct confrontation also translates into an aversion to litigation. The United States is one of the most litigious societies in the world: it has 70 per cent of the world's lawyers, with nearly eighteen million new lawsuits every year. This amounts to an annual outlay of $80 billion in direct litigation costs and $300 billion in indirect costs. This litigious mentality does not carry over well to other countries. In a study of business negotiations between U.S. and Japanese entities, it was found that only 4 per cent of the disputes between the parties were resolved through the combined mechanisms of litigation and arbitration, while 74 per cent of the disputes were resolved by mutual discussion.[31]

Use of Silence

In Japan, vagueness in responses in negotiations is sometimes accompanied by prolonged periods of silence. In Japan the maxim that 'silence is golden' still holds, and may stem from the Japanese desire to avoid confrontation, which is deeply imbued in individuals from childhood. Studies that compared children's quarrels in various European countries with those in Japan found that while prompt retort, in general, was expected in the European countries, Japanese children generally remained quiet even if they felt they were right.[32] When an impasse is reached in a negotiation, the typical Japanese response is silence, withdrawal, or a change of subject. To the Japanese, a period of silence allows people to cool off and gives both sides an opportunity to rethink the issue. North Americans, on the other hand, may feel uncomfortable with silence and have the urge to say something. At these crucial junctures, they are most susceptible to committing tactical errors.

Factors for Success in Cross-National Business Negotiations

In a survey of U.S.–Japan businesses, six factors were found to be responsible for the success of business negotiations: attitude of U.S. firm; cultural awareness; attitude of Japanese firm; product characteristics; personal relationships; and technical expertise provided by the U.S. firm. A similar Canada–Japan study did not examine this dimension, but focused on the problems in alliance formation.

The attitude of the U.S. firm includes items pertaining to the preparation of the firm, patience on the part of the U.S. team, and the latter's sincerity. All these items are related to the willingness of the U.S. firm to devote time and effort to cultivate a business relationship with the Japanese partner, which is perceived to be the most critical factor for success in negotiations. This finding points to the need for U.S. firms to exercise patience and develop a longer-range perspective when investing and doing business in Japan.

Cultural awareness includes items such as familiarity with Japanese customs and business practices. The uniqueness of the product or service that the Japanese firm can offer also relates highly to this factor. A possible explanation is that where a Japanese product or service is unique, the U.S. firm tends to be more accommodating and hence exhibits a greater willingness to adapt to cultural differences in order to obtain access to the product or service. This factor was perceived by most U.S. firms as less important than the previous factor, the attitude of the U.S. firm. Familiarity with a foreign culture is a necessary but insufficient condition for success. There must be a genuine willingness on the part of both sides to work towards some common ground – that is, to accommodate the needs of the other party. It is commendable that Canada's Action Plan for Japan specifically calls for 'increased awareness and knowledge of the Japanese market' and 'product adaptation.'[33]

The factor 'attitude of Japanese firm' includes a single item pertaining to the sincerity, honesty, and good faith exhibited by the Japanese partner in the negotiations. Negotiations, by definition, require the mutual cooperation and efforts of both parties. All parties to the negotiation must possess a genuine desire to work together to accomplish common objectives. Otherwise, there is no basis for cooperation between the parties.[34]

Product characteristics consist of the uniqueness of the product or service offered by the U.S. firm. Given the difficulties encountered by foreign investors in establishing operations in Japan and the general competitiveness of Japanese producers, the product or service offered by the American firm has to be distinctive. Otherwise, the chances of a U.S. firm's gaining successful entry and penetration into the Japanese market may be severely hampered. In fish products, an area the Canadian government has targeted for growth in Japan, there is recognition that the 'processing of seafood products is very specialized in Japan.'[35] Consequently, to increase sales in this sector, Canadian businesses must learn from and adapt to Japanese processing technology and methods.

The 'personal relationships' factor includes the friendly ties built between the parties over a number of years. This again points to the need for patience and the importance of cultivating and developing personal ties to ensure the successful operation of joint cooperative arrangements between the parties.

Technical expertise provided by the U.S. firm to the Japanese partner in the past reflects a combination of the previous two factors, 'product characteristics' and 'personal relationships.' In the early postwar years of U.S.–Japan bilateral relations, Japan imported much technology in the form of licensing agreements and was a major recipient of U.S. technical assistance programs. Although the Japanese have made remarkable strides in technological development since then, many remain grateful for the initial assistance provided them after the war; others concede, however, that the United States still has a technological edge in certain areas. Consequently, technical expertise provided by U.S. firms to their Japanese partners in the past is viewed as a contributing factor to the success of business negotiations.

Factors for Failure in Cross-National Business Negotiations

In the U.S.–Japan study, two factors are responsible for the failure of business negotiations: cultural differences and product characteristics.

In the Canada–Japan study, the problems in alliance formation (in descending order of importance) were finding a suitable company to be an alliance partner; differences in corporate culture/organizational structure; agreeing with a partner on each party's contribution to the alliance; agreeing with a partner on how the alliance is to be managed; differences in personal social/cultural attitudes; agreeing with a partner on how future benefits are to be shared; lack of company resources (human or financial) to enter into alliances; and local government's legal restrictions on collaborative agreements.[36] Factor analysis reveals that these problems can be largely attributed to differences in culture and differences in corporate objectives. The latter can be analysed under 'product characteristics.'

Cultural Differences
This factor includes items pertaining to communication breakdown and differ-

ences in business practices, negotiating styles, and social norms. Many problems in alliance formation identified by Canadian firms fall into this category. In the U.S.–Japan study, the item 'lack of sincerity on the part of the Japanese' also related highly to this factor. A possible explanation for this finding is that perceived insincerity on the part of the Japanese negotiators can be attributed, in part, to cultural differences. For example, in the West, eye contact during handshaking and conversation is considered a sign of honesty and sincerity. In Japan, on the other hand, eye contact is not common during the exchange of greetings nor in the course of conversations. Hence behaviour patterns that are specific to a given cultural environment may be misconstrued by members of other cultures as indications of insincerity and dishonesty.

Two points with regard to cultural differences deserve attention. First, although cultural differences may be viewed as less important than 'attitude of U.S. firms' in the success of business negotiations, ignoring such differences may be detrimental to the outcome of negotiations. Lack of familiarity with cultural differences and an inability to bridge the cultural gap can lead to the collapse of business negotiations. Second, the item 'insurmountable cultural differences' that loaded on this factor was perceived by approximately half the respondents as either irrelevant or responsible 'to a very little extent' for the failure of business negotiations. This suggests that although differences in social customs, negotiating styles, and business practices may pose tremendous obstacles to the progress of negotiations, most respondents perceive these barriers as surmountable. North American firms should take heart that with careful preparation and proper understanding, cultural differences need not impede progress or negatively affect the outcome of business negotiations.

Product Characteristics

In the U.S.–Japan study, this factor includes two items: (1) the Japanese did not need products/services offered by the U.S. firm, and (2) the presence of too many competitors all offering the same products/services that the U.S. company supplies. This finding again points to the extreme competitiveness of the Japanese market and the need for Western firms to offer unique products or services in order to make significant inroads into the Japanese economy. Canadian government and businesses should take heed of this finding. Two areas targeted for growth in Canada's Action Plan for Japan – aerospace industries and information technologies – are highly competitive. Consequently, it is imperative that Canadian firms seek market niches within these two sectors. The inability expressed by some Canadian firms to locate suitable Japanese companies as alliance partners may stem from the highly competitive market situation in Japan.

Relationships between Success and Negotiation Practices
in U.S.–Japan Bargaining

Negotiation practices include the number of previous negotiations with the Japanese; type of industry; type of trade relationship; assets of U.S. firm; types of programs used in preparing for the negotiations (such as studying the host country's business practices and social customs); hired experts to train negotiators; and use of simulated negotiations.

Having had previous negotiations with the Japanese and studying Japanese business practices and social customs were significantly associated with success rates. Other explanatory variables, such as the type of trade relationship, assets of U.S. firm, hiring of experts to train negotiators, and use of simulated negotiations, were not significantly related to success. A marginally significant difference was found for those firms that were engaged in high-technology industries such as engineering, aerospace, and electronics.

These findings have several implications. First, those firms that plan to enter into negotiations with prospective Japanese partners would benefit from learning about other companies' experiences to avoid pitfalls. Second, certain preparatory procedures designed to familiarize North American negotiators with cultural differences, such as reading books on Japanese business practices, can enhance the incidence of favourable outcomes. Third, firms in various industries and of different sizes can be successful in doing business in Japan. Fourth, in view of the extreme competitiveness of the Japanese market, firms in high-technology industries tend to meet with greater success. The aerospace and information technologies industries that the Canadian government has targeted for growth in Japan fit this category. However, as noted earlier, these sectors are highly competitive.

Enhancing Success in Cross-National Negotiations with the Japanese

The growing interdependence in the North Pacific Triangle will mean even closer cooperation among economic entities from the United States, Canada, and Japan. These opportunities are, however, fraught with challenges and frustrations. The common denominators to success in negotiating and doing business with the Japanese may be summarized as follows.

Patience

Most North Americans who have negotiated with the Japanese will readily acknowledge that the experience is unique. Although the negotiations can generally be characterized as cordial, they can also tax one's patience. A North American who hopes to succeed in doing business in Japan has to abandon his or her usual time frame and allow matters to proceed at their own pace, which is characteristically unhurried.

Mutual Trust

Given the Japanese emphasis on human relations and the traditional dislike for law and litigation, business transactions are generally based on mutual trust and respect. Each partner must demonstrate a genuine willingness to understand and respect the interests and desires of the other. Furthermore, because of the Japanese belief that a contractual agreement is an organic document that can change with evolving conditions, the continuation of a mutually beneficial relationship between the parties cannot depend solely on the written contract. Rather, both partners must trust that whatever courses of action may be adopted in the future, these will be in the best interests of the venture as a whole. This points to the need, first, to develop long-term working relationships in Japan, and second, to try to have an intermediary (usually a mutual friend of both partners) who can in a sense vouch for the conduct or behaviour of each party.

To promote mutual trust between the parties, there should be continuity in the relationships. Frequent rotation of personnel on the part of American and Canadian partners is not conducive to the development of trust.

Respect for Cultural Differences

The tremendous differences in cultural systems between the United States and Canada, on the one hand, and Japan, on the other, are reflected in variations in principles of industrial management on both sides of the Pacific. These differences pose problems of adjustment for North American firms. For decades, the Japanese have been assiduous students of North American styles of management and are knowledgeable about North American cultural values and traditions. When Japanese multinationals send people on overseas assignments, they prepare their expatriates through intensive language training programs and study of the cultural norms of the host country, including several months of sharing the same dormitory with Americans and other Westerners so that the Japanese trainees can be steeped in foreign practices.[37]

Americans and Canadians, on the other hand, have generally adopted an ethnocentric (or North American–centric) approach to management, and in most instances expect the foreign partner to make all the necessary accommodations. This attitude is not well received in Japan. Even when U.S. and Canadian firms recognize the need to give their expatriates a nodding familiarity with the country of assignment, this may not be sufficient because mere knowledge of such differences does not necessarily imply the ability to cope with them.

Need to Study the Market and Work within the System

The Japanese market is unique. Despite relatively recent changes, its systems of marketing and distribution are steeped in centuries of tradition. Consequently, they are very different from those found in the United States and Canada. Some North Americans, confusing modernization with Westernization, assume that since Japan is highly industrialized and modern, the North American and Japanese markets are similar, and hence what sells in North America will also sell in Japan. This erroneous assumption could cost a firm millions of dollars in an aborted project.

There are substantial differences between the lifestyles and buying behaviour of North American and Japanese consumers. Given the highly developed Japanese economy, unoriginal products do not sell well in there. A North American investor has to research the Japanese market thoroughly to determine whether there is a demand for its products and, if so, what types of modifications, if any, need to be made. This is particularly important in the case of building products, fish products, processed food products, and auto parts, four areas targeted by the Canadian government for growth in Japan.

Since systems of distribution and relationships between suppliers and customers in Japan are steeped in traditions that date back several centuries, it may be difficult for foreign firms to change them. Rather, they should understand such differences and work with them.

Type of Industry

Given the extremely competitive Japanese market, the products and services marketed by foreign manufacturers have to be distinctive to be successful. Furthermore, they have to fit in with overall national objectives. Japanese businesses operate within the broad framework of their country's industrial policy.

Compatibility of Objectives and Complementarity of Needs

To ensure the continuation of a relationship, the objectives of the partners have to be compatible. Given the differences in perspectives between North American and Japanese entities, the corporate objectives of the companies may often be in conflict. For example, many North American firms are concerned with immediate or short-term profitability, whereas Japanese firms typically are concerned with growth and market share, which often take time to develop and may involving operating losses for several years.

Besides compatibility of goals, a Japanese firm will seldom enter into a collaborative arrangement with a foreign enterprise unless the latter can contribute resources that other Japanese entities cannot provide. The importance of both compatibility of objectives and complementarity of needs to the successful formation and operation of a collaborative agreement points to the need to select one's partner carefully. A North American firm should research thoroughly the capabilities of prospective candidates for contractual agreements in Japan. Again, intermediaries can provide valuable assistance: they can help locate prospective candidates whose objectives and capabilities match and complement those of the North American firm and, if there is interest on either side, facilitate discussion.

Need to Maintain Dialogue

Given the differences in cultural and industrial practices between the United States and Canada, on the one hand, and Japan, on the other, both partners to a venture must maintain constant dialogue to cement the friendly ties between them and avoid misunderstandings. Such dialogue can be maintained through regularly scheduled meetings, after-hours socializing, and almost day-to-day contact at the operational level to keep both sides fully briefed about all aspects of the operation.

Conclusion

Although there are some exceptions, the factors identified here are crucial to the success of negotiating and collaborating in cooperative agreements with the Japanese. Conversely, the absence of such factors may strain the relations between prospective partners and lead to the eventual collapse of any talks.

These factors revolve around two major considerations: cultural awareness and product characteristics. As noted, it is commendable that the Canadian government, in its Action Plan for Japan, has called for 'increased awareness and knowledge of the Japanese market' and 'product adaptation.' With regard to product characteristics, Canadian businesses should be aware of the highly competitive nature of the Japanese auto parts, aerospace, and information technologies industries. Canadian firms have to identify niches within these sectors to seek growth. While Canada should continue to capitalize on its comparative advantage, namely its abundance of natural resources such as lumber and fish, it is better for Canadian business to focus on higher value-added products in these sectors. Otherwise, Canada's export profile will continue to resemble that of a less-developed country.

Although the road to economic cooperation in the North Pacific Triangle may be rough at times, the rewards are indeed great. The experience of many cooperative agreements formed between the United States and Japan and between Canada and Japan has demonstrated that through the correct mix of attributes difficulties can be surmounted, with impressive balance sheets to show for the efforts.

NOTES

1 Tung, 'Toward a Conceptual Paradigm.'
2 Fayerweather and Kapoor, *Strategy and Negotiation.*
3 JEI, *JEI Reports*, 18 March 1994 and 24 June 1994.
4 The definition of 'strategic' is based solely on the host country's perspective of whether the industry is of vital importance to its national security.
5 JEI, *JEI Reports*, 18 March 1994.
6 English, 'U.S. Trade Policy on Japan.'
7 JEI, *JEI Reports*, 18 March 1994.
8 Ibid.
9 Ballon, 'A Lesson from Japan.'
10 Ballon, 'Japan: The Government–Business,' 5.
11 Hall and Hall, *Hidden Differences*, 1987.
12 Ballon, 'Japan: The Government–Business.'
13 Hofstede, *Culture's Consequences*; Ronen and Kraut, 'Similarities among Countries'; Root, *Entry Strategies.*
14 O'Grady and Lane in 'Culture,' for example, have found that Canadian retail managers exhibited a lower need for achievement and were more risk-averse than their American counterparts. In a comparative study of cognitive processing styles among U.S., Canadian, and Japanese MBA students, Abramson, Keating, and Lane in 'Cross-National Cognitive,' reported that Canadians were slower decision-makers than Americans, but were quicker than Japanese. Furthermore, Canadians tended to be more theoretical and imaginative in their problem solving than both Americans and Japanese.
15 Strauss, *Negotiations.*
16 Tung, *Business Negotiations.*
17 Kapoor, *Planning for International*, 2.
18 Tung, *Business Negotiations.*
19 Ibid., 221.

20 Raiffa, *The Art and Science of Negotiation.*
21 Gladwyn and Walter, *Multinationals under Fire.*
22 Canada, *Canada's Action Plan for Japan.*
23 Maruyama, 'Changing Dimensions,' 88–96.
24 Peterson and Shimada, 'Sources of Management Problems.'
25 Tung, 'Strategic Management.'
26 Dore, *British Factory Japanese Factory.*
27 Raiffa, *The Art and Science of Negotiation.*
28 The findings on U.S.–Japan styles are based on a questionnaire survey of cooperative agreements formed between 114 American companies and their Japanese counterparts and case analysis of six U.S.–Japan joint ventures (Tung, *Business Negotiations*). These firms come from a diverse range of industries and business activities, including electronics, aerospace, automotive vehicle and parts, consumer products, sporting goods and equipment, chemical manufacturing, and food processing. The findings on Canada–Japan styles are based on a questionnaire survey of 134 business alliance agreements formed between Canadian and Japanese companies (Hung, 'Use of Business Alliances'). In the Canada–Japan study, some companies included had formed more than one business alliance with the same trans-Pacific partner. According to the International Institute for Management Development's (Switzerland) 1992 'World Competitiveness Report,' Canada ranked seventeenth among the twenty-two OECD member nations in its utilization of international alliances. In the same report, the United States ranked seventh and Japan thirteenth.
29 Graham and Sano, *Smart Bargaining*; Hung, 'Use of Business Alliances.'
30 JETRO, *Japanese Corporate Decision Making.*
31 Tung, *Business Negotiations.*
32 Van Zandt, 'How to Negotiate in Japan?' 45–56.
33 Tung, *Business Negotiations.*
34 Hung, 'Use of Business Alliances.'
35 Canada, *Canada's Action Plan for Japan*, 11.
36 Hung, 'Use of Business Alliances.'
37 Tung, *Key to Japan's Economic Strength.*

II. THE POLITICAL AND SECURITY RELATIONSHIP

8

Cooperative Security in the North Pacific

FRANK LANGDON

Pacific Security in the Nineties

In the nineties, Canada was one of the first Pacific states to urge 'cooperative security' whereby both defenders and potential challengers to Asia Pacific regional peace would meet regularly to consult on security issues.[1] Together with Australia, it strove to persuade a reluctant United States and Japan to join in such a multilateral security approach. The early nineties seemed a good time for this: Australia had already inaugurated the first regional multilateral governmental economic grouping, the Asia Pacific Economic Cooperation forum, in 1989. The nineties also ushered in a new era of comparatively good relations among the major powers due to a decline in Cold War manifestations in East Asia. A sharp decrease in ideological confrontations was apparent among most of the countries of Northeast Asia/North Pacific except North Korea, starting with China under Deng Xiaoping and followed up by Russia under Mikhail Gorbachev.

Although the United States and Japan were content to cling to their bilateral alliances as essential to continued stability in East Asia, Canada was alarmed by the proliferation of modern arms in the area in contrast to the large arms reductions in the Atlantic region with the end of the Cold War. Northeast Asia is one of the most heavily armed regions and is engaged in modernizing its weapons systems. Therefore, in 1991 the Canadian foreign minister urged that a regular North Pacific discussion forum be created among China, Japan, Russia, North and South Korea, Canada, and the United States to discuss security problems. If these countries held regular meetings together, they could build greater confidence among themselves by making their military intentions and preparations more transparent and reassuring, as well as heading off or ameliorating disputes likely to provoke serious conflict in the future.

At first, the United States and Japan feared such meetings might undermine their existing alliances and defence cooperation. But, they became converts to using multilateral confidence-building discussions even in the Asia Pacific region, not just in the Atlantic, if only to supplement their current deployments and alliances and to put regional peace on a firmer basis. However, it was not Canada, but the Association of Southeast Asian Nations (ASEAN) that first succeeded in establishing an Asia-Pacific regional governmental multilateral security body, the eighteen-nation ASEAN Regional Forum (ARF) in 1994. Its members include Canada, Japan, and the United States. Still, it tends to concentrate on Southeast Asian concerns, and its agenda is set by the ASEAN countries that sponsor it. Although ARF touches on security issues of the wider East Asian region, including Northeast Asia, it is not a sufficient substitute for a separate subregional North Pacific or Northwest Pacific body suggested by Canada. The ASEAN Regional Forum also suffers from the absence of North Korea, whose presence is essential for discussing Northeast Asian security problems. However, ARF has the advantage of being a representative multilateral gathering where the presence of the four major regional powers – the United States, Russia, China, and Japan – enables the lesser powers to voice their security fears and requires the big powers to listen and try to reassure them. It also keeps two crucial countries, China and the United States, 'engaged' in dialogue with the others. Without them, any regional security body would have little reason to exist.

Washington's East Asia Strategy

In February 1995, the Pentagon produced a new East Asian Strategy of 'steadfast commitment to sustain a forward military presence of about 100,000 American military personnel in East Asia, of whom 36,000 stand by our ally the Republic of Korea, while 47,000 demonstrate our commitment to regional security and the defence of Japan.'[2] This reversed the plans of the Bush Administration to gradually pull back a substantial portion of its forward deployed forces in East Asia as set forth in its policy documents of 1990 and 1992, and the United States sought to convince the regional countries that it would not greatly reduce its regional presence with the end of the Cold War. The new policy was persuasively presented by Joseph Nye, the assistant secretary of defence for international security affairs, who was on leave from Harvard where he is again the director for the Center for International Affairs.[3] He is also a noted foreign relations analyst and professor of government there. This East Asian strategy seems to give the Pacific and Eastern Asia the same importance as the Atlantic and Western Europe, also garrisoned with 100,000 American military personnel on a long-term basis. If so, it represents a sea change by giving higher priority to the Pacific in what has tended to be an Atlantic- and Middle East–centred foreign security policy.

The new American policy now has a strong economic component, the aspect formerly apt to be ignored in foreign security policy but made explicit in the Nye formulation. The assistant secretary justified the continued American regional military presence and continuing alliances with Japan and South Korea by attributing much of the stability of the region to them, thus making possible the rapid economic growth and development that has become so important to the United States' own prosperity. Indeed, a goal of the Clinton Administration is increased jobs for American workers through expanded exports. Similarly, East Asia keeps increasing in importance for Canada and Japan.

Nye also seems, in effect, to have accepted Canadian officials' arguments in assessing the contribution of multilateral regional security institutions when he wrote, '[T]he Administration has encouraged nongovernmental talks among the Northeast Asian countries in an effort to develop a Northeast Asian security dialogue.'[4] The Canadian government had followed up its proposals through Foreign Minister Joe Clark in 1991 by supporting non-governmental Northeast Asian unofficial security discussions among academic and governmental security specialists and research institutes. These discussions fell under the name of the North Pacific Cooperative Security Dialogue. It was followed by the establishment of the present non-governmental Council for Security Cooperation in Asia Pacific, formed in 1993 by strategic and international relations research institutes throughout the region. Nye looked at those regional security discussions as valuable confidence-building measures.

The argument that the American military presence is a major basis for regional peace and stability and must therefore be continued has not gone unchallenged. But it must be admitted that this presence has probably prevented North Korea from unifying Korea by force. Similarly, the presence of two American aircraft carrier task forces off Taiwan during the 1996 firing of Chinese missiles there may have deterred more aggressive Chinese behaviour. Nye still calls North Korea 'a clear and present danger,' although that country had frozen its attempt to produce its own nuclear weapons since 1994 in return for a gift of fuel oil and two new nuclear power plants by South Korea, the United States, and Japan.[5] But North Korea has continued to develop medium- to long-range missiles and provocatively tested them near Japan and the American bases there to increase its political leverage in negotiating with Japan and the United States.

A strong criticism of the Pentagon–Nye strategy by two academic Japan specialists, Chalmers Johnson and E.B. Keehn, appeared in the same issue of

Foreign Affairs as the article Nye wrote to expound the new American East Asian strategy.[6] The critique argues that the virtual continuation of a fundamentally Cold War defence policy rests on a weak basis of temporary convenience for countries like Japan or those of Southeast Asia that are strong enough to handle their own security needs. But some recent events seem to contradict that argument. After driving out the American bases in 1992, the Philippines does need external support in the face of the challenge from China, which occupied reefs in the South China Sea in 1995 claimed by the Philippines. Nor can South Korea alone stem an invasion from the enormous million-plus hostile North Korean troops, most of which are threateningly poised on its border. Taiwan, too, will purchase new fighter planes from the United States contrary to previous American agreements with China, which is a source of tension between those two countries.

The Clinton Administration's new strategy gives strong endorsement to continuation of the U.S.–Japan Security Treaty, which permits the forward stationing of U.S. garrison forces in Japan. These forces also back up those in South Korea and elsewhere in Asia. This permits much greater global and regional influence for the United States than would a pullback of those forces to U.S. territory. Since Japan has elected to keep its own military preparations small and not shown much initiative in foreign affairs, it is neither a threat to its neighbours nor a competitor of the United States. If Japan has been excessively accommodating to the United States in accepting U.S. security strategies or other policies, and if it has shown weak leadership in its foreign policy, surely that has been due to Japan's own government's decisions and the exigencies of its domestic politics. Its leaders have the power to change the situation if they are willing to do so and can build domestic political support for change. To blame the United States for this, as Johnson and Keehn seem to do, is unfair.

It is likely that, if the United States were to withdraw its forces from East Asia and reduce its presence in Japan, the Japanese public, politicians, and bureaucrats might be sufficiently stimulated to enable Tokyo to assert itself more as some of leaders like Ichiro Ozawa, the president of the leading opposition New Frontier Party (NFP, or *Shinshinto*), wish to do. A more assertive Japan would more fully use its economic, political, and military assets to take a more independent stance towards the United States and its regional partners. It might become a more equal regional partner for the United States under some leaders, or it might relegate the United States to a much smaller regional role under others. If Japan is even less assertive than Canada towards the United States, that is its own fault. The situation is not unlike that of the United States, where many politicians and economists blame Japan for its huge trade imbalance with the United States. Japan's huge trade surplus is largely due to American macroeconomic policies that discourage savings and fail to reduce budget deficits, as Nye points out. The United States could use its regulatory power even more to limit Japanese imports if they affect domestic industry too adversely. That is what the European Union does. In both the United States and Japan, the needs of local politics and politicians may prevent desired solutions, but those are not the fault of foreign countries.

The U.S.–Japan Security Treaty has received almost unanimous support from Japanese politicians – including even the Social Democratic Party of Japan, which opposed it for over forty years until its leader, Tomiichi Murayama, became prime minister in 1994. But the treaty came under sharp public scrutiny for the first time since 1970 with the rape of an Okinawan schoolgirl by three U.S. servicemen in September 1995. Longstanding indignation on the island at bearing the brunt of the foreign military presence in Japan exploded, with public demonstrations drawing up to 85,000 people protesting against the bases. The island, with 0.6 per cent of Japan's territory, hosts nearly 62 per cent of the 47,000 American troops in Japan. Although popular indignation was directed mainly at Tokyo's failure to reduce or move the bases, the inevitable question arose among the Japanese public almost why the American troops should stay on given the end of the Soviet military threat. Some, like Johnson, who believes the balance of regional powers will ensure peace, consider that the American ground forces serve no useful military function and are even a source of instability.[7] Public support of the treaty in Japan grew only slowly through the years, but a newspaper poll of October 1995 showed popular opposition up to 40 per cent from 29 per cent only a few months after the Okinawa incident, when support fell from 60 per cent to 44 per cent, a serious setback.[8]

There was strong resistance in Okinawa to renewing land leases for the bases. Proposals to move some troops to the main islands were rejected by local governments there. Modification of the Status of Forces Agreement or even reduction of bases in Japan began to be discussed. To shore up the alliance, President Clinton made an official visit to Japan in 1996. The joint communiqué with Prime Minister Hashimoto affirmed the continuation of U.S. deployment of 100,000 military personnel in the region and force levels in Japan.[9]

Canada's Pacific Cooperative Security and Multilateralism

Like the United States and Japan, Canada too announced new medium- to long-range security policies with greater attention to Asia Pacific in November 1994. The Parliamentary Joint Committee on Foreign Policy, in a thorough review, reported 'that Canada should support initiatives such as the Association of Southeast Asian Nations Regional Forum (ARF) to develop a cooperative security dialogue in the region, with a view to working gradually toward [more adequate] regional security arrangements. As a Pacific country, Canada should play an active role in these developments, should demonstrate that it has security interests to protect in the Pacific, and should provide a more visible naval presence there.'[10] The Committee also supported Canada's participation in the current non-governmental (track two) Council for Security Cooperation in Asia Pacific (CSCAP) and the 1991–93 North Pacific Cooperative Security Dialogue meetings sponsored by the Centre for International and Strategic Studies at York University, begun with the encouragement of Foreign Minister Joe Clark and ministry officials.

Another committee, the Parliamentary Committee on Defence, reported, '[I]f Canadians want to be able to influence events in the Asia-Pacific region we must show that we have a stake in the region, that we see a Canadian security interest and are prepared to invest resources in protecting that interest ... We must demonstrate a more visible Canadian presence in Pacific waters, both near North America and across the ocean ... We need to engage our Pacific neighbours in a continuing dialogue on security issues.'[11]

In the '1994 Defence White Paper,' the minister of defence not only supported the Asia-Pacific security discussions but also stated, 'We will expand the current program of bilateral military contacts we maintain with a variety of Asian countries, including Japan, South Korea, and members of the Association of Southeast Asian Nations (ASEAN) ... Our activities in the Asia-Pacific region will be broadened gradually to include a more regular program of visits and exchanges in the area of peacekeeping, including programs at the Lester B. Pearson Canadian International Peacekeeping Training Centre.'[12]

Although Canadian military emphasis still remains on traditional commitments to the North Atlantic Treaty Organization (NATO), United Nations peacekeeping, and cooperation with the American ally as in the 1991 Gulf War, the commander of Maritime Forces Pacific has increased naval visits to east Asia. The new Canadian patrol frigates, such as HMCS *Vancouver* in 1994 and HMS *Regina* and *Winnipeg* in 1996, visited Japan about the same time they participated in the Rim of the Pacific (RIMPAC) exercises with American, Japanese, and Australian ships and aircraft. In order to maintain an enduring Canadian regional presence, Westploy 96 was the third consecutive dispatch of a Canadian naval task group across the Pacific.[13] Japanese military personnel were interested in specific equipment and systems they saw on the new Canadian frigates, but the lack of any defence industrial agreement impedes passage of sensitive information needed for potential sales or procurement cooperation. Canada already has a bilateral memorandum of understanding on defence industrial cooperation with South Korea and might benefit from a similar one with Japan.

Canada's increased naval presence in East Asia will bolster efforts of foreign and defence officials to conduct a more active Asia-Pacific security policy as well as other regional objectives. In future, Canadian forces may be called upon to join in Asian peacekeeping or peacemaking operations with the United States or possibly Japan, as it was called upon to do in Cambodia in 1993 and in the Gulf War in 1991. Canada has long participated in the biennial American navy–sponsored RIMPAC joint exercises with other Pacific allies of the United States such as Japan, South Korea, and Australia. While these do not involve any commitment to future joint military action, they do enable the participating navies of the United States, Canada, and Japan to practise joint operations together with their ships and aircraft. This in turn will increase their ability to operate together in the future, especially if Japan should ever expand the limits of its 'individual defence' or put into effect the frozen provisions of its Peacekeeping Law to enable greater joint United Nations security action.

Just before the Clinton–Hashimoto summit in Tokyo in April 1996, the United States and Japan signed an Access and Cross Services Agreement permitting Japan to share such things as fuel, water, and medical services with American forces in peacetime for such things as military exercises or United Nations operations. Such logistics cooperation would normally be expected even during times of hostility in North Korea or the Taiwan Strait, which the U.S.–Japan Security Treaty was designed to deal with. Canada, too, might benefit from a bilateral cross-servicing agreement with Japan.

In 1991, the Canadian and Japanese prime ministers appointed a committee of private citizens called the Canada–Japan Forum 2000, which recommended some ways to strengthen bilateral cooperation between the countries, including security cooperation. A follow-up committee recommended action in six priority areas on such things as closer cooperation at G-7 summits, where the two countries' prime ministers and foreign ministers now regularly hold separate bilateral talks with each other, often covering security problems.[14] It also proposed regional comprehensive security as an added topic at APEC summit meetings as well as those at the annual ASEAN Regional Forum.[15] During Prime Minister Chrétien's November 1996 official visit to Japan, it was agreed that the Canada–Japan Forum would become a permanent body.[16] The newly appointed co-chairmen met in Tokyo during the visit in November just after the two prime ministers had attended the APEC meeting in Manila.

As for military-to-military talks, in September 1996 the Canadian chief of the defence staff visited the Japanese chairman of the joint staff council, and the chief of the Japanese Maritime Self-Defence Force visited the Canadian defence chief in 1992 and 1995 for talks. It is desirable to put some of these high-ranking military exchanges on a regular basis. There are irregular visits between lower-ranking officers, but annual staff study talks alternating between Ottawa and Tokyo are now being held. Also, Japanese students have taken courses at the Pearson Peacekeeping Centre near Halifax.

Of course, Canada continues to take part frequently in joint bilateral exercises with the United States and takes some of the responsibility for sea and air protection in the Eastern Pacific. These military activities are in connection with Canada's role as an ally in the North American Air and Space Command for the protection of the continent, which arose during the Cold War. However, there has been no attempt to form any kind of trilateral military arrangements among Canada, Japan, and the United States, which might be precluded anyway under Japan's present doctrine of individual self-defence and limited security cooperation, mainly with the United States. That does not rule out cooperation in multilateral security operations in future, which might eventually come to include Japan in a naval blockade or some sea or air protection roles in East Asia. Joint disaster relief operations are already possible. The three countries, of course, participate not only in the annual multilateral ARF discussions on regional security issues but also take part in the intercessional meetings and working groups of that body. The unofficial track two Council on Security and Cooperation in Asia Pacific (CSCAP), made up of defence specialists from strategic studies institutes throughout the region, also includes participants from the three countries in their full meetings and working groups. The unofficial CSCAP meetings have had the advantage of sometimes including North Korean participants, which has not been achieved by official government gatherings. It is especially important to include North Korea in an effort to gain its cooperation in resolving tensions in Northeast Asia, something neither ARF nor other multilateral regional bodies are well placed to do. Ever since Foreign Minister Joe Clark's early initiative, North Korean involvement has been a Canadian security goal.

Japan's New National Defence Program and Purely Defensive Policy

The Japanese Liberal Democratic Party (LDP, or *Jiyu Minshuto*) lost its nearly forty-year grip on power in 1993 with the desertion of a large number of members who formed several smaller conservative parties. Together with small centre parties, they formed a series of coalition cabinets under different prime ministers, sometimes changing every few months.[17] One of the non–Liberal Democrat leaders, Prime Minister Hosokawa, appointed a private advisory group of prominent citizens to advise on defence issues in 1993. Their report on 12 August 1994 to Prime Minister Murayama strongly influenced the new basic Japanese defence policy that was authorized by Cabinet in 1995. The new

National Defence Program Outline (NDPO), as it is called, was the result of political compromises among the Murayama Cabinet coalition of the Social Democratic Party of Japan (SDPJ, or *Shakai Minshuto*), the New Pioneers Party (NPP, or *Shinto Sakigake*), and the Liberal Democratic Party.[18] The reduced size of forces and retention of the sharp limits on Japanese combat involvement reflect the strong pacifist sentiments, particularly in the centre-left parties and the public. The Pentagon team working on the new U.S.–Asia Pacific strategy was in touch with the Japanese advisory group, taking its work into consideration in their planning. Both teams were in firm agreement on strengthening the U.S.–Japan security relationship in the new era, strongly supporting continued American troop presence in Japan. The original Japanese National Defence Program Outline of 1976 was superseded by Cabinet approval of the new Outline on 29 November 1995.[19]

The new program ostensively expands the duties of the Japan Self-Defence Forces beyond the old Defence Program Outline of being able to fight alone to repel a 'limited, small-scale aggression' against Japan while relying on the United States to come to its defence in case of any more serious threat. The new program now includes disaster relief, antiterrorism strategy, and peacekeeping under the United Nations, all newly listed responsibilities that Japan had already been carrying out in practice. Until recently, almost any kind of foreign dispatch of defence personnel was forbidden in interpreting the antiwar clause of the constitution. The interpretation was broadened by finally passing a peacekeeping law in 1993 after two failures in Parliament and considerable opposition even within the conservative parties as well by the socialist parties and the public. But severe restrictions remain on any use of force by Japanese forces operating abroad, as insisted upon by the pacifist-minded Socialists, the Pioneers, and the small Democratic Socialist Party (DSP, or *Minshu Shakaito*, later absorbed into the new main opposition party, the New Frontier Party (NFP, or *Shinshinto*).[20] There are provisions in the law for participating in normal peacekeeping duties, such as keeping two hostile armies separated and enforcing disarmament provisions, but these have been frozen by agreement among the parties and not yet put into effect. The frozen provisions also provide for creating a special peacekeeping force separate from the regular Self-Defence Forces.

Japanese personnel are limited to non-combat support operations like logistics and communications duties, or such engineering tasks as building roads and bridges, which it did during UN peacekeeping in Cambodia. But the multi-party government coalition equivocated for three years over sending a fifty-one personnel contingent to the Golan Heights in Syria to relieve a few of the Canadian troops who had served there for twenty years as part of the multinational UN

Disengagement Observer Force (UNDOF). However, some leaders of both the Liberal Democratic Party and the chief opposition New Frontier Party would like to extend the scope of Japan's joint defence cooperation both with the United States and in UN peacekeeping or other joint security measures.[21] Continuing change in the governing party coalition may open up that possibility.

For UNDOF, which served on the Golan Heights in 1996 between Israel and Syria, at the insistence of the Observer Force commander the Japanese government finally agreed to let the first advance contingent participate in military exercises in which they carry weapons just like other UN contingents from Austria, Poland, and Canada. That was achieved over the Social Democrats' opposition from within the coalition and in spite of an earlier agreement in August 1995 that the Japanese troops would not take part in exercises where they had to carry arms. In the Observer Force exercise, Japanese personnel are interpreted to be acting as individuals.[22] One Japanese member of the military said that if the Canadians, who were experienced developed-nation peacekeepers, deemed hand guns, rifles, and machine guns necessary for self-protection, Japan should too, but thinking about guns within Japan was totally unrealistic.[23] Subsequently, the Japanese troops served on the Golan Heights in 1996 when violence did occur.

Japanese seem to have gone to extremes in their continued strong postwar antiwar feelings, in stark contrast to their support of militarism in the thirties and early forties. Such antiwar sentiment even exists in the two main conservative parties, the Liberal Democrats and the New Frontiersmen, although some members favour acting more like other countries that do not put such restrictions on military combat. The two parties are headed by Prime Minister Hashimoto and Ichiro Ozawa, respectively, both of whom favour a more full and normal military role for Japan in peacekeeping. Both are inclined to support unfreezing the relevant clauses of the peacekeeping law, although the law would continue to forbid any military cooperation abroad not authorized by the United Nations. Participation with American ships, and perhaps with Canadian ships also, in a naval blockade to carry out sanctions against North Korea, as was contemplated by the United States in 1994, appears to be out of the question.

The new defence program reduces the authorized size of the standing Ground Self-Defence Forces from 180,000 to 145,000, with plans for a new ready reserve of 15,000. The change is nominal because the ground force numbered only about 150,000 in recent years due to the difficulty of recruiting personnel, partly due to shrinkage in the relevant age cohort and the attraction of better-paying jobs elsewhere. Cuts are also to be made to naval and air force equipment such as ships and planes. However, the stronger fire-power and effectiveness of new equipment will probably still result in a more formidable but defensive military establishment with one of the best navies in the region. This navy cannot have aircraft carriers, long-range bombers, or nuclear weapons, retaining the now traditional 'defensive defence' (*senshu boei*) policy. As currently applied, *senshu boei* means the use of military force is permitted only in self-defence and at only the minimum level necessary for self-defence.

The Clinton–Hashimoto Joint Declaration of April 1996 reaffirmed the importance of the security cooperation between the United States and Japan and described it as the basis of the peace and prosperity of the Asia-Pacific region.[24] The Declaration also confirmed the various additional agreements, like the Access and Cross Servicing Agreement of 15 April 1996, which enables Japanese logistical support to American military units in the form of water, fuel, and medical facilities in peacetime. The two countries agreed to review the 1978 Guidelines for Defence Cooperation to improve planning for joint action during emergencies or joint military operations. A bilateral Special Action Committee on Okinawa (SACO) at work during the year won agreement from both governments that the United States would return one-fifth of the land used by American forces in Okinawa by 2001 but still leave 28,000 American personnel in the prefecture.[25] Strongly welcomed in Okinawa was the return of the U.S. Marine Corps' Futenma Air Station in the densely populated city of Ginowan. The plan to create a $2 billion floating airfield is very striking, something never tried on such a large scale.

After a year of bitter opposition from most Okinawans, including the governor, the central government managed to continue the American use of the periodically expiring land leases, but the Okinawans still want all the American military personnel withdrawn. In Japan there was even some public discussion over whether the country should participate in collective security like other countries or even whether the American alliance was needed, almost for the first time. However, Prime Minister Hashimoto drew the line at widening the constitutional limits on Japan's defence cooperation, a limitation not questioned by the Clinton Administration. Therefore, it is doubtful that the defence cooperation has been significantly increased in any concrete way. The 'new' agreements may even have the effect of being more limiting than before. But, the atmospherics may be more important than the various steps taken if they lead to more cordial behaviour between the two countries and some significant reduction in the severe economic threats and sanctions between them of the last few years.

The subtitle 'Alliance for the 21st Century' of the Clinton–Hashimoto Joint Declaration on Security of 17 April 1996, coming so soon after the missile firing in the Taiwan Strait and the deployment of American carriers nearby, looked more like a policy of containment of China than the proclaimed U.S.

'constructive engagement' policy. However, after the election of Lee in Taiwan, both the Chinese leadership and the Clinton Administration were anxious to calm the troubled waters of China. Soon both China and the United States made overtures to each other. Both Tokyo and Beijing played down the local agitation over the Tiaoyu/Senkaku Islands, where Japanese nationalists had erected a navigational light and Chinese activists from Hong Kong and Taiwan tried to remove it. In January 1997 Chinese Defence Minister Chi Haotian was welcomed in Ottawa on an official visit, as he was again immediately afterward in Washington. The United States also invited Chairman Jiang Zemin for an official visit to Washington in 1997, something proposed by China and pending for a long time despite continuing criticism from civil rights activists and the press for inviting the perpetrators of the Tiananmen Massacre. The willingness of Canada and the United States to emphasize trade over human rights issues points up the importance of the overall relationship with China for the security as well as the prosperity of the Pacific region.

The Pacific in the 1990s: The Era of Constructive Engagement

If the Cold War period was an 'era of containment,' then the 1990s in the Pacific appear to be an 'era of constructive engagement.' And economic power has become the major lever to bring this change about. The strong desire to enjoy the benefits of trade and investment among most of the Asia-Pacific countries in the nineties inclines them to be more conciliatory on security issues. Ever since Canada's and Australia's initiatives in the early nineties, the amount of military exchanges and confidence-building has progressed markedly both bilaterally and multilaterally even across the old Cold War divide, with the possible exception of North Korea.

The Western democratic countries hope that more open economies taking advantage of trade and investment will also bring about more democratic regimes in the autocratic countries, as has happened in South Korea and Taiwan. But Western pressures and sanctions to censure human rights violations in China, Burma, and Indonesia are asserted by some East Asians to be forms of cultural imperialism reminiscent of the behaviour of the former Western powers in Asia. The ASEAN countries have even welcomed the repressive Burman regime as a form of constructive engagement by inviting it to participate in ASEAN meetings and eventually to join their association, despite strong Western disapproval.

Canada's cooperative security approach could also be characterized as constructive engagement in sponsoring regular security discussions across the divide of old hostilities and divergent attitudes towards human rights. Canada has tried (and occasionally succeeded) to draw North Korea further into security cooperation, particularly in non-governmental workshops of the ongoing Council on Security in Asia Pacific (CSCAP) and in the earlier cooperative security dialogues sponsored by Foreign Minister Joe Clark in 1991. Since then, a series of arms control workshops have been held by researchers in Canada and South Korea on confidence-building in the North Pacific in which defence specialists from other Pacific countries also participate.[26] After participating in some of the early Canadian-sponsored security dialogue meetings, North Korean researchers became rather critical of Canadian initiatives. But in November 1995 they invited Canadian academics to Pyongyang, and in May 1996 they visited Canadian universities, where they participated in security discusssions of Asia Pacific.[27] Academics such as Professor Kyung-ae Park of the University of British Columbia were invited back again to exchange views with scholars in Pyongyang in September 1996. A Canada–Korea Forum was begun in 1996 to build a special relationship between South Korea and Canada. The first meeting in Seoul was co-chaired by former Foreign Minister Joe Clark and former Foreign Minister Han Sung-joo.[28]

The Council on Security and Cooperation in Asia (CSCAP) has been successful in persuading China to join. Taiwan is not permitted to join, but individual Taiwanese can take part as participants or observers in working groups. The Democratic People's Republic of North Korea has also joined, so that its coverage now goes beyond any other regional security group. It also has a close relationship with the ASEAN Regional Forum on security, the governmental group sponsored by ASEAN that always supplies the co-chair of CSCAP.[29] Within Canada, CSCAP is backed by a strong group of Asia-Pacific defence specialists, some of whom are members of CSCAP, and it is organized as the Canadian Consortium on Asia Pacific Security with its own conferences and bulletin. Thus, Canadians are an active part of the 'spiderweb of relationships and interests' in the region engaged in community-building in the security field.[30]

U.S. success in negotiating a freeze in North Korea's nuclear weapons program in return for American, Japanese, and South Korean cooperation in aiding North Korea's peaceful nuclear power development is a case of constructive engagement where economic benefits were used to encourage security cooperation. This success was jeopardized in 1996 when a stranded North Korean submarine was found in South Korea that led to the killing of many of the crew and some South Koreans. After delicate negotiations by the Americans, the North Koreans were persuaded to issue an apology, apparently a difficult step for them. This improved relations with South Korea and the United States, enabling the nuclear freeze and provision of fuel and reactors to North Korea to continue. Peaceful mediation managed to mend the faltering engagement with North

Korea, which suffers from deepening economic setbacks and division in its leadership over cooperation with the capitalist world.

In the 1990s, it is surprising the extent to which the smaller powers, including Canada, have created Pacific regional multilateral institutions both in economic and security matters. It was Australia, under Prime Minister Bob Hawke, that successfully inaugurated the APEC forum in 1989, despite the reluctance and suspicion of the ASEAN countries, which did not want their own organization weakened. When Hawke initially proposed to exclude Canada and the United States, the protests of their foreign ministers and the urging of Japanese trade officials resulted in Canberra including them. Although APEC has retained its economic focus, leaders such as President Bill Clinton suggest from time to time that the forum should also include regional security in its agenda. APEC burst into prominence in 1993 when Clinton first added a summit of the heads of state to APEC's annual foreign ministers' meeting, thus providing a kind of Pacific version of the G-7 meetings. It is probably of global importance that the heads of the United States, China, and Japan now meet together regularly to deal with regional affairs, as well as together with most of the heads of other important regional states. Nothing of this nature had been tried before.

The non-major powers prefer dealing with the major powers in an open multilateral forum where they can gain more support and strength than they can when facing a major power on a one-to-one bilateral basis. Thus, in the late eighties and early nineties in the Pacific, it was Canada and Australia that inaugurated the security dialogues and the APEC forum. Of course, the Southeast Asians had created their subregional Association of Southeast Asian States earlier. More recently, they have added to their annual foreign ministers' meeting a separate gathering with foreign ministers of most of the other regional states, including all the major Pacific powers. That group is called the Post-Ministerial Conference (PMC) of foreign ministers, which continues to meet annually and includes Canada as well as the United States, Japan, China, and Russia. It is, thus, actually more representative of the region than even APEC, with the inclusion of the Russian foreign minister and the European Union foreign commissioner.

ASEAN also went further than APEC in setting up the ASEAN Regional Forum, which meets alongside the Post-Ministeral Conferences each summer for security discussions. Although it already included the European Union foreign commissioner in the PMC and in the ARF, in 1996 ASEAN went even further to persuade the fifteen heads of the European Union states to meet with it annually in an East Asian–European Union Summit Meeting (ASEM) and included other major East Asian states: Japan, China, and South Korea, but not Russia, the United States, or Canada. ASEM also covers security as well as economic affairs, although the Europeans no longer have as much interest in, or responsibility for, Asia-Pacific security as they once did.

The new East Asian and West European heads of state gathered for the first time in March 1996 in Bangkok.[31] In the ASEAN-sponsored groups, the Southeast Asian states depend on the multilateral context to strengthen and protect themselves and jealously guard their influence over the agenda. Thus, they have now extended a stronger political reach beyond the Asia-Pacific region of APEC and the PMC to Western Europe, signifying the growth of their global strength and importance. Even in APEC they are favoured by the rule that every alternate year ministerial and summit meetings are in an ASEAN country. ASEAN has succeeded in co-opting in its multilateral diplomacy all the advanced states in the Pacific, including those in North America, and now those in Western Europe as well.

Therefore, the ASEAN members were less than enthusiastic about Prime Minister Hashimoto's proposal, in a speech in Singapore on 14 January 1997, to have an annual summit of Japan and ASEAN leaders as well as parallel 'frank' bilateral security talks.[32] If such a proposal were accepted, it would undercut the strength the Southeast Asians have built in diplomatic and security affairs with the ASEAN forums. Much too late, Japan is attempting to use its large investment in and economic aid to Southeast Asia to formalize the former rather dependent economic relationship by extending it into political and security affairs. With their rapid accumulation of domestic capital and foreign investment, the Southeast Asians are becoming too strong and independent to be captured so easily. Also, it might antagonize China to see Japan gaining a special relationship with ASEAN when it has no such close tie with Beijing. The United States, however, might welcome such a relationship as a stronger regional counterweight to China if it did not see Japan becoming a stronger competitor to its own influence in Asia. Even Prime Minister Mahathir of Malaysia, who has long championed a separate East Asian grouping of states including Japan, but excluding the United States and the other Pacific Anglo-Saxon countries like Canada, has balked at supporting the Hashimoto initiative.

Canada has concentrated its efforts in security cooperation in those ASEAN-sponsored groups both in the regular high-level meetings and in working groups and committees of lower-level officials. Ottawa has also taken minor initiatives of its own, such as giving financial support to the Indonesian-sponsored group of litoral states discussing cooperation in developing resources of the South China Sea. Ottawa hoped that process might lead to future resolution of the serious territorial disputes between the Southeast Asian states and China, which claims all the reefs and islets of the South China Sea and their adjacent economic zones and territorial seas.

On Prime Minister Jean Chrétien's official visit to Japan in November 1996, he and Prime Minister Hashimoto released a Canada–Japan Agenda for Co-operation.[33] It included joint cooperation in Asia Pacific as well as expanded bilateral ties, but extended these to clearly include political cooperation on peace, security, and the environment. To carry out something concrete in security together, they announced that they had commissioned a joint study being implemented by their foreign and defence officials. This is a good example of how much closer the two countries are getting to regional security cooperation. It may also, in effect, carry out the recommendation of some Japanese diplomats and scholars that Japan might improve its handling of relations with its American partner in some of the ways Canada has succeeded in maintaining good relations with the United States despite the same kinds of economic disputes that bedevil Japan's own ties with Washington. After all, Japan and Canada are two of the closest military allies of the United States, as well as the Americans' two most important trading partners, an inescapably trilateral relationship that is growing closer in the 1990s. The three countries' financial ties are so intimate that they strongly influence one another's interest rates, currency values, borrowing capacities, and levels of economic activity. Thus, the theme of broadening trilateral interaction is clearly seen in all these spheres.

The theme of global and Asia-Pacific security cooperation has advanced considerably in the mid-nineties. The Agenda for Cooperation of November 1996 between Canada and Japan calls for promotion of the Comprehensive Nuclear Test Ban Treaty, the Chemical Weapons Convention, and a ban on antipersonnel mines. The two countries already participate in U.S.-sponsored multilateral military exercises. As noted above in the case of the naval Rim of the Pacific exercises, Canadian ships take part with those of the United States, Japan, Australia, and South Korea. Canada's Pacific command has also inaugurated a regular program of naval ship visits to East Asia. The ARF has inaugurated interim meetings of uniformed personnel, in which Canada participates, to give its defence officials more adequate security participation alongside or in addition to the meetings of its foreign and trade officials. These resemble the regional meetings of military officers held by Japan recently. Although some Canadian proposals for joint peacekeeping training with Japan have not worked out, there have been joint peacekeeping discussions between defence personnel and officials of both countries. As noted in the above discussion of Japanese participation in the United Nations Disengagement Observer Force on the Golan Heights, the take-over of some of the logistics duties of Canadian forces by Japanese Self-Defence Forces personnel influenced the desire of the Japanese for more adequate protective arms and Japanese questioning of their own country's severely restrictive arms policies.

In contrast to the Eastern Pacific, Canada has not been a close partner of the United States or Japan in Western Pacific defence where the latter prefer their own bilateral arrangements, but it does participate with them in most of the new multilateral regional organizations, governmental and non-governmental, that deal with security.

The dense network of economic and political ties and exchanges going on in the region are impressive, although their loose consensual nature may not be adequate in the face of severe security threats, which have occurred repeatedly since World War II. But the older Cold War alliances of the United States, Japan, and South Korea continue to underwrite the peace as well as the economic development of East Asia and the Pacific. That peace is in turn supported by the newer multilateral advocacy forums of confidence-building and arms limitations urged strongly by Canada for the region since 1991, an application of constructive engagement to regional security affairs. At the same time, Canada and Japan have stepped up their own bilateral cooperation in security as well as economic and social affairs. As for the theme of Pacific community-building, the three countries – Canada, Japan, and the United States – are drawing closer together in the common task of maintaining an Asian–Pacific community in security as well as in economic affairs.

NOTES

1 David Dewitt, Common, Comprehensive and Cooperative Security.
2 U.S., Department of Defense, *United States Security Strategy for the East Asia-Pacific Region*. See transcript of the Nye briefing to the press also released by the department on the same day.
3 Nye, 'The Case for Deep Engagement,' 90–91. The assistant secretary travelled to give talks in major centres in the United States and Japan to explain and arouse support for the new policy and wrote the article in *Foreign Affairs* for the same purpose.
4 Nye, 'The Case for Deep Engagement,' 96.
5 Ibid., 95.
6 Johnson and Keehn, 'The Pentagon's Ossified Strategy.'
7 Moffett and Holloway, 'Uncertain Future,' 20–21.
8 Holloway and Moffett, 'Patchword Diplomacy,' 17.
9 Japan, 'Japan–U.S. Joint Declaration on Security.'
10 Canada, Parliament, 'Security in a Changing World 1994,' 24. See also Canada, 'Canada in the World,' 30–31.
11 Canada, 'Security in a Changing World 1994.'
12 Canada, '1994 Defence White Paper,' 37.
13 Canada, 'Canadian Naval Task Group to Visit Asia Pacific Countries,' 14.

14 Canada, 'Canada–Japan, Forum 2000,' 10.

15 Ibid.

16 'Ambassador's Greetings,' 2, 6.

17 In 1994, Japan had four different prime ministers.

18 Advisory Group on Defence Issues, 'The Modality of the Security and Defense Capability of Japan.'

19 'Defense Outline Ok'd,' 1. For the complete Japanese text of the new National Defence Outline (*Shin-Boei Keikaku Taiko*), see the 29 November 1995 issue of the *Daily Yomiuri*, 8. The name of the program is 'Boei Keikaku no Taiko,' usually translated as 'National Defence Program Outline.'

20 Japan, *Defence of Japan, 1994*, 118–19. For the severe restrictions on the use of force, see pages 64–65.

21 '"Shudan-teki Jieiken" Nado Shuten ni,' 3.

22 'Goran KaNshigun, "Kyodo Kunren, Jieitai mo,"' 1. For safety, a soldier may carry a gun only when he or she personally decides his or her own life is in danger. He or she may use only the degree of force absolutely necessary. See also 'Gov't Agrees on 51-Member Golan Mission,' 1.

23 'Jieitai Goran Kogen Haken,' 9.

24 Japan, 'Japan–U.S. Joint Declaration on Security.'

25 'Okinawa Report Draws Mixed Reviews,' 4; 'Offshore Airfield Promises Big Rewards,' 1, 27.

26 Bedeski, 'Canada/Korea Arms Control Workshop,' 2–3.

27 Evans, 'North Korean Delegation Visits Canada,' 3.

28 'People and Places,' 6.

29 Narine, 'The ARF and CSCAP,' 4–5.

30 Ibid.

31 Mori, 'Bei, O, Ajia, Shin-Kozu eno Omowaku,' 4.

32 'Fears of Influence,' 14–15.

33 'Prime Minister Chrétien Visits Japan,' *Canada–Japan Trade Council Newsletter*, 8–9; 'Prime Minister Chrétien Visits Japan,' 1, 3; 'Action Plan Unveiled at APEC,' 3.

9

The Future of the U.S.–Japan Security Relationship: A Canadian Perspective[1]

DAVID A. WELCH

It has been suggested that there are three important processes at work in U.S.–Japanese–Canadian relations in the 1990s: a trilateralization of economic interactions, a broadening of the trilateral agenda to include regional and global security issues, and increasing collaboration in multilateral institution building. As a result of these processes, Japan and Canada no longer resemble spokes on a wheel with an American hub, as they did in the heyday of the Cold War. Increasingly they deal with each other – and with the United States – if not as perfect equals, at least as partners with a deeper appreciation for their respective contributions to welfare and security.

This analysis deals with something of an exception to such a portrait. On 'hard' security, Japan and the United States are important players in the North Pacific, while Canada is not. The U.S.–Japan Security Treaty is a strictly bilateral arrangement committing the United States to the defence of Japan; granting the United States facilities in Japan for its land, air, and naval forces; and governing the extensive cooperation between the two countries' armed forces.[2] Canada is not a party to the treaty and has no formal commitment to the defence of Japan.[3] Canada does, of course, have formal security arrangements with the United States (the most important being NATO and NORAD),[4] but these do not entail security commitments in Asia. In short, Canada is a bystander on this issue.

Nevertheless, Canada is not a disinterested bystander. It has an important stake in North Pacific security and is an active player – with the United States and Japan – in regional security arrangements, both formal and informal, whose purposes are to build confidence, increase transparency, slow regional arms races, and provide forums and channels for preventing, managing, and resolving disputes that might otherwise escalate into military confrontation. The purpose of this chapter is to explore Canada's attitude towards the bilateral U.S.–

Japan security relationship, examine its fit with Canada's approach to regional security, and assess its implications for the trilateral relationship.

A Conspicuous Silence

A useful place to begin is with official statements. However, Canada does not have an official position on the U.S.–Japan Security Treaty. There is no reference to the treaty in the statements or speeches of Canadian officials, in the news releases of the Department of Foreign Affairs and International Trade (DFAIT),[5] or in Canadian foreign policy reviews. When officials in DFAIT at both senior and junior levels are asked to comment for the record, they affirm that Canada is 'very interested' in U.S.–Japan relations and note that Canada 'closely follows developments' affecting the security of the Asia-Pacific region, but decline to elaborate further. It seems that the Ottawa foreign policy community considers it indelicate to express an official view on the bilateral defence arrangements of its friends and trading partners.

Off the record, however, Canadian officials readily acknowledge that the treaty has been an historically effective mechanism for promoting Japanese security, U.S.–Japan cooperation, and stability in the northern Asia Pacific. They would consider a disruption of the existing U.S.–Japan security relationship a serious threat to regional peace and stability. While Ottawa would like to see Asia-Pacific security rest increasingly upon multilateral foundations, nevertheless Canadian officials would prefer that these supplement, rather than supplant, the existing U.S.–Japan treaty.[6] It seems, however, that Canada is largely indifferent to the precise *form* the U.S.–Japan security relationship takes in the post–Cold War world, so long as it continues to embody tangible and visible symbols of the American commitment to Japan. Marginal changes and adjustments made necessary by U.S. or Japanese budgets or domestic politics – for example, to basing arrangements, or to the level or kinds of American forces stationed in Japan – would not jeopardize the very tangible benefits the treaty has for stability and security in the Asia-Pacific region. Canadian officials were privately pleased by what appears to have been the successful resolution of the controversy over the presence of American forces in Japan triggered by the 1995 rape of an Okinawan schoolgirl by three off-duty U.S. servicemen.[7] They were also pleased by the Clinton Administration's renewed commitment to the forward deployment of American forces in Asia.[8]

Canada's preference that multilateral security arrangements supplement, rather than supplant, the bilateral U.S.–Japanese Security Treaty reflects mainstream thinking in Canada on foreign and defence policy, and is consistent with the philosophical context of Canadian foreign policy as a whole. Silence in this case reflects not indifference, but merely a sense of decorum.

Canadian Interests and Canada's Role in Asia-Pacific Security

Of all the countries of the Pacific Basin, Canada faces perhaps the fewest direct threats to its physical security. It has no enemies, and virtually no prospect of finding any. Only the United States is physically capable of conquering and occupying Canada, and only those few countries with intercontinental nuclear capabilities are capable of inflicting significant damage upon it. In short, there are no conceivable military threats to Canada it could defend itself against, no matter how much it spent. Largely for this reason, Canada spends relatively little on its armed forces and does not think of itself as a 'player' in Asia-Pacific security in strictly military terms.

Nevertheless, instability in the Asia-Pacific region would be of concern to Canada, primarily for economic reasons. Canadian officials and foreign policy analysts generally maintain that economic stability and economic benefits depend on stable security arrangements.[9] Canada depends heavily for its welfare on international trade, and increasingly on transpacific trade.[10] War in the region would disrupt Canada's trade relations. But even increased political tensions short of war would have economic implications for Canada, threatening Canadian investment in the region. In addition, political tensions complicate regional and global arms control and non-proliferation efforts, which Canada regards as vital to stability in the post–Cold War world.[11] Regional tensions also have the potential to implicate Canada through its human rights and aid policies, and to aggravate ethnic conflict within Canada itself. Moreover, as political tensions in the region become militarized, Canada finds it increasingly difficult to play a role in promoting Asia–Pacific security because its comparative advantages in that regard are not military in nature. This is of concern to Canada because it has a general interest in being seen as a player in, and a contributor to, Asia-Pacific security. One of Canada's greatest fears is that it will come to be seen as irrelevant, because this would silence Canada's voice, threaten the general goodwill with which other states regard it, and consequently erode Canada's ability to defend its interests vis-à-vis the other countries of the region.[12]

Being relevant to Asia-Pacific security is a constant challenge for Canada. Its physical remoteness, negligible military capability, and relatively minor stake in the region (compared with that of virtually everyone else), mean that other Pacific Basin states naturally have difficulty thinking of Canada as a player. This is compounded by the fact that, for better or worse (perhaps on balance for better), Canada's image as an 'unmilitary nation' with a 'voluntarist tradition' constantly in search of 'moral opportunity,' cultivated during the heyday of liberal internationalism, is alive and well.[13] While Canadians and others tend naturally to think of Canada as a country that can perform a variety of useful functions around the globe (such as peacekeeping, election monitoring, relief, and humanitarian aid), they have difficulty imagining Canada playing a significant role in high-politics issues other than as an honest broker. This is compounded by the fact that Canada has a surprisingly small number of strategic thinkers in the government, the military, and the academy, and very few think-tanks or research centres that address traditional 'hard' security issues.[14]

To play a role, and to encourage states of the Asia-Pacific region to think of Canada as an important contributor to regional security, Canadian academics and officials have sought primarily to do two things: first, to broaden the conception of 'security,' and second, to promote an innovative approach to building security that permits Canada to exploit some of its comparative advantages.[15] The most important Canadian innovation was the North Pacific Cooperative Security Dialogue (NPCSD, November 1990–June 1993), which stimulated a host of other initiatives, including the ASEAN Regional Forum, and provided a model for more than thirty regular forums for regional security dialogues that followed.[16] Many of these dialogues take place at the 'Track Two' level (discussions among academics, journalists, and government officials acting in private capacities), rather than at the 'Track One' (official) level, providing room for more creative and free-wheeling discussions of actual or potential regional security problems.

As Frank Langdon notes in Chapter 8, Canada was not the only country in the 1990s advocating a broader conception of regional security or promoting procedural and institutional innovation.[17] Nor were its proposals always welcome.[18] But quite apart from the merits of Canada's efforts for enhancing regional security, they largely succeeded in keeping Canada visible and relevant. They worked precisely *because* Canada was seen as a non-threatening, altruistic, largely disinterested actor with a long history of mediation, a small but skilled collection of committed diplomats and academics, a superb information infrastructure, and an unmatched network of connections to other states, international organizations, non-governmental organizations (NGOs), and universities. The fact that Canada is not a military power of any significance was an advantage – rather than a liability – for the role Canada attempted to play.

Multilateralism vs. Bilateralism

Many advocates of cooperative security would prefer to see multilateral processes and institutions eventually replace bilateral ones.[19] Since Canada champions cooperative security, this might lead one to suspect that Canada would prefer to see bilateral arrangements such as the U.S.–Japan Security Treaty ultimately replaced by multilateral arrangements. Indeed, many analysts of Canadian foreign policy would argue that Canada has a historical and philosophical preference for multilateralism over bilateralism. This is an oversimplification of a more complex reality.[20]

There is no question that Canada has ardently promoted multilateralism in a variety of contexts, including many security issues. Canada's support for multilateralism reflects the beliefs that stability breeds stability, that order breeds order, and that unilateralism and self-help are inconsistent with both of these. It reflects the view that Canada's core interests lie in a stable, orderly, rule-governed international environment.

Canada's interest in multilateralism – and the *kind* of multilateralism in which it has been interested – has changed over the years. For much of the postwar period, Canada's interest in multilateralism reflected fear of a capricious and overbearing United States. Multilateralism was attractive because of Canada's relative weakness and sense of vulnerability. Through multilateralism, Canada found safety in numbers. But multilateralism also brought the *strength* of numbers, and served a much broader array of Canadian interests than merely constraining American unilateralism. Since the global security agenda was relatively clear, unproblematic, and static during much of the postwar period, Canada found both the safety in numbers and the strength of numbers in durable, formal, free-standing institutions such as NATO and the United Nations.

In the post–Cold War era, multilateralism remains valuable – indeed, vital. Peaceful change in the former Soviet Union, including the maintenance of strong central control of nuclear weapons; effective non-proliferation; peaceful management and resolution of international disputes, particularly in economically vital regions such as the Persian Gulf; and progress towards addressing the full range of social, economic, and environmental problems on the global agenda all depend on coordinated multilateral action. But the nature of multilateralism is changing.[21] Neither deterrence nor collective security can play as prominent a role in maintaining international order as it did after 1945. Conflict is becoming increasingly diffuse, subsystemic, and intra-state in origin. It is more difficult to handle through traditional collective security organizations. It requires creative institutional adaptation on both the global and regional scale. The 'new multilateralism' is therefore more complex, more fluid, and more eclectic. Typically, no single institution deals with international conflicts today.[22] The new multilateralism has a crucial advantage over the old: it is unlikely that all security institutions will fail simultaneously and catastrophically. If effective international action is blocked in one forum, it may go forward in another. A dissenter or free rider may find itself outflanked and left behind as responsibility shifts to other institutions in which it has significantly less influence, thereby providing an incentive not to dissent or free ride in the first place. This represents a significant change from the earlier international order built on broadly multilateral, highly formal institutions such as the League of Nations and the UN.

Canada's pursuit of cooperative security in the Asia-Pacific region fits naturally with the new multilateralism. But nothing in the logic of the new multilateralism suggests that *bilateralism* cannot play an important role in maintaining international security. Quite the contrary: owing to the idiosyncrasies of security problems, some may be more amenable to bilateral than multilateral solutions. Canada has always acknowledged this, and has generally acted accordingly. North American air defence, for example, could more effectively be provided bilaterally than either multilaterally or unilaterally, and, accordingly, Canada willingly joined the United States in NORAD in 1957. Indeed, a careful reading of Canadian foreign policy demonstrates that Ottawa has frequently favoured bilateralism over multilateralism when it seemed practical or advantageous to do so.[23]

From a Canadian perspective, the fact that the U.S.–Japan security relationship is a bilateral arrangement – moreover, one that excludes Canada (a country that strongly dislikes being excluded) – does not necessarily imply that it should be scrapped and replaced by some kind of multilateral security arrangement. Since it cannot address the full range of security problems confronting the Asia-Pacific region, it must obviously be supplemented by a variety of institutions and agreements (perhaps mostly multilateral, but conceivably bilateral as well).[24] But if there are good reasons for maintaining it, then from a Canadian perspective it should by all means be maintained.[25]

The Importance of Continuity and the Importance of Change

There is little doubt that the U.S.–Japan security relationship has contributed to peace and stability in the Asia-Pacific region. Arguably, it has done so in a variety of ways. It has tangibly committed the United States to the defence of Japan, reducing the extent to which Japan must prepare to defend itself, and calming those who fear Japanese military capability. By signalling an abiding American commitment to Northeast Asia, it has likewise calmed those who appreciate having a regional counterweight to Russia and the People's Republic of China.[26] In these ways, it has eased tensions in the region generally, has enabled states to devote to more productive uses the resources they might otherwise have spent enhancing their military capabilities, and has moderated arms races. Indeed, when the United States pulled out of its bases in the Philippines and began to discuss further reductions in its Western Pacific presence, the states of the region began to arm themselves at an alarming rate, with predictable effects on the tone and climate of international relations.[27] Ironically, there is no hard evidence to suggest that the U.S.–Japan security relationship succeeded in doing what it was ostensibly intended to do – deter Soviet aggression against Japan – because there is no evidence that the Soviet Union ever seriously contemplated such aggression.

From a Canadian perspective, it is difficult to know what alternative multilateral arrangements could perform the range of security functions that the U.S.–Japan Security Treaty has performed successfully for decades. The U.S.–Japanese relationship has a long track record of accomplishment, and there seems little reason to abandon a formula that appears to work so well in so many ways. While Canadians can be very entrepreneurial when it comes to building and shaping the processes and institutions of international politics, they generally do so only when existing tools and mechanisms are clearly inadequate for the tasks at hand.

But while the dangers of abandoning the existing U.S.–Japan security relationship would be significant, there appears to be no compelling reason from a Canadian perspective not to adjust and tune it to suit the demands of changing circumstances. There is no compelling strategic rationale to maintain existing arrangements unchanged, and it was crucially important to both parties not to permit growing opposition to the American presence in Okinawa to undermine the entire regime. Thus it was clearly prudent for the United States and Japan to attempt to reduce the visibility of the American military presence in Japan so as to contain discontent. Exactly how this ought to have been accomplished is something no Canadian official – and only the most presumptuous Canadian academic – would venture to suggest in detail. But few in Canada would object to marginal adjustments in the numbers and locations of American soldiers in Japan, or to changes in the terms of their deployment, provided that Washington and Tokyo reaffirmed the essence of their security relationship and ensured that the American military presence provided an adequate assurance of the U.S. commitment to Japanese and regional security.

Implications for the Trilateral Relationship

Canada strongly desires to play a role in the maintenance of Asia-Pacific security. It has important interests in the region that can only be harmed by instability, conflict, and Canadian invisibility. By and large Canada has managed to carve out a niche in Asia-Pacific security that prevents other states of the region from entirely forgetting about Canada, and that arguably contributes to mutual understanding, confidence, transparency, and stability. Canada has chosen to do so multilaterally, as has often been the case in Canadian foreign policy, and has managed to articulate a cogent rationale for its efforts. While Canada has not always managed to avoid the hubris of self-importance, it cannot be accused of overreaching.[28] Nor is Canada so enthralled by its multilateralist projects that it fails to acknowledge the place of bilateralism, even a bilateralism that excludes it and over which it has no leverage. Despite Canada's official silence on the future of the U.S.–Japan security relationship, Canada is aware of – and appreciates – the historical and contemporary value of that relationship to the stability and prosperity of the Asia-Pacific region.

As Canada lacks the stake, incentive, and capability to project itself energetically into the hard security sphere in the Asia-Pacific region, it could only damage its two most important relationships by attempting to trilateralize the issue. Washington and Tokyo would consider any such attempt presumptuous and meddlesome. Under the circumstances, given the recently increased delicacy of the issue in both the United States and Japan, even official commentary would be unwelcome.[29] The most that Canada can do is show the flag, provide technical assistance where possible (particularly in the area of its comparative advantage, namely peacekeeping), and promote coordinated international efforts to address select hard-security problems (such as the production and deployment of antipersonnel land mines).[30] Efforts such as these have obvious merit, maintain Canada's regional visibility and reputation, and provide both Japan and the United States with real security benefits. Canada *can* take an active and forward role in multilateral institution building and in creative conflict resolution without stepping on Japanese or American toes, and Canada's efforts in this direction have on balance strengthened the trilateral relationship.[31]

The North Pacific Triangle is therefore strengthened by Canada's official silence on the U.S.–Japan Security Treaty, and its energetic support for the growing multilateral 'soft' security system that supplements it. Historically, Canada has been quick to suggest institutional and procedural innovation whenever it perceives existing bodies and agreements inadequate to their tasks. Canada does not hesitate to involve itself in security issues whenever it perceives an opportunity to do so. That Canada makes no comment on the U.S.–Japan security relationship therefore indicates satisfaction with the essence of the present arrangement, and Canada's hope that it will continue to play a vital role as a bilateral pillar of an increasingly heterogeneous multilateral security structure for the Asia-Pacific region.

NOTES

1 An earlier version of this paper was presented at a workshop on the future of the
   U.S.–Japan Security Treaty held in Osaka, Japan, 19–22 January 1996. The author
   would like to thank the participants and organizers – especially Professors Masayuki
   Tadokoro and Masato Kimura – as well as the helpful comments of two anonymous
   reviewers. The final version of this paper was prepared while the author was on leave
   at the Thomas J. Watson Jr Institute for International Studies, Brown University,
   whose generous support the author would also like to acknowledge.
2 The official title is the 'Treaty of Mutual Cooperation and Security between Japan
   and the United States of America,' signed in Washington, DC, on 19 January 1960,
   which supplants the 1951 Security Treaty signed in San Francisco. The full text of
   the treaty is available on the World Wide Web at http://www2.nttca.com:8010/
   infomofa/ju/q_a/sec/ref_01.html.
3 Despite the absence of formal security commitments, Canada and Japan do have an
   increasingly active bilateral defence relationship. Since 1992, staff of the Japanese
   Self-Defence Forces and the Canadian Armed Forces have held annual talks, alternating between Tokyo and Ottawa, to exchange information on regional defence and
   security. Twice a year, Canadian and Japanese ships participate in bilateral naval
   exercises immediately prior to the multilateral RIMPAC naval exercises involving
   the United States, Japan, Canada, and other Pacific Rim countries. The Japanese
   Training Squadron visits Canada regularly to make port calls and exercise with
   Canadian ships. The two countries' armed forces also participate in a number of
   routine bilateral exchanges (e.g., the Japanese National Defence Academy and the
   Royal Military College of Canada Exchange Program). Canadian and Japanese
   troops also serve side by side in peacekeeping in the Golan Heights, and the
   Canadian Armed Forces has assisted Japanese peacekeeping.
4 North Atlantic Treaty Organization and North American Aerospace Defence Command, respectively.
5 Until 1994, the Department of External Affairs and International Trade.
6 The 'unofficial' Canadian view closely parallels the analysis in Luck, 'Layers of
   Security.'
7 'Okinawa and the Security Treaty,' *Japan Echo*, 32–35; Kristof, 'Doubts Rising in
   Okinawa, 4; Miyagi, 'Redressing the Okinawan Base Problem,' 27–32; Tadae, 'The
   Okinawan Threat,' 46–52; Inoguchi, 'The New Security Setup and Japan's Options,'
   36–39.
8 Nye, 'The Case for Deep Engagement.'
9 CANCAPS, *Canada on Asia Pacific Security in the 1990s*, 1.
10 The Asia-Pacific is Canada's second most important trading region and second-
   fastest-growing export market, after the United States. Canada's transpacific trade is

almost half again as large as its transatlantic trade. In addition, Asians are now major foreign investors in Canada. Smith, 'New Dimensions in Asia Pacific,' in *Canada on Asia Pacific Security in the 1990s*, 66.

11 Smith and Sinclair, 'Arms Control and Security Building in Asia-Pacific: A Canadian Perspective.'

12 Cf. Selin, 'Asia Pacific Arms Buildups Part One.'

13 See for example Eayrs, *The Art of the Possible*; and Hockin, 'The Domestic Setting.'

14 Perhaps the most prominent of these – the Canadian Institute for International Peace and Security – was closed by the federal government in 1992.

15 As former Secretary of State for External Affairs Joe Clark put it in a speech before the United Nations General Assembly, 'Security is more than the absence of war; it is the presence of peace. That requires a shared sense on each side that the survival of the other is in its best interest. This means building trust and confidence.' Clark, 'Notes for a Speech by the Secretary of State for External Affairs, the Right Honourable Joe Clark,' 17.

16 'Canada on Asia Pacific Security,' 2. For a detailed case for cooperative security dialogue, see Selin, 'Asia Pacific Arms Buildups Part Two.'

17 For a detailed exposition as well as a concise statement of competing proposals for Asia-Pacific security systems, see Dewitt, 'Common, Comprehensive, and Cooperative Security'; and Evans, 'Emerging Patterns in Asia-Pacific Security,' 55–61.

18 The NPCSD initiative received decidedly mixed reviews. The USSR and Mongolia supported it, inaccurately claiming that it was an extension of their own proposals. Australia and New Zealand supported the concepts, but disliked the proposed geographic focus. ASEAN initially saw it as an unwelcome, out-of-region initiative. The United States and Japan were the last to be convinced: Japan saw the proposal as a naïve acceptance of the Soviet agenda, and the United States preferred bilateral arrangements. 'North Pacific Cooperative Security Dialogue: Recent Trends,' 37–56, esp. 48–51. Cf. also Evans, 'The Council for Security Cooperation.'

19 Evans, 'The Council for Security Cooperation,' 14.

20 See generally Keating, *Canada and World Order*; and Stairs, 'Choosing Multilateralism.'

21 Welch, 'The New Multilateralism.'

22 Joe Clark writes: '[T]he real art in managing current international relations resides in skilful deployment of resources among all the available channels ... In the current world, Canada has to be adept – as a considerable power – in forming fluid, issue-specific working relations with other countries. It has to draw upon its wealth of affiliations, forming coalitions of common cause as the need arises. This means targeting the most appropriate organizations and being very clear about its agenda. Perhaps the newness of the "New Internationalism" resides partly in this – the unprecedented imperative for multiple but highly selective alternatives, the weaving

of coalitions in an increasingly complex web of institutions.' Clark, 'Canada's New Internationalism.' Holmes and Kirton define the 'new internationalism' as 'all those international institutions and groupings that have sprung to life, within or outside the United Nations galaxy, during the past decade and a half at a time when the old internationalism based on the inherited institutions of the first postwar decade seemed to be in such decay.' Holmes and Kirton, eds., *Canada and the New Internationalism*, Preface, x.

23 See for example Cutler and Zacher, eds., *Canadian Foreign Policy*.

24 Thus Canadians do not regard cooperative security as an alternative to traditional security arrangements. See NPCSD, 'North Pacific Cooperative Security Dialogue, 37.

25 Cf. Tow, 'Contending Security.'

26 On the importance of the United States as a regional power-balancer, see Tow, 'Reshaping Asian-Pacific Security.'

27 '[R]ecent U.S. drawdowns have had a direct effect on arms acquisitions in South Korea and the Philippines. In other cases, including Taiwan, Japan, Australia and ASEAN, the effect is indirect.' Selin, 'Asia Pacific Arms Buildups Part One,' 40–41, 69; see also ibid., 46, and United States Department of Defense, 'A Strategic Framework.'

28 See for example Clark, 'Notes for a Speech by the Secretary of State for External Affairs, the Right Honourable Joe Clark, at a luncheon hosted by the Foreign Correspondents Club of Japan, Tokyo, July 24, 1990,' in 'Canada on Asia Pacific Security in the 1990s,': 'Canada and Japan [are], each in our own way, giants on the North Pacific, each destined to play a decisive but different role in a new world that is building, each aware that the other can be a trusted but reliable partner,' 3.

29 For recent debate on the merits of maintaining the existing treaty, see Okamoto, 'Why We Still Need the Security Treaty'; Moffett and Holloway, 'Uncertain Future'; Mochizuki and O'Hanlon, 'The Marines Should Come Home'; Kitaoka, 'The Case for a Stronger Security Treaty'; Miyazaki, 'Time to Reevaluate the Security Treaty.'

30 See http://www.dfait-maeci.gc.ca/english/foreignp/disarm/mines/menu.htm.

31 But cf., for example, note 18.

10

Japanese and Canadian Peacekeeping Participation: The American Dimension

MITSURU KUROSAWA

With the end of the Cold War and the outbreak of the Gulf War, the issue of Japan's role in the international community and of Japan's contribution to international peace and security became the focus of a debate within Japan over sending national military forces abroad. Japan did take a historic step by sending its Self-Defence Forces (SDF) to Cambodia to serve as part of the United Nations peacekeeping operations in that country. However, UN peacekeeping has a history of more than forty years, with many states, such as Canada, participating since the inception.

In the Cold War era, the Security Council of the United Nations could not function as the collective security mechanism originally devised in the Charter. Thus, a new method of peacekeeping by states other than five permanent members of the Security Council was developed through state practice. The UN peacekeeping tradition that thus developed played a significant role in maintaining international peace and security in the Cold War era.

In the post–Cold War era, however, the demand for peacekeeping operations has increased. Many new operations have been established by the Security Council, some of these differing in important ways from previous ones. Most notably, the United States and other permanent members have become active participants in these operations. It was at this time that Japan agreed to send 600 members of its Self-Defence Forces and seventy-five police officers to Cambodia.

Canada, on the other hand, played a central role in establishing and deploying the first United Nations peacekeeping forces in the Middle East in the 1956 Suez crisis. Canada has been said to have invented peacekeeping operations (PKO). It has participated very actively and often eagerly in almost all of these endeavours. In both the Cold War era and the post–Cold War era, Canada has been very strong in supporting and participating in peacekeeping operations in new international circumstances.

When Japan and Canada make decisions on foreign affairs, the United States often exercises considerable influence over their calculations and ensuing decisions. In particular, the influence of the United States in the field of security is overwhelming. Japan is tightly connected with the United States by a bilateral security treaty that is a cornerstone of Japanese foreign policy. Canada, sharing a long border with the United States, is connected with the United States through North Atlantic Treaty Organization (NATO) membership and through the North American Aerospace Defence Command (NORAD) in the field of security and defence. Considering U.S. influence over their security policies, Japan and Canada display in their peacekeeping activity some common features as well as distinctive elements. The most notable, however, is the critical difference in the role of the United States in propelling Canadian and Japanese peacekeeping participation. For while participation in peacekeeping has meant an independent and autonomous diplomacy for Canada, it has represented an extension of the traditional foreign policy posture of following U.S. direction for Japan.

This chapter first examines Canada's long participation in UN peacekeeping operations. It then explores Japanese participation, focusing on the process for authorizing participation in peacekeeping. It next identifies the causes of both countries' participation in peacekeeping. Finally, it compares U.S. influence on each country with respect to their participation and considers the lessons to be learned by each country from the experience of the other.

Canadian Participation in Peacekeeping Operations

The first case of UN peacekeeping was the United Nations Emergency Force (UNEF) in 1956.[1] At the time of the Suez Crisis, peacekeeping was consciously devised as a new method of security by Canada's Secretary of State for External Affairs, Lester Pearson. He consulted Secretary-General Dag Hammerskjöld on his idea and General Assembly Resolution 998 (ES-1), embodying the concept, was adopted.[2] It 'requests, as a matter of priority, the Secretary-General to submit to it within forty-eight hours a plan for establishing, with the consent of the nations concerned, an emergency international United Nations Force to secure and supervise the cessation of hostilities in accordance with all the terms of the aforementioned resolution.'

The first reason why Canada was so active in establishing this peacekeeping force was Pearson's strong commitment to international peace. In those years Canadian foreign policy was very internationalist in orientation and pursued multilateral diplomacy focused on the United Nations in particular.[3] The second reason was that the United Kingdom and France were the parties to the conflict. The United Kingdom was Canada's mother country and France had a special connection with Canada because of French-speaking Quebec. Canada searched for and found in UN peacekeeping a face-saving formula for the withdrawal of the British and French military forces. The third reason was Canada's desire to support the U.S. position. The United States, which wanted an early withdrawal of the invading troops, was the most important external actor for Canada. Canada played an intermediary role between the United Kingdom and the United States.[4] Canada participated in the resulting force by sending 1,007 personnel at its peak involvement to a UNEF force that numbered 6,000.

In 1960, the UN Security Council adopted a resolution to establish a peacekeeping force in the Congo (ONUC). The Diefenbaker government had not planned to send large-scale numbers of Canadian personnel to this force. However, after the United Nations asked Canada to participate in ONUC, the prime minister promised to send 500 personnel, subject to Parliamentary approval. Canadians were important participants in ONUC because they could speak both English and French in communication units. Canada was also among the few countries that had the necessary military facilities.

In 1962, when the General Assembly approved an agreement on the transfer of Western New Guinea from the Netherlands to Indonesia, another force (UNSF) was established. Canada provided two airplanes, a general, and sixteen military personnel.

In the case of the United Nations Force in Cyprus (UNFICYP), established in 1964, Canada was the only country participating alongside the United Kingdom, whose troops had been stationed there before the operation began. Cyprus was a member of the Commonwealth of Nations. Turkey and Greece were both members of NATO. With this rapid Canadian deployment to UNFICYP, the threat of Turkish military intervention was reportedly avoided. Prime Minister Pearson stated in Parliament in 1967 that 'the purpose of the military presence in Cyprus is for peacekeeping, during which political negotiation should take place. If the negotiation is delayed indefinitely, the reason for the peacekeeping force to stay will have disappeared.' In December 1992, Canada announced the withdrawal of its forces from Cyprus because there was no progress in peacemaking and because Canadian peacekeepers were demanded in other peacekeeping operations.

In the 1970s, three UN peacekeeping operations were established by the Security Council: UNEF II in 1973, the United Nations Disengagement Observer Force (UNDOF) in 1974, and UNIFIL in Lebanon in 1978. Canada was one of the most active participants in those operations.

In the post–Cold War era, UN peacekeeping operations were required much more frequently and in many more locations: in Namibia (UNTAG), in Cambodia (UNTAC), in the former Yugoslavia (UNPROFOR), and in Somalia

(UNOSOM). At times they acquired wider functions than those traditionally per-formed, including observing elections and the conduct of civil administration. In this era, although the United States, the United Kingdom, and France began par-ticipating in the operations, Canada continued to be one of the most active and valuable participants.

In addition to these peacekeeping forces, there are many cases where military observers have been sent as part of peacekeeping operations. In these cases Canada has also been a most active participant.

Japanese Participation in Peacekeeping Operations

Japanese attitudes towards peacekeeping dramatically changed after the Gulf War of 1990.[5] In the face of strong international criticism of Japan for its lack of cooperation in the coalition effort to liberate Kuwait, the Japanese government announced material and financial assistance in August 1990. In spite of this assistance, however, the United States asked Japan for a further contribution through sending military personnel.

In response, the Japanese government in October 1990 submitted a bill to the Japan Diet to enable Japan to engage in United Nations peacekeeping. The bill asked for an authorization of Japan's cooperation, not only in operations taken by the United Nations, but also in activities taken by member states to secure the effectiveness of the UN resolutions, such as the coalition activities taken in the Gulf War and led by the United States. The bill also permitted the corps or members of the Self-Defence Forces to participate in those activities.

Public opinion towards this bill was very negative. A poll taken by the *Asahi Shimbun* on 3–4 November 1990 indicated only 21 per cent approval of and 58 per cent opposition to the bill. More specifically, 67 per cent of respondents thought that the dispatch of Self-Defence Forces abroad based on this bill would be unconstitutional, while only 15 per cent thought it would be constitu-tional. Only 27 per cent supported the proposition that Japan should follow the U.S. initiative in responding to the Gulf Crisis, while 56 per cent argued for Japan's taking an independent response. As a result, the government withdrew the bill in November. The three major parties, including the governing Liberal Democratic Party (LDP), agreed to create a new organization distinct from the Self-Defence Forces to co-operate in UN peacekeeping operations.

After the Gulf War concluded with victory for the coalition forces, the debate shifted focus from cooperation with U.S.-led coalition forces in the Gulf War to cooperation in UN peacekeeping operations. The option of sending members of the Self-Defence Forces themselves was given greater scrutiny. In April 1991, the government decided to send minesweepers of the Marine Self-Defence

Forces to the Persian Gulf. This was the turning point in Japanese military policy. The arguments for a direct international contribution and for securing safety over the oil routes from the Persian Gulf to Japan made it possible for the government to send the Self-Defence Forces abroad for the first time in the post–World War II period.

This measure was quite acceptable to the Japanese mass public. General attitudes towards the involvement of the Self-Defence Forces had by then shifted from negative to positive. According to an opinion poll conducted by *Mainichi Shimbun* in June 1991, the decision to send minesweepers was supported by 61 per cent of respondents, with only 33 per cent opposed.

On 1 August 1991, the government submitted a bill regarding cooperation with UN peacekeeping and similar operations. It included the participation of the Self-Defence Forces in peacekeeping operations whose mission included the disengagement of opposing military forces. The bill stipulated that the implementation of this mission could not include the use or the threat of use of armed force. In addition the government indicated the following five principles as guidelines: (1) there must be an agreement on a cease-fire among the parties to the conflict; (2) the parties to the conflict, including the territorial or host countries, shall have given their consent to the deployment of the peacekeeping forces and to Japan's participation in such forces; (3) the peacekeeping forces shall maintain a strict impartiality, not favouring any party to the conflict; (4) should any of the above guideline requirements cease to be satisfied, the government of Japan may withdraw its contingents; and (5) the use of weapons shall be limited to the minimum necessary to protect the lives of Japanese military personnel.

The bill was submitted to the Diet on 19 September 1991. In doing so, Cabinet Secretary Sakamoto emphasized that Japan should contribute more for international peace not only in the material or financial domain but also by sending personnel, especially in connection with Japan's policy of strengthening the UN.

In March 1992, the UN established its operation in Cambodia (UNTAC). The Japanese government was eager to participate in the operation under the provisions of the new law. However, in the debate in the Diet, some argued that to participate fully in peacekeeping forces was premature and that such action should be delayed. Others called for prior approval by the Diet when Japan was asked to send peacekeeping forces. In this context, 'peacekeeping forces' meant infantry or other units, equipped with small arms, that were given such missions as monitoring the observance of a cease-fire, being stationed within and patrolling buffer zones, inspecting or identifying the carrying in or out of weapons, and disposing of abandoned weapons. This resistance indicated that Japan was still very cautious about becoming involved in military activities, even under UN auspices.

With some amendments to the original bill, including the addition of a requirement for the Diet's approval before sending peacekeeping forces and for a delay in participation in peacekeeping forces, the bill was approved on 16 June. It became effective as law on 10 August 1992.[6] A public opinion poll conducted on the new law by the *Asahi Shimbun* in July 1992 indicated that 36 per cent of respondents agreed with it, while 36 per cent were opposed. The public attitude towards this law was thus completely divided.

Before this law was enacted, Japan's contribution to peacekeeping was restricted mainly to financial assistance. The request by the UN for Japan to send troops to Lebanon for UNOGIL in 1958, two years after Japan's accession to the UN, had been rejected by the Japanese government. Only in 1987 did Japan decide to send civilians to UN peacekeeping operations. One computer engineer was sent to Cyprus for UNFICYP, one civilian to India–Pakistan for UNMOGIP, one to Iran-Iraq for UNIIMOG, thirty-one to Namibia for UNTAG, six to Haiti for ONUVEH, and one to Iran-Kuwait for UNIKOM.

The first effective case of sending personnel after the law became effective was in the UNAVEM II mission in Angola. Here Japan sent three personnel for observing elections from September to October 1992. However, the main purpose for rushing the new law through the Diet was to secure authority for sending a large contingent for UNTAC in Cambodia.

The government group established to examine the Cambodian situation under the framework of the new law and in relation to the UN request for Japanese participation produced a report confirming that the conditions were suitable for Japan to participate. Soon after, informal consultation took place with the United Nations concerning the kind of Japanese contribution that was desired.

Five days after the formal invitation from the United Nations was received, the Japanese government decided on the form of its contribution. This included 8 military observers to monitor the cease-fire, 75 policemen, 600 troops in the engineer battalion to engage in repairing roads and bridges, and 50 election observers.

These forces were sent to Cambodia in September 1992. They returned in September 1993, following the election held in May 1993. According to an opinion survey conducted by the *Asahi Shimbun* in September 1992, 52 per cent of respondents agreed with sending the Self-Defence Forces to Cambodia as part of the peacekeeping operation. Only 36 per cent were opposed. As to the constitutionality of sending troops, 47 per cent believed it was constitutional, while 28 per cent considered it unconstitutional.

The government report on the UNTAC to the Diet suggested it was a great honour for Japan to have been able to contribute, including through sending personnel. The report further suggested that Japanese activities in Cambodia were highly praised by international society, including the Cambodian public and private sectors. They were also understood and supported more deeply by the Japanese public.

The third case of Japanese peacekeeping participation was ONUMOZ in Mozambique. UN Secretary-General Boutros-Ghali had expressed his expectation of Japanese participation in ONUMOZ when he was in Japan in February 1993. However, the Japanese government had been rather reluctant to join another operation before the outcome of UNTAC was clear. Yet because of the delay of the election in Mozambique and the positive report by the government group that surveyed the possibility of Japanese participation, Japan did decide to send about fifty members of the Self-Defence Forces as transport arrangement units. Fifty-three personnel left Japan for Mozambique on 11 May 1993. Of these, forty-eight were assigned for movement control and five officers served as headquarters staff officers.

The fourth dispatch of Japanese personnel abroad in accordance with the law came in March 1994. At that time Japan sent fifteen civilians for elections monitoring as part of UNOSAL in El Salvador.[7]

In connection with, but distinct from UNAMIR in Rwanda, and in response to the request from the United Nations High Commissioner for Refugees (UNHCR), Japan subsequently sent 290 Ground Self-Defence Forces and 180 Air Self-Defence Forces to Zaire. They were dispatched not as part of a peacekeeping operation but as part of a humanitarian relief operation under the new law. Self-Defence Forces participation in the Golan Heights' peacekeeping operation, along with the Canadian unit, was added to this list in January 1996.

Causes of Canada's Peacekeeping Participation

Canada's early and continuing support for participation in UN peacekeeping operations was truly extraordinary. Secretary of State for External Affairs Lester Pearson, after UNEF I was dispatched without much preparation, recommended that every state earmark some forces for UN peacekeeping.[8] Later Canada established the system of stand-by forces for peacekeeping; a part of the Canadian Armed Forces was earmarked and trained for this function.[9]

Canada also emphasized the importance of peacekeeping in its overall defence policy. The *1964 White Paper on Defence* identified military forces for UN peacekeeping operations as one of its top defence priorities.

There are three fundamental causes of Canada's exceptional and enduring support for UN peacekeeping. The first factor propelling active Canadian participation and regular willingness to participate is Canada's overall foreign policy commitment to traditional multilateralism and positive cooperation with the United Nations.[10] Canada realizes that isolationism is not useful for Canada and that its own security is guaranteed by collective security through the United Nations.

Canada's strong support of the UN was shown at the founding San Francisco Conference in 1945. Throughout the Cold War era, Canada kept its allegiance to the United Nations, even though the United States has had a tendency to ignore the UN and search for its security through NATO.[11]

During the Cold War era, the superpowers could not directly play important roles in international peace and security, primarily because of the veto power of the five permanent members of the United Nations Security Council. As a result, middle-sized and small countries expanded their activities. However, small countries did not have sufficient resources and the sense of global responsibility to serve as major contributors to peacekeeping operations. In contrast, middle powers like Canada could perform a very important role in international society through such involvement.[12]

The second cause is Canada's specialized capability and leading performance in having and using well-equipped and well-trained military forces. The United Nations always asked for a Canadian contribution because Canada had very professional forces with state-of-the-art equipment. In establishing peacekeeping operations, one of the core general principles is not to include forces from the five big permanent Security Council powers. As a result, Canadian participation has been indispensable, especially in logistic or communication works, as it is one of a handful of lesser powers with first-tier military capabilities.

The third cause is Canada's international position and reputation. The decision as to which countries will participate in a peacekeeping operation is decided by the United Nations. However, consent by a host state as to which countries would be acceptable is necessary. Although Canada has not always been accepted without reservation, in general it has proven to be very acceptable, along with such neutral states as Sweden, Finland and Austria.

Canada is also a member of NATO and has worked for the interest of the Western alliance. In a sense Canada has played an important role in peacekeeping as a representative of the Western alliance. However, if Canada had pursued the interest of the West only in its participation in UN peacekeeping, it would not have been accepted as warmly by the states concerned.

Although Canada generally has been under the strong influence of the United States, Canadian political or diplomatic positions and activities have not been the same as those of the United States. The attitudes of the two countries towards the United Nations in the 1980s were notably different. Canada's diplomacy has been based not only on bilateral relations with the States, but also on its multilateral relations with NATO, the Commonwealth of Nations, and the United Nations.

Causes of Japan's Peacekeeping Participation

In the Cold War era, participation in UN peacekeeping operations had not been officially discussed by the Japanese government. One reason was the dominant interpretation of the constitution, under which Japan had no right of collective self-defence by sending its Self-Defence Forces abroad. In addition, in an international society based on the Cold War polarity, Japan could depend on the United States through the U.S.–Japan Security Treaty, and thereby avoid becoming actively involved in international affairs.

Japan's position changed radically at the time of the Gulf War. The coalition forces led by the United States demanded Japan's active cooperation. Japan donated U.S.$13 billion for assistance to the Middle East countries and to the coalition forces. This contribution amounted to a U.S.$100 tax increase for every Japanese. However, Japan's financial contribution was not valued highly abroad and Japan was criticized for not sending military personnel.

Japan has traditionally been eager for economic development without emphasizing its role in maintaining international peace and security. It was criticized because, in spite of its economic strength, it made no military contribution to international peace and security. During the Gulf War, Japan did not send any personnel because its government failed to secure adoption of the bill on UN peacekeeping. After the war, Japan sent the Naval Self-Defence Forces for minesweeping in the Persian Gulf. Thus the first cause of Japanese 'peacekeeping' involvement abroad was a desire to respond to U.S. and international criticism.

The second cause was Japan's desire to improve its international status by sending forces abroad as peacekeepers. With the end of the Cold War, the United Nations appeared to regain its power as an organization centrally and effectively promoting world peace. The Japanese government expressed a desire to become a permanent member of the Security Council as part of an overall reform of the Security Council. The Japanese government thought it necessary to participate in UN peacekeeping operations to assist in Japan's campaign to secure permanent Security Council membership.

The third cause was also a consequence of the end of the Cold War. Although there are many non-military contributions to peacekeeping operations, the Japanese government was eager to send the Self-Defence Forces abroad because military power is more visible as a personnel contribution. Moreover, in the post–Cold War era it judged that the Self-Defence Forces must be used for purposes beyond defence against communism. It was thus thought appropriate to use the SDF as peacekeepers.

The American Dimension

What significance does Japanese and Canadian participation in peacekeeping operations have as part of the two countries' relationship with the United States? In the case of Canada, at the time of the Suez crisis Canada's main purpose was to serve as an intermediary between the United States and the United Kingdom, to recover and maintain international peace and security at Canadian initiative, and to persuade the United Kingdom to withdraw, as the United States demanded, while saving face. Canadian participation in Cyprus was based on a desire to act as intermediary between Greece and Turkey and to prevent their dispute from escalating to an armed conflict, because both countries were members of NATO, while Britain was a fellow member of the Commonwealth. Canada, as a member of the Western alliance, was working for Western interests in close consultation with the United States, but also working as a neutral party to prevent an escalation of the conflict.

In the Cold War era, Canada's peacekeeping participation was highly praised. Among Canadians peacekeeping was felt to be something that distinguished their country from the United States.[13] The United States could not participate in peacekeeping as one of the principles it is based on is the exclusion of the big five. Especially during the Cold War era, peacekeeping was one of the strongest and most visible Canadian contributions internationally, and it came to represent a distinct Canadian identity.

In the post–Cold War era, the United States has become a more active peacekeeping participant.[14] It has attempted to expand the function of peacekeeping operations to include peace enforcement in Somalia and the former Yugoslavia. Canada appeared to be rather critical towards such an expansion, with many Canadians advising the United States that it did not understand peacekeeping in the traditional sense.

More recently, mainly because of the failure of peacekeeping in Somalia where the United States was one of the most active participants, the United Nations decided to withdraw from peace enforcement activities and return to traditional peacekeeping. It later withdrew all operations from Somalia. A new U.S. policy on peacekeeping was announced in May 1994, which declared that the United States intended to be more cautious about participation in peacekeeping and to reduce its financial support for such operations.

In Japan's case, there was strong pressure from the United States during the

Persian Gulf War. Japan was asked to play a much more active role as a supporter of a new world order designed by the United States. Japan, which had been enjoying economic prosperity under the security umbrella of the United States, was asked to bear a more proportionate burden in security. Japanese participation in peacekeeping has thus been conducted under overwhelming U.S. initiative and pressure. During the Gulf War, Japan was persistently asked to send personnel in spite of its financial assistance of as much as $13 billion.

In conclusion, participation in peacekeeping constitutes a core component of an independent, autonomous diplomacy in the case of Canada, but a continuation on the whole of the traditional foreign policy stance of deferring to U.S. direction in the case of Japan. Although there are many reasons for this difference, including Japan's and Canada's respective history and tradition, the most important cause is the difference in their overall foreign policy postures. Canadian multilateralism contrasts strongly with Japanese bilateralism as the overall orientation in foreign policy. Both countries do strongly support the United Nations, and Japan's financial contribution to the organization is second only to that of the United States. However, in the substantial work of the UN, Canada has been one of the most active participants. In contrast, the fundamental stance of Japanese foreign policy has been to follow the United States, under the basic structure of the bilateral Security Treaty.

In the post–Cold War era, Japan should move beyond its traditional foreign policy posture of following the United States to develop a more autonomous diplomacy. In this process Japan can learn much from Canada. The most important lesson is the value of Canadian multilateralism: Japan should develop close relationships with many countries other than the United States and act more vigorously, broadly, and cooperatively in the United Nations.

Currently, there are signs of Japan becoming more independent from the United States, in part through active participation in UN peacekeeping operations.[15] Japanese domestic politics are also in transition after the Cold War era. Reconsideration of the U.S.–Japan Security Treaty has recently changed Japanese policies on security issues dramatically, to the point where Japan now accepts the constitutionality of the Self-Defence Forces and the Security Treaty.[16]

In August 1994, the Japanese Prime Minister's Advisory Group on Defence Issues submitted its report *The Modality of the Security and Defence Capability of Japan: Outlook for the 21st Century*. Regarding the missions of the Self-Defence Forces and peacekeeping operations, the report argued that it was important to consider peacekeeping as a major duty of the SDF along with the primary duty of national defence. It further recommended that the SDF participate as actively as possible in various forms of multilateral cooperation that are conducted within the framework of the United Nations for the purposes of international security, including peacekeeping operations.

The Office of the Prime Minister's opinion survey on the SDF and defence issues, conducted in January 1994, revealed that 48.4 per cent of respondents supported Japanese participation in UN peacekeeping operations. This represented a 2.9 per cent increase from the previous poll taken three years earlier. Moreover, in January 1994 only 30.6 per cent remained opposed, representing a 7.3 per cent decrease from the 1991 results.

Although it is true that a segment of the Japanese public still opposes the participation of the SDF in UN peacekeeping and emphasizes instead Japan's non-military contribution to international peace and security, the majority now firmly supports Japanese participation in UN peacekeeping. However, there is no strong support for participating in military coalitions not conducted under UN auspices. It appears that Japan has begun learning from, and should learn more from, Canada on how to become more independent of U.S. influence through actively and autonomously participating in United Nations peacekeeping.[17]

NOTES

1 See Gaffen, *In the Eye of the Storm*; Tackaberry, 'Keeping the Peace'; and Williams, 'International Peacekeeping.' The United Nations Department of Public Information publication *The Blue Helmets* includes UNTSO of 1948 and UNMOGIP of 1949 in its list.

2 For background on the case see Reford, 'Peacekeeping at Suez, 1956.'

3 Buchan, 'Concepts of Peacekeeping.'

4 Spy, 'Canada, the United Nations Emergency Force.'

5 For accounts of Japan's Gulf War debate and peacekeeping participation see Inoguchi, 'Japan's United Nations Peacekeeping,' and 'Japan's Response to the Gulf Crisis'; and Bennett, Lepgold, and Unger, 'Burden-Sharing.' For accounts of comparable Canadian decision-making and attitudes towards participation in the Gulf War see Kirton, 'Liberating Kuwait?' and 'National Mythology.'

6 As to the law, see Yanai, 'Law Concerning Co-operation.'

7 In the elections monitoring field, the government of Japan also sent monitors to Russia in December 1993 and to South Africa in April 1994, but these dispatches were carried outside of the new law.

8 Pearson, 'Force for UN' and 'Keeping the Peace.'

9 Tackaberry, 'Organizing and Training Peace-Keeping Forces.'

10 Williams, 'Canada and International Peace-Keeping Operations.' On the dominance of this liberal–internationalist tradition in Canadian foreign policy, see Dewitt and Kirton, *Canada as a Principal Power*; Nossal, *The Politics of Canadian Foreign*

Policy; Cooper, *Canadian Foreign Policy*; Keating, *Canada and the World Order*; and David and Roussel, 'Une espèce en voie de disparition?'
11 Martin, *Canada and the Quest for Peace*, 1–32.
12 Taylor, 'Peacekeeping.'
13 Granatstein, 'Did Canada Make a Difference?' On current Canadian attitudes, see Martin and Fortman, 'Canadian Opinion and Peacekeeping.'
14 Sokolosky, 'Great Ideals and Uneasy Compromises.'
15 More broadly, see Inoguchi, *Japan's Foreign Policy*.
16 For a review of Japan's policy changes see Sakurada, 'Japanese External Policy.'
17 For an earlier study of this issue, see Kurosawa, 'Comparing Japanese and Canadian National Security Policies.'

11

Environmental Issues: A New International Agenda and Related Domestic Experience

PAUL PARKER

Introduction

Environmental issues highlight the new forms of relations emerging among North Pacific partners.[1] Traditionally, environmental issues were largely a function of domestic considerations and local politics. However, in the 1980s they emerged as high-priority items on the international agenda. This environmental agenda provided a contrast to the prevailing economic and security agendas of earlier international politics. It was not dictated exclusively by a global power such as the United States, but provided an opportunity for smaller countries such as Canada to promote issues such as ozone depletion, acid precipitation, habitat protection, and development assistance. Japan also responded to selected environmental issues to demonstrate its role as a global economic and technological power by becoming the largest source of Official Development Assistance funds for environmental and other projects, as well as becoming a leading source of environmental technologies.

Lessons from these recent experiences are valuable at the turn of the century and beyond. The importance of environmental issues at the international level remains high as people become increasingly aware of the vulnerability of environmental systems and the magnitude of demands human society places on its biophysical surroundings. Environmental issues have thus become part of the security agenda of the post–Cold War period.[2] The rapid evolution of environmental policies and politics demonstrates each of the three main processes apparent in the evolution of the broader triangular relationship among the three North Pacific partners: a shift away from unilateral initiatives, a shift away from the concentration on economic interaction, and the emergence of international community-building initiatives.

The most fundamental change is the recognition of environmental issues at the global level. No single country can dominate the environment, no nation can stop all pollution at its border, and the hegemonic model of one country using its power to control others is inadequate to explain changes in environmental policy, new international standards/targets, and new environmental institutions. The hegemonic model of one country taking initiatives to dictate the terms in bilateral security treaties or special conditions in bilateral trade disputes needs to be replaced with a cooperative model in which many countries become partners to effectively address environmental issues. Canada and the United States have a long history of bilateral environmental initiatives to protect common resources along their 9,000 km border. One innovative mechanism to help solve transboundary problems without infringing national sovereignty is the International Joint Commission established under the 1909 Boundary Waters Treaty.[3] This institution operates by consensus and makes recommendations to government as it monitors and assesses a range of environmental problems in the Great Lakes and other shared resources. The web of interaction is broadened as more partners are required to resolve global environmental issues. Partnerships vary with the particular environmental issue under consideration. Several examples will be provided in this chapter to highlight the varied roles taken by the United States, Japan, and Canada. In many cases, the partnership that stimulated action included members from beyond the North Pacific (from Europe, for example). This illustrates how broad-based, yet dynamic, coalitions were built.

In addition to the shift away from national and bilateral initiatives, the environmental agenda of the 1980s and 1990s proves that the relations among the North Pacific Triangle partners and other countries are no longer restricted to economic matters. The link between domestic economic activity and the environment was proven through local cases of severe urban air, water, and soil pollution.[4] The link between economic activity and its effects on shared environmental resources such as the atmosphere, water, stratospheric ozone, or genetic material required these environmental issues to be addressed at the international level. The severity of environmental damage and its impact on society has led to the inclusion of environmental issues in the security agenda of many countries in the post–Cold War era. For example, the Department of Foreign Affairs and International Trade cites the global environment as one of the five pillars of Canada's foreign policy.

Finally, environmental issues have become a central part of international community-building initiatives. Forums such as the Group of Seven (G-7) and Asia Pacific Economic Cooperation (APEC), which initially focused on the economy, have added the environment as part of their broader agenda. Canada and the United States sponsored environmental initiatives at the Toronto and Houston G-7 summits, respectively, and Japan has joined them in supporting action on selected environmental issues. Japan, the United States, and Canada share many aspirations for the international community and typically overcome their initial differences to reach a consensus that moves them in the direction of improved environmental considerations. In this way the trilateral relationship acts as a dynamic subset of the larger international arena. The negotiations and positions adopted to improve environmental conditions for North Pacific countries are usually set in the context of broader forums or international institutions. National governments are often joined by other actors, including scientists, non-governmental organizations, and corporations in these broad networks of overlapping environmental interests.

The lessons from negotiations and initiatives taken on particular environmental issues may thus serve as case studies to illustrate broader changes in the relations among the three North Pacific partners. They may also provide a base for building international responses to the environmental issues that will arise in the future. Japan, Canada, and the United States have each pursued different sets of environmental policies in the international arena. They agree on some issues and take conflicting positions on others. Current positions are a product of both international objectives and domestic experience.

Each country has claimed environmental leadership in some field, yet lagged in others. Examples of environmental leadership include the 1969 Environmental Protection Act in the United States, which sought to protect the environment by requiring predictions of the impact of projects before projects were approved. Japan followed with special environmental sessions of the Diet in 1970 and 1971 to strengthen its pollution laws and to introduce a series of anti-pollution measures, which stimulated the development of a new generation of technology. Canada also adopted the environment as a priority through the protection of internationally significant habitats and by leading several international efforts to protect shared environmental resources. This chapter introduces not only the policies and politics of change in the international environmental arena but also provides measures of environmental performance over time. These indicators provide evidence as to whether implementation has matched the rhetoric of environmental negotiations and policy.

International Negotiations: Ozone Depletion and Climate Change

International environmental negotiations can lead to conflict or cooperation. Divisions are usually made between polluters and victims. Historically, most pollution was caused by industrialized countries, but the devastating impact that poverty and population growth can generate for the environment are also central to environmental issues such as desertification, deforestation, and endangered species protection. As industrialized countries, Japan, the United States, and Canada might be expected to adopt similar positions on international environmental issues, but such a generalization ignores many of the differences among these three countries. Differences in domestic policies, biophysical environments, industrial structures, access to information, and non-governmental environmental groups all contribute to a unique set of environmental positions being adopted.[5] Two sets of negotiations related to atmospheric pollution (ozone-depleting chemicals and greenhouse gases) illustrate these differences.

Negotiations that led to the Vienna Convention for the Protection of the Ozone Layer in 1985, the Montreal Protocol on Substances That Deplete the Ozone Layer in 1987, the acceptance of the need for faster action at the first Meeting of the Parties in Helsinki in 1989, and the decision to accelerate the phase-out of the eight specified chemicals at the second Meeting of the Parties in London in 1990 achieved a rapid convergence among the positions of most countries.[6] Canada and the Scandinavian countries were early leaders in promoting international action to respond to ozone depletion. The United States was initially strongly opposed to such action, but after a change in national policy in 1983 became an advocate for action and joined the Scandinavian countries as a member of the 'Toronto Group' (Canada, Finland, Norway, Sweden, and the United States, and later Australia, New Zealand, and Switzerland), which promoted the control of chlorofluorocarbon (CFC) consumption. A second group of actors consisted of European Community members, Japan, Chile, and the former Soviet Union. They proposed slower progress and the control of production rather than consumption.

Although the Vienna Convention could not reach agreement on specific measures, it provided the framework for the rapid negotiation of the Montreal Protocol, which was agreed to by the United States, Canada, Japan, and many other countries. The timetable for a 50 per cent reduction of the chemicals specified in the protocol was accelerated and extended to a complete phase-out in subsequent meetings of the parties. As a result of these international negotiations and agreements, individual countries introduced programs to reduce the consumption of specified ozone-depleting chemicals. The success of these programs is demonstrated in Table 11.1, where the consumption of CFCs and related chemicals is shown to have dropped sharply in the United States, Canada, and Japan.

The rapid agreement and international action to protect stratospheric ozone as a common environmental resource was not repeated in the climate change debate, which centred on CO_2 emissions. Some authors have argued that the ozone convention/protocol model would not be repeated in the case of climate change negotiations because of the wide national differences in population, level of development, fuel mix, amount and kind of energy reserves, and varia-

TABLE 11.1
Consumption of chlorofluorocarbons and halons, 1986–93

| | thousand tonnes/yr | | | kg/per capita | | |
	1986	1991	1993	1986	1991	1993
United States	363	207	60	1.37	0.88	0.25
Japan	135	110	47	1.09	0.97	0.39
Canada	23	10	5	0.83	0.58	0.17

Sources: UNEP, *Environmental Data Report 1993–94*; OECD, *OECD Environmental Data: Compendium 1995*.

tions in energy emissions per unit of economic activity.[7] The 1992 Earth Summit (United Nations Conference on Environment and Development) in Rio created the opportunity for most countries to follow up the World Commission on Environment and Development report with new agreements on international environmental issues.[8] Over 100 top leaders attended the conference, including those from the United States, Japan, and Canada. The Framework Convention on Climate Change was signed by 154 nations at the conference and came into effect in March 1994 when more than 50 countries had ratified it.[9] However, the apparent agreement among the signatories disguised significant differences in the negotiation positions adopted.

Canada hosted the 1988 world conference 'Changing Atmosphere: Implications for Global Security.' It called for a 20 per cent reduction in greenhouse gas emissions from 1988 levels by the year 2000 (the Toronto Target). Many European countries joined Canada in calling for both targets and timetables to be included in a proposed Climate Change Convention. However, the United States opposed the inclusion of specific targets or timetables for reductions in CO_2 emissions. Instead, the United States proposed that individual countries set voluntary targets using a comprehensive approach that included all greenhouse gases. Japan was in favour of establishing targets (1990 levels of per capita emissions by 2000), on the condition that other countries took similar action.[10] The Japanese government decided to move with the leaders rather than wait with the laggards on climate change. In 1990 it announced its climate change program of action three months before the United States announced its weaker official policy and three years before the United States released its climate change action plan.[11]

By 1993, the position of the United States had changed as President Clinton included a commitment in his Earth Day speech that the country adopt a national goal of stabilizing all greenhouse gases at 1990 levels by the year

2000. The change in the United States' position was not a direct outcome of isolated Canadian or Japanese actions, but reflected a much broader network of interactions whereby domestic interest groups as well as other national governments interacted in international forums to reach an eventual compromise.

The administration of President Reagan was sceptical of the argument for taking action on the climate change issue, yet was willing to support the formation of an intergovernmental mechanism for the international scientific assessment of climate change. Some American decision-makers saw this international initiative as a way to slow progress towards a convention.[12] The Intergovernmental Panel on Climate Change (IPCC) was jointly established in 1988 by the World Meteorological Organization and the United Nations Environment Program to investigate scientific information and processes, to assess socio-economic impacts, and to formulate response strategies associated with climate change.[13] The United States chaired one of the three main working groups (response strategies), while Canada served as one of five co-chairs to the group, and Japan took the lead role on subsections dealing with industry and energy. Japan also co-chaired the impact group. These working groups enabled scientists from many countries to gain a stronger consensus on the risks associated with climate change and the need to take action. The IPCC and its working groups thus acted as an international forum for the presentation and exchange of information, not exclusively for use by scientists, but also for use by other decision-makers.[14]

The increase in information about climate change was used not only by government agencies and scientists, but also by NGOs, the media, and politicians. Rising public concern over projections of hotter summers and the increased frequency of extreme weather events combined with the efforts of NGOs to stimulate government action. One explanation for the stronger action taken by Japan over that of the United States was the contrasting interpretation of the expected effects on industry. In the United States, energy and industry lobbyists used high cost estimates of measures to reduce CO_2 emissions, for example the controversial costing ($0.8–3.6 trillion) by Manne and Richels, as a large price tag to wave against the unvalued benefits of lower concentrations of greenhouse gases.[15] Despite arguments by Williams and others that the cost of reducing CO_2 emissions could be negative because of the associated increases in efficiency from new technologies, American negotiators adopted a conservative approach and slowed progress towards targets for international climate change programs.[16] In contrast, Japanese policy-makers recognized an opportunity to sell advanced energy-efficient technologies if measures to reduce CO_2 and other emissions were accelerated.[17] This interpretation enabled Japan to move with the global leaders on an important environmental issue while also promoting its economy.

TABLE 11.2
CO_2 emissions from fossil fuel combustion and cement manufacturing, 1960–95

| | million tonnes C/yr | | | | | tC/capita |
	1960	1970	1980	1990	1995	1990
United States	800	1,165	1,259	1,310	1,394	5.3
Japan	64	203	255	289	302	2.3
Canada[a]	53	91	116	115	121	4.4

[a]1995 value refers to 1994 emission level.
Sources: Brown et al., *State of the World 1997*; Canada, *The State of Canada's Environment 1996*; UNEP, *Environmental Data Report 1993–94*.

Although the Bush Administration agreed on the need for a climate change convention, its opposition to specific targets and timetables in the convention was maintained. The 'comprehensive approach' advocated by the United States to limit greenhouse gases overall was easy to promote because the Montreal Protocol and associated agreements already committed countries to phase out CFCs. The United States was the largest single source of CFCs and halons in both absolute and per capita terms in the late 1980s (see Table 11.1). By phasing out these ozone-depleting gases, a reduction was also being achieved in total greenhouse gas emissions because these gases were also very potent greenhouse gases. This avoided the problem of CO_2 emissions where the United States was again the largest contributor (see Table 11.2). The United States maintained this position in the negotiating sessions leading up to the Climate Change Convention, but in the end agreed to exclude CFCs and other gases covered by the Montreal Protocol from the comprehensive approach.[18]

In contrast, Japan not only agreed to phase out CFCs and halons, but also proposed to stabilize CO_2 emissions, which were already less than one-half of the per capita level of the United States (Table 11.2). Despite each of the countries adopting policies to reduce CO_2 and other GHG emissions, all three countries increased their CO_2 emissions in the early 1990s. The weak convention, with its voluntary measures, reflected the limited willingness of governments to actively make changes to the status quo in the early 1990s. However, the IPCC, the Framework Convention on Climate Change, and other international environmental forums continue to promote exchanges among international scientists and policy-makers and to work towards an international consensus on these issues. Participants from Japan, the United States, and Canada are expected to continue to play important roles. For example, Japan will host the 1997 IPCC meeting in Kyoto, where it is expected that participants will endorse a call for binding reductions to replace the voluntary approach adopted earlier.[19]

The different positions brought to such international environmental forums are better understood by examining the relative performance of these countries on several domestic environmental issues. For example, the Japanese proposal to stabilize CO_2 emissions while also promoting economic growth was based on improvements in technical and economic efficiency as well as changes in the mix of fuels used. This approach was in large part an extension of the policies that had improved domestic air quality and stimulated the development of pollution control technology two decades earlier.

Domestic Air Quality

Domestic experience influences the positions that countries adopt in international environmental negotiations.[20] Japanese environmental experience is well illustrated by air quality problems and responses. Rapid economic growth in the postwar period was accompanied by worsening environmental quality. Urban dwellers became accustomed to dark skies with high concentrations of particulates, as well as invisible gases, SO_2, and NO_x. In the late 1960s, local government, the courts, and hundreds of small community groups effectively forced the national government to introduce new environmental laws.[21]

The problem of high levels of urban pollution was recognized throughout the industrialized world. Japan, the United States, and Canada each sought to reduce their levels of urban air pollution and the resulting concentration of SO_2 measured in residential areas of selected major cities (see Table 11.3). These concentrations were lower than those measured in central industrial districts or at major transportation intersections, but are used to illustrate the improvement in air quality as it affected large numbers of urban dwellers. Direct comparisons among cities need to be treated with caution because of different site selection and measuring methods, but improvements were achieved in all three countries. Montreal reported the largest relative improvement from 1975 to 1990 with a two-thirds reduction in SO_2 concentrations, while Tokyo halved its SO_2 concentration and New York cut its SO_2 level by one-third over the same period.

The improvements in SO_2 concentrations were achieved primarily by the control of major point sources through the installation of flue gas desulphurization (FGD) equipment or the change of fuels from high-sulphur coal or oil to other fuels (see Table 11.4). Japan led this trend with the installation of thousands of FGD units and the reduction in total emissions from 5 million tonnes in 1970 to less than 1 million tonnes in 1990. The emission standards for major sources of SO_2, such as coal-fired boilers, have been tightened in all three coun-

TABLE 11.3
Concentration of SO_2 at selected major cities, 1980–92[a]

	# Stations	1975	mean annual values, ug/m³			
			1980	1985	1990	1992
Montreal	7	40	41	14	13	12
Tokyo	20	60	51	29	29	23
New York[b]	15	43	38	34	29	23

[a]Collection methods differ among cities.
[b]1992 value refers to 1993.
Sources: OECD, *OECD Environmental Data: Compendium 1989*,
OECD Environmental Data: Compendium 1995.

TABLE 11.4
Total SO_2 emissions by source, 1970–92

	million tonnes					
	1970	1975	1980	1985	1990	1992
Stationary sources						
United States	27.8	24.9	22.9	20.8	20.1	19.6
Japan	—	2.5	1.1	0.8	0.7	—
Canada	6.6	5.2	4.5	3.6	3.6	2.9
Mobile sources						
United States	0.6	0.6	0.9	0.9	1.0	1.0
Japan	—	0.1	0.1	0.2	0.2	—
Canada	0.1	0.1	0.1	0.1	0.1	0.1
Total emissions						
United States	28.4	25.5	23.8	21.7	21.1	20.6
Japan	5.0	2.6	1.3	0.8	0.9	—
Canada	6.7	5.3	4.6	3.7	3.3	3.0

Source: OECD, *OECD Environmental Data: Compendium 1995*.

tries, although the United States still had one of the most lenient standards among OECD countries in the late 1980s while Japan had one of the strictest limits.[22] Further restrictions were introduced in the United States in the mid-1990s to comply with the agreement reached with Canada to reduce SO_2 emissions and the associated episodes of acid rain.

In addition to urban SO_2 concentrations, total levels of SO_2 emissions were considered important to reduce acid precipitation at the national level. Canada had one of the highest SO_2 per capita emission levels in the world and initiated actions to cut its total SO_2 emissions from 6.7 million tonnes in 1970 to 3.3 million tonnes in 1990. The United States made a more modest reduction from 28.4 million tonnes in 1970 to 21.1 million tonnes in 1990 (Table 11.4). These improvements were achieved not only in urban areas as reported above, but also in the metal-refining and electricity-generating industries. SO_2 emissions form precursors to acid precipitation, and the resulting acidification of sensitive ecosystems resulted in widespread Canadian calls for reductions in emissions.

The international debate over acid rain causing acidification in lakes and the decline or disappearance of fish species commenced with the 1972 United Nations Conference on the Human Environment, where the findings of earlier work by Swedish researchers were presented. However, some countries (the United States and the United Kingdom, in particular) disagreed with the scientific basis of the argument that acidification was caused by long-range transport of pollutants such as sulphur and nitrogen oxides and photochemical oxidants. The UN-ECE Convention on Long-Range Transboundary Air Pollution was signed in 1979 by thirty-five nations, including Canada and the United States. It came into force in 1983. However, its general obligations to develop policies and strategies to protect humanity and the environment needed specific targets to be effective. In 1984 the unofficial '30 Per Cent Club' was formed at a minister's meeting in Ottawa, where ten nations volunteered to reduce their SO_2 emissions by 30 per cent by 1993. In 1985 a protocol to reduce SO_2 emissions by at least 30 per cent was signed by twenty-one nations at Helsinki. Canada signed this SO_2 protocol in the hope that it would increase pressure on the United States, but the American position did not change quickly.[23]

Although the Canadian public and government accepted the evidence demonstrating long-range transport of pollution, U.S. views were slower to change. Concerns about scientific proof were reinforced by the strong lobbies of electric utilities and the National Coal Association highlighting the cost of reducing SO_2 emissions, both in terms of higher electricity charges to pay for scrubbers and more unemployed miners from coal fields containing high-sulphur coal. Negotiations or joint discussions in the form of various international committees had been under way since the late 1970s, but progress was limited. In February 1982 Canada formally proposed that both countries reduce SO_2 emissions by 50 per cent to protect moderately sensitive lake regions. The United States rejected the proposal in June 1982 as premature. Canada continued to promote international initiatives and decided to act unilaterally within North America. The two largest sources of SO_2 in Canada, the Ontario Hydro Electric Company and the International Nickel Company of Canada (INCO), accepted Ontario government control orders to reduce emissions.[24] By the early 1990s, INCO emissions were reduced to one-sixth of their earlier levels.

The 1990s also marked a change in American policy as the government signed the 1991 Air Quality Accord with Canada. The United States had reduced SO_2 emissions by 10 per cent in the 1980s and agreed to the target of reducing emissions a further 29 per cent by 2000. Canada had reduced its emissions by 22 per cent in the 1980s and agreed to cap emissions at 32 per cent below the 1980 level by 2000.[25] Implementation proceeded with the seven eastern provinces achieving their agreed target of a 40 per cent reduction from 1980 levels ahead of the scheduled 1994 date. Persistence was required as well as partnerships before Canada achieved the bilateral reduction in SO_2 it had desired.

Despite domestic improvements, SO_2 emissions remain an important environmental issue in Japan because of increasing concern about acid precipitation resulting from long-distance transport of pollutants, especially from China. International negotiations are again required as the principal parties have different positions. China is expanding its energy systems, especially coal-fired power stations, to meet the needs of its growing economy.[26] The emphasis is on maximum output for a given level of investment. However, Japan and other countries have proven that FGD, fluidized bed combustion, and other techniques can reduce SO_2 emissions by 90 per cent or more. Resolution of the SO_2 issue will require negotiations over questions of technology transfers, various forms of official and other development assistance, as well as the interests of neighbouring countries such as South Korea. Insights from the protracted United States–Canada negotiations may assist in reaching an agreement between Japan and China.

The successful reduction of urban SO_2 concentrations was not equalled by efforts to reduce urban NO_x concentrations. Instead, NO_x levels have typically stabilized. The increased use of automobiles for personal transport and trucks for freight transport have created the need for increasingly stringent emission standards just to prevent increases in the concentration of pollutants. Overall, Japanese regulations on automobile emissions appeared to be stricter for nitrogen oxides (0.48 rather than 0.62 g/km), while American regulations were stricter for hydrocarbons (0.25 rather than 0.39 g/km) and carbon monoxide (2.1 rather than 2.7 g/km).[27] These comparisons are limited by differences in national measurement methods, but the trend of increasingly stringent standards demonstrates that air quality will remain an environmental concern and that transport and other technologies must be continually improved to meet public demands for clean air.

Water Quality

Water quality also received increased attention as an important environmental issue in each of the three countries. In the 1970s the assumption that the largest lakes in the world, the Great Lakes, had an unlimited capacity to assimilate pollution was proven false. Increased concentrations of nutrients, phosphorous and nitrogen in particular, caused the rapid growth of algae. Large quantities of algae increased the biological demand for oxygen when they decayed, and oxygen concentrations in the water fell below the levels required by many species. Photographs of dead fish were featured in newspapers and magazines and action was called for. In response, the 1978 Great Lakes Water Quality Agreement was signed by the governments of the United States and Canada.[28] The International Joint Commission was to coordinate the introduction of new policies to restrict emissions. By the mid-1980s phosphorous levels had been reduced to one-half of their levels a decade earlier in both Lake Erie and Lake Ontario (see Table 11.5).

However, water pollution remains a problem in most countries, as illustrated by a comparison of phosphorous levels in the St Lawrence River in Canada with the Mississippi River in the United States, or the Ishikan River in Japan (Table 11.5). Lakes Biwa (south) and Kasumigaura in Japan also highlight the difficulty in trying to achieve lower levels of nutrients. In both cases, national laws have been reinforced by local laws that, in the case of Lake Biwa, saw the prefectural government ban the use of detergents that contained phosphates in 1980.[29] However, the success achieved in some bodies of water remains to be reproduced in others (e.g., Lake Kasumigaura, Mississippi River). Other nutrients, such as nitrogen, and other pollutants, such as polychlorinated biphenyls (PCBs) and heavy metals, are also problems in many bodies of water. While improvements have been made in some areas, the range of pollutants that have been proven hazardous and in need of control has increased.

The health risks associated with heavy metal concentrations and their bioaccumulation within the aquatic ecosystem were well demonstrated by the methyl mercury poisoning known as Minamata disease. Although official recognition of the link between industrial emissions and health disorders took decades of action by local groups to achieve, recognition was finally gained. The concentration of heavy metals in many Japanese lakes was reported to have declined in the 1980s.[30] Despite similar reductions in emissions in other countries, new problems continue to emerge, as illustrated by the creation of large lakes for hydroelectric generation in northern Canada. These large lakes triggered the release of methyl mercury into the aquatic system because the pH of the lakes changed as large quantities of organic matter decayed in newly

TABLE 11.5
Selected lakes and rivers annual mean concentration of
phosphorous, 1970–93

	total phosphorus (mg/litre as P)					
	1970	1975	1980	1985	1990	1993
Canada/United States						
Lake Ontario	.022	.022	.017	.011	.010	.010
Lake Erie	.017	.023	.011	.012	—	—
Canada						
St Lawrence River	.018	.010	.025	.018	.020	—
United States						
Mississippi River	—	.140	.230	.100	.170	.200
Japan						
Lake Biwa (north)[a]	.012	.008	.009	.007	.009	.009
Lake Biwa (south)[a]	.027	.027	.017	.020	.025	.020
Lake Kasumigaura[b]	—	.040	.080	.060	.066	.097
Ishikan River	—	.090	.090	.070	—	—

[a]1970 data refer to 1971.
[b]1990 data refer to 1989.
Sources: UNEP, *Environmental Data Report 1991–92*; OECD, *OECD Environmental Data: Compendium 1995*.

flooded permafrost areas. Water pollution problems highlight the intricate connections throughout ecosystems and how even relatively small concentrations of some materials can lead to lethal consequences elsewhere in the food chain. Equally important, apparently local environmental problems can have international political dimensions as environmental groups lobby decision-makers in New York and Washington to cancel electricity contracts that create the demand for large hydroelectric plants to be built in Canada.

Habitat Protection

Environmental policies have not been restricted simply to the control of emissions into air or water. In other cases, the habitat itself has been proposed for protection. The movement to form national parks for the protection of areas for future generations began over 100 years ago in the United States and Canada and nearly sixty years ago in Japan. It has grown along with the increased public value placed on the scenic and natural environment. Within the United States, nearly 1,000 areas covering almost 1 million km^2 (two-thirds of which is in Alaska) have been designated for national protection (see Table 11.6). In Can-

TABLE 11.6
Nationally designated protected areas and national parks,[a] 1990

		Protected areas		
	#	km^2	% of territory	ha protected/ 1000 inhabitants
World	6,940	6,514,676	4.9	123
United States[b]	961	982,974	10.5	391
Japan	65	24,024	6.4	19
Canada[c]	523	701,255	7.0	2,634

		National parks		
	#	km^2	% of territory	ha protected/ 1000 inhabitants
World	1,392	3,092,274	2.3	58
United States[d]	59	202,320	2.2	80
Japan[e]	15	12,991	3.4	11
Canada	237	309,529	3.1	1,163

[a]Based on IUCN definitions of national park (category II) and protected areas (categories I–V) each area, unless an island, is greater than 10 km^2.
[b]Includes Alaska: 66 protected areas (698,633 km^2)
[c]Includes Ontario system of 20 nature reserves
[d]Includes Alaska: 11 national parks or equivalent reserves (141,748 km^2)
[e]According to the Japanese classification, there are 28 national parks (20,488 km^2).
Source: OECD, *OECD Environmental Data: Compendium 1993.*

ada, over 500 nationally protected areas cover 700,000 km^2, while in Japan the total size of protected areas is much smaller (24,000 km^2). This measurement can vary as a result of the definition of protected area used. The IUCN (International Union for the Conservation of Nature) definition used by the OECD has a minimum size of 10 km^2 and measures the total protected area in Japan to be one-half that reported by the national government to UNEP, 46,635 km^2 in 684 areas.[31] Large areas are required to protect the habitat of many large animals and the integrity of ecosystems. However, sensitivity needs to be used when comparing the resulting data as an indication of protection efforts.

The relative size of protected areas is also important to note. Protected areas in Canada cover only 7 per cent of the total land area while the value for the United States is 10.5 per cent and that for Japan is 6.4 per cent (IUCN definition) or 12.7 per cent. In addition, the type of habitat or ecosystem protected needs to be considered. Total park area may be large, yet have a few types of habitat (typically mountainous terrain or deserts) overrepresented while other habitats (for example, fertile coasts, fertile flood plains, valleys, or closed canopy forests) are underrepresented. This issue is being addressed in Canada where 217 unique eco-regions have been defined, yet only 160 of these eco-regions are represented in protected areas. In 1992 the federal, provincial, and territorial ministers responsible for environmental protection made a commitment to extend protected coverage to all of the eco-regions by 2000.[32]

In addition to the designation of areas for protection, it is important to provide sufficient resources to protect the habitat. Despite Japan's designation of significant natural areas for parks, the personnel and financial resources allocated to this public service are very limited in comparison to those allocated to parks in the United States or Canada. Japanese national parks face very high usage rates, with the number of visitors reaching 400 million in 1990. The larger and more numerous American parks had only 60 million visitors. This imbalance is further accentuated by the very limited resources provided to Japanese national parks. The total number of national park personnel was reported as only 110 in 1988, while American park personnel numbered 9,500. The result is that each Japanese park employee was responsible for 187 ha on average, while each American counterpart had 20 ha to supervise. Financial resources for Japanese national parks were also very limited.[33]

The very high number and rapid increases in visitors to the twenty-eight Japanese national parks are repeated for the 55 quasi-national parks (1.3 million ha) and the 299 prefectural parks (2 million ha).[34] By 1990 the number of annual visitors to quasi-national parks and prefectural parks each reached 300 million for a total of 1,000 million visitors to the three types of parks in Japan. Given limited human or financial resources to protect the habitat, some of the greatest problems facing the parks were the destruction of habitat caused by the high number of visitors and the damage caused by tourism developments in the parks. Many countries create national parks for the dual objectives of protecting scenic areas for the enjoyment of people and the maintenance of natural ecosystems. In Japan, the first objective appears to outweigh the second, whereas in the United States and Canada more resources are allocated to national parks so that they can balance the two objectives more evenly.

International Habitat Protection

Habitat protection has also been pursued at the international level. The 1971 Ramsar Convention on Wetlands of International Importance Especially as Waterfowl Habitat was the first worldwide conservation treaty and the first to deal only with habitat. It required parties to the treaty to promote the wise use of all wetlands and to protect at least one wetland of international importance.[35]

TABLE 11.7
Internationally designated heritage and habitat areas, 1992

	World Heritage Sites (#)	Biosphere Reserves #	Biosphere Reserves km²	Ramsar Wetlands #	Ramsar Wetlands km²
World	95	300	1,619,445	538	323,362
United States	10	46	191,296	10	11,408
Japan	0	4	1,160	3	99
Canada	6	6	10,500	30	129,373

Sources: UNEP, *Environmental Data Report 1993–94*; OECD, *OECD Environmental Data: Compendium 1993.*

Despite its weak legal obligations, the treaty has been considered successful because of the large number of nations that have become parties to it. More than 500 wetlands have been formally designated worldwide, and the list continues to grow. Canada, Japan, and the United States have each become members and designated wetlands for protection (see Table 11.7). However, the extent of habitat involved varies by orders of magnitude. The thirty wetlands designated in Canada account for over one-third of the area of all Ramsar wetlands worldwide. In contrast, the three wetlands designated in Japan cover just 99 km². The United States lies between these extremes with ten Ramsar wetlands covering 11,000 km². Geographic features, terrain, settlement density, and prior use decisions constrain the abilities of governments to nominate wetlands for protection, but clearly Canada has been a leader in identifying internationally significant wetlands under the Ramsar Convention.

The protection of representative biosphere reserves or world heritage reserves has also been achieved through international mechanisms. In each case, the United States has played a leading role in nominating areas for protection. Japan remains a smaller participant in these international programs. The high density of urban development along the coast of the island nation explains part of this pattern. Overall, habitat protection appears to be a lower priority than reduction of urban pollution levels within Japanese environmental policies.

Environmental Impact Assessment

The United States was a leader in establishing a new form of environmental protection when the National Environmental Policy Act was passed in 1969. The act was based on the application of science to predict impacts and provided review mechanisms that involved the people likely to be affected. This new emphasis on impact assessment prior to project approval was recognized by other countries. In December 1973 the federal government of Canada established the Environmental Assessment and Review Process as a Cabinet directive to require environmental impact assessment. These guidelines were formalized as an order-in-council under the 1984 Department of the Environment Act and were further codified in the 1990 Canadian Environmental Assessment Act.[36] However, Canadian provinces also have important environmental and project approval powers. They also recognized the importance of environmental assessment as demonstrated by Ontario, which passed its Environmental Assessment Act in 1975.

In Japan, the Environmental Agency proposed an Environmental Impact Assessment Bill in 1976, but it was opposed by three powerful ministries and did not become law. Two subsequent attempts failed. Therefore, in 1984 the agency decided to abandon attempts to have a bill passed and instead had environmental impact assessment adopted as an administrative guidance through a Cabinet understanding entitled 'environmental protection measures for various types of public projects.'[37] In the late 1980s the guidelines were being adopted in the evaluation of many public projects, but the degree of use varied by the type of project: expressways (100 per cent), dams (28 per cent), and waste disposal plants (1.4 per cent).[38] In 1994 the Basic Environmental Law was passed by the Japanese Diet to create a more comprehensive basis for environmental protection in Japan.[39]

The Japanese response to international environmental problems illustrates the increasing role of Japan in the international arena. In August 1993, Elizabeth Dowdeswell, the Director General of the United Nations Environmental Program, visited the headquarters of the United Nations University in Tokyo and called for Japan to play an important role in solving global environmental problems as part of its major policy initiative.[40] Japanese domestic environmental policy evolved through a series of stages from ignorance to symbolic steps to substantive technocratic efforts. A similar pattern could be under way in the international arena.[41]

Official Development Assistance

Official development assistance (ODA) is an important part of international environmental initiatives as the issues of poverty, population growth, industrial development, and resource management each affect environmental resources of global importance. The environmental impacts of all international financial transfers (ODA, private investment, or trade) are significant and need detailed examination and evaluation. However, the rapid growth in Japanese ODA (a tenfold increase from U.S.$1.1 billion in 1975 to $11.0 billion in 1991) and the

TABLE 11.8
Official development assistance, 1970–95

| | billion U.S.$ | | | | | | |
	1970	1975	1980	1985	1990	1993	1995
United States	3.2	4.2	7.1	9.4	11.4	9.7	7.3
Japan	0.5	1.1	3.4	3.8	9.1	11.3	14.5
Canada	0.3	0.9	1.1	1.6	2.5	2.4	2.3
	% of GNP						
United States	0.32	0.27	0.27	0.24	0.21	0.15	0.10
Japan	0.23	0.23	0.32	0.29	0.31	0.26	0.28
Canada	0.41	0.54	0.43	0.49	0.44	0.45	0.42

Sources: World Bank, World Development Report 1995; MOFA, ODA Summary 1996.

form of this assistance has made it the subject of severe criticism for causing environmental damage.[42] This is especially true in Asia.[43] In contrast, the United States rapidly retreated from its highest ODA contribution of $11.7 billion in 1992 to just $7.3 billion in 1995. Canada had a smaller total ODA, but allocated a much larger share of its gross national product (GNP) to development assistance than either Japan or the U.S. (see Table 11.8).

The type of ODA flowing to developing countries also changed as environmental issues became a priority in the late 1980s. The generally agreed principle was that environmental ODA was an investment in global environmental security. If the investment was not made now, the larger costs would emerge in the future. International development agencies in Japan, the United States, and Canada each adopted sustainable development as a goal, supported many environment-related projects, and strengthened the environmental evaluation component of projects in other sectors. Japan supported this redirection of international efforts through its proposal to form the World Commission on Environment and Development in 1982 and its coordination of the Tokyo Declaration on Financing Global Environment and Development. The cost of implementing Agenda 21 in developing countries to achieve the objectives of the Earth Summit was estimated at $625 billion per annum. Developed countries were asked to contribute 20 per cent of this total, or $125 billion per annum. Annual ODA allocations from all countries averaged $55 billion in the early 1990s, so a further $70 billion per annum was requested. The total equalled 0.7 per cent of the GNP of the developed countries, and the Tokyo Declaration argued that this should be the minimum contribution.[44]

The Scandinavian countries and the Netherlands are examples of countries that exceed the 0.7 per cent target, but the OECD average remained at one-half that level (0.34 in 1970, 0.35 in 1980, 0.30 in 1993).[45] Japan's contribution remained just below the average for all OECD countries, while the United States let its contribution relative to GNP drop by 50 per cent in the early 1990s. Of the three North Pacific Triangle partners, Canada was well above the OECD average and the closest to achieving the desired level of international contributions to promote environmental protection in developing countries (Table 11.8).

By 1987, Japanese bilateral aid in the environment sector (¥43 billion for water supply, sewerage systems, waste disposal, and forestry) exceeded that of other leading donor countries, such as the United States, Germany, and Canada.[46] Once again, Canadian environmental assistance was smaller in absolute terms ($U.S.1.2 billion over the 1986–92 period), but larger in its relative importance within the Canadian ODA budget. Environmental advisers from each of the three countries have been sent to administrative bodies and research institutes in many countries, and survey teams work on projects identified by recipient countries. Technical cooperation projects combine the transfer of equipment with staff training and project coordination. In addition, it has been suggested that Japan and Canada cooperate in assisting other countries to address environmental issues using their respective strengths in environmental technology management.[47]

The Japanese emphasis on environment sector ODA was further strengthened in 1992 when Prime Minister Miyazawa announced at the Earth Summit in Rio that Japan intended to increase its environment sector ODA to between ¥900 billion and ¥1 trillion over the next five-year period. This target was reached in four years, with a total of ¥980 billion allocated in fiscal years 1992–1995. Most of these funds were spent on projects to improve the residential environment (water supply, sewerage systems, waste treatment, disaster prevention, flood prevention); however, pollution control, forestry conservation, nature conservation, and energy savings are expected to be given a higher priority in the future.[48] Calls have been made for the reform of Japanese ODA, with the government shifting its emphasis in quality, while NGOs call for greater attention to the environmental consequences of ODA.[49]

Japan–Canada Environmental Relations and APEC Initiatives

Japan–Canada relations traditionally concentrated on economic matters such as trade and investment. As the increasing importance of environmental issues was recognized in the 1980s, Japan and Canada also highlighted environmental issues for bilateral initiatives. In the late 1980s, the prime ministers of both countries commissioned the complementarity study that was completed in 1989. One of the six research and development areas identified for immediate cooperation and enhanced collaboration was the environment and sustainable development. Particular attention was to be paid to opportunities created by the complementarity of Japan and Canada. The Foreign Policy Committee of the National Round Table on the Environment and the Economy responded to a Japanese government proposal to arrange a Canada–Japan Workshop on the Environment in June 1991. The workshop was part of the preparations for the Earth Summit in Rio in 1992 and was then followed up by the March 1994 Canada–Japan Environment Conference in Vancouver.

Canadian interest was not restricted to Japanese international policies, but also to the relevance of Japanese domestic experience to environmental issues in Canada. Canadian participants were interested in the innovative financing adopted by Japanese governments to support private investment in pollution control technology. Concern was expressed that the provision of such government funding might be considered an unfair subsidy by the United States under the Free Trade Agreement unless it was made available on a competitive basis through federal financing corporations. The Japanese emphasis on cooperation among diverse stakeholders and a consensus-based approach to long-term decision-making were also considered valuable alternatives to the more adversarial legalistic approach adopted in Canada and the United States.[50]

International issues were considered by the Canada–Japan Forum 2000 established in May 1991. The environment was identified as one of the two principal priorities (along with the multilateral trading system) that emerged in the discussions of the Global Issues Task Force.[51] Recommendations from the forum included a joint bilateral environmental project focused on the stewardship of the North Pacific Ocean: Canada and Japan were to identify and collaborate on the deployment of appropriate strategic technologies to facilitate the monitoring and assessment of pollution and impacts on the sustainability of the fish resource. This initiative followed recent efforts by the United States, Canada, and Japan to limit large-scale pelagic drift-net fishing using UN resolutions and actions, and the extension of fishing controls under the 1952 Tokyo Convention on High Seas Fisheries in the North Pacific Ocean by signing the 1992 Moscow Convention on the Conservation of Anadromous Stocks in the North-East Pacific Ocean. This convention is expected to result in the end of operations of 150 Japanese drift-net vessels in the high-seas salmon fisheries.[52]

More generally, Japan and Canada were to work in partnership on global environmental concerns. The complementarity experience of the Japanese emphasis on technology and the Canadian emphasis on habitat protection and resource management should facilitate creative and balanced responses to some of the regional and global issues that need to be faced. Despite an emphasis on the utility of developing and transferring technology to reduce environmental impacts, it was recognized that more fundamental changes in personal behaviour and lifestyles are required to overcome the conflicting objectives of increased energy and material consumption versus protection of the environment.[53] These Japan–Canada initiatives are typical of new cooperative approaches being adopted and the rapid evolution of international institutional structures.

The Asia Pacific Economic Cooperation (APEC) forum has emerged as an influential consultative forum in which ministers from the member countries exchange ideas on topics of mutual interst. The initial APEC focus on economic issues has broadened in the 1990s to include environmental issues. The APEC Leaders Economic Vision Statement from the 1993 Seattle meeting recognized the importance of the environment to the quality of life and economic vitality of the region. In 1994 the environment ministers of the member countries met in Canada to prepare an Environmental Vision Statement and Framework of Principles for Integrating Economy and Environment in APEC. This was endorsed at the 1994 APEC Ministerial Meeting in Jakarta. An APEC Ministerial Meeting on Sustainable Development was held in Manila in 1996.[54]

An APEC Sustainable Development Training and Information Network has been proposed, and its structure will be considered at the 1997 APEC Ministerial Meeting in Toronto. Canada is an advocate for including environmental issues within the APEC framework. The rapid institutional evolution of APEC highlights how environmental issues have gained a visible position in some of the most important institutions in the region. The principles of cooperation and equity that underlie the APEC initiative are also important for effective decision-making on environmental issues.[55]

Conclusion

Environmental issues are an important part of the international relations among nations at the turn of the century. The relations among the North Pacific Triangle partners illustrate this inclusion of environmental issues at the international level. Valuable experience has been gained in the reduction of some types of pollution emissions, the protection of selected habitats, the transfer of some technology and skills to developing countries, and the international negotiation of conventions to protect common property resources. The United States, Japan, and Canada each have industrialized economies that have caused environmental problems that require domestic legislation and action. However, action at the national level alone has proven ineffective as a means to address the global environmental crises of the twentieth century. Instead, countries must act together in order to be effective. International environmental negotiations are thus a product of both the domestic experience of each country and the need to take cooperative action.

Environmental issues, by nature, cross political boundaries. Their consideration at the international level requires a departure from old approaches to international relations where unilateral initiatives or bilateral initiatives with one party seeking to dictate terms were common. The hegemonic model with a dominant leader must be replaced with a model of coalitions forming to promote particular environmental issues. The common property attributes of the environment imply that all will benefit from improvements, yet no one has the incentive to be the first mover. As a result, many countries must respond to address an issue effectively. The Montreal Protocol and related agreements to cut the consumption of ozone-depleting chemicals demonstrate this process in operation. Smaller countries such as Canada have proven themselves as effective as larger countries such as the United States and Japan in leading international efforts to form coalitions to address particular environmental problems.

Another international trend is that the traditional focus on economic matters has broadened to include environmental issues at most international forums. Indeed, the reduced emphasis on military security in the post–Cold War period has enabled environmental security to grow in priority for the ministry of foreign affairs or the department of state in most countries. New domestic coalitions between environment and foreign affairs departments have thus formed to make this trend operational.

The discussion of environmental matters is not restricted to single, isolated issues, but has become part of more ambitious attempts at international community building where there is a shared interest in addressing critical issues. Collaborative forums such as G-7 or APEC meetings have broadened their agenda to include environmental as well as economic issues. The United States, Japan, and Canada are leading partners in these deliberations and are building the base to address future issues of shared interest.

The increased emphasis on the global environment and sustainable development has also shifted the focus of ODA from the simple transfer of financial resources or industrial technology to a greater emphasis on the sector invested in and its impact on the environment. Japan replaced the United States as the largest provider of assistance for environmental and other ODA projects in the early 1990s. However, Canada continued to allocate a much larger share of its GNP to ODA than either Japan or the United States. Indeed, the requested allocation of increased funds (0.7 per cent of GNP) to address environmental needs following the Rio Earth Summit has not been met by any of the North Pacific partners. This failure of the three countries to achieve financial targets is repeated in the case of greenhouse gas emissions. All three countries continued to increase their emissions of CO_2 in the 1990s despite policies and targets to reverse the trend. If the emission targets negotiated in international forums are to be met, significant measures need to be introduced at the national level before the turn of the century.

Environmental issues also highlight the broadening of the network of actors influencing international relations. National positions are not only a function of various national ministries, but also reflect input from industrial organizations, non-governmental organizations, and groups of scientists. Each of these groups provides information used by the media to influence public opinion and the priorities of politicians. Domestic coalitions and environmental experience thus continue to influence international negotiations.

At the domestic level, the United States, Japan, and Canada have each achieved some success and offered examples of leadership in environmental protection legislation, environmental technologies, and habitat protection. The methods used to achieve these improvements may be helpful for other countries facing similar problems. However, the persistence of some pollutants despite improved technologies and the recognition of the harmful effects of a wider array of pollutants means that more work remains to be done. Common property resources need to be better managed. One example of an area in need of better collaboration is the North Pacific fisheries. The list of global environmental issues is long and growing as global connections in both the economy and environment become better understood. The individual and collective experience of the North Pacific Triangle countries provides a valuable starting point to address not only regional, but also global, environmental issues in the future.

NOTES

1 The author would like to thank the many individuals who assisted with this research. In addition, the Social Science and Humanities Research Council of Canada, the Japan Foundation, the National Institute for Environmental Studies (Japan), and the University of Waterloo provided valuable financial and institutional support.
2 Homer-Dixon, 'On the Threshold'; Homer-Dixon, Boutwell, and Rathjens, 'Environmental Change'; Imber, 'Environmental Security'; Myers, 'The Environmental Dimension.'
3 OECD, *OECD Environmental Performance Reviews: Canada*, 175.
4 Stunkel and Wescott, *The Economic Superpowers and the Environment*; Ui, ed., *Industrial Pollution in Japan*.
5 Pierce, Lovrich, Tsurutani, and Abe, *Public Knowledge*.
6 Szell, 'Negotiations on the Ozone Layer.'
7 Grubb, 'The Greenhouse Effect.'

8 WCED, *Our Common Future.*
9 Hecht and Tirpak, 'Framework Agreement on Climate Change.'
10 IEA, *Energy Policies of IEA Countries.*
11 Park, 'Japanese Policy on Climate Change.'
12 Hecht and Tirpak, 'Framework Agreement on Climate Change.'
13 Obasi and Tolba, 'Preface,' x–xi.
14 Amano et al., eds., *Climate Change*; Houghton et al., eds., *Climate Change 1994.*
15 Manne and Richels, *Global CO$_2$ Emission Reductions.*
16 Williams, *Low Cost Strategies for Coping.*
17 Park, 'Japanese Policy on Climate Change'; Parker, 'Japanese Environmental Policies.'
18 Hecht and Tirpak, 'Framework Agreement on Climate Change.'
19 *Japan Times*, 20 February 1997.
20 Haas, Keohane, and Levy, eds., *Institutions for the Earth*; Parker, 'Japan and the Global Environment.'
21 Pempel, *Policy and Politics in Japan.*
22 IEA, *Coal Information 1992.*
23 Shaw, 'Acid-Rain Negotiations.'
24 Ibid.
25 OECD, *OECD Environmental Performance Reviews: Canada*, 172–73.
26 Parker, P. (ed.), *Pacific Coal Trade.*
27 JETRO, *U.S. and Japan in Figures II.*
28 RCFTW, *Regeneration: Toronto's Waterfront.*
29 UNEP, *Compact-Size Edition of Data Book.*
30 Japan, Environment Agency, *1992 Quality of the Environment in Japan.*
31 UNEP, *Environmental Data Report, 1993–94.*
32 Canada, *The State of Canada's Environment 1996.*
33 JETRO, *U.S. and Japan in Figures II.*
34 Japan, Environment Agency, *1992 Quality of the Environment in Japan.*
35 Estrin and Swaigen, *Environment on Trial*, 328; Lang 'Biological Conservation.'
36 Estrin and Swaigen, *Environment on Trial*, 213–14.
37 Pempel, *Policy and Politics in Japan.*
38 Japan, Environment Agency, *1992 Quality of the Environment in Japan*, 117.
39 Japan, Environment Agency, *White Paper on the Environment 1995.*
40 *Japan Times*, August 24, 1993; *Japan Times*, August 24, 1993, 3.
41 Maull, 'Japan's Global Environmental Policies.'
42 World Bank, *World Development Report 1995.*
43 Cameron, 'Japan and the Environment in Southeast Asia'; *Japan Times*, 24 February, 1997; Japan Center for a Sustainable Environment and Society, *Environment and Sustainable Development.*

44 World Commission on Environment and Development, Brundtland – chair, 'WCED Statement.'

45 World Bank, *World Development Report 1995.*

46 Japan, Environment Agency, *1990 Quality of the Environment in Japan*, 155; JETRO, *U.S. and Japan in Figures II*, 9; OECD, *OECD Environmental Performance Reviews: Canada*, 192.

47 NRTEE, *Canada–Japan Workshop.*

48 Japan, Ministry of Foreign Affairs, 'Japanese Economic Cooperation.'

49 *Japan Times*, 24 February 1997; Japan Center for Sustainable Environment and Society, *Environment and Sustainable Development.*

50 *Canada–Japan Workshop*, 14.

51 CJF, *Partnership across the Pacific.*

52 OECD, *OECD Environmental Performance Reviews: Japan*; *OECD Environmental Performance Reviews: Canada.*

53 NRTEE, *Canada–Japan Workshop.*

54 APEC, 'APEC Declaration,' 1996, http://www.econ.state.or.us/apecdecl.htm; APEC, 'APEC Action Plan,' 1996, http://www.econ.state.or.us/apecacti.htm.

55 'APEC; Community Building in East Asia,' http://www.apec.gspa.washington. edu/appec/us/pub/drysdale/detoc.html; Elek, 'APEC – Motives, Objectives and Prospects.'

III. MANAGING THE NEW RELATIONSHIP

12

Managing Canada–Japan Relations

JAMES H. TAYLOR

It is fair to ask why the question of managing relations between Canada and Japan arises at all. Both countries are free societies with democratic institutions and market economies. Both are members of the small group of advanced industrial economies in the Group of Seven (G-7). Normally the web of connections between countries of this kind is complex. The relationship is shaped by thousands of autonomous decisions, taken by thousands of people. Governments can set national objectives for the development of relations. They can try to create frameworks within which they want parts of the relationship to be conducted. They can seek to encourage the relationship to develop in certain directions, removing obstacles and solving problems where possible. But in a sense, relationships of this nature are not managed by anybody; they are too big and complex, and have enduring structures that make them difficult for any one centre to control. Official communiqués sometimes imply a greater capacity on the part of governments to shape, direct, and control such relations than exists in reality.

Furthermore, the number of actors keeps increasing. In Canada, interest in relations with Japan has traditionally been strongest in Alberta and British Columbia, for obvious reasons. But in the past generation, Japanese interests in Canada and reciprocally Canadian interests in Japan, have spread all across the country. Lumber producers in British Columbia, cattle ranchers in Alberta, canola growers across the West, automobile manufacturers in Ontario, aircraft manufacturers in Quebec, and fisheries interests throughout the Maritimes now have such a stake in the relationship that it is no longer possible to say only Western Canadians care about it. The federal government and many of the provinces borrow funds in Japan. Hundreds of Canadian municipalities are twinned with Japanese counterparts. Interests have grown that are shared by the entire country. Encouraging more Japanese tourists to come to Canada is not an affair confined to a single region. When Japanese bondholders buy or sell Canadian bonds, their decisions can affect all Canadians. Over time, Canada–Japan relations have become more complex, and as they have become more complex, they have become harder to manage, or even conceive of managing, within any single framework. Yet their growing importance is a standing inducement to governments and others to make greater attempts to shape and control them.

Growing complexity can be an argument for laissez-faire. So also is the fact that relations between the two countries are largely trouble-free and self-adjusting nowadays. This was not always the case. Relations, already troubled in the 1930s, were shattered by World War II. Traces of this trauma can still be detected in the relationship half a century later. The treatment of Canadian prisoners of war captured at Hong Kong in 1941 was a subject of discussion when the Canadian prime minister paid an official visit to Japan in 1991, for example. But such issues have long since ceased to dominate relations. True, contemporary relations are not totally trouble-free. Both Japanese investors in Canada and Canadian investors in Japan would attest to this. Yet such problems as exist can be solved either through existing mechanisms or, if necessary, through new devices. None is currently so serious as to colour the entire relationship. The shift from surplus to deficit in Canada's trade balance with Japan, for example, was a source of some anxiety in Canada. The impact of the deficit on Canada–Japan relations, however, is not pervasive. There is no equivalent of the obsessive preoccupations with the trade balance that characterizes relations between the United States and Japan. Trade and economic relations between Japan and Europe, or between Japan and the United States, reverberate with overtones of Great Power rivalry. Such notes are not struck between Japan and Canada for the obvious reason that while both these countries have considerable weight in the international system, they will never be rivals for world power in the sense that Japan rivals the United States. At the same time, Japan and Canada, as members of the same small group of rich industrial democracies, are bound to share a great deal by way of common outlook on the world. A shared world view and the absence of embittering problems or power rivalry combine to encourage smooth relations. Where relations are smooth, there will always be an argument for leaving a good thing alone to manage itself.

For all that, a great deal of effort has been expended, both by governments and by the private sector, in attempts to shape, control, and direct relations between Canada and Japan. Japan's growing importance, to the world and to Canada, as an established economic superpower and an emerging political heavyweight – as a market, a source of capital, and an associate in international cooperation – seemed to demand this degree of attention from Canadians. For the Japanese, Canada gained interest not only as a source of raw materials, but increasingly of manufactures, as a market and field for investment in the world of emerging regional free trade arrangements, and as a source of potentially valuable experience and support in multilateral institutions. There were reasons on both sides for trying to make a good thing better. That, essentially, is what governments and private interests have been engaged in. Some of their experiments are worth examining.

Take, as one instance, relations in the field of international security. For more than a generation, both countries have been separately allied to the United States. Yet their experience of the American alliance has been markedly different. In its alliances, the United States sought to secure certain key strategic areas: in Asia, until the Korean War, the Pacific limit was the Japanese island chain, offshore from the Asian mainland; in North America, the space separating the United States from the Soviet Union; and in Europe, the part of the North European plain occupied by the pre-reunification Federal Republic of Germany. For countries like Canada and Japan, the problem posed by their alliance with the United States was how to engage American power – above all, American nuclear power – in defence of the treaty area while constraining its use and ensuring respect for their own sovereignty. Canada found the answer along with its North Atlantic Treaty Organization (NATO) allies in a multilateral framework. The alternative of a unilateral American guarantee of European territory was an option considered in 1948 by the British, Canadian, and United States negotiators for the Washington Treaty, but was rejected in favour of a multilateral solution.[1] This made sense in Europe where a natural group of allies existed and where France and Germany, as ancient enemies, had determined to turn their backs forever on old quarrels.

NATO countries have no reason to regret their choice. Their alliance has been remarkably successful. It allowed the Western allies to outlast the former Soviet Union and survive the Cold War. It successfully engaged the nuclear might of the United States in defence of the treaty area, yet allowed smaller members like Canada a voice in formulating common policies. NATO powerfully reinforced Canada's multilateral instincts; it was not the only influence in this direction, but it was one of the most important. When new security challenges emerged with the end of the Cold War, it was natural for Canadian policy-makers to search for solutions through adapting the formula that had worked in Europe, first in NATO and then in the Conference on Security and Co-operation in Europe (CSCE): permanent consultation within a multilateral framework.

Japan's experience was different. Circumstances in the North Pacific did not lend themselves to the formation of a multilateral alliance; there was no group of potential, natural allies as there had been in Europe. Reconciliation between

Japan and its neighbours in China, both Koreas, and Russia was a more tentative and slow-moving affair than the parallel process in Germany. The strategic problems were not the same, since they had much more to do with the defence of seas and oceans than of land. There was little possibility of creating a multilateral alliance in the North Pacific and less need for one anyway: the basic security needs of Japan and the United States could be met by a bilateral treaty.

The sudden disappearance of the Soviet Union, along with its empire and its alliance, did not appear to Japanese observers to create the same sort of opportunities to remake the regional security order as had emerged in Europe. The Asian mainland, to their way of thinking, continued to harbour potentially threatening situations in China and Korea. Japan's relations with China and with both Koreas continued to be burdened by a sensitive historical legacy. Beyond that, whereas Britain, China, France, Germany, and even the United States had known periods of friendship and alliance with Imperial Russia and its Soviet successor, the Japanese looked back upon a century of relations with Russia that had rarely been friendly and that had varied over much of that time from indifferent to disastrous. The symbol of this, which the end of the Cold War did nothing to remove, was the unresolved quarrel between Japan and Russia over the Northern Islands. This was the most powerful obstacle to improving relations with post-Soviet Russia: it inhibited the Japanese from joining the Western allies in any rush to aid the new Russia, and the inhibition was effective despite the fact that the Japanese clearly recognized their shared interest in easing the transition of their former adversary to democratic institutions, a market economy, and friendly relations.

In short, there was much in North Asia to stimulate Japanese wariness about parallels between a new dawn in Europe and a new dawn in the Pacific. With the end of the Cold War, Europe 'from the Atlantic to the Urals' ceased to be rhetoric and became a substantial political project. In Asia there was no equivalent. The Japanese believed, with justification, that they had done well throughout the Cold War. They saw no overriding argument to warrant altering an arrangement that had worked as well for them in Asia as NATO had worked in Europe, particularly when they did not believe the threats to Japan's national security had disappeared.

Thus when the Canadian government began early in the 1990s to promote the concept of a broad multilateral approach to cooperative security in the North Pacific, the Japanese were notably reserved. In the face of these and other reservations, Canadian ministers – while continuing to make clear their support and sympathy for the concept – agreed it was preferable to let such an approach be examined further through contacts between academics in Canada and Japan. It engaged the interest of academics in other countries of the region as well. At the level of concepts, much analysis and discussion has been stimulated. Meanwhile governments – inspired in part by the uninhibited exchanges between academics – have flown a skyful of kites about either adapting existing institutions to make them capable of carrying security responsibilities, or creating new ones.

Despite the vivacity of this discussion, it was hard to say five years after the end of the Cold War how much the fundamental attitudes of governments had shifted. In Canada, a new government reviewed its foreign and defence policies. It was not obliged to share the views of its predecessor, although generally speaking the Canadian bias towards multilateralism is not a partisan affair. In Japan, the kaleidoscope of political change made it even harder to fix the image of future policy. For the first time in almost half a century, Japan acquired a socialist prime minister. His party's stock-in-trade traditionally included opposition to the security treaty with the United States, opposition to the Self-Defence Forces, and friendship with North Korea. Policy in Japan was also under review, and it seemed that if change were to come, it might well be in the form of changes in the traditional positions of the socialist party. The new socialist prime minister reaffirmed Japan's attachment to the alliance with the United States. Incidents around the Kuriles suggested that the Japanese approach to the issue of the Northern Islands was not a candidate for change.

If there was a shift in favour of multilateralism, it seemed it might come in relation to North Korea. Given the new uncertainties about North Korea's leadership and the unresolved difficulties with North Korea over the non-proliferation issue, the Japanese might well have had cause to regret that the international community was not better equipped with multilateral instruments to deal with the problems of security in the Korean peninsula. Even here, however, Japanese multilateralism would be different from the Canadian version. As one analyst has observed, 'Although rarely stated explicitly, the underlying logic of this "multilateralism" is the logic of the great power concert. To the Japanese multilateralists, region-wide security forums are a vehicle for regional management by the great powers.'[2] Thus to the extent that peaceful evolution of the Korean peninsula was more than a matter for the Koreans themselves, it would be up to China, Japan, Russia, and the United States to exercise their influence in concert. In calculations of this kind, Canada simply does not count; of the North Pacific countries, it is the least capable of projecting military power. Its assets in any multilateral discussions arise precisely from the fact that it is non-threatening. Japanese policy-makers may be relieved to have one regional neighbour that is neither a threat to be faced nor an ally to be placated, but they would not agree that Canada's relative disinterestedness of itself creates an interest.

As a subject in relations between Canada and Japan, then, regional security has prompted a great deal of lively discussion and activity both within and outside governments; at the same time it has revealed a profound difference in approach between the two countries. This state of affairs seems to alter only slowly over time, and not to be much affected by changes in government in either country.

International security in general, as well as regional security, has been pushed higher up the agenda of relations between Canada and Japan as a consequence of the end of the Cold War. Both countries, in common with the rest of the world, have had to rethink their place in the emerging world order – or disorder. For many Canadians, this process is essentially straightforward: they disliked the world of East–West tension and the constraints of a military alliance dominated by the United States, took pride in what their country had accomplished in peacekeeping under the United Nations, and are now on the whole relieved to envisage a world where Canada may be able to discharge its responsibilities as a decent international citizen mainly under the aegis of the United Nations, while shedding much of the wearying burden of faithful membership in NATO. At least as an initial position, enthusiasm for peacekeeping and for strengthening the United Nations comes easily and instinctively to Canadians.

Sharing this enthusiasm with Japan also comes easily. Over the past generation, successive Canadian governments have welcomed and promoted Japan's progressive return to a prominent place in the international system. They have supported Japan's bid for membership in international bodies and welcomed Japanese candidatures for senior positions. It was consistent with this tradition that, when the question of Japan's becoming a permanent member of the United Nations Security Council began to stimulate active discussion, the first foreign leader to declare publicly, simply, and without qualification that he believed Japan should be a permanent member was the then prime minister of Canada.[3] The Canadian government of the day was well aware of the sensitivity both of the internal debate in Japan on the subject and the complexities of the reform of the Charter of the United Nations. It seemed of overriding importance, however, to set out permanent Japanese membership of the Security Council as a desirable objective, however difficult it might be to reach that goal in practice.

In Japan, these matters have been much less straightforward. Japan's place in the international security system has been the subject of an unresolved running debate ever since the Gulf War of 1990–91. It was clear then and from the long discussion of peacekeeping legislation that followed that Japanese political leaders and Japanese voters are deeply divided about what responsibilities their country should undertake in the field of international security. The Gulf War demonstrated that the world, and in particular the United States, expected Japan to pay a share of the costs of peacekeeping and peacemaking proportionate to its wealth; it also demonstrated this was not enough: ultimately Japan would have to share all the risks of peacekeeping and peacemaking, including the risk of casualties, if international opinion and a certain body of domestic opinion were to be satisfied. What was for many Japanese a serious attempt to arrive at a new national consensus on the issue of using Japanese military force abroad – an awesomely difficult undertaking, given Japanese history and the Japanese constitution – was often treated with scant patience by foreign observers, especially the United States Senate. This was notwithstanding the fact that part of Japan's difficulty arose from applying the 'Peace Clause' of its postwar constitution, imposed on Japan by the United States and its allies for the purpose of ensuring that Japanese military power was never used outside Japan again. Even if this constraint had not existed, the Japanese forces were not organized to permit a rapid response to the special demands of peacekeeping: while they had been expanding steadily as a result of defence spending that, even limited to 1 per cent of GNP, still produced a large budget, they were configured to defend the Japanese islands and the seas immediately surrounding Japan, not to meet UN demands for long-range deployment of peacekeeping specialists.

A more forthcoming position on peacekeeping and permanent membership on the Security Council are separate issues. They are, however, closely related. Were Japan to come not only to underwrite one of the largest shares of the cost of peacekeeping but also assume all of the risks of participating in UN security operations, a corresponding share of political control and responsibility would surely fall to it sooner or later in the Security Council. For a number of Japanese politicians this is the direction in which Japan should be heading. Others are less sure, and for years Japanese opinion has remained divided.

At a time in the early 1990s when it seemed Japan might be moving actively to undertake greater security responsibilities under the United Nations, the official Canadian attitude was to encourage such a development. This was clear from Prime Minister Brian Mulroney's declaration in favour of Japanese membership on the Security Council. It was clear as well from the enthusiasm with which Canada received a variety of Japanese missions – parliamentary, military, and other – that sought information about Canada's experience of peacekeeping. Liberal Foreign Minister André Ouellet confirmed Canada's support for Japan's membership on the Security Council during an official visit to Japan in the summer of 1994. It is hard to imagine that the traditional Canadian support for greater Japanese participation in international organizations will not exert itself in other ways as well the moment Japan itself chooses to resume progress in this direction, despite all the complexities of reforming the Security Council. To the extent that there has been hesitation about a greater Japanese role, it has been more often on the Japanese than on the Canadian side. In a matter of this importance, the normal Japanese preference would be to proceed by consensus. There is no such consensus; indeed, on the part of many thoughtful Japanese there still remains a profound reluctance to see their country use armed force abroad, however circumscribed and respectable the conditions under which it is used.

Trade and economic relations provide further illustrations of interesting experiments in influencing the course of developments between Canada and Japan. Trade has always been a fundamental component of the relationship. Canada had trade interests in Japan, and official government representation to promote these interests, decades before Canada became fully sovereign. When full sovereignty was acquired in the 1920s, Japan was the second country after the United States in which the Canadian government decided to establish an embassy. Trade was a basic factor in this decision. Setting aside the interruption caused by World War II, Canadian exporters to Japan have registered some important successes. Canada continues to be an important source for Japan for wheat, canola, timber, coal, pulp and paper, and uranium; increasingly it has also become a supplier of sophisticated goods such as high-quality food, wood and leisure products, flight simulators and aircraft, communications equipment, and computer software. With a large, prosperous, and demanding consumer market and a rapidly evolving industrial economy, Japan has offered attractive opportunities to Canadian suppliers at a time when the exchange rate generally has favoured Canadian exporters. And Japan was not a closed market. Yet while opportunities were great, difficulties were not negligible. The counterpart of the low dollar, the high yen, made the cost of doing business in Japan prohibitive for small firms. Conditions were different from those in North American markets best known to Canadian firms. Problems arose because of language, because of the Japanese distribution system, because of different approaches to advertising and marketing. All of these added to the difficulties of newcomers to the market. A few troublesome tariff and non-tariff barriers took years to remove.

Individual companies have sought through their own efforts, through association with other private-sector interests, and through cooperation with governments to attack all these problems. Among the active private-sector organizations, the Canadian Chamber of Commerce in Japan has sponsored a variety of programs designed to promote mutual assistance among the community of Canadian business and professional people working in Japan, to encourage contacts between Canadian and Japanese firms with shared interests, and to provide a public platform for distinguished Canadian speakers visiting Japan. Another key organization active now for more than twenty years is the Canada–Japan Business Association. An umbrella organization that organizes an annual conference alternately in Canada and Japan, the association counts among its members virtually all the Canadian and Japanese firms with substantial interests in trade and economic relations between the two countries. Its organization into sectoral groups brings together buyers and sellers in a set of dialogues covering almost the entire range of trade relations. It allows for general discussion of issues of concern to all sectors as well. Growing mutual understanding and confidence between business leaders in the two countries has been an important product of this process.

A newer organization with a different, more general approach to creating mutual understanding is the Japan Society. It functions in Canada through speakers' programs, discussion groups, training programs, and other activities, and includes among its members not only the principal Canadian manufacturing firms with interests in Japan, but also leading firms of lawyers and accountants, hotel chains, transportation companies, and Canadian universities. This by no means exhausts the list of organizations in Canada and Japan that exist to promote the relationship in one way or another. Membership in these various associations and societies, taken together, covers all of Canada. The lion's share of Canadian activity is, however, concentrated in two cities: Toronto and Vancouver. Canadians living elsewhere still have to work hard to maintain a lively sense of contact with Japan.

Fostering closer relations with Japan has been claimed as a foreign policy priority by both Conservative and Liberal governments. Provincial governments have shared this view. The focus has been not just on Japan, but, so to speak, on Japan-in-Asia: not only Japan as the world's second-largest economy and largest source of capital, but Japan as Asia's only fully industrialized economy, a leader of what was until the crisis of 1997 the world's fastest-growing economic region, surrounded by nations apparently well launched on the path of imitating its success. A sign of the times for Canadians arrived in the 1980 when Canada's trade across the Pacific began to exceed its trade across the Atlantic, while for one Canadian province, British Columbia, trade with Japan equalled trade with the United States in importance.

These developments generated strong pressures on governments, both from outside and from within, to ensure that priorities fixed for trade development programs and resources assigned to them were fully adjusted to the growing weight of Asia, and of Japan, in the calculation of Canada's external interests. This was easier said than done. The shift in relative weight was clear beyond a doubt. Yet Japan remained one of the most expensive countries in the world in which to do business. What was desirable, both for governments and the private sector, was often prohibitively expensive. The collapse of the Japanese 'bubble' at the end of the 1980s did not alter this fundamental reality. Urban land values and rents in Japan fell sharply, but so did the dollar against the yen. Throughout this period, governments in Canada struggled with debt and deficits. Pressures to cut government operations were more or less constant from the end of the 1970s. Any investment in improving government services, especially in perennially high-cost Japan, had to fight for its place. Opinion inside and outside government had no difficulty in agreeing that high priority should be given to promoting Canadian interests in Japan. Even so, it took persistence to assemble the resources necessary to give meaning to that priority, and ingenuity to ensure that expenditures were justified in the face of very high costs. Not everyone in the end found that the rewards repaid the investment. On the whole, the federal government stuck to its priorities, put resources for an expanded program into Japan, and justified its costs. Others – some firms, the Ontario government, *The Globe and Mail* – concluded that their interests were better served by running down their operations.

Consistent with the priorities it had assigned in the 'Pacific 2000' program, the federal government decided to strengthen its capacities to serve Canadian interests in Japan. This strengthening took several forms. One was the construction of a long-debated new embassy in Tokyo. The debate had been long because a number of hard choices were involved. Ministers and officials had many difficult discussions of alternatives. The heart of the matter was cost: a new embassy was going to cost some $200 million. There was simply no way to meet a charge like this by following the normal practice of providing the sum necessary out of a departmental budget; neither ministers in the Treasury Board nor Parliament would have approved so large a sum. Furthermore, the site owned by the Canadian government in central Tokyo was enormously valuable – probably the most valuable single piece of real estate the government owned abroad. The temptation to sell it off, or develop it for profit on a commercial basis, was strong.

Some imaginative new solution to the problem had to be found. In the end, the government found it by going into partnership with a major Japanese bank and a construction firm. Canada provided the land for the new embassy without having to sell any of it. In return, it received outright about half the space in a new building, enough for a beautifully designed embassy, with right of reversion to the remainder of the building. This commercial portion, pending reversion, was meanwhile to be leased to business tenants; their rent payments would repay the Japanese partners, who had entirely financed the cost of construction. The trust agreement embodying these arrangements was to have a maximum life of thirty years.

The Canadian government's portion of the building was carefully conceived to meet the needs of the whole range of its programs in Japan. Among these, export promotion was generously provided for. Among the original commercial tenants in the building were the provinces of Alberta and British Columbia. The new building both allowed for and encouraged close cooperation between the federal government and the provinces, as well as between both levels of government and the private sector, in promoting Canadian goods and services in some of the most prestigious and attractive surroundings in Tokyo. For these and its other purposes, the embassy may be the most carefully conceived and built by any government anywhere in the world. Of its total cost of over $200 million, the direct cost to Canadian taxpayers was only $16 million.

The new building was begun in the late 1980s and opened in 1991. During these same years, an equally imaginative solution was found to the problem of regional representation in Japan. The regional markets were large and promising. Osaka's region, the Kansai, for example, had an economy the size of Canada's. The economy of the southernmost of the main Japanese islands, Kyushu, had an economy as large as that of the Netherlands. The regional economies of Japan were bigger than the national economies of some of Japan's Asian neighbours. Their size and prospects fully justified direct Canadian representation, principally for trade purposes, in a number of Japan's main regional centres. Under the National Trade Strategy, a first step was taken with the opening of a consulate-general in Osaka in 1986. Its success was a factor in encouraging a survey of other major regional centres to determine where it would be most rewarding to expand. The Osaka operation had benefited small and medium-sized Canadian producers of high value-added goods. This was just the sort of export promotion the government had sought to encourage in Japan. Furthermore, it suggested that, even in what is arguably the most highly centralized industrial country in the world, there was much to be said for seeking out markets and partners by direct contact with the regions, where the scale of Japanese enterprise itself was often smaller – that it was not necessarily the best course in all circumstances to approach the Japanese market through the large corporations based in Tokyo.

Yet decisions did not come easily. Given the pressure on budgets, any offices opened had to be small. Mini-offices in Japan would have to operate in the Japanese language to a much greater extent than the embassy in Tokyo. To the extent that they were staffed by Canadians, this meant that the Canadian government had to have at its disposal a guaranteed supply of Japanese-speaking trade specialists to serve as consuls. Above all, it was hard to decide where best to locate the new offices. Five cities, each the centre of a large regional economy, were surveyed: Sapporo, Sendai, Nagoya, Hiroshima, and Fukuoka. Each presented attractive prospects. Several had long-standing and important commercial ties with Canada. Yet the government had resources for only two offices staffed by career consuls. It was clear no rationale could be found for selecting two of the five cities and ignoring the other three: all five merited attention. It was finally decided to appoint prominent local business-people as Honorary Commercial Representatives in Sapporo, Sendai, and Hiroshima, and to name career officers to head small consulates in Nagoya and Fukuoka. This program was put in place in 1991 and 1992 and has operated successfully since, although it is too soon to say which of the two formulas of representation is more cost-effective. Canada has as a result a network of points of contact running the whole length of Japan, supported by the strengthened base of the Tokyo embassy.

This description of how an expanded system of support for Canadian interests in Japan was created gives some idea of what is involved for a government in setting priority objectives, assembling the resources necessary to pursue these priorities, and finding new ways to move forward when resources are scarce. Sometimes the course of wisdom in developing relations is simply to go slowly. The approach to multilateral security discussions described earlier provides one instance where prudence was the better course. Another was the approach adopted by the government of the day towards the highly sensitive issue of maintaining the confidence of Japanese investors in Canadian securities.

During the 1980s, Japan had risen to become Canada's third-largest source of foreign capital. The increase in Japanese direct and portfolio investment in Canada was dramatic. Japanese institutions had come to hold in the neighbourhood of $50 billion in long-term Canadian paper, much of this in the form of Canadian government bonds. A number of the provinces, as well as provincial and federal Crown corporations, were important borrowers on the Japanese market also. In the single world of capital markets, the Japan factor had increasingly to be taken into account. The federal government found it sensible to assign an officer to the staff of the Tokyo embassy who devoted his full-time attention to financial affairs. He followed the market, kept in touch with Japanese financial institutions, and reported to the Department of Finance and other interested branches of the federal government; in addition, he was responsible for preparing an annual survey, published by the Department of Finance, of developments in Japanese portfolio investment. The Canadian holdings of particular Japanese institutions were impressive; a number of Japanese houses held portfolios of Canadian securities valued at upwards of $1 billion to $4 billion. These were a small part of the total holdings of these institutions, however, which included some of the largest organizations of their kind in the world. What for them was a minor technical adjustment in their portfolios could have disproportionate and unintended repercussions for particular borrowers. The Canadian government had painful experience of that. It was clear that a two-way flow of authoritative information was needed to guard against unexpected shocks.[4]

Beyond this, Canadians absorbed in the country's unending constitutional debate were concerned that foreign investors unfamiliar with Canadian affairs might overreact as the debate moved from Meech Lake to Charlottetown and beyond. The temptation was strong from time to time to mount a campaign of reassurance: to grab foreign investors, so to speak, by the lapels and insist that Canada was not falling apart. But this risked protesting too much. Any overblown campaign might very well have backfired. Japanese investors, conservative believers in playing a long game, assessed risks across the world and were satisfied anyway that Canada remained a good bet. Regular visits to Japan by senior Canadian ministers, provincial leaders, and prominent business spokespeople, plus careful briefings by senior officials at budget time, provided sufficient occasions to set Canadian constitutional developments in perspective. Financial markets did not overdramatize these preoccupations. From time to time they did, however, provide short, sharp reminders to Canadians of what it meant that their country had borrowed so heavily abroad in recent years, including borrowing on a large scale from new sources in Japan.

A complete review of the management of relations between Canada and Japan would have to extend far beyond these few examples. Most of the preceding discussion looked at developments from a Canadian point of view; much more would need to be added from a Japanese perspective. The history of Japanese trade and economic missions to Canada, notably the Kanao Mission in 1989, would require special attention. So also would Japanese programs designed to promote human contact between Japan and other countries: cultural exchanges and Japanese government initiatives that give young Canadian graduates a chance to work in Japan as English-language teaching assistants in Japanese schools or as aides in government offices. Some hundreds of young Canadians have now seized these opportunities, a fact of great potential significance for the future. Other forms of human contact would need to be reviewed also, notably tourism, which now brings up to half a million Japanese visitors to Canada every year, with potential for considerable further expansion. The special efforts of the Japanese and Canadian governments to encourage closer cooperation in science and technology, through special studies and through funding cooperative venture in joint research, would provide yet another chapter. In particular it would be important to discuss an extraordinary exercise in shaping Canada–Japan relations, Canada–Japan Forum 2000. The forum, a blue-ribbon panel of distinguished Japanese and Canadian leaders from outside government, was established in 1991 by the two governments. Its report the following year contains nineteen recommendations touching on the whole range of relations between the two countries. An exercise of this kind is without precedent in Canada's bilateral relations. The forum's origins, its findings, and the prospects for implementing its recommendations are a story in themselves.

NOTES

1 See Pearson, *Mike*, 49–50; English, *The Worldly Years*, 17; Reid, *Time of Fear and Hope*, esp. Chap. 8.
2 Kawasaki, 'The Logic of Japanese Multilateralism.'
3 Brian Mulroney in a public statement during his official visit to Japan as prime minister in May 1991.
4 For example, as in April 1987, when the unexpected sale of bonds by a major Japanese insurance company triggered a sharp drop in the Canadian dollar.

13

Canada–Japan Forum 2000: A Novel Exercise in Diplomacy

MICHAEL GRAHAM FRY

The legitimation imperative – the need for governments to explain and justify policy to their various constituencies, to engage élites and attentive publics – marks the conduct of foreign policy in open societies. It puts a premium on communication skills and explains the growth of government investment in the apparatus of communication, for if governments cannot explain and justify policy adequately, others will attempt to do it for them, demonstrating official incompetence. That foreign policy must contribute to government credibility and popularity while serving national unity as well as the national interest is an axiom for all governments of whatever political stripe. The apparent end of that phase in U.S.–Russian relations that Raymond Aron described in an exquisitely irreducible phrase as '*guerre impossible, paix improbable*' made these challenges all the more difficult to meet. Indeed, they present the most baffling problem for democratic governments at century's end.

The Canada–Japan Forum 2000,[1] instituted by a Conservative government and inherited by a Liberal government, is part of the Canadian response to these challenges, a response that, in this case, was creative, unprecedented for a bilateral relationship, and virtually without risk.[2] Its origins lay in the Department of External Affairs and International Trade. Joe Clark, participant in the annual ministerial talks with Japan, interested in Pacific security issues, and Minister of External Affairs, with the support of certain senior officials, was its principal animateur from the summer of 1990. It seemed necessary to rethink the relationship, stop it from plateauing, find ways to move it forward, even uncover a vision, and wise to raise Canada's profile in Japan. Prime Minister Brian Mulroney, reaching back to his 1989 Singapore speech, adopted the initiative, gave it energy, and, with the Japanese prime minister, established the forum formally on 28 May 1991. Mulroney's mandate set the forum's agenda from the beginning; officials in the Department of External Affairs and International Trade (especially those involved in the Joint Canada–Japan Economic Committee) gave it shape and form. The Japanese, taken perhaps by surprise, added nothing of substance to it. Rather than having a purely economic agenda, four task forces were required to implement the mandate. Those Canadians who agreed to serve in the spring of 1991 (the list, suitably balanced, was developed in the Department of External Affairs) under the predictably vigorous, persuasive, even commanding chairmanship of Peter Lougheed, former Premier of Alberta and on record on the importance of Canada's relations with Asia Pacific, did so out of a sense of opportunity and obligation. Even then, the point of the exercise required explanation. The bilateral relationship was important, even crucial, for Japan was at the core of Canada's strategy to increases its role in Asia Pacific. Something worthwhile should come out of the foray.

They were a diverse group, differing in experience, knowledge, prominence, intellectual engagement, vigour, and philosophy.[3] They became a Cabinet-like group, finding a cohesion in candour and respectful listening that sensible people do when the challenge is to make practical, short- and medium-term recommendations. Their task was to reanimate, in a businesslike way, a process, to contribute to the continuum that was the Canada–Japan relationship that, in governmental time, had a long history. The group was determined to become knowledgeable on the relationship as briskly as possible, to decide what information was relevant, to discern which advice was valuable, and undeterred by the sceptics, to trust in their collective judgment. The Forum would have something to say. Indeed, by the end, the chairman wrote of them sharing 'a compelling vision of the challenges and possibilities for Canada in the 21st century.' The concern of Lougheed and his colleagues that there be a follow-up mechanism to encourage implementation of their recommendations testified to their confidence. The prime minister must, Lougheed wrote, meet with Japan's leaders, and begin to educate the Canadian public on the importance of the relationship with Japan; he must animate the bureaucracy and engage the provinces in a variety of initiatives while embracing those recommendations that related directly to his Prosperity Initiative.[4]

The Japanese from all accounts were, with significant individual exceptions, initially reluctant, unsure of novelty as they had been regarding the Joint Economic Committee in 1990, even sceptical, or worse. The Canadian initiative was a nuisance, a waste of time, a chore, unlikely to be productive given its general and broad terms of reference, and, possibly, a forum for complaints about Japan's trading practices, among other hidden agendas.[5] The relationship was, after all, uncomplicated and uncontroversial. What Canada coveted was predictable – Japanese direct investment and technology and a greater share of Japan's imports of value-added products to begin to correct the Canadian trade deficit with Japan. So why had Canada singled out the bilateral relationship for such scrutiny? The Canadian constraints on the trade and investment relationships – bound up, for example, in interprovincial trade barriers, widely disparate foreign investment regulations and taxation policies, and thus in federal–provincial relations – were well understood. Canadian attentive publics, except those in the West where knowledge did not always breed understanding, seemed for the most part to be neither well-informed about nor to value sufficiently the relationship. In what sense was Canada a Pacific as well as an Atlantic and North American state? The relationship was, moreover, something of a sideshow to the permanently complex and perennially disputatious relationship with the United States in which, predictably, agreements on trade, arrived at in private and almost immediately interpreted differently in public, were almost more damaging than the absence of agreement.

The Japanese warmed to the enterprise, however, buoyed essentially by anxiety over the implications for Japan of the Canada–U.S. Free Trade Agreement and the prospect of a U.S.–Canada–Mexico North American Free Trade Agreement. The number and profile of Japanese observers to the joint sessions of the Forum were testimony to that concern. The Forum took on promise and provided information. Its agenda, beyond economics, became more welcome and even decisive to Japan's participation. One could begin to say with some conviction that Canada was a Pacific state, a member of a putative North Pacific Triangle, and worthy of close examination. Canada was not the United States in obvious ways, such as the banking system, and in ways that were less than obvious and subtle. Canada had distinct, discrete assets. Canadian negotiators cared and listened; their U.S. counterparts did neither. There were perhaps ways in which Japan could use Canada just as Canada could use Japan.

The Canada–Japan relationship was profoundly different from the U.S.–Japan relationship. Canada, understandably, did not want its relationship with Japan put in jeopardy by Japan's management of its relations with the United States. Perhaps Canada's handling of the United States was worth Japan's scrutiny without ever raising the prospect of a Canada–Japan common front in managing problems with the United States. In that way, as the Japanese became more engaged, and as the Lougheed group identified assets that Canada could use to improve its relations with Japan and saw itself as part of a confidence-building, trust-deepening process, the forum could be candid about differences. These differences – on the dispute-resolution mechanism, on the follow-up and monitoring process by a bi-national, non-governmental review group, on environmental issues such as fish stocks, and on human rights – could be resolved by the forum, finessed, and, at worst, placed in that necessary diplomatic category of 'requiring further study.'

The Lougheed group left the Forum well satisfied with their handiwork, captured in the final report. Their confidence had been justified. They understood the Japanese, just as the Japanese understood and regretted, for example, the complexity of federal–provincial relations in Canada. The group's key members expected their report to be taken seriously, to be acted upon promptly and effectively. It was a wake-up call to the nation to learn, to change its attitudes, and to accept fresh yardsticks for measuring national success – exports sold and foreign direct investment brought in. It identified tasks for the private sector – business, labour, educators, and the media. It asked for a commitment from the public sector – bureaucracies and both provincial and federal governments – as it asserted that traditional approaches were no longer enough. Reliance on traditional markets for Canadian goods and services would no longer suffice; business as usual would not, in the competitive environment of the next century, bring the levels of foreign direct investment that were indispensable to Canada's prosperity. The report was meant to be a rich set of practical and fiscally demanding, but responsible, recommendations, a foundation on which the federal government could proceed to bring Canada's relationship with Japan to a mature, exemplary, and mutually beneficial condition. With that relationship in place, close to the point of 'merging our respective strengths,' Canada and Japan, each in their own way and together, could face more confidently the next century, one of change and opportunity. In that way the uncontroversial, unequal, and bilateral relationship had become part of a vision. Japan was at the core of Canada's future in Asia.

The Report

Everything followed from a single axiom – change – and a set of assumptions about Canada, Japan, and their relationship. Change had two faces: the world had changed and was continuing to evolve, and Canadians at all levels and in all sectors must change their attitudes and responses.[6] No new stable international order had followed the end of the Cold War and bipolarity; interdependence was increasing and the boundary between the domestic and international spheres was disappearing. There existed the prospect of a world that was more free and democratic, and yet potential for conflict lurked in territorial, ethnic, and religious disputes, in terrorism, refugees, inequality, famine, poverty, population pressures, unresolved environmental challenges, drugs and epidemiology (AIDS), nuclear proliferation and the conventional arms trade, and the troubled states and regions formerly under communist control, in the absence of a comprehensive global security system founded on more than military means. There were challenges to be faced and opportunities to be seized if a new sense of purpose were to emerge, if a fresh burst of intellectual and entrepreneurial energy were summoned. That was why the report, while urging Canada and Japan to put their respective houses in order as they restructured their economies, preached more insistently to Canadians than to Japanese.[7]

The report's assumptions were not without their eccentricities. Canada and Japan were dissimilar geographically, historically, politically, institutionally, and ethnically, but they now shared, on Japan's insistence, the same values and an unshakable commitment to democracy and the free market. Both were prepared to accept the international roles and responsibilities befitting their resources and their G-7 and UN membership. Canada always had; Japan, no longer passive and adaptive and willing merely to consume the security and prosperity provided by and at the expense of others, wanted a higher profile. The Japanese admired, respected, and trusted Canada because of the wisdom and courage it had demonstrated as it had helped manage the international system since 1945. Canadians admired Japan because of the economic miracle it had experienced since 1952. The two societies complemented each other; complementarities abounded in the worlds of diplomacy, trade, and investment, pointing to the as-yet-unrealized potential for mutually rewarding, effective cooperation. Canada was becoming a more Pacific and thus less an Atlantic and North American nation. Finally, increased awareness and contact would enhance mutual understanding, richer cultural exchanges would bring greater respect and admiration, dialogue would triumph over indifference, and engagement would make cooperation a habit, en route to a lasting friendship. That was why the framers of the report could not quite decide whether the bilateral relationship was already sufficiently impressive and mature (indeed, was a quietly developed model relationship for cooperation between markedly different societies), or that so much remained neglected that substantial initiatives were required for the relationship to approach its undoubted potential: a creative, mutually beneficial partnership founded on respective strengths. While the Japanese must finally distinguish Canada from the United States, Canadians had a host of corrections to make – to drop outdated stereotypes (that Canada merely produced and Japan consumed natural resources); to build on the necessary but insufficient economic relationship; to create trust, friendship, and mutual understanding by patience, perseverance, and creative mechanisms; to leverage effectively Canada's international reputation; and to reach out in partnership to Asia Pacific and the still-troubled international system.

The model followed from the assumption that a mature bilateral relationship would enable Canada and Japan to reach out regionally into Asia Pacific, and thereby alter their relationship with the United States, and, beyond that, affect decisively the future of the international system. Three concentric circles of action, with their dynamics coming from the core – the bilateral relationship – were devised.

Predictably and unavoidably, the Second Task Force on economic issues dominated the core, the challenge of bringing the bilateral relationship to a mature state. Lougheed, in his letter to Mulroney accompanying the report, found no reason to dwell on the obvious. Japan was identified briskly as Canada's second-largest economic partner, and Canada was identified as Japan's seventh-largest economic partner. Trade between the two countries had grown substantially, from $1.6 billion in 1971 to $17.4 billion in 1991, based on traditional Canadian exports of natural resources principally from Western Canada – coal, minerals, grain, fish, lumber, and pulp – and Japanese exports of consumer products destined principally for Central Canada. The problem was that Canada had not participated in the change in Japan's import mix – from a 75/25 split between raw materials and finished products to a more 50/50 distribution. Indeed, falling prices and tonnages had led to a decline in Canadian exports to Japan and a trade deficit that would continue in the absence of fresh strategies. The problem lay, the report argued emphatically, neither in the lack of import demand nor in a closed Japanese market (a conclusion dramatically opposed to that of the United States, captured in its indictments of Japan), but in unimaginative Canadian business practices rooted in impatience and ignorance. Canadian firms in the finished wood products, processed food, and specialized machinery sectors had registered a certain success in penetrating the Japanese market. Opportunities were at hand in food, software, environmental technology, housing components, and prefabricated houses. These pointed to what was needed – niche marketing of custom-designed, value-added products (seaweed-flavoured french fries in small packages, an Ottawa official with a sense of imagination and humour explained). If non-tariff barriers to trade still existed, and they did, frank and forceful Canadian representations must secure their removal. If the Japanese distribution system was so poor as to create a major impediment to Canadian sales, and it was, Canadian businesses must respond creatively and patiently as they dealt with Japanese trading companies. The key lay in ending Canadian inertia and shedding passé images of a closed Japanese market. Quality of product, consistent quality, timely delivery, adequate inventory, physical market presence, and employment of Japanese must mark the Canadian export effort. The Japanese expected Canadian exporters neither to attempt to sell to Japan those products made primarily for the U.S. market nor to value the Japanese market only when the U.S. market softened. Quality jobs for Canadians would follow. Indeed, job creation was the issue.

Foreign direct investment, the most desirable form of private economic co-operation – transferring capital, business resources, management skills, and technology, and resulting in enhanced exports and job creation – was the other economic pillar of the relationship. Japanese direct investment in Canada traditionally had been in resource industries (pulp and paper, mines, and high-risk oil and gas), but had moved into the automobile, electronic, financial, and tourist industries. Given the United States as the yardstick, in the classic 10/1 ratio, Canada was getting perhaps only 50 per cent of its share of Japanese direct investment. Again the problems lay principally at home in damaging and discriminatory government policies, in interdepartmental disputes, and in inconsistent provincial regulations.[8] Canada, federally and provincially, must mend its ways, provide incentives (for employment-providing plywood mills in the forest industry, for example), open itself to Japanese investment and technology (in, for example, auto parts and oil and gas production in the circumpolar region), create an improved investment climate, and remove the barriers to and attempt to compete with the United States for Japanese capital. Once again, quality jobs for Canadians would follow. There was no hint whatsoever of any negative consequences or public apprehension about increased foreign direct investment.[9] Domestic sources of investment were simply inadequate. Canada, with its taxation policies and banking practices, was capital-deficient. 'Patient capital,' which underpinned research and development and the longer term, was vital. The answer had to lie abroad, and examples existed of the kinds of ventures Canada most needed.

The message, in sum, could not have been more straightforward and categorical – increased Canadian exports to Japan, greater Japanese direct investment in Canada. The Task Force's specific action recommendations followed from this pre-emptive reasoning. Both governments (and in Canada's case it was often an issue of coordinating federal and provincial policies), should adopt strategies to promote rather than obstruct bilateral corporate investment, strategic alliances, technological exchange, and economic partnerships. Investment Canada was a decided improvement on the Foreign Investment Review Agency (FIRA), but just as MITI had begun to facilitate trade and investment, Canada must erase specific obstacles to foreign investment.[10] To enable Canada to benefit from the change in import demand, Japan must enhance the openness of its markets by setting and publicizing its standards and regulations for imports and its prequalification specifications (i.e., the basis of bidding), open up its ports, make its ports and airports more efficient, and improve its distribution infrastructure. Canadian business, facing a market that was protected by few tariff barriers, must adapt its exports to meet changing Japanese demand for value-added products in the manufacturing sector, for example, and become better informed about Japanese business culture and practices. The media could assist in that educational process. Canadian governments, for their part, must sweep away those domestic programs that discriminated in favour of grains and raw materials exports. Finally, the Second Task Force recommended that the two governments explore the creation of a problem resolution mechanism to prevent or resolve disputes promptly, thereby creating a set of clear rules and precedents under which trade, investment, and technology transfer decisions could be made. A four-person commission with a chairperson was envisaged. The economic relationship was to date singularly free of disputes, and the private sector could be relied upon to maintain that enviable record, but this proactive, prescient step should be taken. Some felt that such a step would be entirely in line with Japanese expectations and practices; others were less sanguine.

While the report made light of the need for Canadian business to support education, it made something of the value of the Canadian education system to business, providing, as it did, the skilled, informed, and language-proficient young Canadians and apprentices that could help in the export and investment challenges. In that way at least the Fourth Task Force on cultural issues found a specific and welcome relevance. Lougheed, in his letter to Mulroney, actually singled out the Fourth Task Force as one of six issues worthy of emphasis and funding, while acknowledging that financial constraints, public indifference, and habit made it difficult for cultural issues to find breathing space amidst fundamental economic questions, pressing security concerns, and alluring global initiatives.

The Fourth Task Force was unreserved in its liberal optimism – contact, exchange, familiarity, awareness, and education about the other's cultural heritage and history would breed respect, understanding, and productive relationships, and help avoid undesirable experiences and outcomes 'from personal unhappiness to international crises.' To address cultural issues and educational opportunities, to explore complementarities beyond the economic, and to enable Japanese to understand North America and Canadians to have special insight into Asia Pacific, would be, the Task Force insisted, to provide the social underpinnings of all the other dimensions of the bilateral relationship. They would be, in fact, the key to the success of the relationship. In the absence of a 'ready habit of considering the other's interests and attitudes,' a series of recommendations were made to bring purpose, magnitude, and urgency to the relationship. An endowed fund, a Japan–Canada Fund for Mutual Understanding, would promote exchanges of people in all walks of life; collaboration between scholars, scientists, educators, and artists; and learning from and about each other. Vital, lasting personal relationships would be established as Japanese and Canadians examined issues of mutual interest – the role of culture and devel-opment, the environment, North–South issues, the United States, and non-governmental agencies. Data would be compiled and disseminated on mutual understanding. Teaching materials on history and culture must be developed, the teaching of Japanese in Canadian schools improved, and school libraries enriched. Beyond that, the arts, including the performing arts, of each nation must be introduced to the other. Museums, galleries, and curators must collaborate. Tourism must be promoted, and the broadcast media in all its forms including the respective film industries must begin to collaborate in joint ventures with necessary structural support.

Beyond the core bilateral relationship stood the Asia-Pacific region. The First Task Force, addressing political issues, set out why Canada saw itself as having a Pacific orientation, as becoming a more Pacific nation. In addition to geography, trade, immigration, and diplomacy, involvement in the Korean War and the Indo-China truce commissions and membership in APEC, the Pacific Basin Economic Council (PBEC), the Pacific Economic Cooperation Conference (PECC), and the Post Ministerial Conference of ASEAN gave Canada a vital interest and role in promoting the stability and prosperity of the Asia-Pacific region. This emerging, unavoidable regional involvement would take its place alongside Canada's links with the United States and Europe, and its network of relationships by way of the Commonwealth and the francophone world. The Second Task Force, on economic issues, had pointed to Japan's identical concerns for and growing prominence in the region, thereby magnifying still further Japan's importance to Canada. Regional interests would be best pursued in collaboration with Japan; Japan would help carry Canada into Asia Pacific. Politically, as the potential for conflict remained and the possibility of anarchy in Asia Pacific existed, Japan and Canada must help fill the institutional vacuum and promote the agenda of comprehensive security. It was a matter of building on the existing foundations and institutions of economic cooperation. The Post Ministerial Conference of ASEAN could expand its agenda; the APEC forum, with extended membership, might convene regular summits; and special Canada–Japan working groups could address specific regional disputes and conflicts. A 'Pacific Academy' might evolve and bring together Canadian and Japanese scholars to examine issues of regional cooperation and security.

In economic terms, Canada and Japan should cooperate in ways that brought benefits to Asia Pacific and Latin America. Asia Pacific was the area of future rapid economic growth, and Japan was the key to that dynamic opportunity. Trans-Pacific trade was valued at U.S.$360 billion. A form of regional economic integration could evolve, based on free-market competition, fairness, and transparency. Canadian and Japanese trade and investment in the region would increase. It followed that Canada and Japan, collaboratively, must help maximize the benefits of APEC for the region. They must also ensure that their respective

individual policies towards and behaviour in other bilateral or regional relationships did not damage the interests of the other. While this concern was mutual, its
significance for Japan was immediate and pressing. The prose was pointed:
Japan greatly valued the Canada–U.S. Free Trade Agreement as an instance of
economic cooperation 'that satisfies the requirement of regional openness.' It
appreciated Canada's efforts to ensure '... in certain auto agreements, that
Japanese investment in Canada would not be at a disadvantage.' Japan expected
the NAFTA also to operate on 'the principle of regional openness.'

The Third Task Force, on global issues, could not but address regional matters, given Japan's concern that NAFTA be consistent with and strengthen the
GATT, stimulate trade and investment globally as well as regionally, be outward-looking, and neither divert trade and investment from Asia to North
America nor raise fresh barriers to trade and investment. It recommended,
therefore, that APEC address the problem of trade and investment diversion and
that it, or some other forum, examine the prospects for strengthening ties
between NAFTA and Asia-Pacific states, including Japan. Just as Canada could
be Japan's window on NAFTA, so Japan could help dispel fears of NAFTA in
Southeast Asia. There was absolutely nothing, forum members insisted, overtly
or indirectly anti-American in all this. It was a matter of balance and opportunity, of adding bilateral bonds to those that already existed, of reducing Canada's vulnerability, of reordering priorities somewhat, of not permitting the
United States, formidable as it was, to obscure other prospects, and of prudently
using scarce financial and diplomatic resources. Unavoidably, the closer Canada's bilateral relationship became with Japan and the more oriented toward
Asia Pacific Canada became, the more its relations with the United States
would change.

A variety of concerns, felt particularly by the Canadian side – ecological,
environmental, technological, economic (the development of energy resources,
transportation systems, and new markets), and knowledge-building – led the
Third Task Force also to the northern circumpolar region and to the goals of
mutual discovery and private-sector joint ventures. This recommendation followed logically from the proposal to create a joint environmental project on the
stewardship of the North Pacific Ocean and constituted one of the avenues to
the third circle of the model. There, Canada–Japan cooperation reached beyond
the Asia-Pacific region to the global system, giving bilateralism even greater
multilateral implications and pointing to a framework for global cooperation.

The First Task Force, on political issues, followed precisely that reasoning.
Given the two countries' G-7 membership, common values, global interests,
and complementarities, given Canada's record and Japan's quest for a political
role in promoting peace and stability commensurate with its economic strength

and trading interests, they could increase their joint influence and take the lead in the search for 'comprehensive security.' This phrase came from the Japanese, and meant meeting the challenges of supplying foreign aid; protecting the environment; providing for military security; enhancing trade, investment, and technology transfers; and ensuring financial stability. Specifically, Canada and Japan, at the 1993 G-7 summit and then in the United Nations and the GATT, should redefine summit diplomacy and sponsor an agenda for achieving comprehensive global security that rested on an equitable sharing of responsibilities among states, according to resources and assets. Two or three concrete initiatives were required. It seemed essential, as part of this process, for Japan to become a permanent member of the UN Security Council.

Lougheed, in his letter to Mulroney, gave pride of place to the 'bold and dramatic' recommendation of the First Task Force on peacekeeping to establish the Japan–Canada Centre for Conflict Prevention and Conflict Resolution, probably on Vancouver Island. In collaboration with the United Nations and inviting broader participation, the centre would focus on specific cases of actual or potential conflict and devise appropriate responses. It would help train personnel in peacekeeping tasks, and convene task forces of specialists on 'early-warning,' mediation (i.e., peacemaking), and on peacebuilding through economic, cultural, and environmental projects. The proposed centre met all of the forum's criteria. It responded to a burgeoning need (the 'security gap' born of proliferating conflicts); it was a specific joint initiative; it reflected complementarities (Canada's international expertise and heritage and Japan's awakening sense of responsibility); it was practical and action-oriented and of mutual benefit; and it enabled Canada and Japan, in concert, to influence the international system. The proposed centre represented, moreover, an initiative that was clearly distinct from any facet of the U.S.–Japan relationship. It would be a symbol of Canada's distinctiveness in North America, something that marked Canada as more than an appendage of the United States as it engaged Japan on its own ground. As a study centre, however, it fell far short of being an international peacekeeping staff college for the officers of all nations, staffed by Canada and paid for by Japan.

The Third Task Force, on global issues, rested its recommendations on the twin pillars of international competitiveness, promoting trade in high-quality goods and services, including technology, and the protection of the environment, seeking to strike a balance between liberalized competitive trade and environmental policies that led to sustainable development. It found promise in shared strengths in technology, human resources, and policy expertise and orientation, and complementarities. Specifically, Canada and Japan, to provide a long-overdue institutional basis for multilateral cooperation, and to build on the

Uruguay Round, should promote the creation of a multilateral trade organization (MTO). Its prospects were inviting, its functions many. The MTO would reduce unilateralism, create an improved trade dispute settlement mechanism, promote trade and investment expansion, and bring a degree of coordination into international monetary, trade, and financial policies in cooperation with the IMF and the World Bank. It would moreover – and the re-emphasis was pointed – prevent NAFTA from becoming an inward-looking trading bloc, and ensure both that NAFTA led to enhanced Canada–Japan trade and strengthened GATT.

The pursuit of prosperity through Canada–Japan inspired multilateralism must, however, find a fit with environmental stewardship and the commitment of the Rio conference to global sustainable development. Generally, Canada and Japan, building on their technological proficiencies, would promote the agenda of the Rio conference through the UN Commission on Sustainable Development, the UN Environmental Program, and APEC. They would collaborate to deploy appropriate technologies, and promote the development and transfer of environmentally friendly technologies. They would launch a joint observation satellite by the year 2000 to monitor atmospheric, oceanic, and natural resources, and collect data that contributed to international understanding of environmental problems and solutions. Canada and Japan would cooperate to address threatening environmental problems such as ozone layer depletion, global warming, acid rain, and the spread of radioactive waste.[11] Specifically, they would launch a joint project on the stewardship of the North Pacific Ocean to monitor pollution and the sustainability of fish resources, the latter an urgent Canadian concern, and to coordinate with marine projects launched under APEC.

Beyond multilateral trade and the environment lay the contentious issues of refugees and human rights. Japan's priority lay clearly with the refugee tragedy, supporting as it did the work of the UN High Commissioner for Refugees and other international organizations. The agenda was formidable – to alleviate suffering through resettlement and to eradicate the cause of the international refugee problem. It had both demographic mobility (and guest worker) and security implications. Canada could claim a certain expertise in refugee problems and thus reinforce Japan's activities. But human rights were, most decidedly, not a Japanese priority. They were not about to be lectured on Western versions of human rights. The Third Task Force could, lamely, call merely for an exchange of opinions and information as part of an educational process and the promotion of sound values.

In sum, Canada and Japan, brimming with experience, knowledge, and vitality, adjusting policies, meeting challenges, and taking on fresh responsibilities, would create a mutually beneficial bilateral relationship. That, in turn, would lead them to a form of leadership in Asia Pacific that would enrich the region as a whole. From those foundations they could influence the management of the global system and its pursuit of peace, stability, prosperity, and environmental protection. The dynamics of the model would then become reciprocal. As Canada and Japan acted together globally and regionally, their bilateral relationship would prosper all the more, to the point of a habit of trust.

A Call for Action

By asking that the prime ministers of Canada and Japan each appoint, within 120 days, five citizens to a follow-up review group to monitor 'the earliest and fullest implementation of these recommendations,' and to report to them, the forum said in effect we have done our job, let there be action not the gathering of dust. That request fulfilled the first and only free-standing recommendation of the report, underpinning the eighteen recommendations of the four task forces. Lougheed, in his letter to Mulroney, argued that the fourth recommendation of the First Task Force, on peacekeeping; the third recommendation of the Third Task Force, on the stewardship of the environment; and all the recommendations of the Fourth Task Force be given budgetary priority. He identified the areas requiring prompt action from the federal and provincial governments in tandem, i.e., to remove barriers to economic cooperation and investment, help launch the joint venture on the environmental stewardship of the North Pacific, establish the Fund for Mutual Understanding, and fund the recommendations of the Fourth Task Force.

Lougheed, Geraldine Kenney-Wallace, and Peter Bentley were encouraged by the reception in Ottawa. The prime minister, flanked by Finance Minister Michael Wilson, seemed enthusiastic and picked up the telephone. The Department of External Affairs and International Trade was responsive. Kim Campbell's positive views, and those of Perrin Beatty, became irrelevant almost instantaneously, but the briefing of Liberal leader Jean Chrétien in December 1992 went well. The Liberal Party, in its election manifesto 'Creating Opportunity. The Liberal Plan for Canada,' while getting the date of the forum report wrong, endorsed it and promised to implement many of its recommendations, 'in order to strengthen our trading relationships with the Pacific Rim.' It identified specific products that would add to Canada's export performance – food, telecommunications software, environmental and other technology, housing components, and complete houses. Ontario and Alberta led the provinces in responding positively but waited on Ottawa to take the lead. The Liberal Party swept to victory in the election of October 1993 and then, unavoidably, politics ruled priorities for 1993 and much of 1994. The brief yet embarrassingly protracted delay, in comparison with Japan, itself beset with political problems, in announcing the Canadian contingent for the binational review group by the Liberal government reflected the impact of two changes of government within fifteen months.[12]

Yet, in part because the forum's report pointed in directions in which the Department of External Affairs and International Trade was already going; in part because vigorous, engaged, committed individuals pursued some of those recommendations that were innovative, even unexpected; in part because some progress could be made without either large financial outlay or the commitment of limited diplomatic resources; and in part because the 'vision,' the call to action, was so eminently reasonable, action did occur, and the dynamics of the model demonstrated a certain vitality.

At the bilateral level the Department of External Affairs, in its Action Plan published in May 1993 and revised and reissued in January 1994, responded to the challenge of repositioning Canada and its exports as the Japanese economy changed. Risking the predictable criticism that bureaucrats should not micromanage, the department found for itself the catalytic role of animateur prodding the private sector. The Japanese market was open, tariff barriers were few, and inhibiting regulations were minor. Regional markets were emerging and domestic demand was rising for value-added, tailored products of high and consistent quality with guaranteed supply – processed fish, food and drink products, housing parts and houses, kitchen components, telecommunications equipment, various technologies, and aerospace products. These trends were all underpinned by a resolutely rising yen. Investment in product development, market research, and strategic planning, in harness with carefully selected Japanese partners, in strategic alliances producing joint ventures and package deals, would pay large dividends for Canadian companies and eat into the profits of Japanese intracompany trading. The Canadian embassy in Tokyo and regional representatives were poised to help. Access problems were being resolved and only one unresolved complaint was on the books.[13] Beyond that, Prime Minister Chrétien finally named those who would serve on the binational review group, Alberta and the federal government expressed interest at least in prospects for technology and development in northern regions, and, at the ministerial level, Canada and Japan discussed the Dispute Resolution Mechanism. To some, however, convinced that the Japanese government could not quite see the value and purpose of this mechanism, this ministerial exchange was tantamount to inaction. Finally, steps had been taken to reduce or remove the five obstacles to Japanese direct investment that the Japanese had identified, although a certain degree of imprecision as to the nature of the problem and what had been accomplished remained.[14] Inaction, however, marked the recommendations of the Fourth Task

Force, such as creating the Fund for Mutual Understanding, unless one includes the Japanese tourism mission that went to Canada in the summer of 1993 and the beginnings of cooperation in the film industry. If one found the recommendations flimsy, academic, residual, and not constituting an agenda for governments, as some did, then the inaction was predictable and no cause for great lament.[15] Against that, even though indirect influences and the impact of gradual change are impossible to measure, Canadian government and business will be all the poorer for this inaction.

At the regional level action came on the environment. Geraldine Kenney-Wallace and Toshinobu Wada extracted the resources to stage the Vancouver conference, in March 1994, on the stewardship of the North Pacific. The conference was high-level, brought together the public and private sectors, and, because it identified soluable ocean environmental problems, what data must be collected, and what could be measured, was a distinct success. A working Canada–Japan agreement was to be the basis for broader multilateral action, for international decision-making on the environment.

To some, this marked a genuine shift in Japanese policy, signalling that Japan was serious about combatting environmental problems and cooperating with Canada in developing the environmental sciences. Others detected a degree of Japanese guilt. This venture was both a Canadian sop to Japan and a way for Japan, with its embarrassing record on fish and whales, to cover its tracks. The Japanese agenda, moreover, was scarcely hidden – secure the leadership in developing environmentally friendly technologies and exploit, for example, the burgeoning European market. Only in that sense could one take at all seriously the forum's claims that Japan needed Canada to position itself in Europe. In addition, one might ask how far was this regional initiative to be taken before a Russia that was not alienated by being ignored was brought in? Yet critics of Japan's record on the environment might note, as Statistics Canada has, that while Canada generates 6 tonnes of hazardous waste for each U.S.$1 million of goods and services produced, and the United States 44 tonnes, Japan generates less than a quarter tonne.[16]

Inaction marked the remainder of the regional agenda, including cooperation in APEC on regional security issues and the creation of the Pacific Academy. Japan clearly had its own agenda in APEC, largely to protect its economic policies. Indeed, Canada found more in common with South Korea, New Zealand, and the Philippines on economic issues. The November 1994 agreement at the APEC summit to liberalize trade should benefit Canada as well as the United States, but bore no discernible mark of Canada–Japan joint influence.

At the global level, in both the Uruguay Round and at the G-7 summit, encouraging discussions on cooperation occurred that may well provide a foundation for action. But concrete steps have not been taken towards the global agenda of comprehensive security, the establishment of the Centre for Conflict Prevention and Resolution, and addressing the issue of refugees or human rights. The peacekeeping initiative, like many imaginative schemes, may well have been something of a long shot. Whether Japan will join the Security Council, and on what terms, is by no means clear. Japan, embarrassed by the Gulf War and willing to face the constitutional implications, may well be in search of global status and be willing to shoulder an extended range of responsibilities. Yet Japan's regionalist emphases are surely pre-eminent, and global responsibilities bring their own costs.

Conclusions

The balance sheet of action and inaction, which in any case will change over time, be subject to widely different transactions costs at the bilateral, regional, and global levels, and remain vulnerable to scarce financial and diplomatic resources, is only a part of the issue. So is cataloguing the recommendations that are naïve or realistic, feckless (that Japan needs Canada to position itself in Europe) or pivotal, and routine or imaginative. So is identifying inexplicable omissions, e.g., on nuclear proliferation, Japan's central security concerns (North Korea, Russia, the northern islands and China) and, except inferentially, on regional and global governance. That the forum report, a genuinely joint, negotiated document that fairly reflected the process, was unbalanced in that it said far more to Canada than to Japan was predictable and justifiable.

Beyond lay larger questions. While any Canadian government will not have to ask again, 'Why Japan?' Japanese governments still may well ask, 'Why Canada?' and leave the uncontroversial relationship to develop routinely, without special initiatives.[17] That makes Canada's turn towards China all the more fascinating. While it would be folly to identify a conscious choice here (for China and against Japan), for surely it is not a case of one or the other but both, given the importance of the Asia-Pacific region, the new emphasis is not without import. That is the case even if one assumes that the Japanese government remains indifferent to and not offended by references not merely to a political system in turmoil, but to a bubble that has burst, to a status that has slipped, and to a significance that has waned. At the same time, the Canadian media continues to import images of Japan from the United States to compensate for its inadequate coverage of Japan. Canadian Liberal governments have had both a romance with China of virtually a century's duration, leading to the comforting perception that Canada is well-perceived in China, and an uneven, some would say deplorable, record (especially with FIRA), in dealing with Japan. China is now more than the flavour of the month in Ottawa. The Liberal government, to the applause of certain provincial governments and the banks, looking past human rights or leaving them to the United States, sees significant opportunities in China for investment in resource exploration, energy and water projects, and infrastructure, and for the export of high technology, software, nuclear reactors, medical equipment, telecommunications, and a broad range of value-added products, apart from primary products and natural resources. It is also argued that Canadian–Japanese regional cooperation in Asia Pacific must at some point and on some issues embrace China. Whether China, entering GATT (and now the WTO) on its own privileged terms or not and opening its markets rather than protecting its trade surplus, does become a significant market for Canada remains to be seen. There are early and encouraging signs.[18] Trade may well follow the ministers who made up Team Canada. But clearly and emphatically China will not become a major source of foreign direct or portfolio investment in Canada. And China, like Japan, will not tolerate lectures on human rights.[19]

Such reasoning takes one back to the longer-term significance for Canada of the relationship with Japan and forward to whether the Asia-Pacific region is the key to Canadian export growth and job creation. Richard Wright, in his essay, sets out the consequences for Canada of changes in the Japanese political economy: a marked decline in Japanese foreign investment in North America ($9.1 billion in 1988, $4.1 billion in 1993); a fall in Japanese foreign portfolio investment, with little certainty that there will be compensating flows of direct investment because of NAFTA (i.e., Japan not targeting Canada as a production base for North America); but possible rising export opportunities for value-added products and Canadian firms in the services, capital goods, and construction industries as Japanese markets open further, as *keiretsu* ties weaken, and as Japanese consumers become more discriminating. In addition, investment and other business opportunities may open up for Canadian firms in Japan. The forum report emphasized the need for greater Japanese direct investment in Canada and, seemingly in error, assumed that it could be induced, but pointed in the same direction as Wright on export opportunities if the Canadian private sector, competitive and assisted by government, seized its opportunities.

In the second concentric circle of the forum's model, Canada, in partnership with Japan, was to find immense opportunities – commercial, political, strategic, and environmental – in the Asia-Pacific region. Yet the evidence is that Japan increasingly views and identifies with Asia Pacific in ways that leave little space for a partnership with Canada, and, indeed, that pull Japan 'homeward' and away from North America as a whole. Japan's trade with Asia Pacific is growing twice as fast as with North America; 34 per cent of its imports (from Korea, Taiwan, Malaysia, and China, with manufactured products now comprising 41 per cent) and 35 per cent of its exports are with Asia-Pacific countries. Japan is Asia's principal source of direct investment ($3.6 billion in manufacturing in 1993), technology, and aid. It is Asia's model for the purposes of calculated nationalism, for state activism, for bureaucratic interaction with the private sector, and for government–business cooperation. Asia is now Japan's largest market and principal debtor. Japan expects to take a greater lead politically in Asia: it is working out fresh relationships with China and crafting security arrangements beyond those with the United States against a backdrop of asserting Asian values on human rights and labour codes. Foreign languages studied by Japanese, tourism growth, and attention in the Japanese media point to Asia Pacific. It may well not be a matter of proactive, creative, conscious strategic choice, but as Japan leads Asia Pacific towards greater prosperity by market forces, it is not clear what leverage Canada has to influence the course of events.

Any conscious Japanese strategic choice for Asia Pacific is seen invariably, whether correctly or not, as being made at the expense of North America. It is the equivalent of Canada's 'Third Option,' demonstrating the overwhelming significance for both Canada and Japan of the United States. Lougheed and his colleagues were emphatic – nothing in the forum's report should be seen as directed against the United States; no recommendation threatens the Canada–U.S. economic relationship. To see the forum's work as in any way tainted with anti-American traits is to misunderstand it profoundly. For Canada to attempt to do things differently – to broaden and strengthen its relationship with Japan, to demonstrate its distinctiveness and to convince Japan to see Canada as different, to become a more vital member of the Asia-Pacific region by way of Japan – is neither to turn away from the United States nor to dilute the Canada–U.S. relationship. Yet if the strategy of the model worked Canada's relationship with the United States would change, perhaps markedly, if only because its degree of vulnerability to the United States would be reduced. The same could be said of Japan. The United States would, more emphatically, face a situation where its economic stake in East Asia was rising (33 per cent of U.S. exports flow to Asia Pacific, producing some three million jobs), but its leverage in the region was falling.

Canada, at ease with multilateralism, is inherently wary of bilateral U.S.–Japan arrangements. Like Australia, Canada fears that Japan under U.S. pressure might act in ways that damage Canadian interests. Such 'side-swiping' could mean Japan cancelling orders from Canadian firms and transferring them to U.S. suppliers. The United States is, after all, a competitor in the Japan market. Given the stated policy of the U.S. Export-Import Bank under Kenneth Brody, which is bent on providing 20,000 U.S. export-created jobs for every $1 billion lent to support U.S. trade with China in those niches such as airports and aerospace, power generation infrastructure, high technology, software, and telecommunications that prop up part of Canadian expectations, the United States is a competitor of Canada in the China market. Canada applauds Japan's deregulation and its driving up domestic demand, but fears that U.S. policy, robustly unilateral, is more for trade diversion than trade growth. U.S. officials such as Winston Lord insist that the United States is doing God's work, opening up the Japan market for all trading nations, but Canadian and Australian officials remain unconvinced. As the Japanese market opens further, slowly and painfully, in strategic sectors and procurement, U.S. and not Canadian firms will benefit disproportionately as they always have, despite the barriers in key sectors that produce the disputatious U.S.–Japan trade negotiations. Perhaps trade diversion also marks U.S. policy towards China. Canada, without any leverage of its own, both deplores and sees no utility in Japan-bashing. It can hope to influence Japanese economic behaviour only by reason and moral suasion. Canada plans to continue to do business with Japan, to attempt to increase its exports to and induce investment from Japan, only on Japan's terms, exploiting the Japanese market where it can, not being inhibited by the costs of doing business in Japan that hamper smaller firms, and relying on the Joint Economic Committee and ministerial meetings to foster cooperation. That makes all the more exasperating the sense, the undocumented assertion, that Japan-bashing in the United States actually diverts Japanese investment to the United States away from Canada.

There can be, of course, no question of a Canada–Japan alignment either matching the Canada–U.S. relationship or being aimed at the United States; to think in those terms would be profoundly mistaken. But there may be room for a Canada–Japan dialogue on the issue of managing relations with the United States, on influencing the agenda, on understanding the U.S. Congress, on bargaining techniques and negotiating strategies, on reducing the risk of damaging confrontations, and on altering unacceptable practices (side-swiping Canada and bashing Japan). The Canada–U.S. relationship may be something of a model for Japan. Canada does not want its prospects with Japan or in Asia Pacific forfeited to the U.S.–Japan relationship, even as its economy becomes more, not less, dependent on the U.S. market.

Finally, one returns to the particularly Canadian way of legitimating foreign policy at century's end and the place of the forum in that strategy. It can be argued that complexity requires government and the private sector to find ways 'vigorously and intrusively' to cooperate in managing relationships even when they are relatively free of problems. But not everyone would agree. Why not leave problem-free relationships in the warmth of laissez-faire to the markets, to the private sector, to individual decision under benign and helpful but suitably distant governments, and without the activism of such innovations as the forum? One can imagine, for instance, an accomplished Canadian diplomat being quite unsure of exercises such as Forum 2000, being genuinely puzzled by the initiative, sceptical of its merit, and seeing little by way of predictable impact. And that was, one should recall, the initial reaction from Japan to the Canadian initiative. Yet, as one views the floundering on such matters in the United States, the inability of an opportunistic and garrulous president to legitimate foreign policy and gain political credibility as a result, one may warm to the approach.[20]

APPENDIX 13A: TASK FORCES

One: Political

'Identification of opportunities for Canada and Japan to cooperate on issues of long-term peace and prosperity, globally and within the Asia-Pacific region.'

Coordinators:	Sylvia Ostry	Youichiro Ichioka
Members:	Bernard Wood	Takashi Konami

Two: Economic

'Enhancement of economic ties in such fields as bilateral trade, industrial cooperation, and scientific collaboration in a way which enables the two nations to further invigorate their economies.'

Coordinators:	Peter Bentley	Yoh Kurosawa
Members:	Jack Munro	Koichiro Yoshizawa
	Raymond Royer	

Three: International

'Advancement of international cooperation on global challenges such as preservation of the environment, the protection of human rights, the resettlement of refugees, and the strengthening of the multilateral trade system.'

Coordinators:	Geraldine Kenney-Wallace	Toshinobu Wada
Members:	Rhys Eyton	
	Victor Young	

Four: Cultural

'Promotion of understanding between the Canadian and Japanese people through enhanced mutual awareness of each other's cultural heritage, education system, and historical development.'

Coordinators:	Hartland MacDougall	Susumu Yamaji
Members:	Joyce Zemans	Ayako Sono
	Jacques Bougie	

APPENDIX 13B: THE CANADIAN PANEL

Hon. Peter Lougheed, Co-Chairman
Former Premier of Alberta. Partner in the law firm of Bennet, Jones, Verchere.

Geraldine Kenney-Wallace, Vice Chairman
President and Vice Chancellor, McMaster University, 1987–90. Chair, Science Council of Canada. Chair, Canada–Japan Complementarity Study 1988–89.

Peter G. Bentley
Chairman and CEO, Canfor Corporation and its principal subsidary, Canadian Forest Products Ltd.

Jacques Bougie
President and CEO Alcan Aluminum Ltd. Board member of the Conference Board of Canada.

Rhys T. Eyton
Chairman, President, and CEO, PWA Corporation. Chairman and CEO, Canadian Airlines International Ltd. President, International Air Transport Association (IATA), 1991–92.

Hartland M. MacDougall
Chairman, Royal Trust, Chairman, Pacific First Financial Corp., Seattle, and Deputy Chairman, Trilon Financial Group, London Insurance Group Inc., and London Life Insurance Co. Founding Chairman, Japan Society. Chairman, Canada–Japan Business Committee.

J.J. (Jack) Munro
Chairman, Forest Alliance of British Columbia. Former President, IWA-Canada (woodworkers union). Member, Federal Forest Sector Advisory Council and the BC Forest Resources Commission.

Sylvia Ostry
Chair, Centre for International Studies, University of Toronto. Former Deputy Minister of Consumer and Corporate Affairs, Chair, the Economic Council of Canada, Deputy Minister of International Trade, and Ambassador for Multilateral Trade Negotiations.

Raymond Royer
President and CEO, Bombardier Inc. Adviser on external trade to a number of committees established by the Canadian government.

Bernard Wood
Fellow, Center for International Affairs, Harvard University. Founding Director, North–South Institute. Former CEO of the Canadian Institute for International Peace and Security.

Victor Young
Chairman and CEO, Fishery Products International Ltd. Chairman, International Trade Advisory Committee (ITAC). Chairman, Economic Recovery Advisory Board, Newfoundland.

Joyce Zemans
Professor, and former Dean, Faculty of Fine Arts, York University. Served as Director, Canada Council, 1988–92.

APPENDIX 13C: THE JAPANESE PANEL

Yoshio Okawara, Co-Chairman
Executive Adviser, Federation of Economic Organizations (*Keidanren*). Former Ambassador to the United States and to Australia.

Kiochiro Ejiri, Vice Chairman
Chairman, Mitsui and Company Limited. A leading spokesman for Japanese business.

Youichiro Ichioka
Managing Director/Chief Editorial Writer, *Nihon Keizai Shimbun* (*Japan Economic Newspaper*). Japan's equivalent to the *Wall Street Journal*.

Mikio Kato, Executive Secretary
Associate Managing Director, International House of Japan, Tokyo.

Takashi Konami
Professor of Foreign Studies, Tokyo University. President of the Japan Association for Canadian Studies.

Yoh Kurosawa
President, Industrial Bank of Japan.

Hanae Mori
Designer.

Ayako Sono
Novelist.

Toshinobu Wada
President, Japan Petroleum Exploration Company. Former Vice Minister of Ministry of International Trade and Industry (MITI).

Susumu Yamaji
Chairman of the Board of Directors, Japan Airlines Company, Limited. Former Vice Minister (Management and Coordination Agency) and former official, Transport Ministry.

Koichiro Yoshizawa
Chairman, Honda Motor Company, Limited.

NOTES

1 The Canada–Japan Complementarity Study, from April 1988 to its report in July 1989, on research and development in the sciences, chaired by Geraldine Kenney-Wallace, was a precursor. One can trace links to Forum 2000 through Kenney-Wallace's interests in the environment and sustainable development. The Canada–Japan Workshop on the Environment held in June 1991 was also part of the process. There were also specialist studies of the complementarities between the two economies.

2 So was, from a different perspective, the Canada 21 Council's initiative resulting in the debate over its controversial report, *Canada 21: Canada and Common Security in the Twenty-First Century.* It mentioned Japan but once. The national hearings of the joint Senate–Commons Commission on Foreign Policy were also part of the process.

3 See Appendix 13A. If, for example, one's principal concerns were economic, the agenda of the fourth task force might seem peripheral. Similarly, one might see it as obligatory that the follow-up monitoring group include a person from the West who was experienced in trade and investment or labour matters.

4 Lougheed, in his letter of transmission to Mulroney, a critical and revealing document, summarized the process – an exploratory meeting in Ottawa in September 1991; a learning process, including a meeting with fourteen experts in Winnipeg in November 1991; the first joint session in Tokyo in January 1992 on mandate confirmation and the setting of the December 1992 deadline; five months of exchanges between the joint task forces until June 1992; the April 1992 Canadian meeting in Toronto to set Canadian goals; the second joint session in Banff in July 1992, permitting the task forces to look for specific recommendations and conclusions; the September 1992 Vancouver meeting of the Canadian members to determine, finally, those recommendations most important to Canada that the Japanese would likely accept; the third and final joint session in Tokyo in October 1992 to agree on the report; and the submission of the report, dated 1 December 1992. Stephen Heeney acted as the link between the Forum and the Department of External Affairs; Graeme McDonald was the Canadian executive secretary; Bernard Wood and Youichiro Ichioka drafted the report, which McDonald edited and Lougheed wrote.

5 The Japanese had rejected a previous Canadian initiative to examine comprehensively the bilateral relationship.

6 To aid the changing of attitudes, to promote learning, to develop fresh criteria for a successful foreign economic policy, to alter traditional approaches and business-as-usual assumptions, Lougheed's letter to Mulroney asked various things of the public and private sectors, so as to mark their commitment to deepening the relationship. Beyond the challenges to the provincial governments and the bureaucracy, including a revised mandate for the Export Development Corporation, the public sector must educate Canadians on the significance of the foreign public debt and Japanese holdings of that debt. It should promote specific reform of the Canadian educational system to improve language skills, training in economics, and global awareness ('knowledge of world realities') and explore the feasibility of establishing an accredited Japanese secondary school in Canada. Business and labour must help reverse the situation whereby more than half of Canadian exports to Japan were bought in Canada by Japanese buyers, not marketed directly in Japan, a deplorable state of affairs reflecting the paucity of Canadian skills. It was necessary, therefore, to put young, language-proficient, skilled, and knowledgeable Canadians to work selling in Japan, and to place Canadian interns and apprentices in short-term positions in Japan as part of internationalizing work experiences. It was critical to improve industry-specific information-gathering processes through industry associations and cost-sharing Japanese representative offices (as the Beef Export Federation and the

Council of Forest Industries had done), to adopt some Japanese management methods of employee training, involving employees in product development and improvement, and to improve employee–labour relations in Canada. The media must turn its spotlight on Japan to help educate Canadians rather than focus, for example, on Japan-bashing in the United States.

7 Japan, for example, must reduce working hours, improve its 'living environment,' and increase further domestic demand. Canada must increase its industrial competitiveness, adopt positive fiscal policies, shift to value-added industries and the provision of information and services, and solve debilitating issues in federal–provincial relations.

8 The legislation establishing the Japan National Oil Company specifying that foreign direct investment ventures must secure oil imports for Japan was noted.

9 The Task Force noted both Japanese portfolio investment and modestly growing Canadian direct investment in Japan, reaching $764 million in 1991, and MITTI's limited efforts to facilitate foreign direct investment in Japan.

10 The Japanese had identified the obstacles: discriminatory taxation policies, conflicting federal–provincial and interdepartmental jurisdictions, provincial labour legislation and disclosure regulations for corporations, and disputatious labour–management relations.

11 They included satellite and geographic information systems, ocean engineering and marine technologies, robotics, information technologies, opto-electronics, computer hardware and software, acoustic technology, and materials developed, including biodegradable materials.

12 Less charitable views of Liberal inaction exist: lack of commitment, unsure about the significance of the report, inattention, and floundering as the new government struggled with the processes of reassuming power after the protracted Conservative occupation of Ottawa. The Canadian group was announced in July 1994, and included Peter Lougheed and Geraldine Kenney-Wallace.

13 Japan purportedly welcomed the Action Plan if only because it provided further evidence that the United States, in contrast, had no export strategy.

14 Some argued that discriminatory tax policies did not exist, others that a partial solution had been found to them. The issue of disclosure regulations for corporations had been solved, and clearing up conflicting federal–provincial jurisdictions and interdepartmental conflicts to produce one-stop shopping had begun. Provincial labour laws, especially those in Ontario and British Columbia, and the state of labour–management relations in Canada were, to say the least, large subjects.

15 A significant opportunity for examining how Canada might learn from the Japanese education system, particularly its rigour, habits, and values, had perhaps been missed.

16 Nelson Grabum of the Department of Anthropology at the University of California at Berkeley made these points.

17 Lougheed, in his letter to Mulroney, quoted Hiroshi Kitamura, the former Japanese Ambassador to Canada, on this question of 'Why Canada?' It was not entirely convincing to do so. See H. Kitamura, 'The Position of Canada in Japan's Diplomatic Framework.'

18 In November 1994 Canadian business signed $8.6 billion worth of commercial arrangements with China, including the $3.5 billion agreement between Atomic Energy of Canada and the China National Nuclear Corporation for the sale of two Canadian reactors.

19 The Canadian government sees little advantage in delivering homilies.

20 In addition to meeting with several officials of the Department of External Affairs and International Trade, I consulted Joe Clark informally and briefly, and interviewed Peter Lougheed, Geraldine Kenney-Wallace, Peter Bentley, Jack Munro, Sylvia Ostry, Graeme McDonald, and Jack McKeown.

14

In the Spirit of Nitobe and Norman: Circularity in Japanese and Canadian Approaches to Regional Institution Building

LAWRENCE T. WOODS

In August 1994, Malaysian Prime Minister Dr Mahathir bin Mohamad declared that there was no need for Japan to apologize for its actions during World War II.[1] Central though it might be to any attempt to encourage Japan to play a greater role in Asia, this claim is also significant because of the implicit suggestion that it would be acceptable to ignore part of the past when looking towards the future of institution building in Asia Pacific. An assessment of the diplomatic strategies used by Japan and Canada in their respective current approaches to regional cooperation and institution building challenges this proposition.

With their participation in and support for the creation of the non-governmental Council for Security Cooperation in the Asia Pacific (CSCAP) in 1993 and the governmental ASEAN Regional Forum (ARF, centred on the Association of Southeast Asian Nations) in 1994, Japanese and Canadian strategies have come full circle. The place of the Institute of Pacific Relations (IPR) in our understanding of contemporary regionalism and the observation that Japanese and Canadian approaches today reflect the spirit of two IPR proponents, Inazô Nitobe and E. Herbert Norman, demonstrate this point. CSCAP and ARF represent the reincarnation and extension of the IPR's ideals, although today's indigenous Southeast Asian participation marks a significant departure from the IPR experiment. ASEAN's presence and sensibilities are also pivotal in any assessment of Japanese and Canadian strategies in the mid-1990s. And yet, while the social, economic, and political contexts in which regional cooperation is now being pursued are admittedly quite different, the problem remains much the same: how to build regional institutions amidst rising levels of nationalism, economic competition, and insecurity (personal, national, and regional) that predominate in advance of what some have predicted will be a regional renaissance.[2]

Nitobe, Norman, and the IPR Experiment

The IPR was an international non-governmental organization (INGO) that operated from 1925 to 1960.[3] Multisectoral delegations from Japan and Canada
attended its inaugural session in Honolulu and became full contributors to all of
its activities. The primary focus of the IPR – the search for ways to enhance
regional cooperation on political, economic, and social aspects of security –
meant that national councils were quickly established in each member country
(in Japan, in advance of the first IPR meeting in 1925; in Canada, in conjunction with creation of the Canadian Institute of International Affairs, CIIA, in
1928). Japan and Canada also played host to early IPR conferences (in Kyoto in
1929 and Banff in 1933). However, the Sino-Japanese conflict, the concept of a
Greater East Asian Co-prosperity Sphere, and the looming Pacific War soon left
the liberal internationalist members of the Japanese IPR on the outside looking
in and out of favour in their own land. Japanese participants were ultimately
forced to withdraw from Institute activities by 1939 in protest over the establishment of the IPR's Inquiry series, a controversial research initiative exploring contentious national, bilateral, and regional issues.[4]

Like their Japanese counterparts, early Canadian participants served as their
government's eyes, ears, and, to some extent, voice in the Asia-Pacific region.
However, as the Canadian Department of External Affairs developed its own
representative, information-gathering, and policy-assessment capacities in the
interwar years and during World War II, the IPR's diplomatic utility diminished.
McCarthyism dealt the final blow to the Institute. Canadians involved in the
IPR thus came to share with their Japanese colleagues the stigma that went with
being associated with an organization in disrepute in the United States.[5]

Inazô Nitobe and Herbert Norman are among the persons most often associated with the IPR in Japan and Canada. The Institute benefited from Nitobe's
counsel in its early years. A member of Japan's House of Peers, he became
chair of the IPR's Japan Council in 1929, organized and served as President of
the Kyoto conference that same year, attended three IPR conferences (1929,
1931, 1933), and was a member of the Institute's executive body (the Pacific
Council) until his death in Victoria in October 1933, shortly after he attended
the Banff conference. Norman's association with the IPR began as a research
fellow in the late 1930s and continued throughout his diplomatic career until his
suicide in April 1957. His now classic text, *Japan's Emergence as a Modern
State*, was published by the IPR in 1940 and he attended three IPR conferences
(1942, 1945, 1947). Several articles by and about Norman also appeared in the
Institute's flagship journal, *Pacific Affairs*. Both men are remembered for their
diplomatic contributions (Nitobe for his roles as Under-Secretary General of the

League of Nations and within the IPR; Norman for his efforts to explain Japan to the non-Japanese); both remain controversial (Nitobe because of his statements supporting the Japanese government's policies towards Manchuria and China; Norman because of allegations that he was a communist operative); both are tragic figures (Nitobe because of a course of events that defied his principles; Norman because of his suicide in the face of McCarthyism); and both are commemorated in Japan and Canada (Nitobe's portrait adorns the Japanese ¥5000 note and the Nitobe Memorial Gardens grace the campus of the University of British Columbia; Norman's contributions to the study of Japanese society and politics and his role in the Allied occupation of Japan after World War II continue to be admired). Both were Christians and shared a vision of regionalism that was, like the IPR itself, sparked by a cooperative ethic. Both died with their goals – the enhancement of mutual understanding between Asia-Pacific peoples – unfulfilled and would likely judge themselves failures as a result.[6]

Yet, from another perspective, Nitobe and Norman are major components of the exemplary legacy of the IPR, the organizational structure and mandate of which were reinvented in 1993 in the form of CSCAP and advanced in 1994 with the creation of ARF. What can be learned from the IPR story? Two lessons are particularly pertinent. First, overt politicization of and governmental participation in an INGO may impair that organization's ability to retain its identity; to foster mutual understanding through informal, unofficial, and nonthreatening interactions; and thereby to create and maintain a constituency of support for its contributions to regional diplomacy. In the IPR case, the decision to invite government officials to participate in wartime meetings seemed to confirm charges of interference and a lack of autonomy levied prior to World War II by the Japanese government, and, conversely, left the organization vulnerable to allegations that it had undue influence on the policies of the countries and governments involved. Governmental support for the IPR's regional cooperation efforts fell away in Japan in the 1930s and was only tentative after World War II. In Canada, the allegations made against Norman in the U.S. Senate, although denied by his superiors in the Department of External Affairs, brought the Canadian government under intense scrutiny and, as in Japan, promoted a hands-off attitude on the part of the state towards the IPR to avoid further U.S. criticism.[7]

Second, an INGO's ability to withstand hostile sociopolitical forces is likely to be diminished if the organization is dependent on one country for the provision of key resources such as membership, foundation funding, and administrative support. Events in China in 1949 and the subsequent rise of McCarthyism in the United States made the still highly respected and relatively high-profile IPR a convenient scapegoat for those seeking simple explanations for government blunders. As a result, many U.S. IPR members saw their reputations smeared; some even lost their means of income and/or chose to leave the country.[8] Non-U.S. members, Norman being the most infamous case, were tarred with the same brush. For all intents and purposes, the U.S. Senate investigators saw the IPR as a U.S. organization largely because of its membership list, the non–U.S. national councils and sizeable international membership notwithstanding. Predictably, members everywhere left the organization, nowhere more so than in the United States. The financial support of the Rockefeller Foundation and the Carnegie Corporation for the research and publication efforts of the Institute's international secretariat in New York was withdrawn, and the IPR temporarily lost its status as a charitable organization. No major donors from other countries were in place or in sight. Given these circumstances, Canadian participants, still working from an organizational base within the CIIA, began to push for the disbanding of the IPR as early as 1957.[9]

Rediscovering Non-governmental Diplomacy

It is not, however, a matter of learning only from the IPR's failures. Indeed, it became clear soon after the Institute's passing that the IPR's form of non-governmental diplomacy was viewed by many participants and observers in Japan, Canada, and elsewhere as a good idea gone wrong. It had ceased to exist in an institutional sense; it would now have to be rediscovered or reinvented. Building upon the revival of Japanese participation in the Institute in the 1950s, the IPR model was resurrected in Japan as early as 1961 when the director of the Economic Planning Agency, Saburo Okita (a contributor to IPR publications), addressed the regional cooperation theme as part of a report for the UN Commission on Asia and the Far East. As head of the corporately funded Japan Economic Research Centre in 1963, Okita again suggested the creation of a regional institution bringing together representatives from Japan, Canada, Australia, New Zealand, and the United States. Interestingly, he did not specify whether these representatives should be official or unofficial, unlike Kiyoshi Kojima, an economist at Hitotsubashi University, who took this idea a step further in 1965 when he proposed an intergovernmental agreement to create a Pacific Free Trade Area involving the same five countries.[10]

   Taken together, these proposals suggest that members of the Japanese élite drew three initial conclusions from the IPR experience: (1) that continuing to pursue regional cooperation via non-governmental means remained desirable; (2) that complementing non-governmental efforts with governmental channels was similarly desirable; and (3) that the centrality of economic issues should be acknowledged when considering regional security.[11] One IPR characteristic they seem to have eschewed, however, was inclusiveness. Although the IPR for much of its history could be accused of excluding Asia-Pacific peoples still under colonial rule, this may well have been a constraint that was simply not feasible to overcome until decolonization occurred in India, Korea, Indonesia, and Burma. On the other hand, the notion of limiting participation to the five developed economies of the region seemed starkly paternalistic and brought with it significant costs.

The proposals by Okita and Kojima quickly spawned academic and business initiatives, undertaken with governmental support and in partnership with Australians, that led to the creation of the Pacific Trade and Development Conference (PAFTAD) and the Pacific Basin Economic Council (PBEC).[12] These sectoral non-governmental entities were established in the mid-1960s to pursue two complementary policy objectives: trade promotion and trade liberalization. Today, PAFTAD regularly brings together professional and academic economists to examine regional trade issues and set them in a global context, while PBEC continues to attract chief executive officers from many of the region's largest corporations to its annual general meetings. PBEC's success and utility are more questionable, burdened as it is with its exclusive approach and its image as a rich man's club. PAFTAD's early Asia Foundation funding was granted on the condition that it expand beyond the Pacific Five as rapidly as possible. It is now geographically the most inclusive of any regional institution.[13]

Buoyed by the leadership of Okita and Kojima (which lasted for more than two decades), Japanese participation has consistently been a sizeable and significant feature of each forum. The breadth of participation from the academic and state sectors in Japan is among the most impressive of any member nation. Government support for these forms of unofficial diplomacy has also been unfailing throughout. While Canadians were also among the founding members of each organization and certain individuals have played leadership roles over time, Canadian participation and governmental backing have been neither as sizeable and consistent nor as significant. The federal government has until recently preferred a bottom-up, private-sector-first approach, which could just as easily be interpreted as disinterest or lack of attention.[14]

In 1980, PAFTAD and PBEC proponents saw their efforts give rise to a multipartite organization reminiscent of the IPR in structure. This new INGO, known today as the Pacific Economic Cooperation Council (PECC), was also the product of Japanese–Australian collaboration at the non-governmental and governmental levels. Its mandate encompassed the same trade policy objectives as PAFTAD and PBEC. Canadians were once again present at the creation, but it would be almost a decade before the Canadian government abandoned its passive attitude. Several Japanese academics (including Okita, Kojima, Seizaburo Sato of Tokyo University, and Ippei Yamazawa of Hitotsubashi University) and businesspeople (such as Noburo Gotoh of Tokyu Corporation) retained leadership roles alongside 'unofficial government officials' throughout this period, with far fewer Canadians (H. Edward English of Carleton University and Eric Trigg of Alcan being the most prominent) playing major parts.[15]

Things began to change in the late 1980s. First came the pursuit of a more effective PECC process. Spurred on by bureaucratic interests and demands, the new chair of the Canadian national committee of PECC, William Saywell (president of Simon Fraser University), co-chaired a PECC task force on institutionalization, which resulted in the creation of a permanent international secretariat in Singapore. Second came Canadian support for the establishment of an intergovernmental body now known as Asia Pacific Economic Cooperation (APEC) in 1989. Although Australian Prime Minister Bob Hawke initially included only Western Pacific nations in his APEC blueprint, Canada was quick to express interest and was invited to participate in the inaugural meeting in November 1989, as was the United States.[16]

In 1990, the Canadian government, through Secretary of State for External Affairs Joe Clark, adopted a third approach to things Asian Pacific in the form of a strategy long used by the Japanese under the heading 'private diplomacy.'[17] Believing they were being innovative, Canadian officials and academics began to talk of 'track two diplomacy,' in which state and non-state participants would meet in unofficial, non-governmental settings. These interactions would complement official 'Track One' diplomatic channels. As a result, Canada began to work in tandem with Japan's favourite regional cooperation collaborator – Australia – in an effort to promote a dialogue on security issues. Seeking to ensure a place for itself at the regional diplomatic table, emphasizing the need to work through multilateral institutions, and allegedly taking a broad view of the term 'security,' Canada launched what became known as the North Pacific Cooperative Security Dialogue (NPCSD). This initiative and similarly motivated proposals emanating from Australia encouraged regional leaders to consider the viability of creating an Asia-Pacific version of the Conference on Security and Cooperation in Europe, and of fostering the 'habit of dialogue' critically important to those who sensed that they might not otherwise be consulted.[18]

That such ideas should be floated by middle powers like Canada and Australia is perhaps not surprising, given the rising importance of the Asia Pacific region and the predictable desire to avoid being marginalized within or left out of regional diplomatic settings. In the Australian case, aspects of middle power entrepreneurship had been evident as Australia began in the early 1960s to weigh its location in Asia Pacific and to operate in tandem with another middle power: Japan. When Japan graduated from the middle power ranks, Australia's partner in similar initiatives often became Canada. However, held back by traditional European and Continental perspectives, Canadian officials have had to earn their Asia-Pacific credentials. Today, they are engaged in an ambiguous game of catch-up, working where convenient with the Australians.[19]

In addition, Western bureaucrats want to shape and control any activity in which government is involved or is providing funding. The federal government appoints the members of the Canadian national PECC committee, finances the activities of the committee, and allows state officials to participate in their private capacities. Government support for efforts to improve PECC's effectiveness and an eagerness to move the process to the governmental level via APEC may well have arisen therefore out of the bureaucratic belief that if the state's time, energy, and money are to continue being spent on regionalism, they had best be spent in ways that meet state interests, requirements, and preferences more directly. This willingness to participate in governmental groups such as APEC, or something akin to a Conference on Security and Cooperation in Asia, may also be evidence of a narrow, if not culture-bound, attempt to make Asia-Pacific regionalism fit into organizational models developed and implemented in Anglo-European contexts. What both aspects of this bureaucratic emphasis overlook is the long history of non-governmental diplomacy in Asia Pacific and an arguably dominant regional diplomatic culture in which informal and non-threatening channels of communication and negotiation are preferred.[20]

The Canadian notion of 'cooperative security,' stressing the utility of governmental and non-governmental channels, tempers this criticism somewhat.[21] However, Canadian support for APEC and the NPCSD proposal itself tend to hide the Canadian government's other major reason for moving in these directions: frustration with the slow pace at which the members of ASEAN were willing to allow Asia-Pacific regionalism to proceed in the face of growing European unity, threats of increased U.S. protectionism, and intransigence in multilateral negotiations under the General Agreement on Tariffs and Trade. ASEAN has long been concerned about the impact that more institutionalized or formal pan-Pacific institutions would have on its own organizational integrity and influence. Canada paid particular heed to this concern as it began to participate in the ASEAN Pacific Dialogue (APD) process in 1984, through the annual ASEAN Post Ministerial Conference (ASEAN-PMC). By 1989–90, however, Canada's patience with ASEAN had worn thin. Australia's APEC initiative may well have been a calculated effort to prod ASEAN into action. While not all ASEAN members responded enthusiastically, the association reluctantly agreed to the creation of a governmental forum that might replace the APD as the most meaningful pan-Pacific grouping. Indeed, ASEAN members were among those who insisted on including North American participation in APEC. As for the NPCSD, its geographic specificity suggests that Canada may have been attempting to move towards Asia-Pacific regionalism without ASEAN.

The Japanese, meanwhile, lent their support to the effort to strengthen PECC, having played a seminal role in its founding and continuing to view it as an integral part of Japan's pursuit of 'comprehensive security.'[22] The APEC and NPCSD initiatives were somewhat more problematic from the Japanese perspective. Various Japanese ministries (including Foreign Affairs, and International Trade and Industry) supported calls for a pan-Pacific intergovernmental institution, issued by former national leaders such as Yasuhiro Nakasone in the run up to 1989. But infighting between departments prevented a consensus from being achieved. The fear of adverse reactions from other Asian nations, moreover, undercut forceful endorsement.[23] Yet, such support would have been consonant with the concept of comprehensive security, which acknowledges the multidimensional nature of security, advocates a larger international role for Japan, and stresses the value of working through multilateral institutions. Given the record of organizational initiatives within the region, it is likely that there was some collaboration between Australia and Japan in the crafting and timing of the Hawke proposal. The Australians might have been the 'Trojan Horse' of the Japanese, who would have been equally pleased at the ASEAN members' request that Canada and the United States be included. Clearly, an overt Japanese attempt to take the lead would not have been feasible lest Japan be perceived by the developing and newly industrialized economies of East and Southeast Asia as aligned with or manipulated by other developed countries. As a result, when confronted by the subsequent Southeast Asian backlash against APEC's initial activities – the proposed East Asian Economic Grouping – Japan avoided a leadership role and tempered its statements on the ASEAN–APEC relationship so as to placate all interested parties.[24] Significantly, what is now referred to as the East Asian Economic Caucus remains within APEC.

The Japanese reaction to the NPCSD idea was even more reserved, if not dismissive, leaving Canadian bureaucrats and academics in a quandary.[25] Why, they asked, were the Japanese reluctant to endorse regional cooperation overtures emanating from Canada? Perhaps these Canadian observers were ignoring Canada's reluctance to endorse earlier Japanese ideas on similar themes, the overwhelming Japanese focus on relations with the United States and East Asia, the perennial lack of Canadian interest in things Pacific (and hence Canada's credibility problem when it comes to projecting itself as a legitimate, full-time Pacific partner or power), and Canada's pursuit of continental free trade agreements with the United States and Mexico. It was unlikely, therefore, that Japan would respond with rampant enthusiasm to the NPCSD proposal and the prospect of an institution over which Japan would exercise little control. This was especially the case given Southeast Asian pressure for Japan to play a larger role in Asia and Japan's preference to increase its regional and international presence firmly within the context of the U.S.–Japan security relationship.[26]

Japanese and Canadian Involvement in CSCAP and the ARF

Despite the similarities between the Japanese conception of comprehensive security and the Canadian strategy of cooperative security, a diplomatic impasse had been reached by the early 1990s when it came to regional institution building. Today, Japanese and Canadian proponents of Asia-Pacific regional institutions appear to have undergone a process of role reversal. Whereas the use of non-governmental channels was championed in Japan from the 1960s through the 1980s, a newfound willingness to play a larger and potentially more independent role in regional security and a concomitant desire to be seen as supportive of ASEAN led Japanese officials to promote the creation of the intergovernmental ASEAN Regional Forum in 1994. On the other hand, Canadian élites, while involved in the ARF, can now be seen among the prime movers within the recently established CSCAP, a direct non-governmental complement to the ARF that also plays to the reassertion and centrality of Southeast Asian interests within the pan-Pacific cooperation movement.

Two factors have conditioned each national strategy in recent years: the U.S. attempt to control APEC's agenda, and the attendant realization that non-governmental diplomatic channels remain important. The formation of APEC put into question the future of pre-existing regional economic cooperation institutions of the non-governmental variety, given their reliance on governmental recognition and support. At the same time, efforts in academic and state circles to broaden the meaning of the term 'security' caused many to wonder if an organization like APEC, dealing primarily with trade enhancement and liberalization issues, could be reformed to meet more complex demands. The promotion of an alternative forum now known as the ARF began at the July 1991 ASEAN-PMC in Kuala Lumpur when Japan proposed the institutionalization of an annual regional security dialogue centred on ASEAN. Southeast Asian leaders responded cooly to this idea, uncertain about Japanese motives, seeking Japanese development assistance but at the same time concerned about the resurgence of Japanese militarism, and reluctant to allow the scrutiny of their own internal affairs that might result from such deliberations. They became even more uneasy in 1992 when the Japanese government's suggestion that APEC be converted into a regional security forum was greeted enthusiastically in the United States. Japan's motives were twofold: to signal a willingness to play a larger role in Asia in cooperation with ASEAN (as most ASEAN nations had requested, Indonesia being the most cautious) and to encourage the United States to remain engaged in Asian affairs (again desired by ASEAN leaders in order to offset growing Japanese influence). In January 1993, the Japanese prime minister affirmed this position during a speech in Bangkok.[27]

At the November 1993 APEC summit meeting in Seattle, it became evident that the United States was trying to use APEC for its own purposes, possibly even to drive a wedge between Japan and ASEAN. The Japanese reaction to the U.S. domination of the gathering and the U.S.-driven proposal of a pan-Pacific free trade agreement – like that of most other nations, Canada included – was to recoil from this ploy and to move quickly to rekindle the process of making the dominant regional security institution one in which ASEAN played a central role. Reflecting the hurried and urgent manner in which this initiative was pursued, the ARF's first session in July 1994 was relatively informal, had few agenda items, and lasted only a few hours. The non-governmental CSCAP, initiated in 1993, complements the ARF. Each has adopted a mandate that treats security as a multidimensional objective.[28]

In many ways, the process that culminated in the creation of CSCAP can be seen as a direct outgrowth of the NPCSD initiative: it reasserted the importance of 'Track Two' diplomacy, incorporated ideas consonant with the Canadian notion of cooperative security, and was crafted in part by the same Canadian academics who coordinated the NPCSD. Evidently possessing neither a standalone capacity for Asia-Pacific policy development nor the analytical expertise necessary to cope with a rapidly changing world, the bureaucracy has recently called out for an advisory societal structure akin to the Canadian component of the IPR. Recognition of this need became pronounced as the NPCSD process ran its course in 1993 and manifested itself in the creation of the Canadian Consortium on Asia-Pacific Security (CANCAPS).[29]

Aware that the response to the NPCSD by major players such as Japan had been less than overwhelming and wondering what to do next, the Canadian government chose to pursue its regional concerns and aspirations by blending together support of Southeast Asian research institutes with the momentum arising from NPCSD activities. Since 1987, the Canadian International Development Agency (CIDA), as part of its regional strategy, has been funding an annual Asia Pacific Roundtable (APR), borrowing directly from a format used by the IPR and organized by the Institute of Strategic and International Studies Malaysia (ISIS Malaysia) on behalf of the ASEAN Institute of Strategic and International Studies (ASEAN-ISIS). This has been CIDA's way of addressing the nontraditional side of development assistance, that of research and dialogue. The emergence of the APR as one of the region's largest and potentially most significant annual gatherings of academics, businesspeople, and diplomats coincided with the winding down of the NPCSD. Seeking to capitalize on both the positive and the negative aspects of this experience, the academics who spearheaded the NPCSD and CANCAPS turned their attention to shaping the creation of a pan-Pacific non-governmental institution aimed at fostering confidence-building measures of utility to great, middle, and lesser powers. Working through and with ISIS Malaysia and ASEAN-ISIS has helped to give Canada and Canadians an enviable profile within CSCAP, the policy statements of which indicate an intention to work with and as the non-governmental arm of the ARF.[30]

While some observers will note that the 'Pacific Academy' recommendation contained in the 1992 *Canada–Japan Forum 2000* report appears to have been acted upon with APEC's decision to establish a study centre housed within the Vancouver-based Asia Pacific Foundation of Canada, an even more effective and interdisciplinary network of specialists may have been initiated almost simultaneously in the form of CSCAP. Ironically, a CSCAP working group on enhancing security cooperation in the North Pacific is now co-chaired by Canada and Japan.[31]

Conclusion

Earlier this century, Inazô Nitobe and Herbert Norman dedicated themselves to bridging the Asia-Pacific region through the enhancement of mutual understanding. Limited though their successes may have been, the contributions of and controversies surrounding Nitobe and Norman suggest lessons for contemporary proponents of regional institutions. The recent diplomatic impasse between Japan and Canada will be overcome only if the people of both lands understand the motives, strategies, choices, and shortcomings evident on the parallel but contrasting and at times checkered paths their respective states have already travelled in the name of Asia-Pacific regionalism. A window of opportunity now exists. As the *Canada–Japan Forum 2000* report urged, these two countries must learn about and from each other.[32] Nitobe and Norman would, with some disappointment at the lack of progress, concur.

Japanese and Canadian support for the complementary CSCAP and ARF initiatives has arisen in response to a U.S. attempt to control the regional cooperation agenda at the governmental level and in recognition of the need to encourage and maintain non-governmental linkages that allow the discussion of security, broadly defined. This support also demonstrates renewed Japanese and Canadian affinity for the earlier IPR approach to regional cooperation. A worthy idea has been rediscovered, and the form and function of a path-breaking institution has been revisited and recycled.

Just like Nitobe and Norman within the IPR, Japanese and Canadian élites have played important roles within CSCAP and the ARF thus far. The multidimensional concept of security explored by each of these multilateral institutions fits with contemporary Japanese thinking about comprehensive security and the Canadian pursuit of cooperative security. Still, although IPR conferences during World War II came close to being official diplomatic meetings, the creation of the ARF is a marked departure from the IPR model, as is Southeast Asia's prominence within emerging Asia-Pacific forums. Whether formally 'going governmental' – moving beyond informal community building – proves a successful means of addressing and resolving post–Cold War security challenges may well depend on whether CSCAP and ARF leaders, participants and supporters learn from the past in the sense of acknowledging, evaluating, and drawing lessons from the IPR experience. Otherwise, while acting in the spirit of Nitobe and Norman, they may encounter the same failures and thereby lead us around the same unfulfilled circle of regional institution building once more.[33]

NOTES

1 Canadian Broadcasting Corporation Radio News, 27 August 1994. This pronouncement came during Japanese Prime Minister Tomiichi Murayama's tour of Southeast Asia, during which he announced plans to atone for Japanese actions in World War II. It became part of a debate inside and outside Japan as to whether or not apologies are appropriate or necessary. See, for example, the following series of reports in the Vancouver *Sun*: 'Women Throw Eggs at Japanese Embassy,' 1 September 1994, A16; 'Japan to Spend $1.3 Billion U.S. Righting Wrongs,' 30 August 1994, A13; 'Japanese PM Faces Protest by Ex-Sex Slaves,' 24 August 1994, A14; 'Japan Still Deeply Divided about Accountability for Past Militarism,' 15 August 1994, A9; and 'Defence of Japan's War Role Sets Off New International Row,' 13 August 1994, A16. It is usually assumed that there is an ongoing debate within Japan on this issue and the related matter of what Japan's contemporary international role should be. See, for example, Inoguchi, *Japan's Foreign Policy*, 139–55; and Drifte, *Japan's Foreign Policy*, 1–27. For a dissenting view, see van Wolferen, *The Enigma of Japanese Power*, 408–33.
2 Commission for A New Asia, *Towards A New Asia*; 'The Asian Way,' *Asiaweek*, 2 March 1994, 22–25; Mahbubani, 'The Pacific Way.'
3 On the origins, structure, mandate, activities, contributions, and fate of the IPR, see Woods, *Asia-Pacific Diplomacy*, 29–40; Hooper, 'The Institute of Pacific Relations'; Holland, 'Source Materials on the Institute of Pacific Relations'; and Hooper, ed., *Remembering the Institute of Pacific Relations*.
4 On Japanese participation in the IPR, see Wilson, 'The Manchurian Crisis'; Yamaoka, 'The Activities of the Japan Branch'; Katagiri, 'A Reappraisal of the

Japanese IPR'; and Katagiri and Oshiro, 'The Beginnings of "An Adventure in Friendship."'

5 On Canadian participation in the IPR, see Greathed, 'Antecedents and Origins'; Ohara, 'J.W. Dafoe and Japanese-Canadian Relations'; and Woods, 'Implications for Theory and Practice.' On the downfall of the IPR in the American context, see Thomas, *The Institute of Pacific Relations.*

6 On Inazô Nitobe, see Howes, ed., *Nitobe Inazô*; Oshiro, 'A Reevaluation,' 1–26; and Oshiro, 'Internationalist in Pre-War Japan.' On E. Herbert Norman, see Miwa, 'E.H. Norman Revisited'; Bowen, *Innocence Is Not Enough*; Bowen, ed., *E.H. Norman*; Dower, ed., *Origins of the Modern Japanese State*; and Maruyama, 'Affection for the Lesser Names.'

7 Whitaker and Marcuse, *Cold War Canada*, 402–25.

8 See Lattimore, *China Memoirs*, 219–37; Lattimore, *Ordeal by Slander*; and Lauren, ed., *The China Hands' Legacy.*

9 Edgar McInnis, Institute of Pacific Relations Papers; Woods, 'Learning from NGO Proponents'; Woods, 'Recipient Dependence.'

10 Woods, *Asia-Pacific Diplomacy*, 41–65.

11 Woods, 'Japanese and Australian Approaches.'

12 For a prime example of the Japanese–Australian partnership, see Crawford et al., eds., *Raw Materials and Pacific Economic Integration.*

13 Woods, 'Nongovernmental Organizations.'

14 Soesastro, 'The Pan-Pacific Movement'; Woods, 'The Business of Canada's Pacific Relations.'

15 Woods, 'The Asia-Pacific Policy Network.'

16 Cooper, Higgott, and Nossal, *Relocating Middle Powers*, 81–115.

17 Bryant, *Japanese Private Economic Diplomacy.*

18 CANCAPS, 'Canada on Asia Pacific Security'; Dewitt and Job, 'Asia Pacific Security Studies'; Cooper, Higgott, and Nossal, *Relocating Middle Powers*, 152–56; Henderson, 'Zone of Uncertainty'; Evans, 'The Emergence of Eastern Asia.'

19 Job and Langdon, 'Convergence and Divergence'; Job and Langdon, 'Canada and the Pacific'; Sato, 'Canadian–Japanese Economic Relations: A Japanese Perspective'; Ross, 'Canadian Foreign Policy.' On Japan as a contemporary middle power, see Cox, 'Middlepowermanship.'

20 On this theme, see Palmer, *The New Regionalism.*

21 Dewitt, 'Common, Comprehensive, and Cooperative Security'; Dewitt and Evans, 'The Changing Dynamics.'

22 Kaneko, 'A New Pacific Initiative.' On the concept of comprehensive security, see Dewitt, 'Common, Comprehensive, and Cooperative Security,' 2–4; Morimoto and Kikuchi, 'Security Issues and Studies in Japan'; and Drifte, *Japan's Foreign Policy*, 28–75.

23 Holloway, 'An Idea before Its Time.'

24 Low, 'The East Asian Economic Grouping.'

25 Langdon, 'Japan and Minor Powers'; Kawasaki, 'The Logic of Japanese Multilateralism'; Hervouet, 'Le Canada face à l'Espace Asie-Pacifique.' For an example of a Japanese analysis of the cooperative security idea that does not even mention Canada's NPCSD initiative, see Soeya, 'The Evolution of Japanese Thinking and Policies.'

26 On this theme, see Morimoto, 'Regional Dialogues and Processes in Northeast Asia'; Fujisaki, 'Enhancing Regional Security'; Sato, 'Security in the Asia Pacific Region'; Kaneko, 'An Analysis of Japanese Capability'; Kikuchi, 'Japan and Regional Cooperation'; Arase, 'Japan in Post–Cold War Asia,' Soeya, 'Japan's Policy towards Southeast Asia'; Domoto, 'Le rôle du Japon'; Polomka, 'Asia Pacific Security'; and Hawes, 'Japan and the International System.'

27 Brown, 'Japanese Security Policy'; Ichimura, 'Regional Integration Issues'; and Tow, 'Northeast Asia and International Security.' For detailed analyses of Japan–ASEAN relations, see Paltiel, 'Japan's Innovative East Asian Policies'; Stubbs, 'Reluctant Leader, Expectant Followers'; Saito, *Japan at the Summit*, 119–88; Drifte, *Japan's Foreign Policy*, 92–110; and Quo, 'Japan's Role in Asia.' On APEC's role, see Elek, 'APEC – Motives, Objectives and Prospects'; Soesastro, 'Economic Development'; Harris, 'Enhancing Security'; and Rudner, 'APEC: The Challenges.'

28 Higgott, 'APEC – A Sceptical View'; English, 'U.S. Trade Policy on Japan'; Woods, 'Clinton "Sheepless in Seattle".' On the ARF, see Smith, 'Multilateralism and Regional Security'; Narine, 'Evaluating the ASEAN Regional Forum'; Greaves, 'ASEAN Regional Forum'; Greaves, 'First ASEAN Regional Forum'; Kawasaki, 'The Logic of Japanese Multilateralists'; and Kawasaki, 'The Geostrategic Foundations.' For an insider's analysis of the origin, mandate, structure, and evolution of CSCAP, see Evans, 'The Prospects for Multilateral Security,' 210–17; Cossa, ed., *Asia Pacific Confidence*; Evans, 'Building Security'; Job, 'CSCAP Steering Committee Meeting'; and Job, 'CSCAP Finds Its Stride.'

29 Dewitt and Job, 'Asia Pacific Security Studies,' 87–101.

30 Dewitt and Evans, eds., *The Agenda for Cooperative Security*; Job, 'Eighth Annual Asia-Pacific Roundtable.' The proceedings of the 1993 APR are presented in Nagara and Balakarishnan, eds., *The Making of a Security Community.* For a review of CIDA's activities in Asia, see Rudner, 'Canadian Development Assistance to Asia.'

31 Asia Pacific Foundation of Canada, *Canada–Japan Forum 2000*; Chow, 'Vancouver Group Bags $12 Million,'D1; CANCAPS, 'Canadian Participation,' 8–9. Highlighting the value of INGO networks in a broadened regional security dialogue, the *Canada–Japan Forum 2000* report also cites the utility of APEC and the ASEAN-PMC. A Japanese scholar has referred to persons engaged in such networks as 'action intellectuals.' See Takahashi, 'Challenges of Civilization,' 7–8. On CSCAP and its North Pacific Working Group, see Evans, 'CMC Update,' 13.

32 Asia Pacific Foundation of Canada, *Canada–Japan Forum 2000*, 21–24.
33 For a survey of some of the grassroots issues and challenges confronting regional
cooperation forums, see 'Women's Conference Warns of Threat,' 3; Barlow, 'Free
Trade Meets the Tiger'; Jaffer, 'APEC and Global Capitalist Imperialism'; Woods,
'A Voyage of Rediscovery'; and Woods, 'Economic Cooperation and Human
Rights.'

15

The Emerging Pacific Partnership: Japan, Canada, and the United States at the G-7 Summit

JOHN KIRTON

Since the 1975 creation of the annual Seven-Power Summit, both Japan and Canada have shared a strong interest in having it and its associated institutions develop as the primary instrument through which to pursue their foreign policy priorities and to shape international order. The Summit gives both Japan and Canada a unique opportunity to act as equal, influential 'principal powers' in an informal, adaptable, and at times highly effective club that collectively controls a commanding share of economic and other capabilities in the international system.[1] In sharp contrast to the security and political institutions of the United Nations and Atlantic institutions, the Summit acknowledges Japan's status as a legitimate major power, gives the country a valuable entrée into the still heavily Eurocentric multilateral system, and allows it to 'plurilateralize,' and thus temper and diversify, its vital bilateral relationship with the United States.[2] The Summit also stands as the primary international recognition of Canada's principal power position, and enables it to mobilize its traditional European and Pacific affiliates to constrain and orient in desired directions its pre-eminent continental partner, the United States. Finally, the 'Summit system' allows both Japan and Canada to engender an international order that bridges rapidly developing regional arrangements, and that adequately reflects the interests and values of the powers of the Pacific region, which will have an increasing impact on the world economy, ecology, and security in the coming decades.[3]

Thus far, however, this strong shared Japanese–Canadian interest in forging a bilateral partnership at the Summit has gone largely unrecognized by scholars in both countries. The one account comparing Japanese and Canadian behaviour at the Summit points out the basic differences between the highly open Canadian economy and the relatively closed Japanese and American ones, and between the Canadian–American and the Japanese responses to the 1973 and 1979 oil shocks. It also notes Japanese lack of support for Canadian and British mediatory efforts on trade liberalization at the 1985 Bonn Summit. While recognizing the growing dependence of the Japanese, Canadian, and American economies on international exchanges, the Japanese and Canadian emphasis on multilateralism, and the common focus of Prime Ministers Nakasone and Mulroney on maintaining good relations with the United States, nowhere does it suggest that Japan and Canada have or should stand together at the Summit, apart from or against the United States.[4]

Within Japan the literature on that country's involvement in the Summit ignores how Japanese behaviour compares with that of Canada, how the two countries collaborate, compete, or otherwise connect at the Summit, and how they do or might combine to successfully influence the United States. The primary English-language accounts of Japan's Summit diplomacy have emphasized Japan's use of the institution as a point of entry into multilateral diplomacy and its role as a contributor of macroeconomic stimulus, representative of the Asian region, and mediator between the United States and the European Community.[5] Moreover, the major treatments of the Summit's workings have also omitted Japanese–Canadian comparisons or collaborative activity.[6]

Within the Canadian literature, a similar situation exists. The early accounts touched on the Summit's importance to Japan's growing responsibilities for the international economic system in the wake of U.S. decline, Japan's role as an economic 'locomotive' at London 1977, and Canada's vulnerability to U.S.–Japanese disagreements.[7] More recent works recognize Japan's support for Canada's 1976 admittance to the Summit, Japan's emphasis on anti-inflationary fiscal restraint, and Japan's alliance with Europe against Canada, the United States, and Britain over agricultural subsidy restraint.[8] The major account of the Trudeau years notes how the close relationship between Japanese Ambassador to Canada Yasuhiko Nara and Prime Minister Trudeau engendered Japan's support for Canada's membership, and the similarity between Canada's 'third option' policy of overseas diversification and Japan's own 'Takaku Gaiko' or 'diplomacy for diversification.'[9] Others have pointed to Canada and Japan's 'burgeoning relationship across the Pacific' and argued that 'Canada's Japanese and European connections have proven invaluable in forging a coalition to cope with the United States within the Summit Seven.'[10] But beyond this recognition of initial Japanese–Canadian mutual support, and the natural incentives for an expanding partnership, the literature remains silent on what form it has, will, can, or should take.

This lack of attention to the real and potential Japanese–Canadian Summit partnership flows from the heavy emphasis both countries place on their Summit diplomacy on the United States, the country that remains the Summit's largest member and that was responsible for getting Japan, and especially Canada, admitted to the Summit club.[11] Yet since 1975, both Japan and Canada have in fact slowly, if usually silently, moved to acquire more equal involvement, advanced autonomous positions and agenda items, and even taken initiatives, over initial American resistance, that are at times accepted and reliably implemented by Summit members. More importantly, they have attempted with increasing success to shape the Summit institution in their preferred image, as a concert of equal major powers, with a determining role in collectively managing major world issues.[12] In their efforts to secure national positions within the Summit, and move it in their desired manner, they have increasingly come to develop a de facto and deliberate partnership, usually with, but at times without, the still-central United States.

This movement towards a still fragile Japanese–Canadian Summit partnership has been most pronounced in building the Summit system as a central, well-developed, broadly relevant, and effective international institution. In contrast, the United States' leading power position has given it a penchant for unilateralism and a preference for the United Nations and Atlantic institutions in which it exercises a veto. The Japan–Canada partnership has also appeared over trade, where both Japan and Canada often favour a multilateral, rules-based, liberalizing regime as a constraint on the much larger United States and European Union. Finally, it has emerged more recently on political subjects, particularly where Japan and Canada's deeply embedded identity as non-nuclear weapons powers provides a shared interest in furthering non-proliferation, reducing tensions between nuclear powers, and preventing nuclear accidents.

The movement towards Japanese–Canadian Summit partnership has been driven most generally by the profound shift in relative capabilities among the world's major powers and Summit members. From the late 1960s to the mid-1970s, the end of the United States post–World War II pre-eminence, the sharp increase in Japan's weight, and the more modest increase in that of Canada, led to the creation of the Summit with Japan and Canada as members, as active participants forwarding their distinctive concerns, and as collaborators in making the new institution work effectively. From 1975 to 1980, the continuing American decline and Japanese rise led to increasing Japanese and Canadian assertiveness and bilateral cooperation.[13] From 1980 to 1985 this pattern was reversed as the Reagan revival in the United States, a sharply declining Japan, and a slowly falling Canada led to increased American assertiveness, greater Japanese acquiescence, a slow shift by Canada to follow the American lead, and diminished Japanese–Canadian cooperation. From 1985 to the present, however, the sharp drop in America's capabilities and the striking rise in Japan's have brought Japanese and Canadian Summit activism and cooperation to an unprecedentedly high, if still less-than-possible, level.

Although these substantial shifts in relative capability broadly determine

Japanese, Canadian, and American activity, association, and success at the Summit, the philosophy of the party in power and the perspective of the particular leader in all three countries also have an impact in defining the timing, strength, and form of these transitions. For the United States, by far the most powerful Summit country throughout the period, President Reagan's commitment to restore American primacy through unilateral leadership had a particularly strong impact, while the 'trilateralist' approach of the two Democratic Party administrations (Carter 1976–80, Clinton 1993–) generated a more cooperative approach. For Japan, which by the 1980s had become by far the Summit's second most powerful member, the internationalist views of Prime Minister Nakasone (1982–86) bred some Japanese assertiveness and attempts at cooperation with Canada, while the domestic political weakness of many of Nakasone's LDP and Socialist Party successors had the opposite effect. For Canada, almost always the Summit's weakest member, greater continuity has been evident. However, Conservative governments (Clark 1979, Mulroney 1985–92, and Campbell 1993), with their greater support from Western Canada, have been more willing than their Liberal counterparts (Trudeau 1968–78 and 1980–84, and Chrétien 1993–) to recognize the potential for partnership with Japan, even as they have been less willing to do so at the expense of the United States.

Trends in Relative Capability

To understand the evolving pattern of Japanese and Canadian Summit participation and partnership, it is important to examine the dramatic changes in relative capability among the world's major powers that have taken place from the 1960s to the present.[14] Table 15.1 displays these changes.

The table shows that following the end of World War II, the United States alone possessed a majority of capability in the major power system and among its future Summit partners. However, it lost its singular dominance in the former during the 1960s and in the later from 1970 (when it possessed 54.9 per cent of G-7 capabilities) to 1975 (when it fell sharply, under the impact of its defeat in Vietnam, dollar devaluation, 1973 oil shock, and resulting recession, to 45.5 per cent). America now commanded a minority of 'Western' major power capabilities and had Europe arrayed against it under the leadership of the French in pioneering a separated Eurocentric, rather than trans-Atlantic and American-centric order. The United States thus for the first time needed to combine with its 'Western' partners to maintain control of the full major power system against the vibrant communist rivals of the USSR and China, and to mobilize its two Pacific partners, Japan and Canada, to cope with the French-led European 'Big Four.'

TABLE 15.1
Relative capability of major powers in the international system, 1950–95, ratio of U.S. GNP in current U.S.$ exchange rates

	1950	1955	1960	1965	1970	1974	1975	1976	1977
U.S.A.	100.0	100.0	100.0	100.0	100.0	100.0	100.0	100.0	100.0
Japan	3.8	5.5	7.6	12.2	19.8	32.3	32.9	33.3	36.7
Germany	7.3		16.5	16.9	18.8	27.3	27.5	26.3	27.4
France	9.0		14.2	13.5	14.5	18.8	22.2	20.1	20.2
Italy	4.5		8.5	9.4	9.3	10.8	11.5	11.1	11.4
UK	15.3		14.7	12.3	12.1	13.6	14.9	13.1	13.2
Canada	5.4	6.4	6.5	7.9	8.3	10.3	10.7	11.5	10.5
USSR*	5.6	7.1	8.7	34.2	32.2	32.5	32.9	30.1	29.0
China	NA	9.6	NA	6.8	9.1	9.9	10.2	8.6	8.8
U.S.A. % 9	NA	59.4	NA	46.4	44.6	39.1	38.0	39.3	38.9
U.S.A. % 8	NA	NA	NA	NA	52.0	44.8	43.4	44.6	43.8
U.S.A. % G-7	68.6	65.9	62.0	57.4	54.6	46.9	45.5	46.4	45.6

	1978	1979	1980	1981	1982	1983	1984	1985	1986
U.S.A.	100.0	100.0	100.0	100.0	100.0	100.0	100.0	100.0	100.0
Japan	46.1	41.9	40.0	39.3	35.5	36.0	33.7	33.5	46.7
Germany	30.4	31.9	31.3	23.5	21.6	20.0	16.6	15.7	21.2
France	22.4	24.1	25.1	19.6	17.8	15.8	13.4	13.2	17.4
Italy	12.4	13.6	15.2	12.0	11.4	10.8	11.0	10.6	14.3
UK	14.9	17.1	20.1	17.1	15.8	13.9	11.4	11.4	13.6
Canada	9.7	9.6	9.8	9.8	9.8	9.9	9.2	8.8	8.6
USSR*	29.5	28.2	27.4	23.2	23.6	22.5	18.8	17.5	19.9
China	10.1	10.8	11.5	9.6	9.0	8.9	8.0	7.3	6.7
U.S.A. % 9	36.3	36.1	35.4	39.3	40.9	42.0	45.0	45.9	40.2
U.S.A. % 8	40.6	40.2	39.3	43.3	45.3	46.4	49.2	49.9	43.8
U.S.A. % G-7	42.4	42.0	41.1	45.2	47.2	48.4	51.2	51.7	45.1

Through the initiative of Henry Kissinger, the United States created the Summit as an exclusive concert of the leading 'Western' powers. In constructing this coalition against the initial rival designs of the French and the Germans, the United States had a particular incentive to expand the club beyond the Berlin Dinner, the CSCE-Helsinki, and the Guadeloupe Big Four (all composed of the United States, the United Kingdom, France, and Germany) to include Japan and Canada. The relative capability of either one, when added to that of the United States, was sufficient to restore the majority that America alone had lost at a time when America's historic transatlantic associate, the United Kingdom, had been induced by its new European Community membership to support France.

TABLE 15.1 (concluded)

	1987	1988	1989	1990	1991	1992	1993	1994	1995
U.S.A.	100.0	100.0	100.0	100.0	100.0	100.0	100.0	100.0	100.0
Japan	53.0	60.3	55.9	53.4	59.2	61.5	67.1	68.4	71.6
Germany	24.9	25.0	23.2	27.3	28.1	30.0	27.2	26.1	30.1
France	19.7	19.9	18.7	21.8	21.1	22.2	19.9	18.9	20.9
Italy	16.9	17.3	16.9	19.9	20.4	20.5	15.8	14.9	15.3
UK	15.2	17.3	16.3	17.8	17.8	17.5	14.4	14.4	15.6
Canada	9.2	10.1	10.6	10.4	10.3	9.5	8.7	7.9	7.8
USSR/Russia	21.2	21.6	20.9	NA	13.8	5.3	1.7	1.3	NA
China	6.8	7.9	6.6	6.2	6.6	7.0	8.5	8.9	NA
U.S.A. % G9	37.5	35.8	37.2	NA	36.1	36.6	38.0	36.0	NA
U.S.A. % G8	40.7	38.9	40.3	38.9	37.9	37.3	38.2	36.1	NA
U.S.A. % G-7	41.8	40.0	41.4	39.9	38.9	38.3	39.5	39.9	38.2

U.S.A. % G9 = U.S.A. as percent of G7 plus Russia and China
U.S.A. % G8 = U.S.A. as percent of G7 plus Russia
U.S.A. % G7 = U.S.A. as percent of G7
Source: IMF, *International Financial Statistics*; OECD, *Main Economic Indicators*; UN, *National Accounts Statistics*; *The Economist*.
Note: 1995 figures are as of 1 January 1995. At 5 May 1995 exchange rates and growth rates, the ratios were as follows: U.S.A. = 100, Japan 81.5, Germany 31.6, France 21.9, Italy 14.7, UK 15.1, Canada 8.2, Russia .7, and China (PRC) 10.3.

Japan was by far the preferred partner on grounds of overall capability and was admitted to the Summit from the start. Canada, which contributed a far smaller margin of majority and whose case rested as much on geographic proximity, historic alliance, and specialized commodity power, had to wait for actual entry until 1976.

Common membership, however, did not mean partnership. Because the United States could secure a de facto majority by mobilizing either Japan or Canada, rather than both, America had an incentive to maintain its separate special bilateral relationships with each rather than to forge a trilateral partnership or to encourage a bilateral Japanese–Canadian relationship to develop. Should Japan or Canada be tempted to depart from an American-centric partnership to create or join a competing coalition, the absence of a clear second-ranked power to serve as the core for such a coalition, the number of relatively equal (and geographically and historically distant) countries required to be mobilized to create one, and the ease with which America could stop the process (by activating Japan or Canada alone) provided formidable obstacles. Thus only in rare moments, such as in the immediate aftermath of the August 1971 Nixon shock, were such comprehensive all-but-America coalitions likely.

From 1975 to 1980, America's share of global and G-7 capabilities continued to decline (by close to 4 per cent of the group total in each case), while those of Japan rose (by 8 per cent vis-à-vis the U.S.) and those of Canada fell only slightly (by .4 per cent). These shifts increased the United States' need for Summit partners, particularly by 1980 when it had only 35.4 per cent of major power system capabilities and 41.1 per cent of the G-7's. By then Japan's capabilities, representing 40 per cent of America's and 16.5 per cent of the G-7's was America's preferred Summit partner. Japan's capabilities had pulled well ahead of those of third-ranked Germany and could still give the Japanese–American duo a commanding 56.6 per cent share. But as this duo had had 60.2 per cent in 1975, there was some incentive, if no necessity, to include Canada in a coalition. By 1980 Canada contributed 4 per cent of G-7 capabilities (down from 4.8 per cent in 1975), a level insufficient to make it the first and only partner of a majority-seeking America. However, Canada remained the most available third partner to a 'defensive positionalist' United States seeking to maintain its former share.[15]

Although Japan had by 1980 become the Summit's second-ranking power by a wide margin, the American lead and the dispersion of capabilities below was still too great for Japan to seek to construct a counter-coalition, and certainly to look to little Canada as a preferred partner in this quest. Given the still formidable American lead over Japan, and the consequent absence of any potential Japanese challenge, there was no particular reason for Canada to fear an outbreak of sustained U.S.–Japanese conflict that would sideswipe Canada or endanger the multilateral system Canada preferred.

From 1980 to 1985 the distribution of capabilities, and the accompanying incentive structure, changed considerably. The United States (driven by the rising exchange rate of its dollar) soared to command 51.7 per cent of G-7 capabilities and 45.9 per cent of the major power system's. With its sole majority in the Summit club restored, the United States no longer needed Japan, whose capabilities had declined from 40 per cent to only 33.5 per cent of America's (even if its lead over third-ranked Germany continued to increase). Nor did the United States need Canada, whose capabilities declined from 9.8 per cent to 8.8 per cent of America's. The United States' 51.7 per cent and Japan's 17.5 per cent of G-7 capabilities did give the American–Japanese duo an unprecedentedly high 69.7 per cent of the G-7's total, rendering irrelevant Canada's small additional contribution of only 4.6 per cent. With their capabilities no longer needed to give the United States a majority, and a rapidly declining share vis-à-vis the dominant and rising United States, there was a strong incentive for both Japan and Canada to align themselves with American leadership and to forego any bilateral cooperation between themselves. The only exception was keeping alive the plurilateral Summit forum on which they both depended for their now imperilled principal power status in the face of America's early Reaganesque disregard for, and unilateralist assaults on, the G-7 club.[16]

From 1985 through to 1995, however, there was an even greater reversal as the historic pattern of American decline and Japanese and Canadian rise reasserted itself even more strongly. From 1985 to 1988 American capabilities (led by the falling exchange rate of the U.S. dollar) plummeted from 51.7 per cent to 40 per cent of the G-7 total, and continued a slower decline to a historic low of 38.2 per cent by 1995.[17] By 1995, then, the Americans had an unprecedented need for allies to maintain their control within the Summit club.

Here Japan stood alone as the make-or-break power. Its capabilities had doubled from 33.5 per cent of America's in 1985 to 60.3 per cent in 1988, and 71.6 per cent by 1995. If Japan's 24.1 per cent of G-7 capability were added to America's 40 per cent in 1988, the duo would represent a 64.1 per cent share of the G-7, (with Japan for the first time accounting for more than one-third of the duo's share). But with 71.6 per cent of U.S. capabilities by 1995, and more than double those of third-placed Germany, Japan had become an alternative pole around which a winning coalition without America could coalesce. It was thus in a position to undertake initiatives on major issues that were divergent from U.S. preferences and to sustain them with some reasonable prospect of success. At the same time, because the United States had an unprecedented need to construct coalitions to win at the Summit, it now had a real incentive to adjust its positions to accommodate the preferences of a now genuinely powerful Japan.

Despite the broad link of the Canadian with the U.S. dollar, Canada's G-7 leading GNP growth during the last half of the 1980s increased its relative capability from 8.8 per cent of America's in 1985 to 10.6 per cent by 1989. With only 4.4 per cent of the G-7's total capability in 1989, Canada still could not bilaterally combine with the United States (now at 41.4 per cent) to restore an American-led North American majority. However, given the presence of an alternative Japanese pole, Canada could combine with Japan to exert even stronger influence on, and mount alternative coalitions to, the United States. In addition, if Canada's 4 per cent of G-7 capabilities were added to the 64.1 per cent of the American–Japanese duo in 1988, the three Pacific powers, with 68.1 per cent, would still dominate the Summit at levels just below their 1985 high.

The Importance of the Summit Institution

These differences in relative capability have affected the approach of the United States, Japan, and Canada to the G-7 as an institution. The United States, as the world's most powerful country, possesses an array of unilateral and bilateral options and a plethora of international institutions in which it stands at the centre, exercises a unilateral veto, and claims pride of authorship. It can be expected to attach the least importance to the Summit among G-7 members and to invest the fewest of its foreign policy resources in it. As its relative capability has declined over the past two decades, however, despite the 'Reagan reversal' of 1980–85, the States can be expected to place greater emphasis on the Summit forum in a more (1975–80), less (1980–85), and much more (1986–) cadence.

In contrast, Japan is a substantially less powerful country, with few other privileged international institutional entrées into the world and with no other institutionalized opportunities beyond the G-7 to shape global order as a legitimate principal power. It can be expected to give pride of place to its Summit involvement, to invest heavily in ensuring that the institution is a success, and, secondarily, that Japan is successful within it. As its relative capability has increased to a strong second-place level during the past several years, however, Japan should shift from a focus on the collective success of the institution to Japan's national success within the forum. Moreover, as its rising capability has increased its position in other international institutions (notably its increased quota share in the IMF, its position as the second-ranked power in the annual APEC Summit created in 1993, and the prospect of permanent membership in the United Nations Security Council), Japan's propensity to invest to ensure Summit success should diminish.[18]

Finally, Canada, as the least powerful Summit member, is the most dependent on the development of a rules- or regime-based international system and on contributing to show that it is a country committed to the collective task and thus deserving of its membership in the club. It can thus be expected to invest the most in ensuring the Summit's collective success. Moreover, Canada, like Japan, looks to the Summit as the primary international institution that affirms its principal power status. However, unlike Japan, Canada has a vast array of alternative international institutional affiliations, from its charter membership in the United Nations and Atlantic institutions, to its position as the second most powerful country in the Commonwealth and francophonie (where the United States is not present) and NAFTA, and the third or fourth most powerful country in APEC.[19] As Canada has increasingly become the Summit's least powerful member, as the gap between it and sixth-placed Italy and Britain has widened, Canada should be investing increasingly in the Summit's collective success.

One measure of a country's investment in the institution is its skill in hosting Summits that are regarded as a collective success. Although some national benefit derives from the prestige of hosting a successful Summit, the prerogatives of hosting are accompanied by attendant responsibilities to contribute disproportionately to achieving consensus at the Summit table and to fostering agree-

TABLE 15.2
Seven-power summit success

Summit year		International cooperation	Sherpa consensus	*Globe and Mail* editorials
1975		A–	A	B
1976	(San Juan)	D	B–	C+
1977		B–	B+	B+
1978		A	A–	A–
1979	(Tokyo 1)	B+	A–	A+
1980		C+	B	A–
1981	(Montobello)	D	C	B+
1982		C	C–	E
1983	(Williamsburg)	B	C	B–
1984		C–	C–	C–
1985		E	C+	D
1986	(Tokyo 2)	B–	B+	B+
1987		D	B	F
1988*	(Toronto)	B		A
1989*		A–		A
1990*	(Houston)	B+		B+
1991*		B+		C
1992*		B		
1993*	(Tokyo 3)	B+		

*From 1988 onward the judgment is provided contextually from the writings of Bayne alone.
Source: Putnam and Bayne, *Hanging Together*. Kirton, 'Contemporary Concern Diplomacy.'

ments that adequately address the pressing issues of the day. Thus countries that are committed to the institution, but also sufficiently powerful to make agreements possible, should host Summits that are a success.

Table 15.2 reports the success of each annual Summit according to three criteria: its production of international policy coordination, with a premium on macroeconomic package deals (as identified by Putnam and Bayne); the public consensus of the participating personal representatives or 'sherpas,' and the editorial assessment of Canada's élite daily newspaper, *The Globe and Mail*.

It is clear from the table that patterns of relative capability, and the varying commitment to the G-7 institution that in part flow from them, account well for the record of the three Pacific powers in hosting successful Summits. Thus the United States, with high capability (as the Summit's first-ranked power) but very low commitment, produces only moderately successful Summits. Japan, with relatively high capability (as the Summit's second-ranked power) but also high commitment (given its lesser power and lack of other international institutions in which it is a member of the governing core), consistently mounts successful Summits. Indeed, it is the only Summit member to do so. Canada, with low capability (as the Summit's seventh-ranked member) but moderately strong commitment (deriving from its low capability but tempered by its broad array of alternative international institutional affiliations), stages Summits not regarded as successful (beyond the judgments of the local *Globe and Mail*).

Changing configurations of capability also account well for trends in the three countries' staging of successful Summits over time. Thus the United States, in the 1975–80 period when it had relatively high capability, produced an unimpressive first Summit at Puerto Rico in 1976, but at a time of lower capability from 1985–90 staged a reasonably successful Summit at Houston in 1990. The anomaly is Williamsburg 1983, a relative success mounted at a time of high U.S. capability.

In the case of Japan, its growing capability has led, as predicted, to the hosting of less successful Summits. Thus a relatively weak Japan produced a highly successful 1979 Summit, while a far more powerful Japan did less well in 1986 and 1993. For Canada, the Summit's least powerful member, the relationship is reversed, as weakness produced failure in 1981 while strength led to success in 1988.[20]

The importance of relative capability again appears when Summit success is measured in the post-Summit period, by the compliance of Summit members as a collectivity with their agreed-upon communiqué-encoded commitments in the macroeconomic and energy sphere. Von Furstenberg and Daniels score each Summit on this dimension, as shown in Table 15.3.[21]

By this criterion it is evident in the table that the powerful United States produces poor Summits, and that its high and rising capability during the 1980–85 Reagan resurgence lowered its success (1976 = .264, 1983 = .062). Similarly, Japan always stages Summits whose agreements are complied with, and again is the only member to do so (1979 = .622, 1986 = .757). In sharp contrast, seventh-ranked Canada is the only country to consistently stage failures, even if its higher capability in 1988 compared with 1981 produced an improved result (1981 = .256, 1988 = .439).

A far more precise indicator of a country's willingness to invest in Summit success is its individual national performance in complying with collective commitments. Table 15.4 shows Von Furstenberg and Daniels' ranking of the seven members' record in compliance from 1975 to 1989 as a whole.

As predicted, the United States has a very low record of faithfully fulfilling Summit commitments, securing the lowest score among the seven members except for France. Japan has the third worst compliance record, suggesting that

TABLE 15.3
Compliance with summit macroeconomic/energy
agreements by year, 1975–89

Summit	Ambition	Compliance
Rambouillet	9	.404
San Juan	16	.264
London 1	10	.362
Bonn 1	22	.350
Tokyo 1	15	.622
Venice 1	14	.159
Ottawa	12	.256
Versailles	14	.797
Williamsburg	19	.062
London 2	19	.402
Bonn 2	14	.201
Tokyo 2	4	.757
Venice 2	8	.857
Toronto	14	−.439
Paris	13	.187

Source: Figures for Ambition: John Kirton; figures
for Compliance: Von Furstenberg and Daniels,
'Economic Summit Declarations, 1975–1989.'

TABLE 15.4
Compliance with summit macroeconomic/energy
agreements by country, 1975–89

Britain	.413
Canada	.409
Germany	.346
Italy	.274
Japan	.262
U.S.A.	.246
France	.240

Source: Von Furstenberg and Daniels, 'Policy
Undertakings by the Seven Summit Countries.'

the opportunities for defection provided by its second-ranked capability are far
more salient than its institutional need for the Summit forum. Canada comes
second only to Britain as the most committed implementor of Summit commitments.[22]

Although Von Furstenberg and Daniels deny any relationship between rela-

TABLE 15.5
Assessment of national summit success in
Canadian élite editorials

Summit	Source	
	Globe and Mail	Le Devoir
1975	E	
1976	B	
1977	A–	A
1978	B+	B–
1979	A	B
1980	B	A–
1981	B+	B+
1982	F	E
1983	D	
1984	B	
1985	B	B
1986	B+	
1987	B+	B+
1988	A+	A
1989	B	
1990	B	B
1991	B	
1992	C	
1993	C	

tive capability and national compliance, relative capability acting in combination with post–World War II status does account well for this ordering and
spread. Thus, the Summit's weakest members (Canada, Britain, Italy) rank in
the top tier of Summit compliers. The Summit's largest members (United
States, Japan, France) are at the bottom. Only Germany (the third most powerful country but the third-highest complier) provides an exception, which can be
accounted for by Germany's unique position as the declared initiator and major
defeated power of World War II. This is especially true if Germany's guilt-
ridden compliance is partly inspired by, and serves as compensation for, the
exceptionally low score of victorious but devastated (by Germany) France. In
sharp contrast, Japan has been successful in warding off any tendency to bear a
similar burden on behalf of the United States. Indeed, Japan's compliance score
is only slightly ahead of the much larger country that devastated it in 1945. The
exceptional international economic openness (in trade as a share of GNP and
overseas investments) of Germany along with Canada and Britain, (compared
with the relatively closed economies of Japan and the United States) provides

an additional incentive for reliable implementation, in that generalized lack of compliance will harm the internationally exposed countries first.

A further measure of Summit success focuses on the domestic face of the Summit by examining how each country was thought to have done at the annual event in the opinion of editorialists in élite daily newspapers. Table 15.5 shows the results for Canada by reporting the assessments each year in the élite dailies of Canada's anglophone and francophone communities.

The record suggests that Canada values highly its Summit's membership and the honour of hosting. The year 1975 (when Canada was campaigning for admission) reaped an E, while 1981 and 1988 (when Canada hosted) were accorded a B+ to A+ score. More importantly, the marks fall as expected according to the three-stage cadence defined by American decline, power diffusion, and enhanced relevance for Canada. Thus from 1976 to 1980, Canadian editorialists gave the country grades of B to A. The Reagan resurgence of 1982–85 saw Canada's scores drop significantly, to range from F to B. From 1986 to 1993, when U.S. decline returned in intensified fashion, Canada's score rose substantially to range from B to B+ (save for the C of Munich 1992 and Tokyo 1993).

The composite picture is clear. The United States, with its league-leading capability, hosts rather unsuccessful Summits, although its record has improved as its relative capability has declined. U.S.-hosted Summits do not produce agreements that generate a good record of collective compliance. The Reagan resurgence of 1983 generated, as expected, a decline. Moreover, the United States is second only to France in not abiding by the commitments it has agreed to at the Summit table.

In contrast, Japan, alone among Summit members, hosts very successful Summits (although it did not face the challenge of delivering one during the resurgent early Reagan years). Japanese-hosted Summits produce commitments that are complied with to an unusually high degree. However, Japan itself has a rather low record of compliance. This seems surprising for a World War II vanquished power and relative international institutional isolate. But it is consistent with Japan's relative capability position as the Summit's second-most-powerful member.[23] Indeed, the fact that Japan's record of national compliance is almost as low as that of the United States, even though its relative capability is much lower, suggests that Japan, far from being the Summit stabilizer always giving in to American pressure, is particularly skilful at not having to bear a burden commensurate with its capabilities.[24]

As by far the Summit's weakest member, Canada hosts rather unsuccessful Summits, even though its record has improved since the late 1980s (as America's lead has declined). Nor do the members 'obey' the commitments made at

Canadian Summit tables, and the record has worsened in the latter years. That this lack of hosting success is due to limited capability rather than low commitment is suggested by the fact that Canada is second only to Britain in complying with Summit commitments (wherever made). And in periods of relative American weakness, Canada does mount a national performance at the Summit that earns accolades from its élite editorialists at home.

Forging the Transpacific Partnership

Taken together, these results provide substantial grounds for believing that the dynamics of relative capability have generated a three-stage progression in Japanese–Canadian cooperation, in relation to the United States, at the Summit. The speed and depth of this emerging cooperation has, however, depended to a substantial degree on the particular leader the three countries (and other members) have sent to the Summit, and in particular on their liberal or conservative disposition and compatibility.

The period 1975–80 was one in which changes in relative capability gave both Japan and Canada a strong incentive to develop the Summit institution as an alternative to the U.S. politically inspired trade and monetary unilateralism displayed in the Nixon measures of August 1971. They also gave the beleaguered, post-Vietnam America of Jimmy Carter an incentive to cooperate in this new emphasis on leadership through concert. However, in dealing with major issues at the Summit, differences in the party-based political philosophy of the leaders placed Canada close to the United States and divided it from Japan. In particular, the very liberal policies of Liberal Prime Minister Pierre Trudeau gave Canada considerable compatibility with, and influence on, a similarly disposed President Carter. In contrast, both countries were less close to the more conservative and less internationally assertive Japanese Prime Ministers Takeo Miki (1975–76), Takeo Fukuda (1977–78), and Masayoshi Ohira (1979).

However, from 1975 to 1980 Japan and Canada did show substantial partnership and mutual support in building the Summit as a strong institution in which both were equal members. Japan was second only to the United States in supporting Canada's initial bid for inclusion, although all Summit members save France favoured this move. Japan's support flowed from a desire to reward Canada for the earlier support Canada had given Japan in the latter's bid for membership in GATT. Japan also had an interest in reinforcing the weight of the Pacific powers at the Summit in response to a European group that had added Italy at Rambouillet in 1975 (and was to add the European Community in the presence of the Commission in 1977). Japan further wished to avoid offending the United States. This shared Japanese–Canadian concern with adequate Pacific balance did lead both Japan and Canada to strongly and ultimately successfully resist any repetition of the 1978–79 Guadeloupe meeting or formulae for political summitry (such as a Berlin Dinner Four configuration that left both countries out). However, the quest for Pacific balance had its limits as neither Canada nor the United States offered any support for Japan's professed desire in the 1970s to add Australia to the Summit as a means of enhancing the Asian dimension and focus of the forum.

Architectural support was reinforced by practical cooperation. Japan gave Canada a detailed report on the leaders' discussions at Rambouillet, and Canada assisted Japan by allowing the latter to use for the 1976 Summit Canadian consular facilities in San Juan, Puerto Rico, where Japan lacked a diplomatic presence. Neither Canada nor the United States, however, provided any visible support for Japan's bid, evident from 1976 onward, to serve as host of the Summit the following year, or to provide a regular location (in a European–North American–Asian arrangement) for meetings of personal representatives in the preparatory process.

On substantive issues, however, Japanese–Canadian support and cooperation were far less evident. In the nuclear field, Canada's emphasis on strong safeguards on the export of nuclear materials placed it in opposition to a Japan that, with few energy sources, preferred a less restrictive regime. Only in the field of trade did both countries come together, under American leadership, in 1977 and 1979 to forge the Summit deals that produced a successful conclusion to the Tokyo Round.

From 1980 to 1985, the surging strength and unilateralist, pro-military, and free-market predispositions of Ronald Reagan's United States gave Japan and Canada a much wider area of agreement at the Summit and distinct differences with the United States. Both Japan and Canada (usually with most other Summit members save Margaret Thatcher's Britain) sought to curtail the soaring U.S. dollar and U.S. interest rates, and to cope with the looming Third World debt crisis by such means as transferring more financial resources to multilateral development banks. Here they enjoyed little success as the reluctance of the Japanese to criticize the American president, the deep conviction of Ronald Reagan (and often Margaret Thatcher) in the long-term correctness of his laissez-faire economic policies, and the relatively rising power of the United States (bred by both vibrant growth after 1982 and exchange appreciation) made the Americans unwilling to adjust.

In the fields of trade and East–West relations, however, where U.S. preferences were compatible or less fixed, more influence was evident. Thus Japan and Canada joined the United States (and Britain and Germany), over the reluctance of France, Italy, and the European Community, to stave off substantial protectionist pressures fuelled by the deep recession of 1981 and the failure of the GATT ministerial meeting in November 1982. In the political domain, Canada's Pierre Trudeau received only tacit support from Japan in his somewhat successful effort to temper the American–British aggressive approach to East–West relations. Here Prime Minister Nakasone continued to place priority on his relationship with the U.S. president and was more prepared than his predecessors to articulate Japan's willingness to accept security commitments as part of the western alliance.

The same pattern arose in issues relating to the Summit's membership and institutional development. By the early 1980s Ronald Reagan had adopted Japan's earlier enthusiasm for sponsoring Australia's admission to the Summit, but the reluctance of Canada and the European members ultimately prevailed over the predispositions of the club's most powerful country. American initiative, supported by Japan and Canada, led by 1982 to the creation of the Trade Minister's Quadrilateral, whereby the Summit's trade ministers (with all European members represented by the European Community alone) met by themselves two or three times a year to give guidance to the multilateral trade system. Canada also pressed vigorously for the inclusion of political issues on the Summit agenda, and as early as 1980 for the Summit's foreign ministers to meet as a group. Again Japan, fearful of fuelling debates as divisive and as critical of the Americans as those at Williamsburg in 1983, resisted. However, by 1984 the Summit's foreign ministers' forum was born through annual meetings at the autumn opening of the United Nations General Assembly in New York.

From 1985 onward a more modest and multilaterally inclined America provided more scope for Japanese–Canadian cooperation and influence. However, the new enthusiasm of Canadian Conservative Prime Minister Brian Mulroney for a close relationship with Presidents Reagan and Bush, and the continuing concern of Canadian prime ministers with France and Europe, acted as powerful inhibitors to joint initiatives.

Both Japan and Canada shared an interest in Third World debt and development questions, particularly as Japan emerged as the world's largest official development assistance donor. Yet Japan offered only passive support for Canada's 'Toronto terms' for relief of the debt of the poorest in 1988. Canada offered no support for Prime Minister Miyazawa's plan for middle-income debt relief the same year. Moreover, while Canada from 1988 onward became the Summit's leading enthusiast for vigorous action on global environmental issues, Japan (relative to Germany and Italy) remained reluctant.

In the political domain, Japan opposed Canada's (and France's) desire for a strong Summit condemnation of China for its 1989 murder of students in

Tiananmen Square. Reciprocally, Japan was slow to support Canada's desire to have the Summit take up the issue of reform of the United Nations system. Even on the question of nuclear non-proliferation, where the two countries were in the vanguard of international regime building, the 1993 Tokyo Summit featured a Japanese–Canadian disagreement over how strong the Summit's commitment to an indefinite extension of the Non Proliferation Treaty should be, and how closely it should be linked to arms control measures on the part of existing nuclear weapons powers. By the 1995 Halifax Summit, however, the Japanese–Canadian political partnership flourished. Canada as host was able to secure Summit endorsement, over American, British, and French resistance, for a demand that lending by multilateral development banks be conditional on recipients not engaging in excessive military spending.

In the trade field the potential for partnership was more readily realized. Here Canada's early enthusiasm for having the 1993 Tokyo Summit take concrete measures on multilateral trade, in order to catalyze the successful completion of the long overdue Uruguay Round was accepted by the Japanese. After initial American reluctance, a consensus was built for bringing the Quadrilateral's trade ministers to the Tokyo Summit in order to complete the market access package that swiftly generated a successful conclusion to the long overdue Uruguay Round.

On questions dealing with Summit membership, there appeared to be an increasing Japanese–Canadian divide. Canada, along with Germany, was an early enthusiast for involving the Soviets and Russians in the Summit (and providing them with generous financial assistance). In contrast, Japan – conscious of Russia's continued military occupation of Japan's northern territories, the strength of Stalinist impulses within Russia, and the long, troubled history of Russo–Japanese relations – was the leading advocate of a cautious approach. Canada's concern with its American and French special relationships and its Commonwealth and francophone colleagues, led it to mediate Franco–American disagreements over President Mitterrand's proposal to bring several Third World leaders in for a dinner dialogue with the seven at Paris in 1989. However, Canada displayed no similar interest in helping Japan accomplish its desire to have Indonesia's President Suharto come to Tokyo in 1993.

A similar pattern prevails in regard to the development of the Summit institution. Although at the 1986 Tokyo Summit Canada and Italy joined the existing G-5 to form a new G-7 Finance Ministers group (and one that soon came to take over from the older G-5), it was American support and Italian activism that led to the creation of, and Canada's inclusion in, this group. Japan and Canada did work, together with the Americans, to produce the G-7 ministerial meeting on assistance to Russia in April 1993 and on employment in the spring of 1994.

But in contrast to Canada, Japan proved reluctant to develop a G-7 forum for ministers of the environment based on a spring 1992 meeting in the lead up to the United Nations Conference on Environment and Development, a spring 1994 meeting in Florence, and an April 1995 meeting in Hamilton.

Conclusion: The Potential for Partnership

As the record of the past decade indicates, there has been substantially less Japanese–Canadian cooperation at the Summit than changing relative capability patterns in the world and among the seven would predict or permit. Responsibility for the gap lies in the first instance with Canada. With the rare exceptions of the single outings of Alberta's Joe Clark in 1979 and British Columbia's Kim Campbell in 1993, the prime ministers Canada has sent to the Summit have come exclusively from Quebec, where geography, history, and language orient them strongly towards Europe. Whether through Pierre Trudeau's close personal relationship with Germany's Helmut Schmidt and affinity for socialist leaders from France, Britain, and Italy, or Brian Mulroney's and Jean Chrétien's focus on France and Britain, this deeply embedded Eurocentric bias has endured. The reluctance of Canadian prime ministers to engage in bilateral contact with their Japanese counterparts, either at or apart from the Summit, has diminished the prospects for a genuine understanding of the nuances of the others' positions and domestic constraints, the large measure of foreign policy compatibility between their two countries, and the value of joint initiatives. Nor have Japanese prime ministers, still fixated on Washington, been eager to establish or enrich a high-level link with Canada and to explore the relevance of the Summit's third Pacific partner for the pursuit of their priority concerns.

NOTES

1 On the concept of principal powers see Dewitt and Kirton, *Canada as a Principal Power*. On the G-7's commanding share of global capabilities see Bergsten and Henning, *Global Economic Leadership*.
2 Plurilateralism refers to working through limited membership, manageable groupings of individually appropriate and collectively influential countries, rather than relying on the traditional broad multilateralism of the UN and Atlanticist system, on bilateralism, or on unilateralism.
3 The 'Summit system' refers to the interconnected network of increasingly institutionalized processes centred on the annual gathering of the leaders of the United States, Japan, Germany, France, Italy, Britain, and Canada, together with the European Community since 1977, the post-Summit meeting with the Soviet/Russian

leader since 1991, the G-7/P8 tandem that evolved from it, and ad hoc gatherings such as the arms control consultation in 1985 and the Moscow nuclear safety P8 summit of April 1996. It includes the consultations among the Seven and the preparatory and follow-up process for the annual event. It includes also regular and ad hoc meetings held at the Summit and, separately, of the Seven's ministers for trade since 1982 (through the four-member Quadrilateral), foreign affairs since 1984, finance since 1986, environment in 1992 and since 1994, employment in 1994 and 1996, information technology in 1995 and 1996, and assistance to Russia in 1993 and to Ukraine in 1994. Finally, it embraces official-level meetings of the Seven (e.g., policy planning directors), and the working groups and regimes (the latter often involving additional countries, as with the Missile Technology Control Regime) that the Summit Seven founded. For an overview see Kirton, 'The Seven-Power Summit as a New Security Institution,' 335–57. On the G-7's role in bridging regionalism, see Kirton, 'Le rôle du G7.'

4 McMillan, *Comparing Canadian and Japanese Approaches.*

5 There is no serious treatment of Canada in Sakurada, *Japan and the Management*; Funabashi, *Managing the Dollar*; and Owada, 'A Japanese Perspective,' 95–112. See also the special issue of the *Japan Review of International Affairs* 7 (1993); Kobayashi, *The Japanese Perspective*, does note Canada's G-7 leading economic growth performance in the late 1980s and Canada's particular concern with the agricultural subsidies and supply management issue.

6 Putnam and Bayne, *Hanging Together.*

7 Gotlieb, *The Western Economic Summits.*

8 Ibid.; Hollohan, 'The Magnificent Seven'; and Solomon, 'Summit Reflections.'

9 Granatstein and Bothwell, *Pirouette*, 174.

10 Kirton, 'Further Challenges,' 143. I have shown that during the first two-and-a-half years of the Mulroney government, Japan ranked fourth (just behind France, the United States, and the leading United Kingdom) as a Summit diplomacy partner of Canada, with half of Japanese–Canadian Summit encounters taking place within the Summit context. Kirton, 'Managing Global Conflict.'

11 The Japanese prime minister and foreign minister were absent from the 31 July 1975 lunch among the four Western powers (the United States, France, Germany, and Britain) at the British Embassy in Helsinki, the gathering that marked the genesis of the Summit.

12 Several authors have argued that the Summit is best conceived of as an international concert, notably Wallace, 'Political Issues at the Summit'; Ikenberry, 'Salvaging the G-7'; Kirton, 'The Seven Power Summit'; and Kirton, 'The Diplomacy of Concert.'

13 Because Canada is the smallest major power and Summit member, it is the decline of system-controlling capabilities in the system-leading United States and then the diffusion of capabilities to the second-ranked and rising power Japan, rather than

small shifts in Canada's own relative capability, that primarily determine patterns of Canadian activity, association, and approaches to world order.

14 This analysis assumes that states strive in the first instance for a majority of capability in the system or club (preferably by themselves and then with the fewest number of controllable coalition partners), in the second for a lead as large as possible, and in the third to maintain their position as a major power and hence membership in the system/club. Although this GDP-based analysis adequately reflects broader indices of capability share and change, and thus soundly uses relative capability to explain Summit behaviour, it ignores the reciprocal linkage of how Summit behaviour nationally and collectively can change overall G-7 GDP and members' relative shares thereof through the exchange rate and growth mechanism. This analysis also argues that GDP is the appropriate measure for a Summit designed in the first instance as an economic institution, while current exchange rates are important as cross-national measures of capability in that they largely (since 1975) reflect real market forces more than governmentally administered decisions, and are directly relevant to behaviour in the international system. Other data series, such as those produced by the U.S. Bureau of Labour Statistics, show less dramatic fluctuations, but still support the analysis presented here.

15 Grieco, *Co-operation among Nations*.

16 The peak of American unilateralism came in the pipeline sanctions debacle at the 1982 Summit. If the success of the annual Summit depended on the absence of American hegemony and the emergence of effective equality among the members, it is not surprising that the 1985 Bonn Summit was such a failure. See Kirton, 'Contemporary Concert Diplomacy,' available at http://www.g7.utoronto.ca.

17 The 1985 fall in the exchange rate of the U.S. dollar was importantly determined by the Plaza and Louvre Accords mounted by the G-5 and G-7 respectively, although they were responding to major economic imbalances that had accumulated.

18 The point should not be exaggerated. The United States retains its unique veto power within the IMF and current reform proposals envisage Japan being given permanent membership without a veto in the United Nations Security Council (UNSC). Moreover, on grounds of relative capability as well as geographic location, historical affiliation, and national foreign policy priorities (notably its non-nuclear weapons identity), it is not clear why Japan would decisively prefer China and Russia (in a new P7 UNSC) over Italy and Canada (in the existing G-7).

19 As Joe Clark put it: 'No other major power has Canada's institutional reach.' In Holmes and Kirton, eds., *Canada and the New Internationalism*. Within the United Nations system, in the monetary field Canada since 1945 has had a permanent seat on the Executive Board of the International Monetary Fund, and more recently became part of the six major donors of the International Bank for Reconstruction and Development. At the GATT/WTO Canada's major power position has been con-

firmed by its selection as a country requiring annual review under the Trade Policy Review Mechanism.

20 The fact that both strength at the top and weakness at the bottom produce unsuccessful Summits suggest that the equality and equalization of capability among members is the key to Summit success, as the 'concert' model predicts.

21 Von Furstenberg and Daniels, 'Policy Undertakings.' Countries.' See also Von Furstenberg and Daniels, 'Economic Summit Declarations.'

22 It is possible but unlikely that Canada's skill at Summit diplomacy, its small size, and the unique protection afforded it by the United States mean that the Summit reaches agreements that are especially easy for Canada to meet, making internationalist good citizenship through high compliance a far from onerous task. However, evidence of the fact that it is the weak that adjust is offered by the electoral defeat of two Canadian prime ministers as a partial consequence of their efforts to comply with their Summit commitments. Pierre Trudeau's imposition of a fiscal austerity program as a result of the Bonn Summit helped lead to his defeat in 1978. Joe Clark's implementation of his Tokyo 1 energy conservation commitments by higher energy taxes led to the defeat of his minority government in the House of Commons and its subsequent defeat at the polls in 1980.

23 The assumption here is that Gilpinesque rather than Kindlebergerian hegemony operates, as the dominant powers do not disproportionately give. See Gilpin, *War and Change*; and Kindleberger, *The World in Depression*.

24 It is, of course, still probable that Japan practises the diplomacy of anticipatory adjustment, giving (to the Summit and to American pressure) in advance of, rather than after, the Summit. Japan may also be particularly poor at helping draft communiqués that allow it to comply with ease.

Abbreviations

AEC	Atomic Energy Commission
ALCM	Air-Launched Cruise Missile
APD	ASEAN Pacific Dialogue
APEC	Asia Pacific Economic Cooperation
APR	Asia Pacific Roundtable
ARF	ASEAN Regional Forum
ASEAN	Association of Southeast Asian Nations
ASEAN-ISIS	ASEAN Institute of Strategic and International Studies
ASEAN-PMC	ASEAN Post Ministerial Conference
ASEM	Asian-European Union Summit
ASIA	MITI's Asia Supporting Industry Action Program
BIS	Bank for International Settlements
BOJ	Bank of Japan
CANCAPS	Canadian Consortium on Asia-Pacific Security
CFC	chlorofluorocarbons
CIDA	Canadian International Development Agency
CIIA	Canadian Institute of International Affairs
CSCAP	Council for Security Cooperation in Asia Pacific
CSCA	Conference on Security and Cooperation in Asia
CSCE	Conference on Security and Cooperation in Europe
CTDC	Japanese Civil Transport Developments Corporation
DFAIT	Department of Foreign Affairs and International Trade
DFI	direct foreign investment
DSP	Democratic Socialist Party
EAEC	East Asian Economic Caucus
ENDC	Eighteen Nation Disarmament Committee
FDI	foreign direct investment

FGD	flue gas desulphurization
FIRA	Foreign Investment Review Agency
FRB	Federal Reserve Board
FTA	Canada–U.S. Free Trade Agreement
FY	fiscal year
G-5	Group of Five Finance Ministers
G-7	Group of Seven
G-10	Group of Ten
GDP	gross domestic product
GNP	gross national product
GATT	General Agreement on Tariffs and Trade
IAEA	International Atomic Energy Agency
IMF	International Monetary Fund
INGO	international non-governmental organization
IPCC	Intergovernmental Panel on Climate Change
IPR	Institute of Pacific Relations
ISIS	Institute of Strategic and International Studies
IUCN	International Union for the Conservation of Nature
JAMA	Japan Automobile Manufacturers Association of Canada
JETRO	Japan External Trade Organization
JNTO	Japan National Tourist Organization
LDP	Liberal Democratic Party of Japan
MITI	Ministry of International Trade and Industry, Japan
MOF	Ministry of Finance, Japan
MOSS	Market-Oriented Sector-Specific Talks
MTO	multilateral trade organization
NAFTA	North American Free Trade Agreement
NATO	North Atlantic Treaty Organization
NFP	New Frontier Party
NGO	non-governmental organization
NHP	New Harbinger Party
NORAD	North American Aerospace Defence Command
NPCSD	North Pacific Cooperative Security Dialogue
NSG	Nuclear Suppliers Group
NTB	non-tariff barrier
ODA	official development assistance
OECD	Organization for Economic Cooperation and Development
ONUC	United Nations Operation in the Congo
ONUMOZ	United Nations Operation in Mozambique
ONUSAL	United Nations Operation in El Salvador

ONUVEH	United Nations Observers for the Verification of Elections in Haiti
PAFTAD	Pacific Trade and Development Conference
PBEC	Pacific Basin Economic Council
PCB	polychlorinated biphenyl
PECC	Pacific Economic Cooperation Council
PKO	peacekeeping operations
PMC	Post Ministerial Conference
RIMPAC	Rim of the Pacific
ROI	return on investment
SDF	Self-Defence Forces
SDPJ	Social Democratic Party of Japan
SII	Structural Impediment Initiative
SOP	standard operating procedure
TMD	theatre missile defence
TSE	Tokyo Stock Exchange
UN	United Nations
UNAMIR	United Nations Association Mission in Rwanda
UNAVEM	United Nations Angola Verification Mission
UNDOF	United Nations Disengagement Observer Force
UNEF	United Nations Emergency Force
UNEP	United Nations Environmental Program
UNFICYP	United Nations Force in Cyprus
UNHCR	United Nations High Commissioner for Refugees
UNIFIL	United Nations Interim Force in Lebanon
UNIKOM	United Nations Iran-Kuwait Observer Mission
UNIIMOG	United Nations Iran-Iraq Military Observer Group
UNMOGIP	United Nations Military Observer Group India-Pakistan
UNOGIL	United Nations Observation Force in Lebanon
UNOSAL	United Nations Observer Mission in El Salvador
UNOGIL	United Nations Observation Force in Lebanon
UNOSOM	United Nations Operation in Somalia
UNPROFOR	United Nations Protection Force in the former Yugoslavia
UNSC	United Nations Security Council
UNSF	United Nations Special Force in Western New Guinea
UNTAC	United Nations Transitional Assistance Group in Cambodia
UNTAG	United Nations Transitional Assistance Group in Namibia
UNTSO	United Nations Truce Supervisory Organization Palestine
USTR	United States Trade Representative
VER	voluntary export restraint
WTO	World Trade Organization

Bibliography

Abegglen, James C. *Sea Change: Pacific Asia as the New World Industrial Center.* New York: Free Press/Macmillan, 1994.

Abramson, N.R., R. Keating, and H.W. Lane. 'Cross-National Cognitive Process Differences: A Comparison of Canadian, American and Japanese Management Students.' *Working Paper.* 1994.

'Action Plan Unveiled at APEC.' *Japan Report* 44, 5 (October–December 1996).

Adams, F. Gerard, Byron Gangnes, and Shuntaro Shishido. *Economic Activity, Trade and Industry in the U.S.–Japan–World Economy: A Macro Model Study of Economic Interactions.* Westport, CT: Praeger, 1993.

Advisory Committee on Trade Policy and Negotiations. *Analysis of the U.S.–Japan Trade Problem.* 1989. Photocopy.

Advisory Group on Defence Issues. 'The Modality of the Security and Defense Capability of Japan, Outlook for the 21st Century' (12 August 1994).

Allison, Graham. *Essence of Decision: Explaining the Cuban Missile Crisis.* Boston: Little Brown, 1971.

Allison, Graham, and Morton Halperin. 'Bureaucratic Politics: A Paradigm and Some Policy Implications.' In Robert Tanter and Richard Ullman, eds., *Theory and Policy in International Relations.* New York: Princeton University Press, 1972.

Alston, Julian M., Colin A. Carter, and Lovell S. Jarvis. 'Discriminatory Trade: The Case of Japanese Beef and Wheat Imports.' *Canadian Journal of Agricultural Economics* 38 (1990).

Altman, Roger C. 'Why Pressure Tokyo?' *Foreign Policy* 73 (May/June 1994).

Amano, A., B. Fisher, M. Kuroda, and S. Nishioka. eds. *Climate Change: Policy Implements and Their Implications.* Tsukuba, Japan: Centre for Global Environmental Research, National Institute for Environmental Studies, 1994.

'Ambassador's Greetings.' *Japan Report* 44, 5 (October–December 1996).

American Chamber of Commerce. *Making Trade Talks Work*. Tokyo: American Chamber of Commerce, 1997.

Anchordoguy, Marie. 'Mastering the Market: Japanese Government Targeting of the Computer Industry.' *International Organization* 42 (Autumn 1988).

– *Computers Inc. Japan's Challenge to IBM*. Cambridge, MA: Harvard University Press, 1989.

Ando, Hiroshi. *Sekinin to Genkai Jou*. Tokyo: Kinyu Zaisei Jijo, 1987.

Andrews, David M. 'Capital Mobility and State Autonomy: Towards a Structural Theory of International Monetary Relations.' *International Studies Quarterly* 38 (June 1994).

Angel, Robert. *Explaining Economic Policy Failure: Japan in the 1969–1971 International Monetary Crisis*. New York: Columbia University Press, 1991.

Arase, David. 'Japan in Post-Cold War Asia.' In Chandran Jeshurun, ed., *China, India, Japan and the Security of Southeast Asia*. Singapore: Institute of Southeast Asian Studies, 1993.

Armacost, Michael H. *Friends or Rivals?* New York: Columbia University Press, 1996.

Asahi Shimbun. Various issues.

Asia Pacific Foundation of Canada. *Canada–Japan Forum 2000, Partnership across the Pacific*. December 1992.

'The Asian Way.' *Asia Week* (2 March 1994).

Axelrod, Robert. *The Evolution of Cooperation*. New York: Basic Books, 1984.

Axelrod, Robert, and Robert O. Keohane. 'Achieving Cooperation under Anarchy.' *World Politics* 38 (October 1985).

Balassa, Bela, and Marcus Noland. *Japan in the World Economy*. Washington, DC: Institute for International Economics, 1988.

Baldwin, David. *Economic Statecraft*. Princeton: Princeton University Press, 1985.

Baldwin, David A., ed. *Neorealism and Neoliberalism: The Contemporary Debate*. New York: Columbia Press, 1993.

Ballon, R.J. 'A Lesson from Japan: Contract, Control, and Authority.' *Journal of Contemporary Issues* 8 (1979).

– 'Japan: The Government–Business Relationship.' In R.L. Tung, ed., *Strategic Management in the United States and Japan: A Comparative Analysis*. Cambridge, MA: Ballinger, 1986.

Bamba, Nobuya. *Japanese–Canadian Relations: An Overview*. Toronto: Joint Centre on Modern East Asia, 1983.

Bamba, Nobuya, and Tadayuki Okuma. 'The Post War Years.' Translated by Peter Currie in *Canada and Japan in the Twentieth Century*. Toronto: Oxford University Press, 1991.

Barlow, Maude. 'Free Trade Meets the Tiger: Canada's Deadly Role in APEC.' *Canadian Forum* 75 (January/February 1997).

Barry, Donald. 'The Politics of "Exceptionalism": Canada and the United States as a Distinctive International Relationship.' *Dalhousie Review* 60 (Spring 1980).

Beaton, Leonard, and John Maddox. *The Spread of Nuclear Weapons*. London: Chatto & Windus, 1962.

Beaton, Leonard, and John Maddox. 'Nuclear Fuel For-All.' *Foreign Affairs* 45 (July 1967).

Bedeski, Robert E. 'Canada/Korea Arms Control Workshops' *CANCAPS Bulletin* 10 (August 1996).

Bendor, Jonathan, and Thomas Hammond. 'Rethinking Allison's Models.' *American Political Science Review* 86 (June 1992).

Bennett, Andrew, Joseph Lepgold, and Danny Unger. 'Burden-Sharing in the Persian Gulf War.' *International Organization* 49 (Winter 1994).

Bergsten, C. Fred. 'The United States–Japan Economic Problem.' *Policy Analyses in International Economics* 14 (1987). Washington, DC: Institute for International Economics.

– 'APEC and World Trade.' *Foreign Policy* 73 (May/June 1994).

Bergsten, C. Fred, and C. Randall Henning. *Global Economic Leadership and the Group of Seven*. Washington, DC: Institute for International Economics, 1996.

Bergsten, C. Fred, and Marcus Noland. *Reconcilable Differences: United States–Japan Economic Conflict*. Washington, DC: Institute for International Economics, 1993.

Bhagwati, Jagdish. 'Samurais No More.' *Foreign Policy* 73 (May/June 1994).

Blain, R., and G. Norcliffe. 'Japanese Investment in Canada and Canadian Exports to Japan 1965–1984.' *Canadian Geographer* 32 (1988).

Blaker, Michael. *Japanese International Negotiating Style*. New York: Columbia University Press, 1977.

Blank, Stephen, and Earl Fry. 'The Impact of NAFTA on Japan.' Americas Society, 1993. Photocopy.

Blustein, Paul. 'Japan Approaches Tax-Cut Package.' *The Globe and Mail* (9 February 1994).

Bovard, James. *The Fair Trade Fraud*. New York: St. Martin's Press, 1991.

Bowen, Roger W. *Innocence Is Not Enough: The Life and Death of Herbert Norman*. Vancouver: 1986.

Bowen, Roger W., ed. *E.H. Norman: His Life and Scholarship*. Toronto: 1984.

Brady, Linda. *The Politics of Negotiation*. Chapel Hill: The University of North Carolina Press, 1991.

Brandon, Henry. *The Retreat of American Power: The Inside Story of How Nixon and Kissinger Changed American Foreign Policy for Years to Come*. New York: Doubleday, 1973.

Brazeau, M. *The Directory of Canadian Business in Japan, Volume Two*. Tokyo: Peter Steele, 1990.

Brown, Eugene. 'Japanese Security Policy in the Post–Cold War Era: Threat Perceptions and Strategic Options.' Paper presented to the 34th annual meeting of the International Studies Association, Acapulco, March 1993.

Brown, L., J. Abramovitz, C. Bright, C. Flavin, H. French, G. Gardner, H. Kane, A. McGinn, M. Renner, and D. Roodman. *State of the World 1997: A World Watch Institute Report on Progress toward a Sustainable Society.* Washington, DC: Worldwatch Institute, 1997.

Brown, R.J. Barry. *Globalization and Interdependence in the International Political Economy.* London: Printer Publishers, 1995.

Brownsely, Lorne. *Canada–Japan: Policy Issues for the Future.* Ottawa: Institute for Research on Public Policy, 1989.

Bryant, William E. *Japanese Private Economic Diplomacy: An Analysis of Business-Government Linkages.* New York: Praeger, 1975.

Buchan, Alastair. 'Concepts of Peacekeeping.' In Michael Fry, ed., *Freedom and Change: Essays in Honour of Lester B. Pearson.* Toronto: McClelland and Stewart, 1975.

Buchanan, Gregg, and Charles Macli. 'Getting Tough with Japan.' *Report on Business Magazine* (October 1991).

Buckley, Roger. *U.S.–Japan Alliance Diplomacy, 1945–1990.* Cambridge: Cambridge University Press, 1992.

Burns, E.L.M. 'Can the Spread of Nuclear Weapons Be Stopped?' *International Organization* 19 (Autumn 1965).

Bussey, John, Clay Chandler, and Michael Williams. 'Japanese Recession Prompts Corporations to Take Radical Steps.' *Wall Street Journal* (24 February 1993).

Byers, R.B., ed. *Canadian Annual Review of Politics and Public Affairs* (1980–85, various issues). Toronto: University of Toronto Press.

Campbell, John Creighton. 'Japan and the United States: Games That Work.' In Gerald L. Curtis, ed., *Japan's Foreign Policy.* New York: M.E. Sharpe, 1993.

Canada. Department of External Affairs. *External Affairs* (September, October 1971).

Canada. Department of External Affairs and International Trade. Historical Section. File No. 35–1–USA-1971–SITREP. Vols. 1–11.

– *Canada–Japan Business Conference Background Paper.* Halifax, 12–15 May 1991.

Canada. Department of Foreign Affairs and International Trade. *Canada's Action Plan for Japan.* Ottawa: Department of Foreign Affairs and International Trade, 1994.

– *Canada in the World, Government Statement 1995.*

Canada. Department of National Defence. *1994 Defence White Paper.*

Canada. Environment Canada. *The State of Canada's Environment 1996.*

Canada. Maritime Forces Pacific Headquarters. 'Canadian Naval Task Group to Visit Asia Pacific Countries.' *CANCAPS Bulletin* 8 (March 1966).

Canada. Parliament. Special Joint Committee on Canada's Defence Policy. *Security in a Changing World 1994, Report of the Special Joint Committee on Canada's Foreign Policy.*

Canada. Senate. Standing Committee on Foreign Affairs. *Canada–United States Relations, Vol. 1: The Institutional Framework for the Relationship.* 1975.

– *Proceedings* 9 (1975).

Canada 21 Council. *Canada 21: Canada and Common Security in the Twenty-First Century.* Toronto: University of Toronto Centre for International Studies, 1994.

– *Partnership across the Pacific.* Joint Forum Report. December 1992.

Canada–Japan Forum 2000 (CJF). 'Canada–Japan, Forum 2000, Follow-Up Committee Report: Partnership across the Pacific.' May 1995.

Canada–Japan Trade Council, ed. *Japan's Changing Needs for Canadian Housing Products.* Ottawa: Canada–Japan Trade Council, 1995.

Canada–Japan Trade Council Newsletter. Various issues.

The Canadian-American Committee. *The U.S. Import Surcharge and Canada.* Washington, DC: National Planning Association, 1971.

Canadian Annual Review of Politics and Public Affairs. Various years.

Canadian Broadcasting Corporation (CBC), Radio News, 27 August 1994.

Canadian Consortium on Asia Pacific Security (CANCAPS) (March 1994). *Canada on Asia Pacific Security in the 1990s.*

Canadian Embassy in Tokyo. *Japanese Portfolio Investment in Canada 1994 Survey.* Tokyo: Canadian Embassy, 1994.

Canadian Institute of International Affairs (CIIA). *International Canada* (July & August, September, October, November 1971).

CANCAPS. 'Canadian Participation.' *CANCAPS Bulletin* 3 (July 1994).

Cartwright, D. *Canadian Wood and Building Product Exports to Japan.* Ottawa: Canada–Japan Trade Council, 1995.

Cassuto, Aldo. 'Hiroshima's Japan Goes Nuclear.' *World Today* 28 (August 1970).

Chanda, Nayan. 'Divide and Rule, Beijing Scores Points on South China Sea.' *Far Eastern Economic Review* (11 August 1994).

Ching, Frank. 'Creation of a Security Forum Is a Feather in ASEAN's Cap.' *Far Eastern Economic Review* (12 August 1993).

– 'ARF Off to a Good Start.' *Far Eastern Economic Review* (11 August 1994).

Choate, Pat. *Agents of Influence.* New York: Knopf, 1990.

Chow, Wyng. 'Vancouver Group Bags $12–Million Training Deal.' Vancouver *Sun* (9 September 1994).

Clark, Joe. 'Canada's New Internationalism.' In John Holmes and John Kirton, eds., *Canada and the New Internationalism,* pp. 3–11. Toronto: Canadian Institute for International Affairs, 1988.

– 'Notes for a Speech by the Secretary of State for External Affairs, the Right Honour-
   able Joe Clark, at a Luncheon Hosted by the Foreign Correspondents Club of Japan.'
   Tokyo, 24 July 1990. *Statement* 90/14.
– 'Notes for a Speech by the Right Honourable Joe Clark, Secretary of State for Exter-
   nal Affairs, to the North Pacific Security Dialogue in Victoria, British Columbia.'
   Statement 91/17.
– 'Notes for a Speech by the Secretary of State for External Affairs, the Right Honour-
   able Joe Clark, to the 45th Session of the United Nations General Assembly, New
   York, 26 September 1990. In 'Canada on Asia Pacific Security in the 1990s,'
   CANCAPS Paper 1 (March 1994).

Cohen, Stephen D. *Cowboys and Samurai*. New York: Harper Business, 1991.
– *Uneasy Partnership: Competition and Conflict in U.S.–Japanese Trade Relations*.
   Cambridge, MA: Balinger, 1985.

Cohen, Stephen D., ed. *The Making of United States International Economic Policy*.
   Fourth ed. Westport, CT: Praeger, 1994.

Colliers International Hotel Realty. *The West Coast Hotel Investment Report*. Vancouver:
   Colliers International Hotel Realty, 1994.

Commission for A New Asia. *Towards A New Asia: A Report of the Commission for A
   New Asia*. Kuala Lumpur: 1992.

Constand, Richard, Lewis Freitas, and Michael Sullivan. 'Factors Affecting Price–
   Earnings Ratios and Market Values of Japanese Firms.' *Financial Management* 20
   (Winter 1991).

Cooper, Andrew. *Canadian Foreign Policy: Old Habits and New Directions*. Toronto:
   Prentice-Hall, 1997.

Cooper, Andrew F., Richard A. Higgott, and Kim Richard Nossal. *Relocating Middle
   Powers, Australia and Canada in a Changing World Order*. Vancouver: UBC Press,
   1993.

Cossa, Ralph A., ed. *Asia Pacific Confidence and Security Building Measures*. Washington, DC: Centre for Strategic and International Studies, 1995.

Courtis, Kenneth S. 'Opportunity Knocks.' *The New Pacific* (Summer 1994).
– 'Japan's Tilt to Asia Gaining Momentum.' *Nikkei Weekly* (28 March 1994).

Cowhey, Peter F. 'Domestic Institutions and International Commitments: Japan and the
   United States.' *International Organization* 47 (Summer 1993).

Cox, Robert W. 'Middlepowermanship, Japan and Future World Order.' *International
   Journal* 44 (Autumn 1989).

'A Crack in the Wall.' *The Economist* (11 December 1993).

Craib, B. Anne. 'NAFTA's Implications for Canada–Japan Relations.' Special Supplement to *Canada–Japan Trade Council Newsletter* (originally published as *Japan
   Economic Institute Report* 11A (18 March 1994).

Crane, David. *The Next Canadian Century: Building a Competitive Economy.* Toronto: Stoddart, 1992.

Crawford, Sir John, Saburo Okita, Peter Drysdale, and Kiyoshi Kojima, eds. *Raw Materials and Pacific Economic Integration.* London: Croom Helm, 1978.

Croci, Osvald. 'The American Friend: Canadian Decision-Making during the 1971 International Monetary Crisis.' Paper presented at the annual meeting of the Canadian Political Science Association, Dalhousie University, 27 May 1981.

'CSCAP Finds Its Stride.' *CANCAPS Bulletin* 12 (February 1997).

Cuff, R.D. and J.L. Granatstein. 'Canada and the Perils of 'Exemptionalism.' *Queen's Quarterly* 79 (Winter 1972).

Curtis, Gerald, ed. *Japan's Foreign Policy.* New York: M.E.Sharpe, 1993.

Curtis, John. 'Summitry: Keep Talking.' *Policy Options* 3 (September/October 1982).

Cutler, A. Clair, and Mark Zacher, eds. *Canadian Foreign Policy and International Economic Regimes.* Vancouver: UBC Press, 1992.

Dai, Poeliu. 'Treaty on the Non-Proliferation of Nuclear Weapons with Special Reference to Canada's Position.' *Canadian Yearbook of International Law* 6 (1968).

Daily Yomiuri. Various issues.

David, Charles-Philippe, and Stéphane Roussel. 'Une espèce en voie de disparition?' *International Journal* 52 (Winter 1996–97).

'Defense Outline Ok'd, SDF Gets Bigger Role.' *Daily Yomiuri* (30 December 1995).

Destler, I.M. *American Trade Politics.* Washington, DC: Institute for International Economics, 1992.

Destler, I.M. et al., eds. *Managing an Alliance.* Washington, DC: Brookings Institution, 1976.

– *The Textile Wrangle.* Ithaca, NY: Cornell University Press, 1979.

Destler, I.M., and C. Randall Henning. *Dollar Politics: Exchange Rate Policymaking in the United States.* Washington, DC: Institute for International Economics, 1989.

Destler, I.M., and Hisao Mitsuyu. 'Locomotives on Different Tracks: Macroeconomic Diplomacy, 1977–1979.' In I.M. Destler and Hideo Sato, eds., *Coping with U.S.–Japanese Economic Conflicts.* Lexington, MA: D.C. Heath, 1982.

Destler, I.M., and Hideo Sato, eds. *Coping with U.S.–Japanese Economic Conflicts.* Lexington, MA: D.C. Heath, 1982.

Dewitt, David. 'Japan's Role in Regional and International Security.' In Don Daly and Tom Sekine, eds., *Discovering Japan: Issues for Canadians.* Ottawa: Captus University Publications, 1989.

– 'Common, Comprehensive, and Cooperative Security.' *The Pacific Review* 7, 1 (1994).

Dewitt, David, and Paul M. Evans. 'The Changing Dynamics of Asia Pacific Security: A Canadian Perspective.' *NPCSD Working Paper* 3. North York, Ont.: North

Pacific Cooperative Security Dialogue Research Program, York University, January 1992.

Dewitt, David, and Paul Evans, eds. *The Agenda for Cooperative Security in the North Pacific: Vancouver, March 1993 – Conference Report.* North York, Ont.: North Pacific Cooperative Security Dialogue Research Program, 1993.

Dewitt, David, and Brian Job. 'Asia Pacific Security Studies in Canada.' In Paul Evans, ed., *Studying Asia Pacific Security: The Future Research, Training and Dialogue Activities.* Toronto: Joint Centre for Asia-Pacific Studies, University of Toronto–York University, 1994.

Dewitt, David, and John Kirton. *Canada as a Principal Power: A Study in Foreign Policy and International Relations.* Toronto: John Wiley, 1983.

Dickerman, C. Robert. 'Transgovernmental Challenge and Response in Scandinavia and North America.' *International Organization* 30 (Spring 1976).

Dickey, John S. 'The Relationship in Rhetoric and Reality: Merchant-Heeney Revisited.' *International Journal* 27 (Spring 1972).

Dobell, Peter. *Canada in World Affairs, 1971–1973.* Toronto: Canadian Institute of International Affairs, 1985.

Dobson, Wendy. 'A Canadian Perspective.' In Wendy Dobson, ed., *Canadian–Japanese Economic Relations in a Triangular Perspective.* Toronto: C.D. Howe Institute, 1987.

– *Economic Policy Coordination: Requiem or Prologue?* Washington, DC: Institute for International Economics, 1991.

Dobson, Wendy, ed. *Canadian–Japanese Economic Relations in a Triangular Perspective.* Toronto: C.D. Howe, 1987.

Domoto, Kenji. 'Le rôle du Japon dans le dynamisme du bassin du pacifique.' In Gérard Hervouet, ed., *Asie-Pacifique: Les Nouveaux Espaces de Coopération et de Conflits.* Sainte-Foy, Que.: Les Presses de l'Université Laval, 1991.

Donnelly, Michael. 'Japanese–American Relations: The Costs of Brinkmanship.' *International Journal* 46 (Autumn 1991).

– 'On Political Negotiation: America Pushes to Open Up Japan.' *Pacific Affairs* 66 (1993).

Doran, Charles. *Forgotten Partnership: U.S.–Canadian Relations Today.* Baltimore, MD: Johns Hopkins University Press, 1984.

Doran, Charles, et al. *Pacific Partners: Canada and the United States.* Washington, DC: Brassey's Inc., 1994.

Dore, R. *British Factory Japanese Factory: The Origins of National Diversity in Industrial Relations.* London: George Allen & Unwin, 1973.

Dougherty, James. 'Nuclear Proliferation in Asia.' *Orbis* 19 (Fall 1975).

Dower, J.W. *Empire and Aftermath.* Cambridge, Mass.: Harvard University Press, 1979.

Dower, J.W., ed. *Origins of the Modern Japanese State: Selected Writings of E.H. Norman.* New York: 1976.

Drifte, Reinhard. *Japan's Foreign Policy.* London: 1990.

Eayrs, James. *The Art of the Possible: Government and Foreign Policy in Canada.* Toronto: University of Toronto Press, 1961.

Eckert, Paul. 'Defence Agency White Paper Singles Out North Korea, Report Cites Nuclear Threat from Pyongyang.' *Nikkei Weekly* (2 August 1993).

The Economist. Various issues (esp. 6 March 1993, 29 May 1993, 31 May 1997).

Edgington, D.W. *Japanese Business Down Under: Patterns of Investment in Australia.* London: Routledge, 1990.

– 'Japanese Perceptions of the Canada–U.S. Free Trade Agreement.' *Canadian Journal of Regional Science* 13 (1990).

– 'The Economic Impact of Tourism.' In Canada–Japan Trade Council, ed., *British Columbia and Japan: Aspects of Tourism in the Nineties.* Ottawa: Canada–Japan Trade Council, 1991.

– 'Japanese Manufacturing in Australia: Corporations, Governments and Bargaining.' *Pacific Affairs* 64 (1991).

– 'Japanese Direct Investment in Canada: Recent Trends and Prospects.' *BC Geographical Series* 49. Vancouver: Department of Geography, University of British Columbia, 1992 (updated).

– 'The Globalisation of Japanese Manufacturing Corporations.' *Growth and Change* 24 (1993).

– 'Japanese Investment in Canadian Real Estate.' In J. Kovalio, ed., *Japan in Focus.* Ottawa: Captus University Publications, 1994.

– *Japanese Property Investors in Canadian Cities and Regions.* Vancouver: Centre for Human Settlements, University of British Columbia, 1994.

– '"The New Wave": Japanese Investment in Canada during the 1980s.' *Canadian Geographer* 38 (1994).

– 'Dreams of Pacifica: Integration in the Pacific Northwest Region.' *Ritsumeikan Social Sciences Review* 30 (1995).

– 'Japanese Manufacturing Companies in Southern Ontario.' In M.B. Green and R.B. Naughton, eds., *The Location of Foreign Direct Investment: Geographic and Business Approaches.* Aldershot, U.K.: Avebury, 1995.

– 'Trade, Investment and the New Regionalism.' *Canadian Journal of Regional Studies* 18 (1995).

– 'Japanese Real Estate Investment in Canadian Cities and Regions.' *Canadian Geographer* 40 (1996).

– *Japanese Property Investors in Canadian Cities and Regions.* Vancouver: Centre for Human Settlements, University of British Columbia, 1997.

Edgington, D.W., and W.M. Fruin. 'NAFTA and Japanese Investment.' In Allan M. Rugman, ed., *Foreign Investment and NAFTA.* Columbia, SC: University of South Carolina, 1994.

Edgington, D.W., and R. Hayter. 'International Trade, Production Chains and Corporate Strategies: Japan's Timber Trade with British Columbia.' *Regional Studies* 31 (1997).

Ekonomisuto, ed. *Sengo Sangyoshi eno Shogen 4*. Tokyo: Mainichi Shimbunsha, 1978.

Elek, Andrew. 'APEC – Motives, Objectives and Prospects.' *Australian Journal of International Affairs* 46, 2 (November 1992).

Emmot, Bill. *Japan's Global Reach: The Influences, Strategies and Weaknesses of Japanese Multinational Companies*. London: Century, 1992.

Encarnation, Dennis. *Rivals Beyond Trade*. Ithaca, NY: Cornell University Press, 1992.

Encarnation, Dennis J., and Mark Mason. 'Neither MITI Nor America: The Political Economy of Capital Liberalization in Japan.' *International Organization* 44 (Winter 1990).

English, H. Edward. *Tomorrow the Pacific*. Observation Number 34. Toronto: C.D. Howe Institute, 1991.

– 'U.S. Trade Policy on Japan Undermines Wider Cooperation.' *Asian Pacific Research and Resource Centre Newsletter* (4 June 1994).

English, John. *The Worldly Years: The Life of Lester Pearson, Vol. 2: 1949–1972*. Toronto: Vintage Books, 1993.

Ennis, P. 'Canada Set for a Bigger Share of Japanese Auto Investment.' *Tokyo Business* (February 1995).

Epstein, William. 'Canada.' In Joref Goldblat, ed., *Non-Proliferation: The Why and Wherefore*. Philadelphia: SIPRI, Taylor & Francis, 1985.

Estrin, D., and Swaigen, J. *Environment on Trial*. Toronto: Emond Montgomery Publications, 1993.

Evans, Paul M. 'Emerging Patterns in Asia Pacific Security: The Search for a Regional Framework.' Paper presented at the ISIS (Malaysia) Roundtable in Kuala Lumpur, June 1991.

– 'The Emergence of Eastern Asia and Its Implications for Canada.' *International Journal* 47 (Summer 1992).

– 'Building Security: The Council for Security Cooperation in the Asia-Pacific (CSCAP).' *Pacific Review* 7 (1994).

– 'The Council for Security Cooperation in the Asia Pacific: Context and Prospect.' *CANCAPS Papier* 2 (March 1994).

– 'CMC Update.' *CANCAPS Bulletin* 10 (August 1996).

– 'North Korean Delegation Visits Canada.' *CANCAPS Bulletin* 10 (August 1996).

– 'The Prospects for Multilateral Security.' In Desmond Ball, ed., *The Transformation of Security in the Asia/Pacific Region*. London: Frank Cass, 1996.

Evans, Paul M., ed. *Studying Asia Pacific Security: The Future of Research Training and Dialogue Activities*. Toronto: Joint Centre for Asia-Pacific Studies, University of Toronto–York University, 1994.

Evans, Peter B., Harold K. Jacobson, and Robert D. Putnam., eds. *Double-Edged Diplomacy: International Bargaining and Domestic Politics*. Berkeley, CA: University of California Press, 1993.

Falk, Richard. *Legal Order in a Violent World*. Princeton, NJ: Princeton University Press, 1968.

Fallows, James. 'Containing Japan.' *The Atlantic* 263 (May 1989).

Far Eastern Economic Review. Various issues.

Fayerweather, J., and A. Kapoor. *Strategy and Negotiation for the International Corporation*. Cambridge, MA.: Ballinger, 1976.

'Fears of Influence.' *Far Eastern Economic Review* 160, 5 (23 January 1997).

Financial Post. Various issues.

Financial Times. Various issues.

Fisher, Roger, and William L. Ury. *Getting to Yes*. New York: Harper and Row, 1981.

Florida, R., and M. Kenney. 'The Globalization of Japanese R and D.' *Economic Geography* 70 (1994).

Fortune. Various issues.

Fox, Annette Baker, Alfred O. Hero, and Joseph Nye, Jr., eds. *Canada and the United States: Transnational and Transgovernmental Relations*. New York: Columbia University Press, 1976.

Frantz, D., and C. Collins. *Selling Out: How We Are Letting Japan Buy Our Land, Our Industries, Our Financial Institutions, and Our Future*. Chicago: Contemporary Books, 1989.

Friedland, Jonathan. 'Bust Bankers.' *Far Eastern Economic Review* 155 (26 November 1992).

Fujisaki, Ichiro. 'Enhancing Regional Security in the Asia Pacific Region – Conventional Wisdom and Future-Oriented Dialogue.' A paper presented to the eighth Asia Pacific Roundtable, Kuala Lumpur, June 1994.

Fukushima, Glen. *Nichibei Keizai Masatsu no Seijigaku*. Tokyo: Asahi Shimbunsha, 1992.

Funabashi, Yoichi. *Nichibei Keizai Masatsu*. Tokyo: Iwanami Shincho, 1987.

– *Managing the Dollar: From the Plaza to the Louvre*, 2nd ed. Washington DC: Institute for International Economics, 1989.

– *Tsuka Retsu Retsu*. Tokyo: Asahi Shimbunsha, 1989.

Gaffen, Frank. *In the Eye of the Storm: A History of Canadian Peacekeeping*. Toronto: Deneau and Wayne, 1987.

Gale, Roger W. 'Nuclear Power and Japan's Proliferation Option.' *Asian Survey* 18 (November 1978).

George, Alexander L. 'Case Studies and Theory Development: The Method of Structured Focused Comparison.' In Paul Gordon Lauren, ed., *Diplomacy: New Approaches in History, Theory and Policy*. New York: The Free Press, 1979.

George, Aurelia. 'Japan's America Problem: The Japanese Response to U.S. Pressure.' *The Washington Quarterly* (Summer 1991).

Gilpin, Robert. *War and Change in World Politics.* New York: Cambridge University Press, 1981.

– *The Political Economy of International Relations.* Princeton, NJ: Princeton University Press, 1987.

Gladwyn, T., and I. Walter. *Multinationals under Fire.* New York: John Wiley & Sons, 1980.

The Globe and Mail. Various issues.

Golub, Stephen S. 'Is Trade between the United States and Japan Off Balance?' *Finance and Development* 31 (September 1994).

'The Good News from Japan.' *The Economist* (29 January 1994).

'Goran KaNshigun, "Kyodo Kunren, Jieitai mo"' ('Golan Observer Force, Joint Exercise, Self-Defence Force too'). *Yomiuri Shinbun* (30 January 1996).

Gotlieb, A.E. 'The Western Economic Summits.' Notes for remarks to the Canadian Institute of International Affairs, Winnipeg, 9 April 1981.

– *The Western Economic Summits.* Toronto: Centre for International Studies, 1987.

'Gov't Agrees on 51-Member Golan Mission.' *Daily Yomiuri* (16 December 1995).

Government of Ontario. *Japanese Investment Profile.* Tokyo: Ontario House, 1993.

Gowa, Joanne. *Closing the Gold Window: Domestic Politics and the End of Bretton Woods.* Ithaca, NY: Cornell University Press, 1983.

Graham, J.L., and Y. Sano. *Smart Bargaining.* Cambridge, MA.: Ballinger, 1984.

Granatstein, J.L. 'Did Canada Make a Difference?' In John English and Norman Hillmer, eds., *Making a Difference? Canada's Foreign Policy in a Changing World Order.* Toronto: Lester Publishing, 1991.

Granatstein, J.L., and Robert Bothwell. *Pirouette: Pierre Trudeau and Canadian Foreign Policy.* Toronto: University of Toronto Press, 1990.

Greathed, Edward D. 'Antecedents and Origins of the Canadian Institute of International Affairs.' In Harvey L. Dyck and H. Peter Krosby, eds., *Empire and Nations: Essays in Honour of Frederic H. Soward.* Toronto: Canadian Institute of International Affairs, 1969.

Greaves, Rosemary. 'ASEAN Regional Forum Firmly Established.' *Insight* (15 August 1994).

– 'First ASEAN Regional Forum Aims to Build Trust.' *Insight* (18 July 1994).

Grieco, Joseph. 'Anarchy and the Limits of Cooperation: A Realist Critique of the New Liberal Institutionalism.' *International Organization* 42 (Summer 1988).

– *Cooperation among Nations: Europe, America and Non-Tariff Barriers to Trade.* Ithaca, NY: Cornell University Press, 1990.

Grubb, M. 'The Greenhouse Effect: Negotiating Targets.' *International Affairs* 66 (1993).

Haas, Peter M., ed. 'Knowledge, Power and International Policy Coordination.' Special issue of *International Organization* 46 (Winter 1992).

Haas, Peter, R. Keohane, and M. Levy. *Institutions for the Earth*. Cambridge, MA: MIT Press, 1990.

Hall, E.T., and M.R. Hall. *Hidden Differences: Doing Business with the Japanese*. Garden City, NY: Anchor Press, 1987.

Hampson, H. Anthony. *Nikka Kankei: Japanese–Canadian Relations, The Opportunities Ahead*. Observation Number 33. Toronto: C.D. Howe Institute, 1988.

Harris, Stuart. 'Enhancing Security: Non-Military Means and Measurements II.' In Bunn Nagara and K.S. Balakarishnan, eds., *The Making of a Security Community in the Asia-Pacific*. Kuala Lumpur: ISIS Malaysia, 1994.

Hawes, Michael. 'Canada–U.S. Relations in the Mulroney Years: How Special the Relationship?' In Brian W. Tomlin and Maureen Appel Molot., eds., *Canada among Nations: The Tory Record, 1988*. Toronto: James Lorimer, 1989.

– 'Japan and the International System: Challenge from the Pacific.' *International Journal* 46 (Winter 1990–91).

– *Atlantic Past, Pacific Future*. Toronto: Prentice-Hall, forthcoming 1999.

Hay, Keith A.J. *Manufactures: Has Canada Got the Goods for Japan?* Ottawa: Canada–Japan Trade Council, 1991.

Hay, Keith A.J., ed. *Canadian Perspectives on Economic Relations with Japan*. Montreal: Institute for Research on Public Policy, 1980.

Hay, Keith A.J, and Victoria R. Fiander. *Canada–Japan: The Import–Export Picture 1989*. Ottawa: Canada–Japan Trade Council, 1990.

Hay, Keith A.J, and Colin A. Saravanamuttoo. *Canada–Japan: The Export–Import Picture 1988–1991*. Ottawa: Canada–Japan Trade Council, 1992.

Hayami, Masaru. *Hendo Sobasei 10 Nen*. Tokyo: Toyo Keizai Shimposha, 1982.

Hayashi, Taizo. 'Arufa (Enkiriage) Sagyo Shimatsuki.' *Kinyu Zaisei Jijo* (24 June, 1 July 1974).

– 'Enkiriage Sagyo no Zasetsu Kara Furoto made.' *Kinyu Zaisei Jijo* (31 January, 7 February, 14 February 1977).

Hecht, A., and D. Tirpak. 'Framework Agreement on Climate Change.' *Climate Change* 29 (1995).

Helliwell, John F. 'Some Comparative Macroeconomics of the United States, Japan, and Canada.' In Robert Stein, ed., *Trade and Investment Relations Among the United States, Canada and Japan*. Chicago: University of Chicago Press, 1987.

Henderson, Stewart. 'Zone of Uncertainty: Canada and the Security Architecture of Asia Pacific.' *Canadian Foreign Policy* 1 (Winter 1992/93).

Hervouet, Gérard. 'Le Canada face a l'Espace Asie-Pacifique.' In Gerard Hervouet, ed., *Asie-Pacifique: Les Nouveaux Espaces de Coopération et de Conflits*. Sainte-Foy, QC: Les Presses de l'Université Laval, 1991.

Hervouet, Gérard, ed. *Asie-Pacifique: Les Nouveaux Espaces de Coopération et de Conflits*. Sainte-Foy, PQ: 1991.

Hesse, S. 'Japan's Chance for Quality ODA.' *Japan Times* 35, 192 (24 February 1997).

Higashi, Chikara, and G. Peter Lauter. *The Internationalization of the Japanese Economy*. Boston: Kluwer Academic Publisher, 1987.

Higgot, Richard. 'APEC – A Sceptical View.' In Andrew Mack and John Ravenhill, eds., *Pacific Cooperation: Building Economic and Security Regimes in the Asia-Pacific Region*. Boulder, CO: Westview Press, 1995.

Hirano, Minoru. *Gaiko Kisha Nikki: Fukuda Gaiko no Ichi Nen*. Tokyo: Seikaioraisha, 1977.

Hockin, Thomas. 'The Domestic Setting and Canadian Voluntarism.' In Lewis Hertzman et al., eds., *Alliances and Illusions*. Edmonton: M.G. Hurtig, 1969.

Hofstede, G. *Culture's Consequences: International Differences in Work-Related Values*. Beverly Hills, CA: Sage, 1980.

Holland, William L. 'Source Materials on the Institute of Pacific Relations.' *Pacific Affairs* 58 (Spring 1985).

Hollohan, Brian. 'The Magnificent Seven: A Primer on G-7 Summits.' *Canadian Business Review* (Autumn 1989).

Holloway, Nigel. 'An Idea before Its Time.' *Far Eastern Economic Review* (15 June 1989).

Holloway, Nigel, and Sebastian Moffet. 'Patchword Diplomacy.' *Far Eastern Economic Review* (23 November 1995).

Holmes, John, and John Kirton, eds. *Canada and the New Internationalism*. Toronto: Canadian Institute of International Affairs, 1988.

Holroyd, C., and K. Coates. *Pacific Partners: The Japanese Presence in Canadian Business, Society, and Culture*. Toronto: James Lorimer, 1996.

Holsti, Kal J. 'Canada and the United States.' In Steven L. Spiegel and Kenneth N. Waltz, eds., *Conflict in World Politics*. Cambridge, UK: Winthrop, 1971.

Homer-Dixon, T. 'On the Threshold.' *International Journal* 46 (1991).

Homer-Dixon, T., J. Boutwell, and G. Rathjens. 'Environmental Change and Violent Conflict.' *Scientific American* 268, 2 (February 1993).

Honda Announcement. 19 July 1994.

'Honda Expands Canadian Operations.' *Canada–Japan Trade Council Newsletter* (November–December 1995).

'Honda: Is It an American Car?' *Business Week* (18 November 1991).

Hooper, Paul F. 'The Institute of Pacific Relations and the Origins of Asian and Pacific Studies.' *Pacific Affairs* 61 (Spring 1988).

Hooper, Paul F., ed. *Remembering the Institute of Pacific Relations: The Memoirs of William L. Holland*. Tokyo: Ryukei Shosha, 1995.

– *Rediscovering the IPR: Proceedings of the First International Conference on the Institute of Pacific Relations.* Honolulu: Centre for Arts and Humanities, University of Hawaii, 1994.

Horioka, Charles Y. 'Future Trends in Japan's Saving Rate and Implications Thereof for Japan's External Imbalance.' *Japan and the World Economy* 3 (1991).

Hosokawa, Morihiro. 'Text of the Prime Minister's Diet Policy Speech.' *Japan Times* (24 August 1993).

Houghton, L., et al. *Climate Change 1994: Radiative Forcing of Climate Change and an Evaluation of the IPCCIS 92.* Cambridge, UK: Cambridge University Press, 1995.

Howell, Thomas R. et al., eds. *Conflict among Nations.* Boulder, CO: Westview Press, 1992.

Howes, John F., ed. *Nitobe Inazô: Japan's Bridge across the Pacific.* Boulder, CO: Westview Press, 1995.

Hung, C.L. 'Use of Business Alliances by Canadian Companies in Pacific Asia and the Role of Communication.' Paper presented at the Pacific Region Forum on Business and Management Communication, Simon Fraser University, British Columbia, 16 March 1994.

Hunt, Constance. 'Canadian Policy and the Export of Nuclear Energy.' *University of Toronto Law Journal* 27 (Winter 1977).

Ichimura, Shinichi. 'Regional Integration Issues in Asia.' Paper presented to the Eighth Asia Pacific Roundtable, Kuala Lumpur, June 1994.

Ikenberry, John. 'Salvaging the G-7.' *Foreign Affairs* 72 (Spring 1993).

Ikle, Fred Charles. *How Nations Negotiate.* New York: Harper and Row, 1964.

Illgen, Thomas. *Autonomy and Interdependence: U.S.–Western European Monetary and Trade Relations, 1958–1984.* New Jersey: Rowman & Allanheld, 1985.

Imai, Ryukichi. 'The Non-Proliferation Treaty and Japan.' *Bulletin of the Atomic Scientists* 25 (May 1968).

– 'Proliferation and the Indian Test: A View from Japan.' *Survival* 16 (September/ October 1974).

Imber, M.F. 'Environmental Security.' *Review of International Studies* 17 (1991).

Ina, Hisashi. 'Doubts over Cost-Effectiveness Shouldn't Shoot Down Missile-Defence Proposal.' *Nikkei Weekly* (10 October 1994).

Inoguchi, Takashi. 'Japan's Response to the Gulf Crisis, 1990–1991: An Analytic Overview.' *Journal of Japanese Studies* 17 (Summer 1991).

– *Japan's Foreign Policy in an Era of Global Change.* London: 1993.

– 'The New Security Setup and Japan's Options.' *Japan Echo* 23, 3 (Autumn 1996).

– 'Japan's United Nations Peacekeeping and Other Operations.' *International Journal.* 50 (Spring 1995).

International Energy Agency (IEA). *Energy Policies of IEA Countries*. Paris: Organization for Economic Cooperation and Development, 1990.

– *Coal Information 1992*. Paris: Organization for Economic Cooperation and Development, 1992.

– *Climate Change Policy Initiatives: 1994 Update*. Paris: Organization for Economic Cooperation and Development, 1994.

International Organization 28 (Autumn 1974). Special issue entitled *Canada and the United States: Transnational and Transgovernmental Relations*.

Investment Canada. 'Foreign Multinationals and Canada's International Competitiveness.' *Working Paper* 16. Ottawa: Investment Canada, 1993.

'Investors Have Confidence in Canada.' *Japan Times* (17 July 1994).

'Is Japan Unreformable?' *The Economist* (29 January 1994).

Ito, Toshiyuki. 'Kono: UNSC Seat Requires Full Support of the People.' *Daily Yomiuri* (31 August 1994).

Jack, I. 'Toyota Chief: We're Canadian.' *Financial Post* (13 February 1997).

– 'Sales Surge Forecast.' *Financial Post* (14 February 1997).

Jaffer, Fatima. 'APEC and Global Capitalist Imperialism: No No No, Absolutely Not!' *Kinesis* (December/January 1997).

Jaipal, Rikhi. 'The Indian Nuclear Explosion.' *International Security* 1 (Spring 1977).

Janow, Merit. 'Trading with an Ally: Progress and Discontent in U.S.–Japan Trade Relations.' In Gerald Curtis, ed., *The United States, Japan, and Asia*. New York: Norton, 1994.

Japan Automobile Manufacturers Association of Canada (JAMA). *JAMA Canada Annual Report 1993*. Toronto: JAMA Canada, 1993.

– *JAMA Canada Annual Report 1996*. Toronto: JAMA Canada, 1996.

Japan–Canada Forum 2000. *Partnership across the Pacific*. December 1992.

Japan Center for a Sustainable Environmental and Society. *Environment and Sustainable Development in Official Development Assistance since the 1992 Earth Summit*. Tokyo: JACSES, 1996.

Japan. Defence Agency. *Boei Hakusho (Defence White Paper), Heisei Go-Nenban*. Tokyo: Finance Ministry Printing Office, 1993.

– *Defence of Japan, 1994*. English edition. Tokyo: The Japan Times, July 1994.

Japan Economic Almanac: 1997. Tokyo: Nihon Keizai Shimbunsha, 1997.

Japan Economic Institute (JEI). *JEI Reports*. Various issues.

Japan. Economic Planning Agency. *EPA White Paper*. Various years.

Japan. Environment Agency. *1990 Quality of the Environment in Japan*. Tokyo: Environment Agency, 1991.

– *1992 Quality of the Environment in Japan*. Tokyo: Environment Agency, 1993.

Japan. Ministry of Finance. Institute of Fiscal and Monetary Policy. *The Mechanism and Economic Effects of Asset Price Fluctuations*. Tokyo: Ministry of Finance, 1993.

Japan. Ministry of Foreign Affairs (MOFA). 'Japan–U.S. Joint Declaration on Security, Alliance for the 21st Century. 17 April 1996. Unofficial translation, 9 pp.

Japan. Ministry of Foreign Affairs (MOFA). Economic Cooperation Bureau. 'ODA Summary 1996.' Tokyo: Association for the Promotion of International Cooperation (June 1996). (http://www.mofa.go.jp/oda/sum1996/index, htm).

Japan. Ministry of Transport. *Annual Report on the Transportation Economy, Summary (Fiscal 1990)*. Tokyo: Ministry of Transport, 1991.

Japan. Tsusho Sangyo Chosa Kai, ed. *Nichibei Kozo Mondai Kyogi Saishu Hokoku*. Tokyo: 1990.

Japan External Trade Organization. (JETRO). *Japanese Corporate Decision Making*. Tokyo: JETRO, 1982.

– (JETRO). *JETRO Report on Unfair Trade Policies*. Tokyo: JETRO, 1992.

– *U.S. and Japan in Figures II*. Tokyo: JETRO, 1992.

– *1993–94 Directory: Japanese–Affiliated Companies in U.S.A. and Canada*. Tokyo: JETRO, 1993.

– *JETRO Report on Unfair Trade Policies*. Tokyo: JETRO, 1993.

– *Nippon 1993: Business Facts and Figures*. Tokyo: JETRO, 1993.

– *JETRO White Paper on Foreign Direct Investment 1994*. Tokyo: JETRO, 1994.

– 'Eighth Annual JETRO Survey of Japanese-Affiliated Firms in Canada.' Toronto: JETRO, 1996. Photocopy.

Japan Review of International Affairs 7 (1993, Special Issue).

Japan Times. Various issues (see esp. 24 February 1997).

Japanese External Trade Organization. (JETRO). *Directory of Japanese-Affiliated Companies in U.S.A. and Canada: 1997–1998*. Tokyo: JETRO, 1996.

– *JETRO White Paper on Foreign Direct Investment, 1997*. Tokyo: JETRO, 1997.

Japanese Foreign Press Center. *Direct Overseas Investment Recorded in FY 1995*. Tokyo: Japanese Foreign Press Center, 1996.

'The Japanese Have a Yen for Mexico Again.' *Business Week* (28 November 1994).

Japanese Prime Minister's Advisory Group on Defence Issues. *The Modality of the Security and Defence Capability of Japan: Outlook for the 21st Century.* 12 August 1994.

'A Japanese Puzzle.' *The Economist* (19 June 1993).

Jeshurun, Chandran, ed. *China, India, Japan and the Security of Southeast Asia*. Singapore: 1993.

'Jieitai Goran Kogen Haken, "Keiko Buki" Minaoshi Kyumu' ('Self-Defence Force Golan Heights Dispatch, Pressing Need to Rethink Portable Weapons, Let's Learn from Canadian Forces'). *Yomiuri Shinbun* (4 November 1995).

Job, Brian. 'CSCAP Steering Committee Meeting.' *CANCAPS Bulletin* 3 (July 1994).

- 'Eighth Annual Asia-Pacific Roundtable.' *CANCAPS Bulletin* 3 (July 1994).
- 'CSCAP Finds Its Stride.' *CANCAPS Bulletin* 12 (February 1997).
Job, Brian, and Frank Langdon. 'The Evolving Security Order of the Asia Pacific: A Canadian Perspective.' *North Pacific Cooperative Security Dialogue (NPCSD) Working Paper* 15. North York, Ont.: Centre for International and Strategic Studies, York University, September 1992.
- 'Canada and the Pacific.' In Fen Osler Hampson and Christopher J. Maule, eds., *Canada among Nations 1993–94: Global Jeopardy.* Ottawa: Carleton University Press, 1993.
- 'Convergence and Divergence of Interests in the Changing Asia-Pacific Security Setting.' In Charles F. Doran et al., eds., *Pacific Partners: Canada and the United States.* Washington: Brassey's, 1994.
Johnson, Chalmers, and E.B. Keehn. 'The Pentagon's Ossified Strategy.' *Foreign Affairs* 743 (July/August 1995).
The Journal of Japanese Studies. Special Issue: A Forum on the Trade Crisis. 13, 2 (Summer 1987).
Kaneko, Kumao. 'A New Pacific Initiative: Strengthening the PECC Process.' *Japan Review of International Affairs* 2 (Spring/Summer 1988).
- 'An Analysis of Japanese Capability of Playing a Security Role in Asia.' In Kuang-sheng Liao, ed., *The New International Order in East Asia.* Hong Kong: Hong Kong Institute of Asia-Pacific Studies, Chinese University of Hong Kong, 1993.
Kapoor, A. *Planning for International Business Negotiations.* Cambridge, MA: Ballinger, 1975.
Kapoor, S.K. 'The Legality of Nuclear Testing: The Pokharan Explosion.' *Indian Journal of International Law* 14 (July–December 1974).
Kapur, Ashok. 'India and the Atom.' *Bulletin of the Atomic Scientists* 30 (September 1974).
- 'The Canadian–Indian Nuclear Negotiation: Some Hypotheses and Lessons.' *World Today.* 34 (August 1978).
Kase, Shoichi. *Kokusai Tsuuka Kiki.* Tokyo: Iwanamishoten, 1975.
Kashiwagi, Yusuke. *Gekidoki no Tsuuka Gaiko.* Tokyo: Kinyu Zeisei Jijo, 1973.
Katagiri, Nobuo. 'A Reappraisal of the Japanese Institute of Pacific Relations.' In Paul Hooper, ed., *Remembering the Institute of Pacific Relations: The Memoirs of William L. Holland.* Tokyo: Ryukei Shosha, 1995
Katagiri, Nobuo, and George M. Oshiro. 'The Beginnings of "An Adventure in Friendship": The Institute of Pacific Relations and Japan, 1925–1936.' *Journal of Shibusawa Studies* 5 (October 1992).
Katzenstein, Peter J., and Yutaka Tsujinaka. '"Bullying," "Buying," and "Binding": U.S.–Japanese Transnational Relations and Domestic Structures.' In Thomas Risse-

Kappen, ed., *Bringing Transnational Relations Back In*. Cambridge, UK: Cambridge University Press, 1995.

Kawasaki, Tsuyoshi. 'The Canadian–American Economic Relationship, 1963–1977: A Regime Analysis.' Unpublished MA thesis, University of Toronto, 1986.

– 'In Defence of Economic Sovereignty: The Japanese Ministry of Finance in Macroeconomic Diplomacy, 1985–1987.' *Asian Paper* 5. Toronto: University of Toronto–York University Joint Centre for Asia-Pacific Studies, 1993.

– 'Managing Macroeconomic Adjustments: Japanese Fiscal Policy in the Era of Global Capitalism.' Unpublished PhD dissertation, Princeton University, 1993.

– 'Policy Ideas and Change in Japanese Bureaucratic Politics: The Ministry of Finance in International Monetary Crisis, 1969–1971.' *Journal of Public Policy* 13 (April–June 1993).

– 'Pressing Japan for Fiscal Expansion: Lessons from the Late 1970s.' *The Pacific Review* 6 (1993).

– 'The Logic of Japanese Multilateralism.' *CANCAPS Bulletin* (May 1994).

– 'The Geostrategic Foundations of Peace and Prosperity in the Western Pacific Region.' *Working Paper* 3. Institute of International Relations, University of British Columbia, July 1994.

– 'The Logic of Japanese Multilateralism for Asia-Pacific Security.' *Working Paper* 8. Vancouver: Institute of International Relations, University of British Columbia, December 1994.

Keating, Tom. *Canada and the World Order: The Multilateral Tradition in Canadian Foreign Policy*. Toronto: McClelland and Stewart, 1993.

Keenan, G. 'Ontario Toyota Plant Quality Leader in North America.' *The Globe and Mail* (25 May 1995).

– 'Ottawa Dropping Tariff for Honda.' *The Globe and Mail* (20 December 1995).

– 'Toyota Plans $400 Million Retooling of Ontario Plant.' *The Globe and Mail* (6 February 1997).

Keenan, G., B. Jang, and A. Freeman. 'Canada Still Luring Investment.' *The Globe and Mail* (1 July 1995).

Kelly, Donald R., Kenneth R. Stunkel, and Richard R. Wescott. *The Economic Superpowers and the Environment: The United States, the Soviet Union, and Japan*. San Francisco: W.H. Freeman, 1976.

Keohane, Robert. 'The Theory of Hegemonic Stability and Change in International Economic Regimes, 1967–1977.' In Ole Holsti, et al., eds., *Change in the International System*. Boulder, CO: Westview Press, 1980.

– *After Hegemony: Cooperation and Discord in the World Political Economy*. Princeton, NJ: Princeton University Press, 1984.

– *International Institutions and State Power: Essays in International Relations Theory*. Boulder, CO: Westview Press, 1989.

– 'Multilateralism: An Agenda for Research.' *International Journal* 45 (Autumn 1990).

Keohane, Robert, and Joseph Nye, Jr. 'Transgovernmental Relations and International Organization.' *World Politics* 27 (October 1974).

– *Power and Interdependence*, 2nd ed. Glenview, IL: Scott, Foresman, 1989.

Keohane, Robert, and Helen V. Milner, eds. *Internationalization and Domestic Politics*. Cambridge, UK: Cambridge University Press, 1996.

Kernell, Samuel, ed. *Parallel Politics*. Washington, DC: The Brookings Institution, 1991.

Kikuchi, Tsutomu. 'Japan and Regional Cooperation in the Asia-Pacific Region.' In Kuang-sheng Liao, ed., *The New International Order in East Asia*. Hong Kong: Hong Kong Institute of Asia-Pacific Studies, Chinese University of Hong Kong, 1993.

Kimura, Masato, and David Welch. 'Specifying "Interests": Japan's Claim to the Northern Territories and Its Implications for International Relations Theory.' *Working Papers Series* 97-3. Harvard University Centre for International Affairs, March 1997.

Kindleberger, Charles. *The World in Depression, 1929–1939*. Berkeley, CA: University of California Press, 1973.

Kirton, John. 'Further Challenges.' In John Holmes and John Kirton, eds., *Canada and the New Internationalism*. Toronto: Canadian Institute of International Affairs, 1988.

– 'Managing Global Conflict: Canada and International Summitry.' In Maureen Molot and Brian Tomlin, eds., *Canada among Nations: A World of Conflict, 1987*. Toronto: Lorimer, 1988.

– 'Contemporary Concert Diplomacy: The Seven-Power Summit and the Management of International Order.' Paper delivered at the annual meeting of the International Studies Association, London, 29 March–1 April 1989. Available at http://www.g7.utoronto.ca.

– 'Liberating Kuwait?' In Don Munton and John Kirton, eds., *Canadian Foreign Policy: Selected Cases*. Scarborough, ON: Prentice-Hall, 1992.

– 'The Seven Power Summit as a New Security Institution.' In David Dewitt, David Haglund, and John Kirton, eds., *Building a New Global Order: Emerging Trends in International Security*. Toronto: Oxford University Press, 1993.

– 'National Mythology and Media Coverage.' *Political Communication* 10 (October–December 1993).

– 'Promoting Plurilateral Partnership: Managing United States–Canada Relations in the Post–Cold War Period.' *The American Review of Canadian Studies* 24 (Winter 1994).

– 'The Diplomacy of Concert: Canada, the G-7, and the Halifax Summit.' *Canadian Foreign Policy* 3 (Spring 1995).

- 'Canada and APEC: Contributions and Challenges.' *Asia-Pacific Papers* 3 (May 1997).
- 'Le rôle du G7 dans le couple intégration régionale/sécurité globale.' *Études internationales* 28 (juin 1997).

Kirton, John, and Robert Bothwell. 'A Proud and Powerful Country: American Attitudes toward Canada, 1963–1976.' *Queen's Quarterly* 92 (Spring 1985).
- 'A Very Necessary Country: American Attitudes toward Canada, 1976–1980.' *Queen's Quarterly* 93 (Summer 1986).

Kissinger, Henry. *White House Years.* Boston: Little, Brown, 1979.

Kitamura, H. 'The Position of Canada in Japan's Diplomatic Framework.' *Pacific Affairs* 64 (1991).

Kitaoka, Shinichi. 'The Case for a Stronger Security Treaty.' *Japan Echo* 23 (Summer 1996).
- 'Okinawa and the Security Treaty.' *Japan Echo* 23 (Autumn 1996).

Kobayashi, Tomohiko. *The Japanese Perspective on the Toronto Economic Summit and the Uruguay Round.* Toronto: Centre for International Studies, 1988.

Krasner, Stephen. *Defending the National Interest: Raw Materials Investments and U.S. Foreign Policy.* Princeton: Princeton University Press, 1978.

Krauss, Ellis S., and Simon Reich. 'Ideology, Interests and the American Executive: Toward a Theory of Foreign Competition and Manufacturing Trade Policy.' *International Organization* 46, 4 (Autumn 1992).

Kristof, Nicholas. 'Doubts Rising in Okinawa on Giving Up U.S. Bases.' *New York Times* (2 June 1996).

Kurosawa, Mitsuru. 'Comparing Japanese and Canadian National Security Policies in Connection with the U.S.' *Hosei Riron (Niigata University)* 23 (1991).

Kurosawa, Mitsuru, and John Kirton, eds. *Taiheiyo Kokka no Toraianguru: Gendai no Nichibeika Kankei.* Tokyo: Sairyusha Press, 1995.

Laliberté, Lucie. 'Foreign Investment in the Canadian Bond Market.' *Canadian Economic Observer* (June 1991).

Lall, Arthur. *Modern International Negotiation.* New York: Columbia University Press, 1966.

Lang, J. 'Biological Conservation and Biological Diversity.' In G. Sjostedt, ed., *International Environmental Negotiation.* Newbury Park, Calif.: Sage Publications, 1993.

Langdon, Frank. 'Japanese Reactions to India's Nuclear Explosion.' *Pacific Affairs* 48 (Summer 1975).
- *The Politics of Canadian–Japanese Economic Relations, 1952–1983.* Vancouver: University of British Columbia Press, 1983.
- 'Canada and the Growing Presence of Asia.' *Occasional Paper* 9. Vancouver: Institute of Asian Research, University of British Columbia, 1990.

– 'Japan and Minor Powers in Pacific Security.' *Proceedings of the Japan Studies Association of Canada Annual Meeting, Edmonton, 30 September–2 October 1994.* Ottawa: Japan Studies Association of Canada, 1994.

Larwson, Arthur. *Questions and Answers on the Spread of Nuclear Weapons.* Durham, NC: Rule of Law Research Centre, Duke University School of Law, April 1968.

Lattimore, Owen. *Ordeal by Slander.* New York: Bantam Books, 1950.

– *China Memoirs: Chiang Kai-Shek and the War Against Japan.* Tokyo: University of Tokyo Press, 1990.

Lauren, Paul Gordon., ed. *The China Hands' Legacy: Ethics and Diplomacy.* Boulder, CO: Westview, 1987.

Lawrence, Robert Z. 'Imports on Japan: Closed Markets or Minds?' *Brookings Papers on Economic Activity* 2 (1988).

– 'How Open Is Japan.' In Paul Krugman, ed., *Trade with Japan.* Chicago: University of Chicago Press, 1991.

Lebow, Richard Ned. *The Art of Bargaining.* Baltimore: John Hopkins University Press, 1996.

Legault, Albert, and Michael Fortmann. *A Diplomacy of Hope: Canada and Disarmament 1945–1988.* Montreal and Kingston: McGill-Queen's University Press, 1992.

Leyton-Brown, David, and Joseph Jockel, eds. 'Weathering the Calm: The State of the Canada–United States Relationship.' *The American Review of Canadian Studies* 24 (1994).

Liao, Kuang-sheng, ed. *The New International Order in East Asia.* Hong Kong: 1993.

Lincoln, Edward J. *Japan: Facing Economic Maturity.* Washington, DC: The Brookings Institute, 1988.

– *Japan's Unequal Trade.* Washington, DC: Institute for International Economics, 1990.

'Local Content Should Not Be Used to Buy Trade Policy.' *Nikkei Weekly* (14 March 1992).

Low, Linda. 'The East Asian Economic Grouping.' *Pacific Review* 4 (1991).

Luck, Edward. 'Layers of Security.' *Asian Survey* 35 (March 1995).

Magosaki, Ukeru. *Kanada no Kyokun.* Tokyo: Daiamondosha, 1992.

– 'Taibei Senryaku wa Kanada ni Manabe.' *Chuokoron* (December 1992).

Mahbubani, Kishore. 'The Pacific Way.' *Foreign Affairs* 74 (January/February 1995).

Manne, A.S., and R.G. Richels. *Global CO_2 Emission Reductions: The Impacts of Rising Energy Costs.* Menlo Park, Calif.: Electric Power Research Institute, 1990.

Mark, R. 'Japanese Direct Investment in Canada.' *The Canadian* [Tokyo] 3 (1992).

Marks, Thomas. 'The Acquisition of Nuclear Weapons by Japan.' *Military Review* 53 (March 1973).

Martin, Lawrence. *The Presidents and Prime Ministers: Washington and Ottawa Face to Face, the Myth of Bilateral Bliss, 1867–1982.* Toronto: Doubleday, 1982.

Martin, Paul. *Canada and the Quest for Peace.* New York: Columbia University Press, 1967.

Martin, Pierre, and Michel Fortman. 'Canadian Opinion and Peacekeeping in a Turbulent World.' *International Journal* 50 (Spring 1995).

Maruyama, Magoroh. 'Changing Dimensions in International Business.' *Academy of Management Executive* 6 (1992).

Maruyama, Masao. 'Affection for the Lesser Names: An Appreciation of E.H. Norman.' *Pacific Affairs* 30 (September 1957).

Mastanduno, Michael. 'Do Relative Gains Matter?' *International Security* 16 (Summer 1991).

– 'Setting Market Access Priorities: The Use of Super 301 in U.S. Trade with Japan.' *The World Economy* 15 (November 1992).

Mathieson, Robert. 'Pan Pacific Regionalism: Reactions of Japan and Asia to NAFTA.' June 1992. Photocopy.

Matsumoto, M. 'Politically Wary Honda Opens Mexico Plant.' *Nikkei Weekly* (19 September 1994).

Matthew, R., and L. Boownsey, eds. *Japan's Relations with North America: The New Pacific Interface.* Vancouver: The North American Institute, 1990.

Maull, H. 'Japan's Global Environmental Policies.' *Pacific Review* 4 (1991).

McCormack, James. 'The Japanese Way: The Relationship between Financial Institutions and Non-Financial Firms.' *Policy Staff Paper* 94/16. Ottawa: Department of Foreign Affairs and International Trade, 1994.

McInnis, Edgar, President, CIIA, to William L. Holland, Secretary-General, IPR, 16 October 1957. Institute of Pacific Relations Papers. Special Collections. University of British Columbia. Box 42, File 10.

McMillan, Charles J. *Comparing Canadian and Japanese Approaches to the Seven Power Summit.* Toronto: Centre for International Studies, 1988.

– 'Bridge across the Pacific: Trade and Investment.' In John Schultz and Kimitada Miwa, eds., *Canada and Japan in the Twentieth Century.* Toronto: Oxford University Press Canada, 1991.

– *Building Blocks or Trade Blocks: NAFTA, Japan and the New World Order.* Ottawa: Canada–Japan Trade Council, 1993.

Merchant, Livingston T., and A.D.P. Heeney. *Principles for Partnership: Canada and the United States.* Washington, DC: The U.S. Department of State, 1965.

Meyer, A.H. *Assignment: Tokyo.* Indianapolis: Bobbs-Merrill, 1974.

Mikanagi, Yumiko. *Japan's Trade Policy.* London: Routledge, 1995.

Miki, Takeo. 'Japan's Reservation.' *Survival* 9 (May 1967).

Milner, Helen. 'International Theories of Cooperation among Nations: Strengths and Weaknesses.' *World Politics* 44 (April 1992).

Minden, Karen, John Kirton, and Steve Parker. *Linking the APEC Community:*

Canada's Objectives for APEC 1997. Vancouver: Asia Pacific Foundation of Canada, 1997.

Miwa, Kimitada. 'E.H. Norman Revisited.' In John Schultz and Kimitada Miwa, eds., *Canada and Japan in the Twentieth Century*. Toronto: Oxford University Press, 1991.

Miyagi, Etsuji. 'Redressing the Okinawan Base Problem.' *Japan Quarterly* 43 (January–March 1996).

Miyazaki, 'Time to Reevaluate the Security Treaty.' *Japan Quarterly* 37, 4 (October–December 1990).

Mochizuki, Mike, and Michael O'Harlon. 'The Marines Should Come Home.' *Brookings Review* 14 (Spring 1996).

Moffet, Sebastian, and Nigel Holloway. 'Uncertain Future: Is the U.S.–Japan Alliance Past Its Prime?' *Far Eastern Economic Review* (23 November 1995).

Molot, Maureen Appel. 'The Role of Institutions in Canada–United States Relations: The Case of North American Financial Ties.' In Andrew Axline et al., eds., *Continental Community?: Independence and Integration in North America*. Toronto: McClelland and Stewart, 1974.

Molot, Maureen, and Brian W. Tomlin, eds. *Canada among Nations* (various issues 1984–86). Toronto: James Lorimer.

Morganthau, Hans. *Politics among Nations: The Struggle for Power and Peace*. New York: Knopf, 1948.

Mori, Chiharu. 'Bei, O, Ajia, Shin-Kozu eno Omowaku' ('America, Europe, and Asia from the Perspective of a New Configuration'). *Yomiuri Shinbun* (2 February 1996).

Morimoto, Satoshi. 'Regional Dialogues and Processes in Northeast Asia and the North Pacific Region: Prospects and Obstacles.' Paper presented to the Eighth Asia Pacific Roundtable, Kuala Lumpur, June 1994.

Morimoto, Satoshi, and Tsutomu Kikuchi. 'Security Issues and Studies in Japan.' In Paul M. Evans, ed., *Studying Asia Pacific Security: The Future of Research Training and Dialogue Activities*. Toronto: Joint Centre for Asia-Pacific Studies, University of Toronto–York University, 1994.

Morris, J. 'Japanese Manufacturing Investment in Canada: Regional Presence and Integration Strategies.' In J. Morris, ed., *Japan and the Global Economy: Issues and Trends in the 1990s*. London: Routledge, 1991.

– 'Globalisation and Global Localisation: Explaining Trends in Japanese Foreign Manufacturing Investment.' In J. Morris, ed., *Japan and the Global Economy: Issues and Trends in the 1990s*. London: Routledge, 1991.

Mueller, John E. 'Incentives for Restraint: Canada as a Non-Nuclear Power.' *Orbis* 11 (Fall 1967).

Murakami, A. 'UNEP Director Urges Environment-Friendly Aid.' *Japan Times* (24 August 1993).

Murata, Kiyoaki. 'Japan and Non-Proliferation.' *Survival* 9 (May 1967).

Myers, N. 'The Environmental Dimension to Security Issues.' *The Environmentalist* 6 (1986).

Nagao, K. 'Globalization Processes of Japanese Automobile Production: Some Evidence from Southern Ontario.' Paper presented to a seminar at the Centre for Japanese Research, University of British Columbia, 1997.

Nagara, Bunn, and K.S. Balakarishnan, eds., *The Making of a Security Community in the Asia-Pacific.* Kuala Lumpur: ISIS Malaysia, 1994.

Naka, Norio. *Predicting Outcomes in United States–Japan Trade Negotiations.* Westport, CT: Quorum Books, 1996.

Nakamura, Masao, and Ilan Vertinsky. *Japanese Economic Policies and Growth: Implications for Businesses in Canada and North America.* Edmonton: University of Alberta Press, 1998, forthcoming.

Narine, Shaun. 'Evaluating the ASEAN Regional Forum: The Limits of the "ASEAN Way."' *CANCAPS Bulletin* 10 (August 1996).

– 'The ARF and CSCAP.' *CANCAPS Bulletin* 12 (February 1997).

National Planning Association. *The Nth Country Problem and Arms Control.* New York: National Planning Association, 1960.

National Round Table on the Environment and the Economy (NRTEE). *Canada–Japan Workshop on the Environment: a Summary of the Discussion.* Ottawa: NRTEE, 1991.

Nemetz, Peter N., ed. *The Pacific Rim: Investment, Development and Trade, Second Revised Edition.* Vancouver: UBC Press, 1990.

New York Times. Various issues.

NHK Shuzaihan. *Nippon no Jyoken Mane 1: Hendo Soba no Jidai.* Tokyo: Nihon Hoso Kyokai, 1981.

Nicolson, Harold. *Diplomacy.* New York: Brace and Company, 1939.

Nihon Hoso (NHK) Shuppan Kyokai. *Nichibei no Shototsu.* Tokyo: Nihon Hoso Shuppan Kyokai, 1990.

Nihon Keizai Shimbun. Various issues.

Nikiforuk, A., and E. Struzik. 'The Great Forest Sell-Off.' *The Globe and Mail Report on Business Magazine* (November 1989).

Nikkei Weekly. Various issues.

Niosi, Jorge. 'The Place of Canada in MNE Location Decision.' Paper presented to the Conference on Multinationals in North America, Ottawa, 19–21 May 1993.

Nixon, Richard. *Public Papers of the President: Richard Nixon, 1971.* Washington, DC: The U.S. Government Printing Office, 1972.

Noble, John. 'Canada's Continuing Search for Acceptable Nuclear Safeguards.' *International Perspectives.* July/August 1978.

North Pacific Cooperative Security Dialogue (NPCSD). 'North Pacific Cooperative

Security Dialogue: Recent Trends.' *NPCSD Working Paper Number 1*, January 1992, in 'Canada in Asia Pacific Security in the 1990s.'

Nossal, Kim Richard. *The Politics of Canadian Foreign Policy*, Third Ed. Scarborough, ON: Prentice-Hall, 1997.

Nye, Joseph S., Jr. 'Transnational Relations and Interstate Conflicts: An Empirical Analysis.' *International Organization* 28 (Autumn 1974).

– 'The Case for Deep Engagement.' *Foreign Affairs* 74 (July/August, 1995).

Obasi, G., and Tolba, M. 'Preface.' In WMO/UNEP, *Climate Change: The IPCC Response Strategies*. Washington, DC: Island Press, 1991.

Ochiai, Kotaro. *Nichibei Keizai Masatsu Zohoban*. Tokyo: Keiotsushin, 1994.

Odell, John. *U.S. International Monetary Policy: Markets, Power and Ideas as Sources of Change*. Princeton, NJ: Princeton University Press, 1982.

'Offshore Airfield Promises Big Rewards.' *Nikkei Weekly* (16 December 1996).

Ogawa, Yoshihiko. 'Ratification of the Nuclear Non-Proliferation Treaty.' *Jurist* (1 August 1975).

O'Grady, S., and H.W. Lane. 'Culture: An Unnoticed Barrier to Canadian Retail Performance in the United States.' Paper presented at the annual meeting of the Academy of International Business, Brussels, November 1992.

Ogura, Kazuo. *Nichibei Keizai Masatsu*. Tokyo: Asahi Shinbunsha, 1991.

Ohara, Yuko. 'J.W. Dafoe and Japanese–Canadian Relations during the 1920s.' In John Schultz and Kimitada Miwa, eds., *Canada and Japan in the Twentieth Century*. Toronto: Oxford University Press, 1991.

Okamoto, Yukio. 'Why We Still Need the Security Treaty.' *Japan Echo* 22 (Winter 1995).

Okimoto, Daniel. 'Japan's Non-Proliferation Policy: The Problem of the NPT.' *Asian Survey* (May 1975).

'Okinawa Report Draws Mixed Reviews.' *Nikkei Weekly* (9 December 1996), 4.

Organization for Economic Cooperation and Development (OECD).

– *OECD Environmental Data: Compendium 1989*. Paris: OECD, 1989.

– *OECD Environmental Data: Compendium 1993*. Paris: OECD, 1993.

– *OECD Environmental Data: Compendium 1995*. Paris: OECD, 1995.

– *OECD Environmental Performance Reviews: Japan*. Paris: OECD, 1993.

– *OECD Environmental Performance Reviews: Canada*. Paris: OECD, 1995.

Orme, W.A. *Understanding NAFTA: Mexico, Free Trade and the New North America*. Austin, TX: University of Texas Press, 1996.

Oshiro, George M. 'Internationalist in Pre-War Japan: Nitobe Inazo, 1862–1933.' Unpublished PhD dissertation, University of British Columbia, 1985.

– 'A Reevaluation of the Life and Work of Nitobe Inazô.' In Michio Yamaoka,. ed., *International Relations of the Asia-Pacific Region in the Dawn of a New Era: Studies on the Institute of Pacific Relations.* Tokyo: Institute of Social Sciences, Waseda University, 1994.

Ota, Hiroshi. 'Non-Proliferation: Risks and Controls.' *Japanese Annual of International Law* 22 (1978).

Ota, Takashi. *Kokusai Kinyu: Genba Kara no Shogen.* Tokyo: Chuokoronsha, 1991.

Owada, Hisashi. 'A Japanese Perspective on the Role and Future of the G7.' *International Spectator* 29 (April/June 1994), special issue.

Owen, Lattimore. *Ordeal by Slander.* New York: Bantam Books, 1950.

– *China Memoirs: Chiang Kai-shek and the War against Japan.* Tokyo: University of Tokyo Press, 1990.

Oye, Kenneth A. *Economic Discrimination and Political Exchange.* Princeton, NJ: Princeton University Press, 1992.

Oye, Kenneth A., ed. *Cooperation under Anarchy.* Princeton, NJ: Princeton University Press, 1986.

Palmer, Norman D. *The New Regionalism in Asia and the Pacific.* Lexington, MA: Lexington Books, 1991.

Paltiel, Jeremy. 'Japan's Innovative East Asian Policies: Keeping the Flying Geese in Formation.' In J. Kovalio, ed., *Japan in Focus.* North York, ON: Captus Press, 1994.

Parboni, Riccardo. 'The Dollar Weapon: From Nixon to Reagan.' *New Left Review* 158 (July–August 1986).

Park, J. 'Japanese Policy on Climate Change.' *Social Sciences Japan* 4 (August 1995).

Parker, P. 'Japanese Environmental Policies and Technology Trade.' In J. Kovalio, ed., *Japan in Focus.* Ottawa: Captus Press, 1994.

– 'Japan and the Global Environment.' In D. Rumley et al., eds., *Global Geopolitical Change and the Asia Pacific.* Aldershot, UK: Ashgate, 1996.

Parker, P., ed. *Pacific Coal Trade: Energy or Environmental Priorities.* Canberra: Australia–Japan Research Centre, 1993.

Partnership across the Pacific. Report of the Canada–Japan Forum 2000, December 1992.

Pearson, Lester B. 'Force for UN.' *Foreign Affairs* 35 (1956–57).

– 'Keeping the Peace.' *External Affairs* 16 (1964).

– *Mike: The Memoirs of Lester B. Pearson, Vol. 2, 1948–1957.* Toronto: University of Toronto Press, 1973.

Pempel, T.J. 'Japan's Nuclear Allergy.' *Current History* 68 (April 1975).

– *Policy and Politics in Japan: Creative Conservatism.* Philadelphia: Temple University Press, 1982.

'People and Places.' *Asia Pacific Report* 21, 1 (Spring 1997).

Peterson, R.B., and J.Y. Shimada. 'Sources of Management Problems in Japanese–American Joint Ventures.' *Academy of Management Review* 3 (1978).

Pierce, J., N. Lovrich, T. Tsurutani, and T. Abe. *Public Knowledge and Environmental Politics in Japan and the United States*. Boulder, CO: Westview Press, 1989.

Plumptre, A.F.W. *Three Decades of Decision*. Toronto: McClelland and Stewart, 1977.

Polomka, Peter. 'Asia Pacific Security: Towards a Pacific House.' *Australian Journal of International Affairs* 44 (December 1990).

Porges, Amelia. 'U.S.–Japan Trade Negotiations: Paradigms Lost.' In Paul Krugman, ed., *Trade With Japan*. Chicago: University of Chicago Press, 1991.

Powell, Robert. 'Anarchy in International Relations Theory: The Neorealist–Neoliberal Debate.' *International Organization* 48 (Spring 1994).

Pratt, Larry, and Ian Urquart. *The Last Great Forest: Japanese Multinationals and Alberta's Northern Forests*. Edmonton: NeWest Press, 1994.

'Premier Pledges Active Role if UNSC Bid Is Successful.' *Yomiuri Shimbun* (6 October 1994).

Prestowitz, C.V. *Trading Places*. New York: Basic Books, 1989.

'Prime Minister Chrétien Visits Japan.' *Canada–Japan Trade Council Newsletter*.

'Prime Minister Chrétien Visits Japan.' *Japan Report* 44, 5 (October–December 1996).

Pringsheim, Klaus. *Neighbours across the Pacific: The Development of Economic and Political Relations between Canada and Japan*. Westport, CT: Greenwood Press, 1983.

Public Papers of the President, Richard Nixon, 1972. Washington, DC: U.S. Government Printing Office (USGPO), 1972.

Public Papers of the President of the United States, Jimmy Carter, 1980–81. 1981 (I), 1982 (II, III) Washington, DC: USGPO, 1982.

Public Papers of the President of the United States, Ronald Reagan. 1981, 1982 (I, II), 1983 (I, II), 1984 (I, II), 1985 (I, II), 1986 (I, II), 1987 (I, II), 1988 (I), 1988–89 (II). Washington, DC: USGPO, 1981–91.

Putnam, Robert. 'Diplomacy and Domestic Politics: The Logic of Two Level Games.' *International Organization* 42 (Summer 1988).

Putnam, Robert, and Nicholas Bayne. *Hanging Together: Cooperation and Conflict in the Seven Power Summits, Revised and Enlarged Ed.* Cambridge, MA: Harvard University Press, 1987.

Putnam, Robert, and C. Randall Henning. 'The Bonn Summit of 1978: A Case Study in Coordination.' In Richard N. Cooper et al., eds., *Can Nations Agree? Issues in International Economic Cooperation*. Washington, DC: The Brookings Institution, 1989.

Pyle, Kenneth B., ed. *A Forum on the Trade Crisis*. Washington, DC: Society of Japanese Studies, 1987.

Quester, George. 'Japan and the Nuclear Non-Proliferation Treaty.' *Asian Survey* 10 (September 1970).

Quo, F. Quei. 'Japan's Role in Asia: A United States Surrogate?' *International Journal* 38 (Spring 1983).

Raiffa, Howard. *The Art and Science of Negotiation*, Cambridge, MA: Harvard University Press, 1982.

Reford, Robert. 'Peacekeeping at Suez, 1956.' In Don Munton and John Kirton, eds., *Canadian Foreign Policy: Selected Cases*. Scarborough, ON: Prentice-Hall, 1992.

Reid, Escott M. *Time of Fear and Hope: The Making of the North Atlantic Treaty 1947–49*. Toronto: McClelland and Stewart, 1977.

Reston, James. *The Lone Star: The Life of John Connally*. New York: Harper and Row, 1989.

Richardson, T. 'Reaping the Yen: Japan's Stake in Canada.' *Canadian Business* (August 1990).

Robertson, G., and T.R. Waggener. 'The Japanese Market for Softwood and Changing Pacific Rim Wood Conditions: Implications for the U.S.' *CINTRAFOR WP* 52. Seattle, WA: College of Forest Resources, University of Washington.

Ronen, S., and A.I. Kraut. 'Similarities among Countries Based on Employee Work Values and Attitudes.' *Columbia Journal of World Business* 12 (1977).

Root, F.R. *Entry Strategies for International Markets*. Lexington, MA: LexingtonBooks, 1987.

Rosati, Jerel A. 'Developing a Systemic Decision-Making Framework.' *World Politics* 33 (January 1981).

Ross, Douglas A. 'Canadian Foreign Policy and the Pacific Rim: From National Security Anxiety to Creative Economic Cooperation?' In F. Quei Quo., ed., *Politics of the Pacific Rim: Perspectives on the 1980s*. Burnaby, BC: SFU Publications, 1982.

Royal Commission on the Future of the Toronto Waterfront (RCFTW). *Regeneration: Toronto's Waterfront and the Sustainable City*. Toronto: Queen's Printer for Ontario, 1992.

Rudner, Martin. 'Canadian Development Assistance to Asia: Programs, Objectives, and Future Policy Directions.' *Canadian Foreign Policy* 1 (Fall 1993).

– 'APEC: The Challenges of Asia Pacific Economic Cooperation.' *Modern Asian Studies* 29 (May 1995).

Rugman, Alan M. *Japanese Direct Investment in Canada*. Ottawa: Canada–Japan Trade Council, 1990.

Sagami, Takehiro. 'Tenno Heika to En no Kiriage.' *Shukan Toyo Keizai* (16 October 1982).

Saito, Shiro. *Japan at the Summit: Japan's New Role in the Western Alliance and Asian Pacific Cooperation*. London: Routledge, 1990.

Sakurada, Daizo. *Japan and the Management of the International Political Economy: Japan's Seven Power Summit Diplomacy*. Toronto: Centre for International Studies, University of Toronto, 1988.

- 'Sengo Kanada Gaiko Seisaku no Rironteki Tenkai: Hozu no Riron Ruikei o Chushin ni.' *Gaiko Jiho* 1278 (May 1991).
- 'For Mutual Benefits: The Japan–U.S. Security Treaty from a Japanese Perspective.' *CSS Working Paper.* Wellington, NZ: Centre for Strategic Studies, 1997.
- 'Japanese External Policy in the Post-Cold-War Era: The Emerging Consensus in Uncertainty.' *Social Sciences Research (University of Tokushima)* 10 (1997).
Sakurada, Daizo, and Patricia Lynn Elmhirst. 'The Myth of Constraints on Canadian Foreign Policy: Quebec and the "Nixon Shocks" of 1971.' *Bulletin of Shinshu Junior College* 5 (1993).
Sanwa Bank, 'Responding to Rising Costs due to the Greying of the Japanese Population.' *Economic Letter (Sanwa Bank)* (August 1992).
- 'The Effects of Increased Domestic Demand and the Yen Appreciation on Reducing Japan's Trade Surplus.' *Economic Letter (Sanwa Bank)* (October 1992).
Sato, Hideo. 'A Japanese Perspective.' In Wendy Dobson, ed., *Canadian–Japanese Economic Relations in a Triangular Perspective.* Toronto: C.D. Howe Institute, 1987.
- *Taigai Seisaku,* Tokyo: University of Tokyo Press, 1989.
- *Nichibei Keizai Masatsu, 1945–1990.* Tokyo: Heibonsha, 1991.
Sato, Saizaburo. 'Security in the Asia Pacific Region: Threats, Risks and Opportunities.' Paper presented to the Eighth Asia Pacific Roundtable, Kuala Lumpur, June 1994.
Saxonhouse, Gary. *The Economics of the U.S.–Japan Framework Talks.* Stanford, CT: Hoover Institution, 1994.
Scalapino, Robert A. 'The United States and Asia: Future Prospects' *Foreign Affairs* 70 (Winter 1991/1992).
Schelling, Thomas. *The Strategy of Conflict.* New York: Oxford University Press, 1963.
Schoppa, Leonard J. 'Two-Level Games and Bargaining Outcomes: Why *Gaiatsu* Succeeds in Japan in Some Cases but Not Others.' *International Organization* 47 (Summer 1993).
- *Bargaining with Japan.* New York: Columbia University Press, 1997.
Schultz, John, and Kimitada Miwa, eds. *Canada and Japan in the Twentieth Century.* Toronto: Oxford University Press, 1991.
- *Kanada to Nihon: 21 Seiki eno Kakehashi.* Tokyo: Sairyusha Press, 1991.
'SDJP Drafts Policy to Scale Down SDF.' *Daily Yomiuri* (1 September 1994).
Sebenius, James. 'Challenging Conventional Explanations of International Cooperation: Negotiation Analysis and the Case of Epistemic Communities.' *International Organization* 46 (Winter 1992).
- 'The Law of the Sea Conference: Lessons for Negotiations to Control Global Warming.' In G. Sjostedt, ed., *International Environmental Negotiation.* Newbury Park, CA: Sage Publications, 1993.
Seki, Hiroharu. 'Nuclear Proliferation and Our Options.' *Japan Quarterly* 22 (January–March 1975).
Sekiguchi, Sueo. 'The Structural Impediments Initiative and Recent Japan–U.S. Rela-

tions.' In Peter Gourevitch and Paolo Guerrieri, eds., *New Challenges to International Cooperation*. Manuscript, 1993.

Selin, Shannon. 'Asia Pacific Arms Buildups Part One: Scope, Causes and Problems.' *Working Paper* 6. Vancouver: Institute for International Relations, University of British Columbia, November 1994.

– 'Asia Pacific Arms Buildups Part Two: Prospects for Control.' *Working Paper* 7. Vancouver: Institute for International Relations, University of British Columbia, November 1994.

Shale, Tony. 'The MOF's Get-Fit Class.' *Euromoney* (May 1992).

Sharp, Mitchell. *Which Reminds Me: A Memoir*. Toronto: University of Toronto Press, 1994.

Shaw, R. 'Acid-Rain Negotiations in North America and Europe: A Study in Contrast.' In G. Sjostedt, ed., *International Environmental Negotiation*. Newbury Park, CA: Sage Publications, 1993.

'Shin-Boei Keikaku Taiku (National Defence Outline).' *Daily Yomiuri* (29 November 1995).

Shiota, Ushio. *Kasumigaseki ga Furueta Hi*. Tokyo: Simul Press, 1983.

– *Issen-nichi no Joho: En wa Doru ni Kattanoka*. Tokyo: Shinchosha, 1988.

– '"Shudan-teki Jieiken" Nado Shuten ni, Genjitsu Chokushi no Kenpo Rongi e Kyo Kenpo Kinenbi' ('Focus on Right of Collective Self-Defence, Etc., Facing Up to a Realistic Debate on the Constitution on Constitution Day'). *Yomiuri Shinbun* (3 May 1994).

Sinhal, I.K., and Keith A.J. Hay. *Dispute Settlement Mechanisms: Lessons for Canada–Japan Commercial Relations*. Ottawa: Canada–Japan Trade Council, 1993.

Smith, Gary. 'Multilateralism and Regional Security in Asia: The ASEAN Regional Forum (ARF) and APEC's Geopolitical Value.' *CANCAPS Bulletin* 13 (September 1996).

– 'New Dimensions in Asia Pacific.' Address to the Canadian Institute of International Affairs Conference on Trends in Canadian Foreign Policy, Kingston, ON, January 1994. In *Canada and Asia Pacific Security in the 1990s*. Canadian Consortium on Asia Pacific Security [CANCAPS] Paper No. 1 (March 1994).

Smith, Gary, and Sinclair, Jill. 'Arms Control and Security Building in Asia-Pacific: A Canadian Perspective.' *Canada on Asia Pacific Security in the 1990s*. Canadian Consortium on Asia Pacific Security [CANCAPS] Paper No. 1 (March 1994).

Soesastro, Hadi. 'Economic Development: The Security Impact.' In Bunn Nagara and K.S. Balakarishnan, eds., *The Making of a Security Community in the Asia-Pacific*. Kuala Lumpur: ISIS Malaysia, 1994.

– 'The Pan-Pacific Movement: An Interpretative History.' In Barbara K. Bundy, Stephen D. Burns, and Kimberley V. Weichel, eds. *The Future of the Pacific Rim: Scenarios for Regional Cooperation*. Westport, CT: Praeger, 1994.

Soeya, Yoshihide. 'Japan's Policy towards Southeast Asia: Anatomy of Autonomous

Diplomacy and the American Factor.' In Chandran Jeshurun, ed., *China, India, Japan and the Security of Southeast Asia*. Singapore: Institute of Southeast Asian Studies, 1993.

– 'The Evolution of Japanese Thinking and Policies on Cooperative Security in the 1980s and 1990s.' *Australian Journal of International Affairs* 48 (May 1994).

Sokolsky, Joel. 'Great Ideals and Uneasy Compromises.' *International Journal* 50 (Spring 1995).

Solomon, Hyman. 'Summit Reflections.' *International Perspectives* (July/August 1988).

Solomon, Robert. *The International Monetary System, 1945–1976*. New York: Harper & Row, 1977.

'South Korea Opposed to Giving Veto Power to Japan.' *Daily Yomiuri* (5 October 1994).

Spy, Graham. 'Canada, the United Nations Emergency Force, and the Commonwealth.' *International Affairs* 33 (July 1957).

Stairs, Denis. 'Choosing Multilateralism.' *CANCAPS Papier* 4 (July 1994).

Statements and Speeches. Various issues.

Statistics Canada. *Canada's International Investment Position*. Cat. 67-202.

– *Travel Between Canada and Other Countries*. Cat. 66-001.

Stein, Arthur. *Why Nations Cooperate*. Ithaca, NY: Cornell University Press, 1990.

Stein, Janice Gross, ed. *Getting to the Table*. Baltimore: Johns Hopkins University Press, 1989.

Stein, Janice Gross, and Louis W. Pauly, eds. *Choosing to Cooperate: How States Avoid Loss*. Baltimore: Johns Hopkins University Press, 1993.

Stern, R.M. ed. *Trade and Investment Relations among the United States, Canada and Japan*. Chicago: University of Chicago Press, 1989.

Stewart, Walter. 'The Week of the Great Ultimatum.' *Maclean's* (March 1972).

Strange, Susan. *States and Markets*. New York: Basil Blackwell, 1988.

Strauss, A.L. *Negotiations, Varieties, Contexts, Process, and Social Order*. San Francisco: Jossey-Bass, 1978.

Stubbs, Richard. 'Reluctant Leader, Expectant Followers: Japan and Southeast Asia.' *International Journal* 46 (Autumn 1991).

Stubbs, T. 'Japanese Travel Market Growth and Change, 1952–1983.' *Working Paper* 10 Canada and the Changing Economy of the Pacific Rim. Vancouver: Institute of Asian Research, University of British Columbia, 1988.

Sumiya, F. 'Toyota to Hike North American Output 50 Percent.' *Nikkei Weekly* 19 (September 1994).

Summary of the address and answers by Mitchell Sharp to Canada–U.S. Relations Colloquium at the University of Toronto, 23 November 1979.

Sung-Joo, Han. 'South Korean Perspectives on International and Regional Security

Issues.' Paper for Workshop on Changing Perceptions of National Military Security, 28–29 August 1992.

Szell, P. 'Negotiations on the Ozone Layer.' In G. Sjostedt, ed., *International Environmental Negotiation*. Newbury Park, CA: Sage Publications, 1993.

Tackaberry, R.B. 'Keeping the Peace.' *Behind the Headlines* 26 (September, 1966).

– 'Organizing and Training Peace-Keeping Forces: The Canadian View.' *International Journal* 22 (1966–67).

Tadae, Takubo. 'The Okinawan Threat to the Security Treaty.' *Japan Echo* 23 (Fall 1996).

Takahashi, Kazuo. 'Challenges of Civilization.' Paper presented to the Eighth Asia Pacific Roundtable, Kuala Lumpur, June 1994.

Takeuchi, Kenji. 'Does Japan Import Less Than It Should? A Review of the Econometric Literature.' *Asian Economic Journal* (September 1989).

– 'Managed Trade vs. Free Trade in Japan's Trade Policy.' *Journal of Asian Economics* 3 (1992).

Tasker, Rodney, and Adam Schwartz. 'ASEAN: Preventive Measures.' *Far Eastern Economic Review* 157 (11 August 1994).

Taylor, Alastair M. 'Peacekeeping: The International Context.' In Alastair M. Taylor et al, eds., *Peacekeeping: International Challenge and Canadian Response*. Toronto: Canadian Institute of International Affairs, 1968.

Thayer, Nathaniel B., and Stephen E. Weiss. 'Japan: The Changing Logic of a Former Minor Power.' In Hans Binnendijk, ed., *National Negotiating Styles*. Washington, DC: Foreign Service Institute, U.S. Department of State, 1987.

Thomas, John N. *The Institute of Pacific Relations: Asian Scholars and American Politics*. Seattle: University of Washington Press, 1974.

Thordarson, Bruce. *Trudeau and Foreign Policy: A Study in Decision Making*. Toronto: Oxford University Press, 1972.

Thornell, M, and K.J. Pringsheim. *Japanese Travel to Canada*. Ottawa: Canada–Japan Trade Council, 1993.

Tiessen, J. *Canada–Japan Trade Perspectives*. Ottawa: Canada–Japan Trade Council, 1996.

Tourism Canada. *Proceedings, Canada–Japan Tourism Conference*. Montreal, 21 September 1993. Ottawa, 1993. Photocopy.

– 'Meeting Highlights: Japan MOT Challenge Canada Committee Meeting.' Vancouver, 23 February 1994. Photocopy.

Tow, William T. 'Northeast Asia and International Security: Transforming Competition into Collaboration.' *Australian Journal of International Affairs* 46 (May 1992).

– 'Contending Security Approaches in the Asia-Pacific Region.' *Security Studies* 3 (Autumn 1993).

– 'Reshaping Asian-Pacific Security.' *Journal of East Asian Affairs* 8 (1994).

'"Trading System" Would Let Nations Pay for Pollution.' *Japan Times* 35, 188 (20 February 1997).

Tung, R.L. *Business Negotiations with the Japanese.* Lexington, MA: D.C. Heath, 1984.

– *Key to Japan's Economic Strength: Human Power.* Lexington, MA: D.C. Heath, 1984.

– 'Toward a Conceptual Paradigm of International Business Negotiations.' In R.D. Farmer, ed., *Advances in International Comparative Management*, Vol. 3. Greenwich, CT: JAI Press, 1988.

– 'Strategic Management Thought in East Asia.' *Organizational Dynamics* 22 (1994).

'Two Japanese Firms Moving Out of Quebec.' *Mainichi Daily News* (3 September 1995).

Tyson, Laura D'Andrea. *Who's Bashing Whom? Trade Conflict in High-Technology Industries.* Washington, DC: Institute of International Economics, 1992.

Ui, Jun., ed. *Industrial Pollution in Japan.* Tokyo: United Nations University Press, 1992.

Umeda. 'Strong Yen Boosts Overseas Touring.' In *Nikkei Weekly*, ed., *Japan Almanac 1996.* Tokyo: Nihon Keizai Shimbunsha, 1996.

United Nations Environment Program (UNEP). *Environmental Data Report, 1991–92.* Oxford: Blackwell Publishers, 1991.

– *Environmental Data Report, 1993–94.* Oxford: Blackwell Publishers, 1993.

– T. Kira., ed., *Compact-Size Edition of Data Book of World Lake Environments.* Kusatsu: International Lake Environmental Committee Foundation and Lake Biwa Research Institute, 1995.

United Nations. Department of Public Information. *The Blue Helmets: A Review of United Nations Peace-Keeping*, 2nd ed. New York: 1990.

United States Congress. Senate. Committee on Finance. Subcommittee on International Trade. *United States–Japan Structural Impediments Initiative (SII).* 101st Congress, 1st session (part 2 of 3), 6–7 November 1989.

– *United States–Japan Structural Impediments Initiative.* 101st Congress, 2nd session (part 3 of 3), 5 March 1990.

– *United States–Japan Trade Relations.* 101st Congress, 2nd session, 25 April 1990.

United States Congress. House Committee on Foreign Affairs. *United States–Japan Economic Relations: Structural Impediments Initiative.* 101st Congress, 2nd session, 20 February and 19 April 1990.

United States. Department of Defense. 'A Strategic Framework for the Asia Pacific Rim: Looking toward 21st Century.' April 1990.

United States. Department of Defense. Office of the Assistant Secretary of Defense for

International Security Affairs (East Asia and Pacific Region). 'A Strategic Framework for the Asia Pacific Rim.' *Report to Congress.* 1992.

United States. Department of Defense. Office of International Security Affairs. *United States Security Strategy for the East Asia–Pacific Region.* 27 February 1995.

United States Government. *United States–Japan Structural Impediments Initiative (Parts 1–3).* Hearings before the Subcommittee on International Trade of the Senate Committee on Finance, July 1989, November 1989, and March 1990.

– *Joint Report of the U.S.–Japan Working Group on the Structural Impediments Initiative.* 28 June 1990.

– *First Annual Report of the U.S.–Japan Working Group on the Structural Impediments Initiative.* 22 May 1991.

– *Second Annual Report of the U.S.–Japan Working Group on the Structural Impediments Initiative.* 30 June 1992.

United States International Trade Commission. *Phase II: Japan's Distribution System and Options for Improving US Access.* USITC Publication 2327, 1990.

Ursacki, Terry. 'The Internationalization of the Japanese Pulp and Paper Industry: Implications for Canada.' *University of British Columbia Forest Economics and Policy Analysis Research Unit Working Paper* 172 (1992).

Ursacki, Terry, and Ilan Vertinsky. 'Canada–Japan Trade in an Asia-Pacific Context.' *Pacific Affairs* 69 (Summer 1996).

Ushiba, Nobuhiko. *Gaiko no Shunkan.* Tokyo: Nihon Keizai Shimbunsha, 1984.

Van Cleave, William, and S.T. Cohen. 'Nuclear Aspects of Future U.S. Security Policy in Asia.' *Orbis* 19 (Fall 1995).

Van Wolferen, Karel. *The Enigma of Japanese Power: People and Politics in a Stateless Nation.* London: Macmillan, 1989.

Van Zandt, H.F. 'How to Negotiate in Japan?' *Harvard Business Review* (November–December 1970).

Vancouver *Courier.* Various issues.

Vancouver *Sun.* Various issues.

Volcker, Paul, and Toyoo Gyohten. *Changing Fortunes: The World's Money and the Threat to American Leadership.* New York: Times Books, 1992.

Volger, John. 'Interdependence, Power, and the World Administrative Radio Conference.' In R.J. Barry Jones and Peter Willetts, eds., *Interdependence on Trial: Studies in the Theory and Reality of Contemporary Interdependence.* London: Frances Printer, 1984.

Von Furstenberg, George M., and Joseph Daniels. 'Policy Undertakings by the Seven "Summit" Countries: Ascertaining the Degree of Compliance.' *Carnegie-Rochester Conference Series on Public Policy* 35 (Autumn 1991).

– 'Economic Summit Declarations 1975–1989: Examining the Written Record of International Cooperation.' *Princeton Studies in International Finance* 72 (February 1992).

Wagner, J. Richard, and Daniel O'Neil. 'Canadian Penetration of the American Political Process: A Case Study.' Paper presented at Western Social Science Association Annual Meeting, Lake Tahoe, Nevada, 26–27 April 1979.

Wagner, R. Harrison. 'Economic Interdependence, Bargaining Power, and Political Influence.' *International Organization* 42 (Summer 1988).

Walczak, James R. 'Legal Implications of the Indian Nuclear Development.' *Denver Journal of International Law and Policy* 4 (Fall 1974).

Waldie, P. 'Canada Losing Sole TV Tube Factory.' *The Globe and Mail* (23 March 1996).

Wallace, William. 'Political Issues at the Summit: A New Concert of Powers.' In Cesare Merlini, ed., *Economic Summits and Western Decisionmaking*. London: Croom-Helm, 1984.

Walton, Richard, and Robert B. McKersie. *A Behavioral Theory of Negotiations*. New York: McGraw Hill, 1965.

– *A Behavioral Theory of Labor Negotiations*. Ithaca, NY: ILR Press, 1965.

Webb, Michael C. 'International Economic Structures, Government Interests, and International Coordination of Macroeconomic Adjustment Policies.' *International Organization* 45 (Summer 1991).

Welch, David. 'The New Multilateralism and Evolving Security System.' In Fen Osler Hampson and Christopher Maule, eds., *Canada among Nations, 1992–1993: A New World Order?* Ottawa: Carleton University Press, 1992.

– 'The Organizational Process and Bureaucratic Politics Paradigms.' *International Security* 17 (Fall 1992).

Westney, D. Eleanor. 'Japanese Investments in North American Bloc.' Paper presented to the Conference on Multinationals in North America, Ottawa, 19–21 May 1993.

Whitaker, Reg, and Gary Marcuse. *Cold War Canada: The Making of a National Insecurity State, 1945–1957*. Toronto: University of Toronto Press, 1994.

'Why America's Levers Will Not Shift Leveraged Japan.' *The Economist* (5 February 1994)

Williams, D. Colwyn. 'Canada and International Peace-Keeping Operations.' *Saskatchewan Bar Review* 29 (March 1964).

– 'International Peacekeeping: Canada's Role.' In Ronald MacDonald et al., eds., *Canadian Perspectives on International Law and Organization*. Toronto: University of Toronto Press, 1974.

Williams, R.H. *Low Cost Strategies for Coping with Carbon Dioxide Emission Limits*. Princeton, NJ: Princeton University, Center for Energy and Environmental Studies, 1989.

Wilson, Sandra. 'The Manchurian Crisis and Moderate Japanese Intellectuals: The Japan Council of the Institute of Pacific Relations.' *Modern Asian Studies* 26 (July 1992).

Winham, Gilbert R. 'Negotiation as a Management Process.' *World Politics* 30 (October 1977).

Wiseman, Geoffrey. 'Common Security in the Asia-Pacific Region.' *Pacific Review* 5 (1992).

'A Wobbly Time for Japan's Workers.' *The Economist* (18 December 1993).

'Women's Conference Warns of Threat to Food Security from Trade Reforms.' *Japan Times* (18 November 1996).

Wood, C. *The Bubble Economy: The Japanese Economic Collapse.* London: Sidgwick and Jackson, 1992.

Woods, Lawrence T. 'The Business of Canada's Pacific Relations.' *Canadian Journal of Administrative Sciences* 4 (December 1987).

– 'Japanese and Australian Approaches to Regional Economic Diplomacy.' *Asia Pacific Review* 8 (Winter 1988).

– 'Nongovernmental Organizations and Pacific Cooperation: Back to the Future?' *Pacific Review* 4 (1991).

– *Asia-Pacific Diplomacy: Nongovernmental Organizations and International Relations.* Vancouver: UBC Press, 1993.

– 'Clinton Sheepless in Seattle as APEC Wary of U.S. Role,' *APRRC Newsletter* 3 (January 1994).

– 'The Asia-Pacific Policy Network in Canada.' *Pacific Review* 7 (1994).

– 'Economic Cooperation and Human Rights in the Asia-Pacific: The Role of Regional Institutions.' In James T.H. Tang, ed., *Human Rights and International Relations in the Asia-Pacific Region.* London: Pinter Publishers, 1995.

– 'Implications for Theory and Practice Arising from Canadian Participation in the Institute of Pacific Relations: A Research Agenda.' In Paul F. Hooper, ed., *Remembering the Institute of Pacific Relation: The Memoirs of William L. Holland.* Tokyo: Ryukei Shosha, 1995.

– 'Learning from NGO Proponents of Asia-Pacific Regionalism: Success and Its Lessons.' *Asian Survey* 35 (September 1995).

– 'Recipient Dependence and the Redemption of a Philanthropic Villain: The Rockefeller Foundation's Support of the Institute of Pacific Relations and the Canadian Institute of International Affairs.' Paper presented to the Association of Asian Studies, Honolulu, Hawaii, 11–44 April 1996.

– 'A Voyage of Rediscovery.' Victoria *Times Colonist* (11 February 1997).

World Bank, *World Development Report 1995: Workers in an Integrating World.* Oxford: Oxford University Press, 1995.

World Commission on Environment and Development (WCED). G.H. Brundtland, chair. *Our Common Future.* Oxford: Oxford University Press, 1987.

Wright, Gerald. 'Persuasive Influence: The Case of the Interest Equalization Tax.' In

Andrew Axline et al., eds., *Continental Community?: Independence and Integration in North America*. Toronto: McClelland and Stewart, 1974.

– 'Cooperation and Independence: Canada's Management of Financial Relations with the United States, 1963–1968.' Unpublished PhD dissertation, Johns Hopkins University, 1976.

Wright, Gerald, and Maureen Appel Molot. 'Capital Movements and Government Control.' *International Organization* 28 (Autumn 1974).

Wright, Richard W. *Japanese Investment in Canada: The Elusive Alliance*. Montreal: The Institute for Research on Public Policy, 1984.

– 'The Unrealistic Hopes for Japanese Foreign Investment.' *Financial Times of Canada* (26 March 1990).

– 'Head for the Rising Sun.' *Business Quarterly* 59 (Winter 1994).

– *Japanese Finance in Transformation: Implications for Canada*. Ottawa: Canada–Japan Trade Council, 1994.

– 'Hidden Linkages in Japanese Business.' In Wendy Dobson and A.E. Safarian, eds., *East Asian Capitalism: Diversity and Dynamism*. Toronto: University of Toronto Press, 1996.

– 'A Big Bang for Japan?' *Canada–Japan Trade Council Newsletter* (January–February 1997).

Yabunaka, Mitoji. *Taibei Keizai Kosho*. Tokyo: Simul Press, 1991.

Yamakage, Susumu. 'Sogoizonron.' In Makoto Aruga et al., eds., *Koza Kokusaiseiji 1: Kokusaiseiji no Riron*. Tokyo: University of Tokyo Press, 1989.

Yamamoto, Yoshinaru. *Sengo Nihon Gaikoshi 5, Keizai Taikoku eno Fuatso*. Tokyo: Sanseido, 1984).

Yamamoto, Yoshinobu. *Kokusaiteki Sogoizon*. Tokyo: University of Tokyo Press, 1989.

Yamamura, Kozo, ed. *Policy and Trade Issues of the Japanese Economy*. Seattle: University of Washington Press, 1982.

– *Japan's Economic Structure: Should it Change?* Seattle: Society for Japan Studies, 1990.

Yamaoka, Michio. 'The Activities of the Japan Branch of the IPR in the Pre-War Era.' In Paul Hooper, ed., *Rediscovering the IPR: Proceedings of the First International Conference on the Institute of Pacific Relations*. Honolulu: Center for Arts and Humanities, University of Hawaii, 1994.

Yanagida, Kunio. *Nippon wa Moeteiruka*. Tokyo: Kodansha, 1983.

Yanai, Shunji. 'Law Concerning Cooperation for United Nations Peace-Keeping Operations and Other Operations.' *Japanese Journal of International Affairs* 36 (1993).

Yarborough, Beth V., and Robert M. Yarborough. *Cooperation and Government in International Trade*. Princeton, NJ: Princeton University Press, 1992.

Yatabe, Atsuhiko. 'A Note on the Treaty on the Non-Proliferation of Nuclear Weapons: The Japanese Point of View.' *Japanese Annual of International Law* 14 (1970).

Yomiuri Shinbun. Various issues.

Yoshino, Toshihiko. *En to Doru: Endaka eno Kiseki to Haikei.* Tokyo: Sanseido, 1984.

Young, H. Peyton. *Negotiation Analysis.* Ann Arbor, MI: The University of Michigan Press, 1991.

Young, Oran R. 'Strategic Interaction and Bargaining.' In Oran R. Young, ed., *Bargaining: Formal Theories of Negotiation.* Urbana, IL: University of Illinois Press, 1975.

Yuasa, Hiroshi. *En to Doru no Kobo.* Tokyo: Asuka Shinsha, 1988.

Zartman, I. William, and Maureen R. Berman. *The Practical Negotiator.* New Haven, CT: Yale University Press, 1982.

Zielinski, Robert, and Nigel Holloway, *Unequal Equities: Power and Risks in Japan's Stock Market.* Tokyo: Kodansha International, 1991.

Index

Access and Cross Services Agreement, 173, 176
Andrews, David, 54
Angola, 201
Anti-Monopoly Law, 81
Appel Molot, Maureen, 53
Arctic Waters Pollution Prevention Act, 21
Armacost, Michael H., U.S. Ambassador to Japan, 73
arms control, 4, 5, 187, 254; and anti-personnel landmines, 5, 182
arms race, 6
Aron, Raymond, 251
Asia Pacific Economic Cooperation Forum (APEC), 5, 167, 173, 180–81, 210, 229–30, 259, 262, 265, 282–83, 285, 286, 300; and East Asian Economic Grouping, 284; and Leaders Economic Vision Statement, 229
Asia Pacific Roundtable (APR), 286
Association of Southeast Asian Nations (ASEAN), 172–73, 178–81, 188, 259, 277, 283–87; and Asia Pacific Dialogue, 283
Association of Southeast Asian Nations Post Ministerial Conference (ASEAN-PMC), 5, 283, 285
Association of Southeast Asian Nations Regional Forum (ARF), 5, 11, 168, 174, 180, 182, 285, 287–88
Australia, 268, 280, 282–84

balance of payments policy, 37; and imbalances, 37, 40
Bank for International Settlements (BIS), 114
Beatty, Perrin, 263
Benson, Edgar, Finance Minister, Canada, 22
Bently, Peter, 263
Black Monday (1987), 51
Boundary Waters Treaty, 210
Bretton Woods monetary system, 19, 42, 43
Brody, Kenneth, 268
Burma, 178, 281
Burns, Arthur, Chairman of the U.S. Federal Reserve Board, 24, 30, 31
Bush, George, President of the United States, 61, 66, 67, 68, 77, 78, 79, 81, 168, 215, 308

Cambodia, 4, 173, 175, 196–200
Campbell, Kim, Prime Minister of Canada, 263, 310
Canada, 237; and 'Action Plan for Japan,' 142, 149, 156–58; and Alberta, 237, 245, 263–64; and Bank of Canada, 27; and banking services, 257; and British Columbia, 237, 244–45, 310; and Canadian dollar, 20, 21, 22, 23, 27, 97; and Department of Foreign Affairs and International Trade (DFAIT), 142, 186, 210, 251, 263–64; and Education System, 258; and Embassy in Tokyo, 245–47, 264; and Environmental Assessment and Review Process, 225; and environmental issues, 228; and exchange rate regime maintenance, 8; and exports, 11, 21, 157, 237, 256–57, 263; and foreign exchange reserves, 47; and Foreign Investment Review Agency (FIRA), 257; and foreign policy, 245, 269; and Foreign Policy Committee of the National Round Table on the Environment and Economy, 228; and interprovincial trade barriers, 253; and Japanese investment, 4, 8, 11, 85–88, 94, 135, 137, 157, 244–48; and Japanese tourism, 8, 97, 98, 237; and job creation, 256; and Ministry of Finance, 38; and Ontario, 237, 246, 263; and provincial regulations, 257; and Quebec, 12, 237, 249; and Soviet–Canada détente, 21; and taxation policies, 257; and trade, 238
Canada–Japan Business Association, 244
Canada–Japan Environmental Conference, 228
Canada–Japan Forum 2000, 11, 173, 249, 251–77, 287; Global Issues Task Force, 228; Task Forces, 270–71
Canada–Japan Workshop on the Environment, 228
Canada–Korea Forum, 179
Canada–United States Autopact (1965), 8, 17, 23, 27, 97
Canada–United States Balance of Payments Committee, 54
Canada–United States Free Trade Agreement (CUFTA), 4, 36, 38, 87, 94, 135, 142, 143, 228, 253, 260
Canada–United States Interparliamentary Group, 23
Canadian–American Committee, 30
Canadian Chamber of Commerce in Japan, 244
Canadian Consortium on Asia-Pacific Security (CANCAPS), 286–87
Canadian Institute of International Affairs (CIIA), 278, 280
Canadian International Development Agency (CIDA), 286
'capital mobility hypothesis,' 54
Carnegie Corporation, 280
Carter, Jimmy, President of the United States, 44, 45, 50, 54, 306
Centre for Conflict Prevention and Resolution, 266
Centre for International and Security Studies, 172
chemical weapons, 182
China. See People's Republic of China
Chrétien, Jean, Prime Minister of Canada, 11, 182, 263–64
Clark, Joe, 169, 172, 179, 275, 282, 310
Climate Change Convention, 213–15
Clinton, William J., President of the United States, 61, 82, 177, 180, 213
Cold War, the, 4, 167–68, 170, 174, 178, 183, 196, 239, 242; end of, 254

Conference on Security and Co-operation in Asia, 283
Conference on Security and Co-operation in Europe (CSCE), 239
Congo, 198
Connolly, John, Secretary of the Treasury, United States, 22, 23, 24, 27, 30
Council on Security Co-operation in Asia Pacific (CSCAP), 5, 11, 169, 172, 174, 179, 277, 279, 285–88
cross-national political alliances, 64
Cyprus, 201, 205

'debt crisis,' 307–8
defence policy, 9
Defence White Paper, 172
Denmark, 24
development, 258; assistance, 10, 12

Earth Day, 213
Earth Summit, 213, 227–28, 230
East Asian–European Union Summit Meeting (ASEM), 180
Economic Framework talks, 82
El Salvador, 202
Employment Support Act, 22
environment, 10, 93, 182, 253, 261–63, 265, 308; and 'Agenda 21,' 220; and environmental technology management, 227; and habitat protection, 221–22; and impact assessment, 224–25; and protected areas, 223; and technology transfers, 229; and voluntary targets, 213
European Community (EC), 293
exchange rate policy, 7, 37, 39–41, 50–52, 64; and fixed exchange rates, 19, 42, 43; and trade, 244

fiscal policy, 7, 39, 40, 41

foreign aid, 261, 268; policies, 187
foreign exchange market, 50, 51, 52
foreign investment, 4, 7, 37, 43, 254–57, 259–61, 264, 266–67, 269; and barriers, 260
Framework Convention on Climate Change, 213, 215
France, 25
Fukuda, Takeo, Prime Minister of Japan, 44, 45, 49, 50, 54, 306

gaiatsu, 61, 75
General Agreement on Tariffs and Trade (GATT), 19, 65, 68, 79, 306; and Kennedy Round, 22; and Uruguay Round, 11, 262, 265
Germany, 41, 227
globalization, 12, 60
Golan Heights, 175–6, 182
Gorbachev, Mikhail, 167
'governmental politics' model, 19
Gramm-Rudman-Hollings law, 51
Great Lakes, 210, 220
Greece, 205
Group of Five Finance Ministers, 52. See also Group of Seven Finance Ministers
Group of Seven (G-7), 5, 11, 12, 38, 44, 54, 68, 72, 79, 142, 210, 230, 237, 255, 260–61, 265, 291–310
Group of Seven Finance Ministers, 67
Group of Ten (G-10), 26, 27
Gulf War (1990–91), the, 3, 4, 97, 172–73, 199, 204, 206, 242
Gyohten, Toyoo, 43

Haiti, 201
Haotian, Chi, Chinese Defence Minister, 178
Hashimoto, Prime Minister of Japan, 171, 176–77, 182

Hawke, Bob, Prime Minister of Australia, 180, 284
Head, Ivan, 24
Hills, Carla, Head of USTR, 67, 71, 77
Hirohito, Emperor of Japan, 26
Hosaka, Prime Minister of Japan, 174
human rights, 178, 187, 253, 262, 266, 268

Income Equalization Tax, 46
India, 201, 281
Indo-China truce commissions, 259
Indonesia, 198, 281, 285
Institute of Pacific Relations (IPR), 277–88
Institute of Strategic and International Studies Malaysia (ISIS Malaysia), 286–87
Interest Equalizaton Tax, 21, 29, 38, 42, 43, 47, 48
Intergovernmental Panel on Climate Change (IPCC), 214–15
International Monetary Fund (IMF), 67, 262, 300
International Nickel Company of Canada (INCO), 218–19
International Union for the Conservation of Nature (IUCN), 222
Iran, 201
Iraq, 201

Japan, 240; and aging population, 8, 126, 127, 128, 129; and allied occupation, 279; and Bank of Japan (BOJ), 24, 25, 28, 109; and 'bubble economy,' 55, 85, 109, 245; and Democratic Socialist Party, 175; and direct investment overseas, 8, 9, 78, 85, 87, 89, 90, 106, 130, 131, 132, 134, 141; and economic agenda, 251; and Economic Planning Agency, 70, 74, 80, 115; and exports, 50, 124; and external trade surplus, 9, 123, 125; and Fair Trade Commission, 70, 74; and fiscal policy, 50; and foreign policy, 61, 171; and House of Councillors, 69; and Japanese External Trade Organization (JETRO), 86, 88, 101; and Japanese Management and Coordination Agency, 108; and Japanese Ministry of Agriculture, 26; and Japanese Ministry of Finance (MOF), 24–26, 28, 43, 44, 67, 69, 78, 116, 118, 119; and the Japanese Ministry of Foreign Affairs (MOFA), 69, 80; and Japanese Ministry of International Trade and Industry (MITI), 25, 26, 69, 80, 82, 258; and Japanese National Land Agency, 117; and Japanese National Tourist Organization (JNTO), 97; and Liberal Democratic Party, 8, 24, 63, 66, 68, 69, 72, 75, 78, 174–76, 199; and National Defence Program Outline (NDPO), 175; and New Frontier Party, 170, 176; and New Pioneers Party, 175–76; and peace-keeping deployments, 12; and 'post-bubble' economic changes, 8, 100, 106, 119, 125; and Research Institute of Construction and Economy, 117; and role in Asia, 245; and Social Democratic Party, 171, 175; and 'Ten Million Program' (1987), 97; and trade imbalances, 51, 64, 66, 97; and yen, 20, 22, 25–28, 45, 51, 85, 88, 97, 116, 124
Japan–Canada Fund for Mutual Understanding, 258, 264
Japanese Self-Defence Forces, 175–76, 182, 196, 199–204, 206, 241
Johnson, Lyndon, President of the United

States, 19, 40, 41, 42, 43; and 'Great Society' program, 19
Joint Canada–Japan Economic Committee, 252
Joint Canada–United States Committee on Trade and Economic Affairs, 53
joint ventures, 259

Keehn, E.B., 169
keiretsu, 267
Kennedy, John F., President of the United States, 40, 41, 42
Kenney Wallace, Geraldine, 263, 265
Kissinger, Henry, National Security Advisor, United States, 24, 30, 31, 296
Korean War, 259
Kuwait, 201

labour codes, 268
Large-Retail Store Law, 81
League of Nations, 190, 279
Lebanon, 201
Lester B. Pearson Canadian International Training Centre, 172
Lord, Winston, 269
Lougheed, Peter, former Premier of Alberta, 252, 256–57, 262
Louvre Accord, 52

Mahathir bin Mohamed, Prime Minister of Malaysia, 181, 277
Malaysia, 267
Mandatory Capital Control measures, 38, 42, 43, 48
McCarthyism, 278
Mexico, 284
Mieno, Yasushi, Governor of the Bank of Japan, 116
Miki, Takeo, Prime Minister of Japan, 306

Miyazawa, Prime Minister of Japan, 227, 308
Mizuta, Mikio, Finance Minister, Japan, 27
monetary policy, 7, 19, 39, 40, 41, 45
Montreal Protocol on Substances That Deplete the Ozone Layer, 212, 215, 230
Mozambique, 4, 202
Mulroney, Brian, Prime Minister of Canada, 243, 251, 256–57, 262, 293, 308
Muruyama, Tomiichi, Prime Minister of Japan, 171, 174

Nakasone, Yasuhiro, Prime Minister of Japan, 44, 45, 51, 52, 284, 293–95, 308
Namibia, 201
Nara, Yasuhiko, Japanese Ambassador to Canada, 293
National Coal Association, 218
'national compliance,' 304
Netherlands, 198
New Zealand, 265, 280
Nichi-Bei Kozo Mondai Kyogi (Japanese–American Discussions of Structural Problems), 69
Nitobe, Inazo, 277–88
Nixon regime, 20, 24, 26, 30, 306
Nixon, Richard, President of the United States, 18, 23, 24, 25, 26, 29; and 'New Economic Policy,' 20, 24, 25
Nixon Shocks ('Nixon Shokku'), 17, 18, 20, 21, 24, 25, 27–29, 31, 297
Non-governmental organizations, 258, 278–79; and the environment, 215, 226, 230
Norman, E. Herbert, 277
North American Aerospace Defence Command (NORAD), 5, 29, 174, 190, 197

North American Free Trade Agreement
(NAFTA), 4, 8, 86–88, 94, 95, 97, 100,
101, 134, 135, 253, 259, 262, 266, 300
North Atlantic Treaty Organization
(NATO), 21, 26, 172, 185, 189, 197,
203, 205, 239, 242; and defence burden sharing, 26
North Korea, Democratic People's
Republic of, 4, 6, 167, 179, 239–40,
266, 281
North Pacific Co-operative Security Dialogue (NPCSD), 5, 10, 169, 172, 188,
282–84, 286–87
nuclear weapons and deterrence, 6, 179,
182, 189, 254, 266, 294, 307
Nye, Joseph, 168–69

Official Development Assistance (ODA),
225–27, 230
Ohira, Masayoshi, Prime Minister of
Japan, 44, 49, 50, 306
oil shock, 295
Okinawa reversion treaty, 24, 26
Okita, Saburo, Director of the Economic
Planning Agency, 280
Omnibus Trade and Competitiveness Act
(1988) (also known as the Super 301),
67, 68, 72, 75, 77
Ontario Hydro Electric Company, 218
Organization for Economic Cooperation
and Development (OECD), 67, 127
'organizational process' model, 19
Ouellet, André, Foreign Minister of Can-
ada, 243
Ozawa, Ichiro, 170, 176

Pacific Basin Economic Council (PECC),
11, 259, 281–84
Pacific Trade and Development Conference (PAFTAD), 11, 281

Pakistan, 201
'parallel politics,' 66
Pearson, Lester B., Prime Minister of
Canada, 197–98, 202
People's Republic of China (PRC), 4, 6,
11, 26, 30, 190, 219, 239–40, 266–67,
269, 279, 308
Pepin, Jean-Luc, Trade Minister, Can-
ada, 22
Philippines, 265
Plaza Accord, 51, 52, 88, 109
Post-Ministerial Conference (PMC),
180–81
President's Advisory Committee on
Trade Policy and Negotiations, 67
Putnam, Robert, 71, 80

Ramsar Convention on Wetlands of Inter-
national Importance, 223
Rasminsky, Louis, Bank of Canada Gov-
ernor, 47, 48
Reagan, Ronald, President of the United
States, 44, 45, 51, 52, 213, 308
Recruit Cosmos Scandal, 68
regionalism, 13
Reisman, Simon, Deputy Minister of
Finance, Canada, 20, 21, 27, 28
'relative capability,' 295, 298–99,
301–4
research and development, 228, 257
Rim of the Pacific (RIMPAC) exercises,
172–73
Rockefeller Foundation, 280
Russia, 4, 6, 190, 240–41, 265–66, 309.
See also Soviet Union
Russian reforms, 3
Rwanda, 202

Sasaki, Tadashi, BOJ Governor, 26
Sato, Eisaku, Prime Minister of Japan,

21, 24, 25, 28, 43; and the Nixon Shocks, 21, 24

Schmidt, Helmut, 310

security, 4, 6, 8, 9, 11, 12, 13, 141, 167–79, 185–86, 209, 239, 251, 254, 261, 277, 285, 287–88

Sharp, Mitchell, External Affairs Minister, Canada, 22

Shin, Kanemaru, 78

Smithsonian Settlement, 26

South Korea, 219, 240, 265

Southeast Nations Regional Forum (ARF), 171

Soviet Union, 21, 30, 189, 239, 309; and Soviet–Canada detente, 21. *See also* Russia

Special Action Committee on Okinawa (SACO), 177

Strange, Susan, 63

Structural Impediments Initiative (1989–90), 8, 61–3, 66–9, 71, 72, 75, 78–81; and the SII working group, 69

Suez Crisis, 197, 205

Super 301. *See* Omnibus Trade and Competitive Act

surcharge crisis (1971), 5, 8, 17, 20–25, 27, 29

Syria, 175

Taiwan, 26, 177–78

technology, 268–69; transfers, 261

Tiananmen Massacre, 178, 309

Tokyo Convention on High Seas Fisheries in the North-East Pacific Ocean, 228

Tokyo Declaration on Financing Global Environment and Development, 226

tourism, 8, 98, 259, 268

trade, 7, 157–9, 187, 244–45, 254–55, 259–61, 266, 269; and environment, 227; and multilateral trade system, 12, 19; and trade barriers, 22, 62, 65, 244, 260, 264; and trade disputes, 210; and trade liberalization, 12, 23, 293; and trade negotiations, 3, 62, 65

Trade and Tariff Act (1974), 67

transactions costs, 266

transgovernmental alliances, 62

Trudeau, Pierre, Prime Minister of Canada, 21, 22, 23, 29, 30, 293, 306, 308–9; and the Nixon Shocks, 21; and the Trudeau government, 21

Turkey, 198, 205

'two-level games,' 71

United Kingdom, 292, 296

United Nations (UN), 4, 242–43, 255, 261, 280, 300, 308; and election monitoring, 188; and environmental program, 214, 218, 225, 262, 310; and General Assembly, 26, 162; and humanitarian aid, 188; and peacekeeping, 10, 12, 172–73, 176, 182, 187, 196–207, 242–43; and UN Disengagement Observer Force (UNDOF), 176, 182; and UN Emergency Force (UNEF), 197

United States: and budget deficits, 50, 51; and Department of Commerce, 67; and Department of Defense, 67; and Department of External Affairs, 279; and Department of State, 67; and Environmental Protection Act, 210; and foreign economic policy, 49 and foreign exchange reserves, 47; and global security endeavours, 3, 6, 243; and hegemony, 54; and macroeconomic policy, 8, 40, 41, 44, 49, 50; and military presence in Japan, 3, 64, 68, 141, 145; and trade deficits, 50, 51, 71; and

trade imbalances, 51, 64; and trade
negotiations with Japan, 3, 40, 41, 44,
50, 61, 62, 64, 65; and Treasury
Department, 24, 43, 47; and unilateral
capital control measures, 48; and U.S.
dollar, 20–22, 26–8, 42, 47, 52; and
U.S. Customs, 143
United States Trade Representative
(USTR), 67
Uno, Sosuke, Prime Minister of Japan, 68
U.S.–Asia Pacific Strategy, 175
U.S. Export-Import Bank, 268
U.S.–Japan Security Treaty, 5, 10, 170–
71, 173, 185–86, 189, 190, 204, 206
U.S.–Japan Working Group, 78

Vienna Convention for the Protection of
the Ozone Layer, 212
Vietnam War, 19, 295
Voluntary Capital Control, 38, 42, 43

Wada, Toshinobu, 265
Western New Guinea, 198
Westploy 96, 172
Williams, Linn, USTR, 67
Wilson, Michael, Finance Minister of
Canada, 263
World Commission on Environment and
Development, 213, 226
World Meteorological Organization, 213
World Trade Organization (WTO), 79, 82
World War II, 182, 199, 238, 277–78, 288
Wright, Gerald, 48

Xiaoping Deng, 167

Zaire, 202
zaitech ('fund engineering'), 110
Zemin, Jiang, 178